A HUNDRED AND FIFTY YEARS OF ARCHAEOLOGY

By the same Author

1942. The Three Ages

1950. The Prehistoric Chamber Tombs of England and Wales
A Hundred Years of Archaeology

1951. A Picture Book of Ancient British Art (with Stuart Piggott)

1955. Lascaux and Carnac

1956. Barclodiad y Gawres (with T. G. L. Powell)

1958. The Megalith Builders of Western Europe

1960. The Prehistoric Chamber Tombs of France

1961. The Idea of Prehistory

1963. The Hungry Archaeologist in France

1964. New Grange and the Bend of the Boyne (with S. P. ORiordain)

1966. Man Discovers his Past

1967. The Origins and Growth of Archaeology

1968. The First Civilisations

1972. Megaliths in History

A HUNDRED AND FIFTY YEARS OF ARCHAEOLOGY

GLYN DANIEL

Disney Professor of Archaeology
in the University of Cambridge
and Fellow of St. John's College

DUCKWORTH

This impression 1978
Second edition 1975 *Reprinted* 1977
First published as A Hundred Years of Archaeology February 1950
Reprinted 1952

To
MY WIFE

Printed in Great Britain by
REDWOOD BURN LIMITED
Trowbridge & Esher

CONTENTS

PREFACE TO THE SECOND EDITION

This book, entitled *A Hundred Years of Archaeology*, was first published in 1950, and re-issued, with a few minor corrections of spelling, in 1952. It is now re-issued with the addition of an eleventh chapter taking in some of the major developments between 1940 and the present day. It has been given a new title, not only for bibliographical convenience, but because the field it now covers is well over a hundred years. Indeed if one had to select a moment when it seemed that archaeology was really coming into existence as a separate discipline, wresting the facts of history from the material remains of the past, then it might be the second decade of the nineteenth century. It is roughly a hundred and fifty years since the Danish National Museum was opened to the public and Thomsen's arrangement of the museum, according to the three successive ages of Stone, Bronze and Iron, was shown to all.

Only minor changes of spelling and date have been made in the first ten chapters, which have not been revised in substance. They were all written between 1945 and 1949 and refer to that time when they speak of "recent" developments or things that have happened "in the last ten, twenty or thirty years". I have re-cast, revised and considerably added to the bibliography, and brought up to date the calendar of events which in the old book ended at 1940. New maps by Mr H. A. Shelley replace those in the first edition.

The new text has incorporated corrections and suggestions made by several friends among which must be specially mentioned Professor C. F. C. Hawkes, and the late George Yule of Cambridge and H. J. A. Randall of Bridgend, Glamorgan. The new chapter has been read through by Professor Stuart Piggott whose comments I have valued. My wife has been most helpful, patient and kind in the preparation of this new version.

The Flying Stag,
Bridge Street, Cambridge.
Michaelmas, 1973.

G.E.D.

PREFACE TO THE FIRST EDITION

Archaeology has at the present day two meanings—the study of the material remains of man's past, and the study of the material remains of man's prehistoric past. The first meaning, which for convenience we may refer to as general archaeology, comprises both prehistoric archaeology and historic archaeology; it deals with everything from eoliths to time capsules, and covers such an enormous field that much of it is dealt with by specialist studies such as the history of art or the history of architecture. In this book our concern is mainly with prehistoric archaeology, with the development of what, in the last hundred years, has come to be known as prehistory. We shall only touch in a very general way on the archaeology of historic times.

There is this very important difference between the prehistoric and the historic archaeologist. In the later periods of man's development the archaeologist is the handmaiden of history and supplements the story provided by written records. But in the earlier periods the archaeologist is not merely the handmaiden: he is the prime source for writing early history. Prehistory is written from many sources—the material remains of the past, deductions from language, physical anthropology, place names and comparative ethnology. All these are sources which in historical times are auxiliary to the written sources. But in prehistory they are the main sources, and archaeology is by far the most important of them. This is then the great interest of the development of prehistoric archaeology; we are not studying merely the development of a technique, or watching the growth of knowledge regarding man's artifacts; we are studying the development of our main source regarding the history of man before writing. That is our main theme in this book — the discovery and description of prehistoric man, and the change in our perspective of our own remote past because of these archaeological discoveries.

It is a theme which most appropriately falls within the limits prescribed by this series of books, since it is the period from 1840 to the 1939–45 War that has seen the birth and growth of prehistoric archaeology. Archaeology was the creation of the Victorians. The period from 1840 to 1900 was the creative period in archaeological discovery and method and more space has therefore been devoted here to these sixty years than to the four or five decades of the twentieth century, the discoveries and methods of which it is less easy to see in their proper historical perspective.

There were, of course, students of man's prehistoric artifacts before 1840, but they were mainly antiquarians and art historians, interested as dilettantes in the curious, the beautiful and the old. The essential of the archaeologist, as we interpret his function to-day, is that he is an historian, and his aim is the writing of history by the methodical study of all objects—beautiful or ugly, important or trivial—that survive from the prehistoric past. The development of antiquarianism is another story, and a most fascinating one; it has only been touched on here to provide a background for the beginnings of archaeology.

The detailed history of prehistoric scholarship has yet to be written. This present book is no more than a discussion of some of the significant discoveries and developments of the last hundred years. I have had to select what is to be included, and shall be accused of treating some subjects superficially and others in too great detail. I have thought that a personal emphasis on what seems to me important was better than a catalogue of discoveries and details, and I have particularly stressed the development of changes in the conceptual basis of prehistory.

In writing this book I have had especially in my mind the serious student of prehistory and have throughout given references to the literature describing the discoveries being made. I have therefore confined my short bibliography to secondary sources, that is to say sources dealing in whole or in part with the history of archaeology, and have not cited again all the primary works of archaeological scholarship unless they contain historical material of special value. As the treatment of the book has been topical rather than chronological, a chronological table of some of the most important events and publications has been added.

I am indebted for information and helpful criticism to Professor Stuart Piggott, Dr J. G. D. Clark, and the editors of *The Times*, the *Daily Telegraph*, and the *Illustrated London News*. Sir John Myres has very kindly allowed me on several occasions to tap his own unrivalled personal knowledge of the development of prehistoric archaeology. My thanks are due to the American School of Prehistoric Research for permission to reproduce here, as Fig. 5 (p. 245), a figure from MacCurdy's *Human Origins*. Professor W. B. Dinsmoor of Columbia University has read through the book in proof and made many suggestions and corrections, for which I am most grateful.

Cambridge, 1949. G. E. D.

TEXT-FIGURES

CHAPTER ONE

THE ANTIQUARIAN BACKGROUND

FOUR natural curiosities have prompted the study of the prehistoric human past—that study usually referred to as prehistoric archaeology or prehistory. The first is an interest in the immediate ancestors of known historic peoples. The French have naturally been interested in the Gauls and the Celts, the Danes in the Goths, and we, in the British Isles, in the Ancient Britons and Picts. The second is a natural interest in the non-functional aspects of the present landscape, and in the objects belonging to early man which turn up from time to time through ordinary activities such as ploughing, gardening, or digging drains. The ruined abbey and the worn coin can be explained with reference to written history, but the grass-grown banks of a hill-fort, the ruined stones of a megalithic monument, the bronze spearhead—these objects keep their own secrets. To whom did the hill-forts and barrows and stone circles belong? Who built these obvious monuments of the everyday landscape? And who fashioned and used the stone and bronze tools? Were stone tools, as some suspected, meteors, or fairy arrows, or were they the work of men who lived before writing? Were the megalithic monuments the works of giants or fairies, of heroes of old like Arthur, or were they, also, the buildings of people who have left no name in history? These are all natural questions, and they have for hundreds of years predisposed curious men to an interest in antiquarian studies.

Then again, in the last few centuries, travellers have observed and described from parts of the world, other than Europe and the Mediterranean, primitive or preliterate folk who now coexist with civilised men. It has been natural to ask how this could be, and what it implied. What was the origin of these savages or barbarians? Are they the impoverished and degraded remnants of former civilisations, or are they the survivals of stages in our own prehistoric past? And to all these questions we must add a fourth, natural curiosity, which has prompted an interest in prehistory—the natural curiosity as to how man and his culture came into being, the mechanics of cultural origins and change.

1. *The Classical World and Antiquities*

It was these last two reasons that prompted the Greeks to take an interest in prehistory, and they were the first people in history known to us to take such an interest. The Greeks were interested in the problem of the origin and development of man as part of their general philosophical speculations. Their philosophy—the parent of modern science even if not science in the sense western European scholars have used that word since the Renaissance—was vitally concerned with the nature of man, and this problem was obviously much bound up with man's origin and the development of his culture. The Greeks were also stimulated to an interest in prehistory and ethnography by their contacts with existing savages and barbarians. By the time of Aeschylus they had some knowledge of many savage or semi-savage peoples, as well as of the ancient civilisations of the Persians and Egyptians. Herodotus, on his travels, met the Scythians, and described their material culture with an accuracy proved by modern excavation of Scythian graves, and in Macedonia he met and described people living between the rivers Struma and Vardar in lake villages rather like the prehistoric lake villages of the Bronze and Iron ages in Switzerland. Herodotus has been variously described as the father of history and of anthropology and archaeology. The Greeks did not recognise anthropology as a branch of knowledge: the ἀνθρωπολόγος was no more than a gossip or busybody, but they were interested in the problem of savage communities and their relation to civilisation, a state which Plato and Aristotle identified with the Greeks.

It seems clear, too, that the earliest Greeks had some memory of their own prehistoric past. Homer reflects a bronze-using civilisation, Hesiod seems aware that bronze preceded iron in the history of civilisation *as a fact*, and not as a matter for speculation: in his *Works and Days* he envisages the past of man as falling into five stages: the Age of Gold and the Immortals, who "dwelt in ease and peace upon their lands with many good things, rich in flocks and loved by the blessed gods"; the Age of Silver, when man was less noble by far; thirdly, the Age of Bronze, when the world was peopled by "a brazen race sprung from ash-trees, who delighted in war and were the first to eat animal food . . . their armour was of bronze, and their houses of bronze, and of bronze were their implements; black iron was not yet", fourthly, the age of the Epic Heroes, who were an improvement on the brazen race, and, lastly, the Age of Iron and Dread Sorrow, when " men never rest from labour and sorrow by day and from perishing by night". Hesiod deplores that his own lot was cast in this fifth age, an age full of crime and violence, and forecasts worse to come, even an age when "men will be born with grey hair on their temples". Hesiod's scheme was, in part, a philosophical scheme, but was also, in part, derived from genuine traditions of a Bronze Age and of the destruction of the Minoan civilisation.

While the Greeks, and the Romans who followed Greek traditions, assumed the priority of the Bronze Age over the Iron Age as a matter beyond doubt, they were not all agreed on the significance of these developments. Plato, while sometimes arguing that "the ancients were better than ourselves and nearer the Gods", also realised that behind the earliest Egyptian annals lay an immense period of uncivilised life. Herodotus had also been greatly impressed by the strength and antiquity of Egyptian civilisation. Aristotle argued that the shepherd preceded the farmer, and Pausanias describes the progress of man from a diet of acorns and dwelling in huts, to a knowledge of agriculture and other arts.

The Romans had, in Tacitus and Julius Caesar, ethnographers as accurate as Herodotus. Indeed Tacitus's *Germania* is one of the finest ethnographical memoirs, and so, in its way, is Caesar's description of the Ancient Britons and Gauls in the *De Bello Gallico*. And in Lucretius, who has also been claimed as the father of prehistoric archaeology and anthropology, they produced a poet and philosopher whose analysis of man's early history was a very shrewd guess at what had actually been the industrial development of early man in Europe. In his *De Rerum Natura*, perhaps reflecting Epicurus, Lucretius contended that man first used his nails, teeth, stones, wood and fire, and then later copper, and then, still later, that iron gained in popularity. But, like the five ages of Hesiod, the stages of Lucretius were just a general scheme of the development of civilisation based on philosophical speculation. It was not based, like the formulation of the three-age scheme by the nineteenth-century Danish archaeologists, on museum analysis, stratigraphy and comparative ethnography.

The Greeks and the Romans, though they were interested in the early development of man and in the status of their barbarian neighbours, did not develop the necessary prerequisites for writing prehistory, namely the collection, excavation, classification, description and analysis of the material remains of the human past We cannot really claim the fifth-century Thracian princess who had a collection of neolithic axes in her grave, or Germanicus, the adopted son of Tiberius, who set out for Egypt, *cognoscendae antiquitatis*, as Tacitus says, as the first archaeologist. In any case, if we were trying to establish a claim for antiquaries in ancient history we should have to go back to Nabonidus, the last king of Babylon, who devoted much of his life to antiquarian research, excavated below the pavement of the temple of Shamash at Sippar, and found, eighteen cubits down, a foundation stone laid by Naram-Sin, son of Sargon of Akkad, "which for 3,200 years no previous king had seen". But Nabonidus and the Thracian princess are exceptions. The ancient world developed historians, geographers and ethnographers, but not archaeologists. Prehistoric archaeology is one scholarly discipline that we cannot trace back to the Greeks.

2. *The Rise of Antiquarianism*

The decay of the ancient world meant the loss of even those speculative notions of early man that the Greeks and Romans had produced. The story of the creation of the earth and man as set forth in Genesis now replaced the schemes of Hesiod and Lucretius. There was no further advance towards a prehistory of man until the end of the Middle Ages, with the return of humanism to Italy. The Renaissance revived interest in the classical world, and the ideas of Herodotus, Aristotle and Lucretius were read again. But the classical writers not only revealed to the sixteenth century their speculations on early man; they displayed the ancestors of at least north-western and northern European scholars as barbarian Celts, Germans and Goths, with strange customs and strange priesthoods like the Druids. They provided a puzzling early chapter to the history of north-west Europe concerning which there were no written records in Europe north of the Mediterranean. Was it possible, scholars began to ask, that some of the curious antiquities of northern and western Europe belonged to this period, and were in fact the work of such as the Druids? Here was the first stimulus to antiquarianism.

But the classical civilisation of Greece and Rome survived to the sixteenth century, not only in its literature but archaeologically. The sixteenth-century scholars in Italy, and travellers from other countries to Italy and Greece, found and studied the material remains of the ancient past which were all round them. Here, in the discovery and description of classical antiquities, was the second stimulus to the development of antiquarianism.

In Rome the collector's zeal first began to manifest itself during the last decades of the fifteenth century—it had appeared slightly earlier in Florence. The Popes, men like Sixtus IV, his nephew Julius II, and Julius III, started the habit in Rome of collections of antiquities. Their examples were followed by cardinals and other distinguished men, who furnished their villas to be treasure houses of ancient art. To add to these collections private excavations were conducted. It was this age in Italy that produced the word *dilettanti*—those who delighted in the arts. The *dilettanti* must certainly be reckoned among the founders of archaeology.

By the eighteenth century the habit of art-collecting was dying away in Italy and much of the Roman collections had been dispersed to places like Venice, Paris, Madrid, Munich and Prague. Yet when Winckelmann, in the middle of the eighteenth century, came to write his famous *History of Art* (1763–68), it was still Rome that provided him with the greater part of his material. Winckelmann has been called, together with so many others who will be mentioned in this book, the father of archaeology, and it is true that he was the first to study ancient art from the historical point of view. But the study of ancient art is not prehistory. Winckelmann stands as a great pioneer in one, only, of the strains of antiquarianism which eventually gave rise to archaeology.

During the period from the sixteenth to the eighteenth century, when antiquarian interest was being born in Italy, antiquarian studies of a different kind were coming into existence in England. Indeed, it may fairly be claimed, as Taylor has done recently,[1] that formal historical antiquarianism as distinct from dilettantism and the history of art, began in England in the sixteenth century.

[1] W. W. Taylor, *A Study of Archaeology*, 12.

Here men like John Leland, John Stow, William Camden, Humfrey Lhwyd and John Norden were writing enthusiastic topographical studies, and some of the chief visible antiquities of Britain were being described for the first time. Leland, the first and to this day the only man in England to hold the high-sounding title of King's Antiquary, toured England and Wales listing and describing objects of antiquarian interest. He was chiefly concerned with the names of towns and villages and with genealogies, but he did include prehistoric sites. Humfrey Lhwyd described the prehistoric antiquities of Anglesey. Camden, whose *Britannia* was first published in 1586, travelled widely in the British Isles, visited Hadrian's Wall and Stonehenge, and concluded that the latter was *insana substructio*.

The strength of antiquarian interests in England in the late sixteenth century is further shown by the formation in 1572 of a society for the preservation of national antiquities. The prime movers in the foundation of this society—the ancestor of the Society of Antiquaries of London—were Archbishop Matthew Parker and John Stow, together with Camden and his pupil, Sir Robert Cotton. Application was made to Elizabeth for the grant of a charter to the society, but after her death James I opposed this and the society was abolished as political in aim. The papers submitted and read at the meetings of this pioneer but shortlived society were published by Thomas Hearne in 1720 under the title of *A Collection of Curious Discoveries by Eminent Antiquaries*.

Despite the suppression of the embryo Society of Antiquaries, and of the office of King's Antiquary, antiquarian studies flourished in the seventeenth century in England. County historians like William Dugdale, Thomas Habbington, Robert Plot, Antony à Wood, and Edward Lhwyd carried on the traditions of Leland and Camden. They were topographers as well as historians, noting and describing any curious features that came their way. Some of the questionnaires which they sent out indicate the catholicity of their interest in the curious. Robert Plot, whose *Natural Histories* of Staffordshire and of Oxfordshire were published in the sixteen-seventies, asks: "Are there any ancient sepulchres hereabout of Men of Gigantic Stature, Roman Generals, and others of ancient times?"; and Machell, in his questionnaire, invites answers to these questions: "What memorable places where Battles have been fought? Round heaps of stone or earth cast up in Hills, trench'd round about or otherwise? What fortifications, camps?" Edward Lhwyd, who was keeper of the Ashmolean Museum at the end of the century, had been employed by Dr Gibson to collect materials in Wales for a new edition of Camden's *Britannia*, and to do this he set out on a lengthy tour of the scientific and antiquarian curiosities of Wales. Here indeed was the birth of serious field studies. Lhwyd was studying antiquities for themselves and not merely as one element in the cultural landscape; and so was John Aubrey, justly the most famous of the seventeenth-century antiquaries. Aubrey worked mainly in Wiltshire; encouraged by Charles II he wrote detailed accounts of Stonehenge and Avebury, arguing that they were places of religious observance, probably Druidical temples. Lytton Strachey has called Aubrey "the first English archaeologist": he may perhaps with justice be called the first English field archaeologist of importance. Aubrey, and perhaps Lhwyd as well, blazed a trail which leads from Leland and Camden to Stukeley, Colt Hoare, Cunnington, and to the great field archaeologists of the last fifty years, such as Williams-Freeman, Crawford and Fox.

It was not only field archaeology that flourished in the seventeenth century. That century saw the first collection of curios, formed by the Earl of Arundel, who sent his agent, William Petty, to collect antiquities from Greece. The Duke of Buckingham vied with Arundel and created a rival collection of curios. Charles I himself began a collection of antiquities, employing one of his admirals as a collecting agent in the Aegean. Other less distinguished persons began similar collections, notably John Tradescant, once gardener to Queen Henrietta Maria. Tradescant's "Closet of Curiosities", a remarkable collection of "varieties and oddities" popularly known as Tradescant's ark, formed the nucleus of the Ashmolean Museum. James I, despite his disapproval of the embryo Society of Antiquaries, had commissioned Inigo Jones to examine Stonehenge. Jones made the first official plan, declaring that Stonehenge was a Roman temple. Seven years later Charles I, in an Order in Council, stated that "the study of antiquities is by good experience said to be very serviceable and useful to the general good of the State and Commonwealth".

We may say, then, that antiquarianism was born in England in that century and a half between 1533 when Leland was appointed King's Antiquary and 1697 when Aubrey died. It was the product of a new interest in nature and antiquity brought about by the Renaissance of learning. It was a substitute for the study of classical antiquities. It may also be a reflection of the new national pride in England that existed from Tudor times. It may also be in part due to the Reformation, for the antiquaries saw the monasteries destroyed and libraries disposed, and, as Sir Kenneth Clark has written, "were moved to perpetuate their vanishing glories. Though there seems little of the crash and swagger of Elizabethan patriotism in these dull volumes, yet they too were written for patriotic ends, and boasted their country's treasures as poets did her wars".[1]

In the eighteenth century the study of antiquities, still youthful despite the official recognition of its usefulness, was invigorated by three things—the discovery of Greece, the Romantic Movement, and the development of natural history. The writing of county histories and topographies continued to flourish in the eighteenth century. Sacheverell's *History of the Island of Man*, Bridges's *Northampton*, Hutchins's *Dorset*, Hasted's *Kent*, Morant's *Essex*, and the work of Samuel and Daniel Lysons on Gloucestershire carry on the traditions of Plot, Dugdale and Wood, and now we also find scholars studying antiquities more and more for their own sake, and not merely as part of some wider historical or topographical scheme of work. The interest in England in classical antiquities was a great fillip to the study of our own antiquities. In the first renaissance of Greek scholarship in England, the interest was almost wholly linguistic and literary. The second renaissance of Greek scholarship in England took place in the second half of the eighteenth century.[2] During the period 1750–1830 the antiquities of classical Greece were "discovered" by English scholars, just as the main antiquities of England had been discovered between the time of Leland and

[1] *The Gothic Revival*, London, 1928, 19–20. There is as yet no general account of the English antiquaries, but see T. D. Kendrick, *The Druids*, H. B. Walters, *The English Antiquaries of the 16th, 17th and 18th Centuries*, E. G. R. Taylor, *Tudor Geography* and *Late Tudor and Early Stuart Geography*, Anthony Powell, *John Aubrey and his Friends*, and Stuart Piggott's articles in *Antiquity* (1935 and 1937).

[2] On this see especially M. L. Clarke, *Greek Studies in England, 1700–1830* (1945).

Aubrey. Collectors and travellers now visited classical lands making notes, drawings and excavations. The work of the agents of Lord Arundel and Charles I was slight compared with the collectors of the late eighteenth and nineteenth centuries.

The great age of collectors began with the travels of Stuart and Revett in 1751–53, and may be said to extend to the work of Lord Elgin in the early years of the nineteenth century. The painter James Stuart and the architect Nicholas Revett arrived in Athens in 1751; they spent three years measuring, drawing, recording. Their great work on the *Antiquities of Athens* was very long delayed; the first volume appeared in 1762, but the fourth not until 1816. Meanwhile the Society of Dilettanti, who had financed the publication, sent out a fresh expedition at their own expense—the "first Ionic expedition" of 1764—which consisted of Revett, Richard Chandler and William Pars. The results of this first Ionic expedition were published in the volumes of the *Antiquities of Ionia*, which appeared in quick succession between 1769 and 1797. At the same time as Stuart and Revett had been working in Athens, two other Englishmen, Robert Wood and James Dawkins, were engaged on a tour of parts of Greece, Asia Minor, Syria, Palestine and Egypt, the results of which appeared in two volumes from Robert Wood, the *Ruins of Palmyra* (1753) and the *Ruins of Baalbec* (1757).

These eighteenth-century travellers opened the eyes of Englishmen to the artistic achievements of the ancient Mediterranean civilisations. Sir William Hamilton's *Antiquités Etrusques, Grecques, et Romaines* (1766–67) inspired the potter Wedgwood with new ideas, and the Wedgwood works in Staffordshire still bear the name Etruria in recognition of this inspiration. These early collectors brought back with them antiquities for their closets and cabinets of curiosities—the forerunners of our archaeological museums.

A knowledge of Egyptian antiquities was added to the growing knowledge of East Mediterranean antiquities by Napoleon Bonaparte's Egyptian expedition. From the time of Herodotus onwards the wonders of Egyptian antiquity were known of, and even the Greeks themselves regarded Egypt as the seat of a civilisation older than their own. It was not, however, until the nineteenth century that modern Western civilisation recovered, through archaeology, a full knowledge of the extent and glory of prehistoric and protohistoric Egypt; but they were given their first taste of Egyptian archaeology by Bonaparte. Napoleon deliberately equipped his expedition with skilled draughtsmen and scientists to investigate the geography and antiquities of Egypt, notable among them being Dolomieu, the mineralogist, and Denon, the artist. The expedition arrived in Egypt in 1798 and, despite Nelson's destruction of the French fleet in Aboukir Bay, the French Egyptian Institute was founded in Cairo. It was impossible for the Institute not to be interested in Egyptian antiquities, as it was impossible for the more obvious antiquities not to be observed by all. Napoleon even used the Pyramids for a pep talk to his troops. "Soldiers," he cried, "forty centuries look down upon you from the top of the Pyramids!" The staff and draughtsmen of the Institute carried on their work with great thoroughness and energy. No excavations were undertaken, but portable antiquities were collected, among them, of course, the Rosetta Stone. When the French were compelled to evacuate Egypt in 1801 their collection of Egyptian works of art had to be surrendered to England, and found their way into the British Museum, not into the Louvre, which was opened in November of that year and contained only 117 objects—mainly Roman. The work of the Institute, however, remained in the hands of the French, and after years of editing was issued in the numerous volumes of the *Déscription de l'Egypte* (1809–13).

But it was not everyone who could afford to travel widely in classical lands, and, for such, the study of British antiquities provided a cheap and interesting substitute near at hand. Dr William Borlase, in his *Antiquities of Cornwall* (1754), says that he carried out his Cornish researches as a substitute for the classical travels he could not undertake. The literary movement known as the Romantic Revolt clothed in attractive garments the British substitute for classical archaeology. Scholars turned away from the classical light to barbarian gloom, and romanticised the Ancient Britons and the Druids, and the local British antiquities attributed to them. The study of the picturesque in the landscape promoted an interest in those obvious picturesque and romantic features—the ancient barrows, forts, standing stones and hut circles—about which written history said so little. And what could be more romantic and exciting than the excavation of these strange antiquities? In the work of the Rev. James Douglas, the Rev. Bryan Faussett in Kent, Henry Rowland in Anglesey, and Charles Warne in Dorset we may see the beginning of serious excavation in Britain. Faussett's work on the Kentish Anglo-Saxon barrows was carried out between 1757 and 1773. Douglas's *Nenia Britannica, or a History of British Tumuli*, published in 1793, is a good picture of the state of antiquarian knowledge at the end of the eighteenth century.

The finest example of the romantic British archaeologist was, of course, William Stukeley (1687–1755). His greatness as a field archaeologist must not be obscured by our interest in his eccentric Druidomania, and by our vision of him sitting in his "garden of the Druids" with an apple-tree sprouting mistletoe in the middle. He was a very great field archaeologist both in practice and theory. In his *Itinerarium Curiosum* (1724) he says it was his object "to oblige the curious in the Antiquities of Britain: it is an account of places and things from inspection, not completed from others' labours, or travels in one's study".

The great interest in natural history which began to develop in Britain at the same time as the Romantic Revival was due much to the personal teaching and appeal of Linnaeus. The Linnaean Society was founded in 1790. Country gentlemen and clergy had long been interested in natural history. Now they were reinforced by the scientific tastes of the rising and wealthy industrial class. The study of nature became fashionable and societies for its study flourished. Eminent and typical figures of this late eighteenth-century vigorous interest in nature and natural history were Gilbert White, Joseph Banks and William Kirby.

The seventeenth century had witnessed the formation of the first scientific societies, such as the Academia dei Lincei in Rome, to which Galileo belonged, and which flourished from 1603–30, the Academia del Cimento of Florence founded by the Medici in 1650, the Royal Society of London between 1660–62, and the Académie des Sciences of Paris in 1666, while the Academia Secretorum Naturae in Naples had been founded as early as 1560. In 1707 an association of antiquaries was formed in London on much the same lines as the Elizabethan Society. This was formally constituted as the Society of Antiquaries of London in 1718, and received its charter from George II in 1754. The first number of the journal *Archaeologia* was published in 1770, with the avowed purpose "to explode what rested upon only the vanity of the inventors and propagators" of fantasies. Ten years later the Society of Antiquaries of Scotland was formed.

The Society of Dilettanti first met in 1732. It was founded by a group of learned men in London and its first purpose was merely to bring together for discussion travellers who had "done" Italy and the grand tour. The origin of the Dilettanti is described in the preface to Chandler's *Ionian Antiquities* as follows: "Some Gentlemen who had travelled in Italy, desirous of encouraging, at home, a Taste for those objects which had contributed so much to their entertainment abroad, formed themselves into a Society, under the name of the DILETTANTI." Soon after the Society lent itself to serious undertakings, as we have seen, like its expeditions to the East Mediterranean.

Between them, the Society of Antiquaries and the Society of Dilettanti admirably illustrate the interests of the eighteenth-century antiquaries in the early remains of Britain and the Mediterranean. It is difficult to assess the relative importance of the Romantic Movement, the discovery of Greece, and the development of natural science, in the birth of archaeology from antiquarianism. Piggott would attribute the origin of British prehistoric archaeology to the Romantic Movement [1]: M. L. Clarke, on the other hand, stresses the effect of the discovery of Greek antiquities: "The expedition to Greece of Stuart and Revett in the middle of the eighteenth century may be taken as the beginning of scientific archaeology," he writes. "Before then the history of English archaeology is rather the history of collecting and of taste." [2]

We must remember, however, that English antiquarianism was a flourishing plant before the eighteenth century. The Romantic Movement and the discovery of Greece nurtured that plant until it grew into a sturdy sapling. But the ground in which that sapling was securely bedded was the advance of natural science at the end of the eighteenth century and the beginning of the nineteenth. There could be no real archaeology before geology, before the doctrine of uniformitarianism was widely accepted.

Of course, there were those who, in the eighteenth century, thought that there never could be such a subject as prehistoric archaeology, and that no new source of information about the

[1] "Prehistory and the Romantic Movement," *Antiquity*, 1935, 22 ff.
[2] M. L. Clarke, *Greek Studies in England, 1700–1830*, 175.

human past was possible. Such a one was Dr Johnson, who declared roundly: "All that is really known of the ancient state of Britain is contained in a few pages. We can know no more than what old writers have told us." Dr Johnson, if he reckoned at all in this matter, was reckoning without geology. The pages which geologists were to write in the early nineteenth century would show that we can know more than what is written by the ancient historians, and that the labour of three centuries of antiquarians was concerned not only, as some of them supposed, with the Celts, Romans and Saxons of history, but also with the nameless peoples of prehistory.

3. *Stone Tools and the Geologists*

The great contribution which geology made to the development of archaeology in the early nineteenth century was the recognition that associations of human bones or stone tools with extinct animals were authentic, and involved the great antiquity of these human remains. It now appears that one such association was actually observed and commented on in 1771, when Johann Friedrich Esper discovered in the Gaylenreuth cave, near Bamberg, in the German Jura, human bones associated with cave bear and other extinct animals. Esper published his finds in 1774 in his *Detailed Report on Recently Discovered Zooliths of Unknown Quadrupeds and the Caves containing them . . . in the upper mountainous countries of the Margravate of Bayreuth.* He asked this question regarding the human bones: "Did they belong to a Druid or to an Antediluvian or to a Mortal Man of more recent times?"—and concludes: "I dare not presume without any sufficient reason these human members to be of the same age as the other animal petrifactions. They must have got there by chance together with them." [1]

Before these associations could be accepted it needed a revolution in geology—the revolution produced by the acceptance of uniformitarianism, and it needed the further realisation that stone tools were artifacts and not—as they had earlier been described—thunderbolts, fairy arrows, or elfshot. Aldrovandus, in the mid-seventeenth century, describes stone tools as "due to an admixture of a certain exhalation of thunder and lightning

[1] I am indebted to Dr Hugo Gross of Bamberg for this information and for the translation of Esper's work.

with metallic matter, chiefly in dark clouds, which is coagulated by the circumfused moisture and conglutinated into a mass (like flour with water) and subsequently indurated by heat, like a brick", and Tollius, at about the same time, claimed chipped flints to be "generated in the sky by a fulgurous exhalation conglobed in a cloud by the circumposed humour".

Mercati, however, as early as the end of the sixteenth century, had maintained that the so-called thunderbolts were the arms of a primitive folk ignorant of a knowledge of metallurgy, and at about the same time Sir William Dugdale, in his *History of Warwickshire*, declared that they were "weapons used by the Britons before the art of making arms of brass or iron was known". Dr Plot, in his *History of Staffordshire* (1686), reaffirmed this view, and later, de la Payrère stated his view that the thunderbolts were really the tools of some early primitive and pre-Adamitic race. A century later Bishop Lyttelton gave it as his view to the Society of Antiquaries that, "There is not the least doubt of these stone instruments having been fabricated in the earliest times and by barbarous people before the use of iron and of other metals was known, and from the same cause spears and arrows were headed with flint and other hard stones." But there were considerable doubts in the minds of many, and Bishop Lyttelton, with his enlightened views, was in a small minority. And many of even those few who recognised the thunderbolts as humanly fashioned tools had little idea of how they would demonstrate not merely that man once used only stone tools, but the immense antiquity of the stone-using phase of human history. Yet by 1800 there was evidence of how this demonstration could be used, if only that evidence were properly appreciated.

At the end of the seventeenth century a flint hand-axe was found near Gray's Inn Lane associated with the skeleton of an "elephant"—presumably a mammoth, by a Mr Conyers. John Bagford, who describes this find in a letter dated 1715, accepts the association of human artifact and extinct animal, but thought that the "elephant" was a Claudian import. In 1797 John Frere wrote to the Secretary of the Society of Antiquaries enclosing some flint implements found at Hoxne, near Diss, in Suffolk, which, he says, "if not particularly objects of curiosity in themselves, must, I think, be considered in that light, from the situation in which they were found". They were Acheulian hand-axes and were found twelve foot below the surface of the ground in the bottom layer of some undisturbed strata, and were associated with the bones of extinct animals. Frere described them, very properly, as "weapons of war, fabricated and used by a people who had not the use of metals", and added "the situation in which these weapons were found may tempt us to refer them to a very remote period indeed; even beyond that of the present world".[1]

At the time, John Frere's wise words attracted little attention. They were made in a climate of thought unwilling as yet to accept the great antiquity of man and firmly convinced that the Old Testament gave the facts about the origin and early development of the earth and man. At the end of the eighteenth century and at the beginning of the nineteenth century there was prevalent what Wood Jones calls "a most satisfying and spiritually comfortable conception of the universe".[2] The whole realm of nature, it was believed, had been designed in perfection—God, being good, could not have created anything evil—and with purpose underlying everything, and man was a special creation made in God's image. It was believed that the date of creation was a recent one, certainly not before 5000 B.C., and many accepted Archbishop Ussher's date of 4004 B.C. which was printed in the margins of the authorised version of the Bible.[3] The creation was thought to have taken six days, and Adam, the first man, to have been created on the sixth day. Adam was created perfect, but fell, and his descendants suffered for his fall and shared in his sin. It was believed that a universal deluge had wiped out the world except for a few human and animal survivors collected together by Noah in his ark. These were the notions set out clearly in the Bridgewater Treatises written upon the direction of the Trustees of the Earl of Bridgewater by authors selected by the President of the Royal Society in consultation with the Archbishop of Canterbury and the Bishop of London. These treatises, designed to illustrate and elaborate Paley's *Natural Theology*,[4] were written by Prout, Whewell, Buckland, and others, and published in 1833. The world was thought by Paley to "teem

[1] "Account of Flint Weapons discovered at Hoxne in Suffolk," *Archaeologia*, XIII (1800), pp. 204–205.

[2] *Design and Purpose* (1942), 41.

[3] Bishop Lightfoot asserted that it was nine o'clock on the morning of October 23, 4004 B.C.

[4] Paley's *Natural Theology; or Evidences of the Existence and Attributes of the Deity collected from the appearances of Nature*, was published in 1802.

with delighted existence", but not to have done so for more than about 6,000 years. The civilisation of Egypt and the Bible took up so much of the 6,000 years that there was, anyhow, no time for prehistory!

The facts of geology and archaeology had, therefore, at the beginning of the nineteenth century, to be explained in terms of these Creationist and Diluvialist beliefs. The study of antiquities was held to illumine only history or peoples on the verge of history. In the first sixty years of the nineteenth century, four things shattered the satisfying and comfortable conception of the universe propagated by Paley and the Bridgewater Treatises. The first was Lyell's formation of the doctrine of uniformitarianism, the second the development by Danish antiquaries, such as Thomsen and Worsaae, of a relative chronology for Danish prehistoric antiquities, the third the proof of the antiquity of man by the demonstration of the association of his fossil bones and artifacts with extinct animals in ancient strata, and, fourth, the popularisation by Darwin of the doctrine of evolution and the mutability of species. *The Principles of Geology* was published between 1830–33; the *Origin of Species* in 1859, the same year in which Boucher de Perthes's finds on the Somme were accepted as authentic by Evans and Prestwich at meetings of the Royal Society and the Society of Antiquaries. It was not until 1859 that prehistoric archaeology could be said to have come into being. Its immediate foundations were the discoveries and disputes of geologists, archaeologists and historians in the first half of the nineteenth century, to which we must now turn our attention. Its ultimate foundations, as we have seen, lay with the antiquarians and natural historians of the sixteenth, seventeenth and eighteenth centuries.

CHAPTER TWO

THE ANTIQUARIAN AND GEOLOGICAL REVOLUTIONS

1. *The Development of English Antiquarianism*, 1800–40

THE great interest in classical antiquities which had characterised the second half of the eighteenth century in England continued for a short while in the early nineteenth century. Elgin's work in Athens took place in the years 1801–3, though the famous marbles were not dispatched to England until 1812. William Wilkins, Captain Leake, E. D. Clarke, Cockerell and others were working in Greece and Magna Grecia in the first quarter of the nineteenth century, and the "second Ionian mission" of the Society of Dilettanti set out in 1812; but gradually the English interest in classical antiquities began to decline, while German scholarship in classical antiquities began to establish itself. In the year 1826 Millingen visited England and complained of "the disregard entertained in this country for archaeological pursuits"[1]—by which he meant the study of classical antiquities. The truth was that the English interest in classical antiquities was part of the cultivation of taste in the late eighteenth century, and the great age of dilettantism was now passing away; the Society of Dilettanti itself fell into obscurity, and an interest in non-classical antiquities began in England to replace the classical interest more assuredly than it had in the eighteenth century. As M. L. Clarke has pointed out, Britton's *Architectural Antiquities of Great Britain* (1807–26) and Winkles's *Cathedrals* (1838–42) were beginning to replace the *Antiquities of Athens* and the *Ruins of Palmyra and Baalbec.*[2] And the interest was not only in mediaeval and architectural remains; there was a quickened interest in things prehistoric.

In England, William Cunnington, Sir Richard Colt Hoare and Dean Merewether were excavating and recording antiquities on Salisbury Plain, Lukis in the Channel Islands, Wakeman and

[1] *Ancient Unedited Monuments* (1826), II, preface.
[2] *Greek Studies in England, 1700–1830*, 206.

du Noyer in Ireland, and Thomas Bateman in Derbyshire. Their work and the reports now filling the pages of *Archaeologia* were eloquent testimony to the growing interest in non-classical antiquities.

This new interest is visible in the sections on antiquities in the county histories and topographies which were published in the first half of the nineteenth century, such as Fenton's *Historical Tour through Pembrokeshire* (1811), Sir Henry Englefield's *Description of the Principal Beauties, Antiquities, etc., of the Isle of Wight* (1816), Baker's *History and Antiquities of Northamptonshire* (1822–41), Clutterbuck's *History and Antiquities of Hertfordshire* (1815–27) and—deservedly the most famous of them—Colt Hoare's *History of Ancient Wiltshire* (1810–21). This was also a period of many-volume topographical surveys of the whole country, the forerunners of our County Archaeologies and County Books of the present day. Richard Gough, who had in 1789 produced an expanded edition of the English translation of Camden's *Britannia*, later produced the *Sepulchral Monuments of Great Britain* (1786–99), described by Horace Walpole as the "most splendid work" he had ever seen. Francis Grose produced his *The Antiquities of England and Wales* in 1777–87, his *Antiquities of Scotland* in 1789–91, and his *Antiquities of Ireland* posthumously in 1791. The nine volumes of Britton and Brayley's *Beauties of England and Wales* were published between 1801–14; the first ten county volumes in Daniel and Samuel Lysons's great work *Magna Britannia* between 1806–22.[1] All this indicates a growing interest in antiquities, as do Roach Smith's "Antiquarian Notes" in the *Gentleman's Magazine*, and the appearance of textbooks and manuals such as Fosbrooke's *Encyclopedia of Antiquities and Elements of Archaeology* (1822–23).

Cunnington and Colt Hoare [2] tried hard to eschew the romantic approach of their eighteenth-century predecessors. William Cunnington describes himself digging barrows on Salisbury Plain in 1803 "in the hopes of meeting something which might supersede conjecture", and in his *Ancient Wiltshire* Colt Hoare declares "we speak from facts not theory. I shall not seek among the fanciful regions of Romance an origin of our Wiltshire barrows".

[1] The material collected for the remaining volumes is in sixty-four volumes in the British Museum.

[2] As to the shares of Cunnington and Colt Hoare in this work see *Wiltshire Archaeological Magazine*, 1948, 216.

Colt Hoare dug 379 barrows, recording his observations with care, distinguishing between different types of barrow, different types of interments, and between primary and secondary interments. He abandoned terminologies involving Druids, as far as he could, and distinguished between long barrows and four types of round barrow. Colt Hoare and Cunnington were the first to take note of village sites and to classify camps and earthworks. *Ancient Wiltshire* is a pioneer work of its kind in English and marks a great forward step from antiquarianism to archaeology. It is no longer a book of local genealogies and family histories interspersed with antiquarian details. It deals specifically with the archaeological history of a county, and attempts to be comprehensive and complete. Indeed, it is worth noting that of the seventy to eighty long barrows listed in Wiltshire in the early twentieth century, Colt Hoare lists as many as fifty-six in his survey.

Cunnington and Colt Hoare may very properly be called the fathers of archaeological excavation in England, just as John Aubrey was the father of field archaeology. But, for all their efforts and protestations, they had not entirely succeeded in throwing off the mantle of the romantics. The title-page of *Ancient Wiltshire* is romantic enough, with its archaised spelling and its border of arrowheads. Although Colt Hoare carefully distinguished five types of barrow, one of these he still called the "Druid" barrow. And in describing the finding of a certain skeleton Colt Hoare comments in the best "Gothick" taste that it was "grinning horribly a ghastly smile . . . a singularity that I have noticed before". In spite of their hard work and devotion, antiquaries like Colt Hoare and Cunnington failed to find any way of breaking down the apparent contemporaneity of pre-Roman remains. Colt Hoare describes as his aim: "to ascertain to which of the successive inhabitants of this island they [*i.e.* the prehistoric antiquities] are to be ascribed, or whether, in fact, they are the work of more than one people", but after ten years' work he was forced to confess "total ignorance as to the authors of these sepulchral memorials; we have evidence of the very high antiquity of our Wiltshire barrows, but none respecting the tribes to whom they appertained, that can rest on solid foundations". The prehistoric remains of Wiltshire remained stubbornly "Ancient British".

The same picture is roughly true for French antiquarianism in the early nineteenth century as we have painted for English antiquarianism. We have seen that English antiquarianism was the result, first, of a romantic interest in the non-functional features of the cultural landscape, secondly, of a patriotic interest in local and national antiquities, and, thirdly, a substitute for the study of classical antiquities. The development of French antiquarianism seems to have followed much the same lines. The early French antiquaries, such as Peiresc, Spon and Caylus in the seventeenth century, dealt with classical antiquities. Then, perhaps influenced by English antiquaries, there developed in France Celtophiles—French antiquaries proud of their own local and national archaeology. *L'Académie Celtique* was founded in 1804 and the *Société Royale des Antiquaires de France* developed from it in 1814. In 1810 questionnaires were sent from the Ministry of the Interior to the prefectures requesting information on local antiquities, and in 1818 a commission was formed to investigate "all the national monuments . . . the Gallic, Greek and Roman antiquities, the vestiges of the ancient roads, the milestones, etc." Here was a great interest in national antiquities, but still no way had been found in France of dealing with this problem of the apparent contemporaneity of prehistoric remains. The terms Celtic, Gallic, Ancient British blanketed everything pre-Roman.

This was the fog of which Rasmus Nyerup complained in Denmark.[1] But whereas Cunnington and Colt Hoare and the members of the Académie Celtique were unable to penetrate the fog, the successors of Nyerup in Denmark and Sweden were able to disperse it completely. Yet, even if the antiquaries of western Europe were unable to take the great forward step that bridged the gap between antiquarianism and archaeology—the step here described as the antiquarian revolution—there was in one respect hope for British archaeology. The great development of British geology was bringing more and more scientists interested in that period of recent time between geology proper and history proper—that period which has become the domain of the prehistoric archaeologist. And a popular interest was beginning. The great popular interest was still of course to come, stimulated as it would be by *The Antiquity of Man*, *Nineveh and its Remains*,

[1] See p. 38 *infra*.

Prehistoric Times, *The Descent of Man*, and the popular lectures of Lyell, Pengelly, Evans and Lubbock.

To break through the fog of apparent contemporaneity which surrounded prehistoric remains three things were needed: the clear proof that some of the remains were immeasurably more ancient than the pre-Roman verge of history, second, the reasoned belief that all remains of pre-Roman or heathen times were not contemporaneous and must be arranged according to a chronological scheme, and, thirdly, the stratigraphical proof of this reasoned belief. The proof of the great antiquity of man had been available since the discoveries of Conyers near Gray's Inn Lane and John Frere at Hoxne: it was made over again by MacEnery and Schmerling and others between 1800–50, but had to wait until the excavation of the Brixham Cave, Pengelly's re-excavation of Kent's Cavern and the acceptance by British scientists of Boucher de Perthes's finds before it became part of general scientific thought. The reasoned belief in a relative chronological succession of prehistoric remains was born in Denmark in the period 1800–50, and was later demonstrated stratigraphically as a fact in the same country.

2. *The Antiquity of Man: Catastrophists and Fluvialists*

In the first half of the nineteenth century there were made many discoveries of artifacts and human bones in association with extinct animals and, sometimes, sealed between layers of stalagmite. Some of these discoveries were made in error—they were claims which could not later be substantiated—but others were genuine, and provided accurate information about the great antiquity of man. Among the pioneers of this period, Schmerling of Belgium and MacEnery of England are the names most often remembered, but contemporary with them Jouannet, de Saussure, Tournal, Dumas and de Christol were making similar discoveries in the caves of southern France.

In 1828 Tournal, the curator of the Narbonne Museum, published in the *Annales des Sciences naturelles* [1] his discoveries in the Grotte de Bize (Aude), where he had found human bones and pottery associated with bones of animals, some of which were extinct, some still surviving. Tournal does not describe any

[1] XV, 348.

stratigraphical sequence at the Grotte de Bize, but Marcel de Serres insisted that the human bones were in the same state of preservation as the extinct animal bones. Next year Tournal announced that he had found bones of extinct animals which bore the marks of cutting tools.[1] In the following year de Christol of Montpellier published his findings at a cave shelter near Pondres where he claimed to have found human bones associated with bones of hyena and rhinoceros.[2] Similar discoveries were reported by Dumas in the Grotte de Souvignargues near Sommières (Gard), and by Pitore at Fauzan near Cesseras (Hérault).

Spurred on by the researches in the south French caves, Dr P. C. Schmerling began to work in several caves at Engihoul, near Liége, of which the most famous was Engis. The results of Schmerling's researches were published in his *Recherches sur les Ossements Fossiles découverts dans les Cavernes de la Province de Liége* (Liége, 1833–34). His discoveries included seven human skulls, many artifacts, some associated with the skeletons of rhinoceros and mammoth. "There can be no doubt", wrote Schmerling, "that the human bones were buried at the same time and by the same cause as the other extinct species."[3] His discoveries, however, were not considered seriously by his contemporaries. Lyell, who visited Schmerling's sites on more than one occasion, paid a great tribute to his work. "To be let down, as Schmerling was," he wrote, "day after day, by a rope tied to a tree so as to slide to the foot of the first opening of the Engis cave, where the best-preserved human skulls were found; and, after thus gaining access to the first subterranean gallery, to creep on all fours through a contracted passage leading to larger chambers, there to superintend by torchlight, week after week and year after year, the workmen who were breaking through the stalagmite crust as hard as marble, in order to remove piece by piece the underlying bone breccia nearly as hard; to stand for hours with one's feet in the mud and with water dripping from the roof on one's head, in order to mark the position and guard against the loss of each single bone of a skeleton, and at length after finding leisure, strength and courage for all these operations, to look forward, as the fruits of one's labour, to the publication of un-

[1] *Annales des Sciences naturelles*, 1829, XVIII, 244.

[2] In a pamphlet entitled *Notice sur les Ossements Humains des Cavernes du Gard* (1829).

[3] *Recherches*, p. 59.

welcome intelligence, opposed to the prepossessions of the scientific as well as of the unscientific public—when these circumstances are taken into account, we need scarcely wonder, not only that a passing traveller failed to stop and scrutinise the evidence, but that a quarter of a century should have elapsed before even the neighbouring professors of the University of Liége came forth to vindicate the truthfulness of their indefatigable and clear-sighted countryman." [1]

The same fate befell MacEnery's work in Kent's Cavern, Torquay, as had befallen Schmerling—it had to wait a quarter of a century for recognition. Kent's Cavern was first excavated in 1824 by a Mr Northmore, of Cleve, near Exeter, and Sir W. C. Trevelyan, with the double object "of discovering organic remains, and of ascertaining the existence of a Temple of Mithras" —both of which objects were apparently fulfilled. In the following year Father J. MacEnery, a Roman Catholic priest, began excavations in the Cavern. These he continued until 1829, and during these four years found flint implements associated with the remains of extinct animals such as rhinoceros, under the stratified unbroken floor of stalagmite of the Cavern. These discoveries seemed to MacEnery to demonstrate beyond doubt the coexistence of man and the extinct animals at a very remote time in the past—certainly before 4004 B.C.—but his views were not shared by many of those with whom he discussed his excavations. MacEnery went on working in Kent's Cavern until his death in 1841.

At the same time as Tournal and de Christol were working in the south of France, Schmerling in Belgium and MacEnery in Britain, Ami Boué dug in the quaternary deposits of south Austria, and also claimed to have found the remains of fossil man in association with extinct animals.[2] Later, in 1835, an ancient skull, found at Cannstadt in 1700, was described scientifically after it had lain in the Stuttgart Museum for 135 years, but, again, no attention was paid to this description of what was the first ancient skull that had ever been found. In 1844 Aymard, the secretary of the Société Académique du Puy, announced to the French Geological Society the discovery of human remains under lava from the extinct volcano of Denis at Espaly (Haute Loire).[3]

[1] *Antiquity of Man*, 68–69.

[2] *Annales des Sciences naturelles*, 1829, XVIII; *Bull. Soc. Géol. de France*, 1830–31, I, 105.

[3] *Bull. Soc. Géol.*, II, vol. 1, pp. 107–110.

His discovery, like all the others, was disbelieved, but he championed it vigorously until the scientific world, persuaded by finds elsewhere, was prepared to accept the great antiquity of man. In 1848 a skull of the type now known as Neanderthal Man was found at Gibraltar. It attracted no attention at all: in fact it was not properly described until as late as 1907.

The reason why it took so long to persuade people of the relevance and significance of discoveries such as those of Schmerling and MacEnery was, in the first place, that they were sceptical of the evidence and thought it could be interpreted in other ways. It was known that caves were occupied by a succession of inhabitants, that they were sometimes used for burials, and that their deposits could be and were altered by burrowing animals, floods and rivers. Desnoyers advanced an exclusively archaeological argument against accepting the great antiquity of man on the evidence of cave deposits, declaring that the artefacts were the same as those found in megalithic monuments and therefore on the fringe of recorded history!

But the real reason behind the slow acceptance of the evidence from the French, Belgian and British caves was that most geologists were still Catastrophists in their interpretation of sedimentary deposits. Cuvier (1769–1832) held that the record of the rocks could only be interpreted by supposing that there had been a series of great catastrophes in the earth's history, and that in the Genesis narrative of the Noachian Flood was preserved an historic account of the most recent of these catastrophes. He expressly denied the existence of fossilised man of great antiquity, and said that such things could not be. Conybeare (1787–1857) postulated three deluges before the Noachian, and Buckland (1784–1856) wanted many more catastrophic convulsions and all but universal deluges.

Dean Buckland, the first Reader in Geology at Oxford, and afterwards Dean of Westminster, is the best representative of the Catastrophic geological approach to the problem of early man. He published his views in his *Reliquiae Diluvianae; or Observations on the Organic Remains contained in Caves, Fissures, and Diluvial Gravel and on other Geological Phenomena attesting the action of an Universal Deluge* (1823), and his *Geology and Mineralogy considered in relation to Natural Theology* (1836), which was a summary of geological knowledge as a proof of "the power, wisdom and goodness of God as manifested in creation". His problem was to reconcile the apparent evidence of fossils and geological deposits with the Biblical story and the Mosaic chronology as laid down by Archbishop Ussher, and in doing this by invoking catastrophes he was forced to find alternative explanations for the apparent facts proving the antiquity of man. Buckland himself explored the Goat's Hole Cave at Paviland on the Gower coast of Glamorgan in 1823 and found the skeleton of a young man—the so-called "Red Lady of Paviland"—associated with Palaeolithic flint implements. This skeleton he declared to be "clearly not coeval with the antediluvian bones of the extinct species", and dated it to the Romano-British period. The discovery of human bones encrusted with stalactite in a cave at Burringdon, in the Mendips, Buckland explained by the cave "having either been used as a place of sepulture in early times or resorted to for refuge by the wretches that perished in it, when the country was suffering under one of our numerous military operations"! "The state of the bones affords indication of very high antiquity," he admitted, "but there is no reason for not considering them postdiluvian."

MacEnery was in communication with Dean Buckland and other geologists while preparing his discoveries for publication. Buckland refused to accept MacEnery's inferences, arguing that the "Ancient Britons", whose artifacts MacEnery had found, had scooped ovens in the stalagmite at Kent's Cavern and that their implements had penetrated the stalagmite only through these holes. Out of deference to Buckland, MacEnery refrained from insisting on the contemporaneity of implements and rhinoceros bones, and abandoned his intention of publishing his discoveries, which therefore passed unnoticed at the time.[1]

Opposition was, however, gradually growing to the Catastrophist interpretation of geology advocated by followers of Cuvier, Conybeare and Buckland. James Hutton (1726–97) in his *Theory of the Earth* (1785) showed that he realised the stratification of the rocks was due to processes which were still going on in seas, rivers and lakes. "No processes are to be employed that are not natural to the globe," he wrote, "no action to be admitted except those of which we know the principle." This was the beginning of the theory of uniformitarianism. William Smith

[1] His manuscripts were lost until 1859, when an abstract of them was published by Mr Vivian. Subsequently they were published in full by Pengelly, in 1869.

(1769–1839)—"strata Smith" as he was called—assigned relative ages to rocks by noting their fossil contents in his *Strata identified by Organised Fossils* (1816), and argued for the orderly deposition of strata over a long period of time.

The most cogent of the Fluvialists, as they were called, in opposition to the Catastrophic Diluvialists, was Charles Lyell (1797–1875), whose *Principles of Geology* was first published between 1830–33. Lyell argued that geologically ancient conditions were in essence similar to those of our own time; in short, that the geological strata could be interpreted correctly only by assuming that the agencies forming them had proceeded in a uniform way and at a uniform rate comparable with similar present-day agencies. The implications of this doctrine of uniformitarianism were considerable for the study of prehistoric man: it meant that human bones and artefacts buried under layers of stalagmite or thick layers of earth must have been originally deposited there very long ago, and that there was no *a priori* reason why one should doubt the findings of John Frere, Schmerling and MacEnery. But the doctrine was not universally accepted, and the records of mid-nineteenth-century geological meetings are filled with disputes between the Diluvialists and the Fluvialists.

3. *The Northern Antiquaries and the Three-Age System*

We have already mentioned the first of the nineteenth-century Danish pioneers of prehistoric archaeology, namely Professor Rasmus Nyerup. In 1806 Nyerup published *Oversyn over foedrelandets mindesmaerker fra oldtiden*, in which he advocated the formation of a National Danish Museum of Antiquities, urging that only by means of such a comprehensive collection, and its careful study, could any exact knowledge be obtained of the prehistoric past. For many years Nyerup had been privately collecting antiquities and had formed them into a small museum at the University of Copenhagen, of which he was librarian. But he had been unable to classify them in any significant or helpful way, confessing that "everything which has come down to us from heathendom is wrapped in a thick fog; it belongs to a space of time which we cannot measure. We know that it is older than Christendom, but whether by a couple of years or a couple of centuries, or even by more than a millennium, we can do no more than guess". This oft-quoted remark epitomises the attitude of so many antiquaries of the early nineteenth century. It is the same *cri de coeur* that we have found in Colt Hoare's confession of "total ignorance" of the authors of the Wiltshire barrows.

In 1807, the year after the publication of Nyerup's book, and following the request of several literary men, the Danish Government set up a "Royal Committee for the Preservation and Collection of National Antiquities". This committee was charged to form a national museum of antiquities, to see to the preservation of ancient and historic monuments, and to make known to the general public the importance and value of antiquities. The secretary was Professor Nyerup, and the collections which he and his staff made in the burial chambers, bogs and kitchen middens of Denmark, as well as his own private museum, formed the nucleus of the National Museum in Copenhagen. It is interesting to remember that for its first seven or eight years the work of the committee was hindered by the war with England.

The despairing confessions of Nyerup and Colt Hoare are typical of the attitude of informed antiquaries at the turn of the eighteenth century and the beginning of the nineteenth. They rejected Dr Johnson's claim, believing that we *can* know more than what old writers have told us. They were satisfied that the work of the archaeologist was not merely the romantic ascription of ancient monuments and portable antiquities to Druids and Goths. They attempted to classify and describe what they studied, but they could not get far because there was no chronological *depth* to their ideas of prehistory. The prehistoric past to them was veritably a thick fog. As Worsaae wrote in his *Primeval Antiquities of Denmark*, in 1847: "Although it was now generally acknowledged that our native land had been inhabited by several distinct races, still it was supposed that all these antiquities must have belonged to one and the same people, namely those who were the last that found their way into our country, the Goths of Scandinavia, from whom we derive our descent. By this means objects appertaining to the most different times were naturally mingled together." This was a natural error if the prime source of prehistory was regarded as written and oral. The prime source of prehistory is archaeological, and the great achievement of the Danish and Swedish antiquaries of the early nineteenth century was to realise this, and to realise that written and oral sources were secondary and to be fitted in, where possible, to the facts deduced from archaeology alone. "If we consider the most ancient accounts of Denmark and its inhabitants", said Worsaae, "we shall find that they are enveloped in obscurity and darkness . . . it becomes therefore necessary to look to other sources from which we may not only derive fresh facts, but also obtain confirmation and illustration of those facts which are preserved in our early records." It was this conviction, as well as the pressure of the growing archaeological collections, that achieved the antiquarian revolution in Denmark.

As the collections of antiquities in the Danish National Museum grew, scholars were forced to study them in detail and to try to explain their relation to early Danish history. From these attempts came the birth of the three-age system of prehistory usually associated with the name of Thomsen, and which was the framework of European prehistory during most of the hundred years reviewed in this book. It is difficult to conceive how there could have been any advances in prehistory without some such system as this, and, to that extent, Ingwald Undset is right in claiming that Professor Nyerup and his Commission were the real founders of prehistoric archaeology.[1]

The first person to set out clearly the notion of the three ages seems to have been, not Thomsen himself, but the historian Vedel-Simonsen, in his *Udsigt over Nationalhistoriens oeldste og maerkeligste Perioder*, the first volume of which was published in 1813. "The weapons and implements of the earliest inhabitants of Scandinavia were at first of stone and wood," wrote Vedel-Simonsen. "These folk later learnt the use of copper . . . and only latterly, it would appear, iron. Therefore, from this point of view, the history of their civilisation can be divided into an age of stone, an age of copper and an age of iron. These ages were not separated from each other by such exact limits that they did not overlap each other. Without doubt the poor continued to use implements of stone after the introduction of copper implements, and copper implements after the introduction of those of iron." Vedel-Simonsen's views were not widely accepted: it was left to Thomsen to reaffirm them clearly, and, by his arrangement of the collections in the National Museum, to demonstrate to all their usefulness and their inherent probability.

[1] *Revue d'Anthropologie*, 1887, 313 ff.

Christian Jurgensen Thomsen succeeded Nyerup as secretary of the committee in 1816, and at the same time was appointed the first curator of the National Museum, a post which he held until his death in 1865. Thomsen was the son of a Copenhagen merchant, but had from his earliest youth taken a very great interest in antiquities. His first task was to arrange the growing collections in some sort of order. The collections of antiquities were mixed up with all sorts of non-archaeological curiosities in a small room in the library in the University. Thomsen arranged his collections by classifying them into three ages of Stone, Bronze, and Iron on the basis of the material used in making weapons and implements, dividing the specimens into three groups representing what he claimed were three chronologically successive ages. In 1819 the Museum was open to the public organised on this scheme, which Thomsen expounded in his guide lectures to visitors. He was always present when the Museum was open and he paid very special attention to peasants, "because", as he said, "it is by them that we shall have our collections enlarged". At last the collections were so large that they had to be moved from the University library. Thomsen was allotted rooms in the Christiansborg royal palace, and there he fully carried out his new plan of arrangement of the Danish pagan antiquities, having separate rooms for the Stone Age, the Age of "Brass" or Bronze, and the Age of Iron. It was the first step in dispersing the thick fog, the first step from the ignorance of antiquarianism to the knowledge of archaeology.

In 1825 Thomsen wrote to Professor Keyser, of Christiania, explaining the basis of his classification, and in 1839 Hildebrand studied under him and learnt his scheme. The first clear statement of the concept of the three ages is in a guide-book to the National Museum entitled *Ledetraad til Nordisk Oldkyndighed*, published in Copenhagen in 1836. A German edition of this guide appeared the following year under the title of *Leitfaden zur nordischen Alterthumskunde*, and an English translation by Lord Ellesmere in 1848 entitled *A Guide to Northern Antiquities.* Thomsen was responsible for the section in the guide on the early monuments and antiquities of the north, some parts of his essay being elaborated by other members of the Archaeological Committee of the Royal Society of Northern Antiquaries.

Meanwhile the doctrine of the three ages was gradually

winning acceptance in Sweden. Magnus Bruzelius of Lund accepted Vedel-Simonsen's idea in his *Specimen Antiquitatum Borealium* (1816), and his *Svenska Folketshistoria* (1832), and, as we have mentioned, Dr B. E. Hildebrand of Lund studied under Thomsen at Copenhagen in 1830; he thereafter returned to Lund and classified the museum there on the basis of the three-age system. Three years later Hildebrand went to Stockholm and took charge of the museum there, also arranging it on the three-age system. He was appointed King's Antiquary in 1837, and for many years, until his retirement in 1879, exercised a great influence on the development of prehistoric archaeology in Scandinavia, using the three-age system as the basis of his researches and teaching. In 1834 Sven Nilsson, Professor of Zoology at Lund, published, as an introduction to a new edition of his work on the fauna of Scandinavia, an essay on the origins of fishing and hunting in Scandinavia entitled *Udkast til Jagtens og Fiskeriets Historie i Scandinavien*, in which he argued for a Stone Age and a Bronze Age preceding the historic Iron Age. His views were later developed in his *Skandinaviska Nordens Urinvånare*, the first edition of which was published at Lund in 1838–43 and the second in 1862–66. The first part of the second edition was translated into German, and then into English by Lubbock under the title of *The Primitive Inhabitants of Scandinavia* (1868).

In Denmark the work of Thomsen was being developed by his pupils, notably Sorterup Strunk Herbst and J. J. A. Worsaae. Worsaae was successively assistant to Thomsen, Professor of Archaeology in Copenhagen University, Inspector of the Monuments of Danish Antiquities, and finally Supreme Director of the Museums of Ethnography and Northern Antiquities. His views on the three-age system and the classification of northern antiquities were set out in his *Danmarks oldtid oplyst ved Oldsager og Gravhöie* (1842), translated into English by W. J. Thoms under the title of *The Primeval Antiquities of Denmark* (1849).

At the same time as the three-age system was being developed in Denmark and Sweden it appears to have been in use in Germany. In 1836 G. C. Friedrich Lisch was appointed curator of the Grand Duke of Mecklenburg-Schwerin's fine museum at Ludwigslust Castle, and began to classify the collections on the three-age system. He continued a publication begun in 1824 by his predecessor, H. R. Schröter, and called *Friderico-Francisceum*, and in an issue for 1837 sets forth the three-age system as a basis for museum classification. About the same time Danneil, working on the prehistoric graves of the Salzwedel, seems to have been using the same scheme. It is possible that Lisch and Danneil hit upon the three-age system independently of Thomsen, Nilsson and Worsaae, but it seems more likely that they borrowed the notion from the Danish and Swedish archaeologists.

The claims of Thomsen to have invented this basic idea have been often disputed. J. N. L. Myres claims that Thomsen "was merely making practical application of an idea familiar to Greek and Roman thought and so readily accessible to European educated opinion at least since the sixteenth century".[1] It is true that some writers of the eighteenth century seem vaguely to anticipate Thomsen. Rhind,[2] de Mortillet [3] and John Evans [4] have listed some of these writers; they include Professor Iselin of Basle, Professor Eckard in Germany, Mahudel and Goguet in France, Pennant, Dr William Borlase, Littleton and Sir Richard Colt Hoare in England. Rhind even alleges that Thomsen was merely the first to give practical effect in a museum to the three-age technological system. It is true that in the writings of some of these eighteenth-century historians and antiquaries we find the notion of past times in human history when iron was unknown and bronze the chief metal, and before that when metal-working was unknown to man, but these ideas, like those of the Greeks on the human past, were based on abstract speculations. They were philosophical guesses at the early state of man, rather than inductions from carefully analysed archaeological material. Thomsen was the first person to induce scientifically the existence of these ages.

Goldenweiser has claimed that Thomsen's achievement was merely the application to man's technological development of the evolutionary schemes which nineteenth-century anthropologists and historians were devising in all branches of human culture [5]; his scheme would then be parallel to Morgan's ethnic stages, the religious stages proposed by Spencer, Tylor and Jevons, and the stages of social organisation invented by Bachofen,

[1] *English Historical Review*, September, 1946.
[2] *Archaeological Journal*, 1856, pp. 208–214.
[3] *Le Préhistorique*, 1901, chap. ii.
[4] *Ancient Stone Implements of Great Britain* (1897), pp. 3–4.
[5] *Anthropology*, 14.

McLennan and Morgan. But this claim neglects the fact that Thomsen published his scheme in 1836, and had already devised it some sixteen to eighteen years before, and that Vedel-Simonsen had outlined these ideas even earlier. It should be remembered that Thomsen, Vedel-Simonsen and Nilsson were contemporaries of Lamarck, von Baer and Lyell: the work of the early northern antiquaries was done before Spencer and Darwin. The *Ledetraad til Nordisk Oldkyndighed* was contemporary not with the *Origin of Species* but with the *Bridgewater Treatises*.

The lie to the claims of Goldenweiser and Myres is given by Worsaae's own writings. A reading of his *Prehistoric Antiquities* leaves no room for doubt that the concept of the three ages was devised in Denmark by the Danish archaeologists as a classification of antiquities and for the dispelling of the fog described by Professor Nyerup. "This division of the ancient times in Denmark into three periods", writes Worsaae, "is solely and entirely founded on the accordant testimony of antiquities and barrows, for the ancient traditions do not mention that there was a time when, for want of iron, weapons and edged tools were made of bronze."[1] Worsaae admits that "it is stated by Homer, Hesiod, and other authors that the Greeks in the most ancient time, before they had knowledge of iron, used bronze, which was also the case with the Romans",[2] but he does not regard this as evidence of the three ages in Greece itself, let alone Denmark.

Worsaae explains that he was moved to accept the three-age system because he fully appreciated that all the pre-Christian antiquities of Denmark could not possibly belong to one period, and because, having read how stone implements were at present used by Pacific islanders, and knowing that the Goths made no such use of stone implements, he concluded there must have been a Stone Age. "As soon as it was pointed out that the whole of these antiquities could by no means be referred to one and the same period, people began to see more clearly the difference between them." Nilsson had argued for the Stone Age on different grounds. He insisted that objects of stone which resembled familiar objects of iron, such as adzes, axes, chisels and harpoons, must be stone adzes, stone axes, stone chisels and stone harpoons. He then argued that no one who knew the use of iron would have been so stupid as to make objects of stone; the

[1] *Primeval Antiquities*, 124. [2] *Ibid.*, 138.

stone objects must date from a pre-metal age. "People who employed stone for implements of daily use", he wrote, "must have been ignorant of the use of metals."

It is important to realise that the concept of the three ages set out in the writings of Thomsen and Worsaae is not primarily an evolutionary one. They did not regard the three ages as forming a natural succession in Denmark. Worsaae explains many times that the Bronze Age in Denmark did not develop step by step out of the Danish Stone Age: "the transition is so abrupt", he writes, "that the bronze period must have commenced with the irruption of a new race of people, possessing a higher degree of cultivation than the earlier inhabitants." [1] And in the same way the Iron Age was the result of another invasion. Worsaae appreciated that the spread of the bronze users and iron users to Denmark from south and south-east Europe must have been a slow and gradual process and that the terms Bronze Age and Iron Age could have no exact chronological value without a geographical limit. "The universal diffusion of metals could only take place by degrees," he declared. It is interesting to find in these early nineteenth-century Danish writers the ideas of invasion, diffusion and homotaxy which formed the framework of European prehistory in the first half of the twentieth century.

Nilsson, while accepting the view that several waves of invaders had introduced changes in the prehistoric cultures of Scandinavia, was convinced that prehistory as a whole showed the gradual evolution of man and his works. Just as geology showed the long development of the organic world, and physiology the development of the individual, so prehistoric archaeology demonstrated that, "notwithstanding apparent or partial retrogression", the human race was "constantly undergoing a gradual and progressive development". "Nations spring into existence," he wrote in his *Primitive Inhabitants of Scandinavia*, "and, in their turn, decline and fall; but civilisation and humanity are steadily progressing, spreading themselves more and more, and will one day be disseminated over every spot inhabited by man."

The Copenhagen Museum *Guide* of 1836 and Worsaae's *Primeval Antiquities* are probably the most important archaeological works produced in the first half of the nineteenth century. To archaeology they are as important as was Lyell's *Principles* to

[1] *Primeval Antiquities*, 24.

geology. Here, in these two Danish works, are laid down the principles of prehistoric archaeology. The Danish archaeologists had no doubts as to the importance and necessity of studying their prehistoric antiquities. "A nation which respects itself and its independence cannot possibly rest satisfied with the consideration of its present situation alone," wrote Worsaae. "It must of necessity direct its attention to bygone times, with the view of enquiring to what original stock it belongs, in what relations it stands to other nations, whether it has inhabited the country from primeval times or immigrated thither at a later period, to what fate it has been exposed; so as to ascertain by what means it has arrived at its present character and condition." It was clearly appreciated that archaeology could not confine itself to portable antiquities and to museum specimens but must study field monuments as well. "To obtain correct ideas on the subject of the first peopling and the most ancient relations of our native country", says Worsaae, "it will not be sufficient to direct attention exclusively to objects exhumed from the earth."

Thomsen and Worsaae stressed the need for accurate description and classification of antiquities. The *Guide* classifies objects of the heathen period into (*a*) objects of stone, (*b*) urns and funeral vessels, (*c*) articles supposed to have been connected with pagan worship, (*d*) weapons and articles of metal relating to war, (*e*) ornaments, and (*f*) implements of other materials than stone, (*g*) household utensils, and (*h*) sundry articles. This rather arbitrary classification gets into further difficulties in its detailed classification of urns and funeral vessels: "Although the attempts hitherto made to classify them according to their age have not been without success," says the *Guide*, "still the complete development of such a mode of classification would too much exceed our limits, so that we find it on the whole more convenient to arrange them according to the materials of which they are composed." The adoption of this principle produces a classification of pottery as follows: (*a*) vessels designed to be hung up, (*b*) vessels designed to be carried, (*c*) flowerpot-shaped vessels, (*d*) bowl-shaped vessels, (*e*) cup-shaped, (*f*) beaker-shaped, (*g*) can-shaped, (*h*) pitcher-shaped, (*i*) bottle-shaped, (*k*) oval- and oblong-shaped clay urns, and (*l*) closed urns. This seems very strange to us to-day, as does Worsaae's classification of Danish megalithic monuments into Long Cromlechs, Round Cromlechs and Giants'

Graves (Langdysser, Runddysser and Jaettestuer), and Thomsen's classification in the *Guide* of stone groupings into "places for sepulture, places of justice, places of combat, places of sacrifice, shipformed enclosures, triangular and circular enclosures, monumental stones and rocking stones". Equally curious is Nilsson's classification of stone tools, his eight categories being: (i) tools by means of which other tools and weapons of stone were made, (ii) implements for hunting and fishing, (iii) carpenters' and mechanics' tools, (iv) some forms of stone implements which cannot satisfactorily be classed amongst any of the foregoing, (v) ornaments, (vi) vessels of burnt clay or stone, (vii) implements which have become worn out or broken through use, and (viii) implements transformed into implements of another kind!

But, curious though these classifications are, they do represent attempts at descriptive classification. These early archaeologists were wrestling with the difficult problem of accurate description and they realised that taxonomy was at the basis of any method of dealing with the intractable material before them. They were applying the methods of Linnaeus to artifacts. Worsaae stressed the need for classification and accurate nomenclature. "I think that antiquaries can scarcely pay too much attention to the introduction of a fixed terminology," he wrote. "British archaeology has suffered very much from the want of a fixed nomenclature." This was in 1849! Other modern archaeological ideas seem to have been originated or first stated clearly by these early Danish archaeologists. The *Guide* discusses the value of morphological and decorative features in the dating of prehistoric objects: "towards determining the exact age of antiquities", it declares, "there is still another guide which has hitherto been but little followed with respect to the antiquities of the North, viz. an investigation of the *Forms* of the objects and of the *Ornaments* with which they were decorated, with a view that by a careful comparison and by accurately noting what sorts are generally found together, we may ascertain the order in which the successive changes took place and thus determine the periods to which a mere inspection of the ornaments will authorise us to assign the object". Here is the genesis of the typological method.

Nilsson laid down the principles which must determine the archaeologist in his search for movements of culture; he must find out which of his artifacts is the earliest, and how this early form of artifact developed. "For instance," he wrote, "if we wish to examine the origin of the Bronze Age, we must clearly understand which form of bronze sword is the oldest. . . . I may be allowed to request all who may wish to determine the origin of the Bronze Period in Northern and Western Europe carefully to consider this point." Worsaae fully appreciated the time-lags in the diffusion of archaeological types, and the possibility of dating prehistoric objects and cultures in northern Europe by the appearance of such objects in historical contexts in the Mediterranean. Here again is the genesis of the synchronological technique of giving accurate dates to relatively dated cultures, later developed by another Scandinavian, Oscar Montelius.

Both the *Guide* and Worsaae have wise words to say about the technique of excavation. Worsaae stresses that casual excavation by untrained persons is to be deplored. Excavations, he says, "should be carried on with care, and by persons of intelligence, who will know how to apply the objects discovered to the positive advantage of science". Complete descriptions must be made. A barrow should be dug either by a large hole from the top or by a trench eight feet broad from south-east to north-west, "which, in more complete investigations, may again be intersected by a similar trench from south-west to north-east". All "curiosities" should be preserved: even "trifling objects . . . are always worth preserving"; "the bones of those animals which have been interred with the deceased may have a value for science". There is the feeling of a General Pitt-Rivers about these words of Worsaae: that these trivial antiquities "are of common occurrence forms no objection," he says, "for historic results can be deduced only from the comparison of numerous contemporary specimens".

Nilsson argued that the study of artifacts was not the only method by which we could gain knowledge of the prehistoric past. He stressed the value of *traditions* and of what he called the *comparative method*; religious and profane traditions often contained facts of interest whose real significance was forgotten, he argued. "As witnesses throwing light upon ancient times I count not only antiquities, monuments, their different shapes, and the figures engraved upon them, but also *popular tales*, which most frequently originate from traditions, and are therefore remnants of olden times." The comparative method, he declared, ought always to be used, and by this he meant the comparison of prehistoric artifacts with formally and functionally identical objects used by modern primitive peoples. Nilsson remarked on the need for care in the use of the comparative method: "similarities such as the presence of similar stone arrows in Scania and Tierra del Fuego do not always prove one and the same origin", he said, sounding a most salutary warning neglected by the later hyper-diffusionists. He claimed that archaeology "by availing itself of the comparative method" ought to be able "to collect the remains of human races long since passed away, and of the works which they have left behind, to draw a parallel between them and similar ones which still exist on earth, and thus cut out a way to the knowledge of circumstances which have been, by comparing them with those which still exist".

By means of his comparative method Nilsson arrived at a classification of prehistoric man based on the mode of subsistence. He distinguished four stages in man's development: the *savage* stage, the childhood of the human race, when man is a hunter, fisher and collector of berries and fruits; the *herdsman* or *nomad* stage, the youth of the human race, when man subsists on the produce of his herds, with hunting as an occasional occupation; the third stage of man the *agriculturist*, and the fourth and final stage of *civilisation*, which Nilsson defined on the basis of coined money, writing, and the division of labour. Here, in this classification, Nilsson was the pioneer of similar classifications later developed by Tylor and Morgan, and did in fact adumbrate a classification more relevant to history than that of the three-age system of his Danish contemporaries. But he did not pursue his ideas, nor equate his subsistence classification closely with the ages of Stone, Bronze and Iron. Although he was aware of the value of comparative ethnography and of non-archaeological techniques he was in the grip of the archaeological material as much as were Thomsen and Worsaae.

Worsaae faced up resolutely to the task of relating the archaeological remains from Denmark to the known historic inhabitants of the north. He asked the sort of question which has occupied perhaps too much the minds of archaeologists for over a century: were the peoples distinguished by archaeology to be given linguistic and historic labels? The form in which Worsaae asked this perennial question was this: "Were the Stone Age folk which he had distinguished as the first inhabitants of Denmark to be labelled Finns or Laplanders or Celts?"[1] After considerable discussion, Worsaae concludes they could not be dubbed with any of these labels but that they were "an older and still unknown race who in the course of time have disappeared before the immigration of more powerful nations, without leaving behind them any memorials except the Cromlechs of stone in which they deposited their dead, and the implements which, by the nature of their materials, were protected from decay". He goes on from this sensible conclusion to a general statement far in advance of his times: "History", writes Worsaae, "has scarcely preserved to us the memory of all the nations who have from the beginning inhabited Europe; it is therefore a vain error to assume that certain races must incontestably be the most ancient, because they are the first which are mentioned in the few and uncertain records which we possess." Worsaae was criticised for introducing a nameless and hitherto unknown people into the history of Europe: he was told that he was rendering little service to historical knowledge by this conclusion of his. He very properly dismissed as irrelevant a criticism which, if just, would render all prehistory of little service to historical knowledge. But that this criticism could be made shows the sceptical approach of historians at the time to the extension and complication of their problems by archaeology.

Nor was Worsaae afraid of giving an absolute chronology to his Danish relative chronology. He suggested 3000 B.C. as the date of the arrival of the first settlers in Denmark; and dates the decorated objects of the Bronze Age to between 1400 and 1000 B.C.

The real significance of the work of these pioneer Danish archaeologists needs to be stressed. Thomsen's first aim, of course, was to arrange the material in the Museum at Copenhagen of which he was in charge, and to produce some order out of the collections. In so doing he not only introduced the first semblance of order into the study of antiquities, but postulated in man's prehistoric past three successive ages of Stone, Bronze and Iron. Instead of the romantic chaos of Druids and Ancient Britons and Germans that had fogged the picture of pre-Roman Europe, and of which Nyerup had complained, Thomsen provided three successive technological ages. He and his contemporaries and pupils introduced the idea of, and the basis for, the relative

[1] *Primeval Antiquities*, 133.

chronology without which prehistoric archaeology would never have emerged from the mere description of antiquities thought to be pre-Roman but conceived of as vaguely contemporary. By the beginning of the nineteenth century the antiquarianism engendered in the eighteenth century needed a fresh vision and an impetus to research, and these were given at once by Thomsen's systematisation. It is therefore little wonder that, with justice, Déchelette described the three-age system as "the basis of prehistory" and Macalister described it as "the corner-stone of modern archaeology".

Thomsen, Worsaae and Nilsson were not only responsible for the idea of the three ages. Between them, as we have seen, they were responsible for the clear statement of many doctrines and methods essential to the development of prehistory. And their work must be seen against the background of a great interest in prehistoric archaeology in the Scandinavian countries in the first half of the nineteenth century. The work of these three great prehistorians is merely the outstanding labour of many who in Denmark and Sweden at this time were studying seriously their prehistoric antiquities as a source for their early history. The Royal Society of Northern Antiquaries was founded in 1825, and by the middle of the century was publishing four journals, of which one, the *Mémoires de la Société Royale des Antiquaires du Nord*, existed to summarise the advances in northern prehistory in French for the benefit of foreigners. By 1850 the Museum of Northern Antiquities in Copenhagen is described as having its "specimens arranged in 12 rooms of the palace of Christiansborg in chronological order according to the ascertained or conjectured age of the objects, first the articles from the three successive periods of *Heathen Antiquity*, viz. the *Stone Age*, the *Bronze Age* and the *Iron Age*; then the articles from the *Catholic Times* also divided into periods". Worsaae declared in 1847 that there were more than 3,000 implements of bronze, "a very large room filled with antiquities of brass, among which are complete shields and several large trumpets of war, between two and three hundred complete swords and daggers of brass, several hundred celts and brass hatchets, lanceheads, ornaments, etc." [1]

Besides the National Museum there were in Copenhagen at this time a Cabinet for American Antiquities, an Ethnographical

[1] *Journal of the Royal Irish Academy*, 1846–47, 314.

Cabinet, and the Antique Cabinet, or "collection of the classical antiquities of southern countries"; and there were also "Cabinets for Northern Antiquities" in Bergen, Christiania, Stockholm, Lund and Kiel.

The question must now be asked: why did the Danes achieve what Colt Hoare and the Celtophiles of L'Académie Celtique were unable to achieve? How is it that the revolution in antiquarian thought which transformed the dilettantism of antiquaries into the historical research of archaeologists took place in *Denmark* in the early nineteenth century? Worsaae himself supplied one answer. He thought that the French Revolution had a great deal to do with the development of archaeology and prehistory in the early nineteenth century. "With a greater respect for the political rights *of the people*", he declared in an address to the Royal Irish Academy, "there awakened in the nations themselves a deeper interest in their own history, language and nationality." He argued that the Danes turned to a study of their early history after great national calamities, "as a time from the contemplation of which their spirit of nationality might gain support, and in whose memories they found the hope of a new and equally glorious era again".[1]

Ingwald Undset has given two reasons why the great advances in prehistory took place between 1800 and 1850 in Scandinavia rather than in other European countries.[2] Scandinavia is particularly rich in ancient monuments, and the problem of the unexplained features of the cultural landscape was constantly before the eyes of the Danish and Swedish naturalists and historians. Secondly, Scandinavia was not reached by the Roman invasions: history *sensu stricto* began there a thousand years later than it did in England and France. In Scandinavia there were only Heathen and Catholic times, as the Copenhagen Museum realised, and there were no convenient labels derived from history with which to break up Heathen times. The Scandinavian historians did not even have the doubtful assistance of labels such as Celtic, Romano-British and Anglo-Saxon which had stood British antiquaries in such good stead. The urgency of the problem was thus much greater in Scandinavia than it was in northern Europe; it was surely unreasonable that the history of

[1] *Journal of the Royal Irish Academy*, 1846–47, 311–312.
[2] *Revue d'Anthropologie*, 1887, 313 ff.

Denmark and Sweden must be left to begin in the tenth century A.D. when history had been recorded in France for a thousand years and in the east Mediterranean for twice as long. A method must be found to transmute the Scandinavian antiquities into history. The only method was that of archaeology.

But these reasons merely explain that opportunity existed for the early development of archaeology in northern Europe. We must still pay homage to men like Vedel-Simonsen, Thomsen, Hildebrand, Nilsson and Worsaae, who seized and improved on that opportunity. In a Marxian interpretation of the development of archaeology and anthropology [1] Crawford has argued that both these branches of learning came into being as a result of the Industrial Revolution. This view has been widely quoted, though it is little more than a half-truth. Crawford argues that the large-scale digging for coal mines, iron mines, railway cuttings, tunnels and ballast pits, farm and fen drainage, dredging, building, the extension of arable land which we associate with the Industrial Revolution brought with it the discovery of large quantities of "curios" whether in the form of fossils or artifacts, and that from these collections of curios and the observation of stratigraphy was born geology, archaeology, as well as the Darwinian restatement of evolution. This he would regard as the creative result of the Industrial Revolution, while the non-creative result was the growth of a leisured bourgeois class with acquisitive habits who formed private archaeological collections and arranged them typologically, a process leading, especially in Denmark and Switzerland, Crawford alleges, to nothing but a dead end.

The facts may be otherwise. The leisured bourgeois class of collectors were in the nineteenth century merely replacing the leisured aristocratic collectors of the eighteenth century and earlier, as they were themselves replaced by State museums and University collections in the twentieth century. Sir John Evans and his contemporaries were no new phenomenon in history; they came of a long line of collectors going back to the Earl of Arundel, the Duke of Buckingham and John Tradescant. The Cabinets of the Copenhagen museums were lineal descendants of Tradescant's "Closet of Curiosities". Far from the nineteenth-century collections leading to a typological dead end, they lead,

[1] "The Dialectical Process in the History of Science," *Sociological Review*, 1932, 165–173.

as we have seen, directly to the formulation of the three-age system which was without doubt mainly responsible for the nineteenth-century development of prehistory. The three-age system grew up in a country less affected than most at the time by the Industrial Revolution, and one whose antiquarian collections were based mainly on the excavation and analysis of surface antiquities. The human fossils of the palaeolithic would in any case have been missing from the deep excavations of Denmark. It is true, of course, that geology was directly responsible for the knowledge of the antiquity of man, and that geology gave, in the persons of Prestwich, Falconer, John Evans, Pengelly and Boyd Dawkins, very fine scholars to archaeology. But the recognition of the antiquity of man was only one of the two foundation stones of prehistory in the nineteenth century, and it did not take place until after the middle of the century. The other foundation stone was the three-age system, and that was set out clearly forty years before the authenticity of the Somme gravel finds was publicly declared in the Royal Society, and Prestwich and Pengelly dug the Windmill Hill Cave at Brixham.

4. *Archaeology in 1840*

What was then the state of prehistoric archaeology in 1840? The answer is that, apart from a group of intellectuals in Denmark and Sweden, it hardly existed. We have stressed that prehistoric archaeology as we know it has three contributory sources—the advance of geology, the pushing backwards of the frontiers of history by archaeological means and, thirdly, the growth of archaeological technique out of antiquarianism—the deliberate wresting of historical facts from the monuments of the past that have survived.

By 1840 historians had been able to make little impression on the field of prehistory by their unaided labours, though the work of scholars like Champollion and Rawlinson was showing how history could extend itself backwards into a field where languages other than those known at the beginning of the nineteenth century were spoken and written. By 1840 geologists were, however, making a startling and unique contribution to the development of archaeology, although it was still not being appreciated. The Catastrophists were being routed, and Schmerling, MacEnery and Tournal, if not de Christol and Boué, had proved the contemporaneity of man with extinct animals.

The Mosaic cosmogony and Archbishop Ussher's chronology were being disproved, but the full implications of these discoveries were not yet properly understood. "In the 40s", writes G. M. Young, "the religious world was divided into those who did not know what the geologists were saying and those who did not mind." [1] But there were some who began to fear the undermining influence of geology and its child, archaeology; Blomfield would not allow ladies to attend geological lectures at King's College, London.

But it was impossible to muzzle the findings of the geologists. The British Association for the Advancement of Science was founded in 1830. In 1800 George Birkbeck of Glasgow started the first course of lectures which developed into the first Mechanics' Institute. The London Mechanics' Institute was founded by Birkbeck and Brougham in 1826 and Mechanics' Institutes were very important, in the second quarter of the century, in disseminating knowledge to the lower middle classes.[2] G. M. Young has argued that the work of the Society for the Diffusion of Useful Knowledge and the Literary, Scientific and Mechanics' Institutes was mainly literary—the Bible and its commentators, Milton, the economists, philosophers, and historians; science, he says, apart from phrenology (!), "for want of apparatus, did not much affect the workman: the culture of the self-educated man was still literary".[3] This may be true of physical science: but geology and the geological beginnings of archaeology were certainly to find their place in these institutes. Pengelly's first successes as an expositor of the antiquity of man was in the Torquay Mechanics' Institute.

The lower middle classes were also reached through the remarkable publications of William and Robert Chambers, notably *Chambers's Journal*, which began in 1832, the *Educational Course*, the *Miscellany of Instructive and Amusing Tracts*, begun in 1845, and completed in twenty volumes, "to furnish innocent entertainment mingled with correct information and instruction", the *Family Herald*, the *Repository of Instructive and Amusing*

[1] *Victorian England*, 74.

[2] Vide Coates, *Report on the State of Literary, Scientific and Mechanics' Institutes*, 1841.

[3] *Victorian England*, 36.

Tracts (1852), and, of course, Robert Chambers's *Vestiges of Creation*, anonymously published in 1844, and in its way comparable to Wells's *Outline of History* published in 1920. These many works included facts of Pleistocene geology and correct information and instruction about early man. At the same time the upper middle classes were being instructed by the *Spectator*, the *Gentleman's Magazine* and the *Athenaeum*. John Mitford became editor of the *Gentleman's Magazine* in 1824 and filled it with antiquarian and archaeological information and discussion.

Of course there were many journals and men of learning who took no interest in the development of science and field studies. The British Association was much jeered at in its early days: *John Bull* called it in 1835 the most glaring "among the extensive humbugs which so eminently distinguish this very extraordinary enlightened age".

Interest of course was not enough. Only in two countries had an interest in antiquities produced a systematic attempt to wrest out of the antiquities some facts of prehistory. This was in Denmark and Sweden, and here, by 1840, the real foundations of scientific archaeology had been laid. Not only the famous tripartite system, but, as we have seen, ideas of invasion, diffusion and homotaxy, the principles of typology, the comparative method, the synchronological technique had all been set out in the writings of those three great men, Thomsen, Worsaae and Nilsson. They were responsible for what can only be described as a revolution in antiquarianism. As the Swiss scholar Morlot wrote, as early as 1868, the growth of prehistoric archaeology was really due to the diffusion of the ideas of these three men through Europe. To that, and to the proofs given by Pengelly and Boucher de Perthes, that Schmerling and Tournal and MacEnery had been right all the time in their claims for the antiquity of man, and to the demonstrations by Botta, Layard and Sir John Evans that history could extend itself backwards by archaeological methods. If the great event, archaeologically speaking, of the period 1800–40 was the Danish antiquarian revolution, we cannot say that prehistoric archaeology exists until the results of this revolution were spread throughout Europe, and the work of Pengelly, Boucher de Perthes, Botta, Layard and Mariette had taken place. These were achievements of the period from 1840–75.

CHAPTER THREE

THE BIRTH OF ARCHAEOLOGY: 1840–70

1. *The Antiquity of Man*

THE two discoveries that persuaded the scientific world to accept the contemporaneity of man and extinct animals were those of Falconer and Pengelly at Brixham, and of Boucher de Perthes in the Somme valley. The labours of these men crowned the discoveries of John Frere, MacEnery, Tournal, de Christol and Schmerling, which had hitherto been disbelieved or disregarded.

MacEnery's excavations at Kent's Cavern, Torquay, had been continued in 1840 by R. A. C. Godwin Austen. He had no such scruples as Father MacEnery and no respect for the views of the Diluvialists, declaring roundly that "the bones of the cave-mammals and the works of man *must* have been introduced into the cave before the floor of the stalagmite had been formed". In 1846 a committee of the newly founded Torquay Natural History Society was appointed further to explore Kent's Cavern. These excavations were directed by William Pengelly, a local schoolmaster and private coach, with an overmastering passion for geological research. The work of this committee under Pengelly proved that the observations of MacEnery and Godwin Austen had been correct.

It was not, however, until the Brixham Cave had been excavated that the scientific world in England was prepared to accept the South Devon evidence for the contemporaneity of man and extinct animals. In 1858, in quarrying the rock which overlooks Brixham Harbour, a series of fissures was accidentally discovered. Falconer thought this should prove an excellent test section, and one which would avoid the criticisms made of the Kent's Hole finds, namely, that the cave had been disturbed. He interested the Royal and Geological Societies in this cave at Windmill Hill, Brixham, and a committee was set up to take charge of the excavations, consisting of Falconer, Ramsay, Prestwich, Lyell, Godwin Austen and Pengelly. William Pengelly himself superintended the excavations, which lasted from July 1858 to the summer of 1859. They were crowned with success; flint tools were found associated with extinct animals in the cave-earth, "on which lay a sheet of stalagmite from three to eight inches thick; and having within it and on it relics of lion, hyaena, bear, mammoth, rhinoceros and reindeer".[1]

The Brixham discoveries alone convinced many people. Prestwich has described how the Brixham evidence affected him,[2] and in his address to the Geological Section of the British Association in Aberdeen, in 1859, Sir Charles Lyell said: "The facts recently brought to light during the systematic investigation . . . of the Brixham Cave must, I think, have prepared you to admit that scepticism in regard to the cave evidence in favour of the antiquity of man had previously been pushed to an extreme." [3]

When the excavations at Brixham were completed Pengelly returned to his work at Kent's Cavern. He excavated here for nearly twenty years, from 1865 to 1883, under the auspices of a committee of the British Association. He was able to demonstrate further what MacEnery had first demonstrated, and what he himself had proved to sceptics at Brixham, namely, the certain fact that man had inhabited these caves at a time when Devonshire was also inhabited by extinct mammals such as mammoth and woolly rhinoceros. He rescued MacEnery's original account and published it, as well as the full results of his own long years of excavations.[4]

Jacques Boucher de Crêvecoeur de Perthes, a customs official of Abbeville, became interested in archaeology through his friend Picard, who was studying the "Celtic" remains—in reality Neolithic chipped flints, polished axes and broken bones—thrown out by dredging in the Somme canal. But his great interest was in the pre-Celtic or "diluvial" remains of man and extinct animals found in the quarries of Menchecourt and Moulin-Quignon, near

[1] Address to Southport Meeting of the British Association, 1883, reprinted in Pengelly, *William Pengelly*, 74–77.

[2] *Phil. Trans. Roy. Soc.*, 1860, 280.

[3] *Report Brit. Ass.*, 1895: Trans. Sects., 93. The full publication of the Brixham Cave is by Pengelly, Bush, Evans and Prestwick in *Proc. Roy. Soc.*, xx, 514, published in 1873.

[4] Pengelly, "The Literature of Kent's Cavern," *Trans. Devon. Ass.*, XVI, 189-434.

Abbeville. From 1837 onwards he began to collect from the Somme gravels roughly chipped flints associated with bones of extinct animals. These chipped flints, which he termed *haches diluviennes*, were exhibited in 1838 to the Société Impériale d'Émulation de la Somme at Abbeville, and the following year to the Institut at Paris, and were published in his five-volume work, *De la Création: essai sur l'origine et la progression des êtres* (Abbeville, 1838–41). Undaunted by the cold reception which his finds and publications received, he went on collecting and working, and in 1847 published the first volume of a three-volume work entitled *Antiquités Celtiques et Antédiluviennes*. The title of this work indicates at once the result of his researches; the *haches diluviennes*, as he had at first termed them, were in reality, he now believed, *haches antédiluviennes*, and the association of human artifacts and extinct animals in the Somme gravels was not to be explained any longer by the Diluvial theory.

The members of the Société d'Émulation at Abbeville had not taken seriously Boucher de Perthes's discoveries and theories: the Institut had received him with derision. His books were regarded as the work of a crank. "At the very mention of the words 'axe' and 'diluvium'", he said at a meeting of the Société d'Émulation in 1860, "I observe a smile on the face of those to whom I speak. It is the workmen who help me, not the geologists." Most of the geologists were still believers in diluvial catastrophes. But gradually they changed their views in face of Boucher de Perthes's insistence and the evidence from the Somme gravels which he steadily accumulated and persistently displayed.[1]

The first convert was Dr Rigollot of Amiens. Rigollot excavated in gravel pits at Saint-Acheul with the avowed intention of disproving Boucher de Perthes's theories. His excavations, however, achieved the reverse of this purpose; he became converted to de Perthes's views, and in his *Mémoires sur les Instruments en Silex trouvées à Saint-Acheul*, published at Amiens in 1854, he provided further evidence of the contemporaneity of early man and extinct mammals. A young French palaeontologist, Albert Gaudry, conducted further personal excavations at Amiens and Saint-Acheul, and was also convinced by the evidence.

[1] And the Société d'Émulation d'Abbeville eventually made amends. In 1908 a statue to Boucher de Perthes was unveiled at Abbeville! Vide *Bulletin de la Soc. d'Em. d'Abbeville*, 1908.

In 1858 the English geologist Falconer happened to be visiting the Somme valley on his way to examine the caves of Sicily; he saw the chipped flints and thought that Boucher de Perthes's claims were reasonable. On returning to England he explained his views to his colleagues and urged Prestwich and John Evans to visit the Somme gravels. This they did in the following year, spending a considerable time studying the discoveries at Abbeville and Amiens. Before crossing to France, Evans, who had hitherto been mainly interested in early British coins, wrote as follows in his diary of his reactions to the finds at Brixham and Abbeville: "Think of their finding flint axes and arrowheads at Abbeville in conjunction with bones of Elephants and Rhinoceroses 40 ft. below the surface in a bed of drift. In this bone cave in Devonshire, now being excavated by the Geological Society, they say they have found arrowheads among the bones and the same is reported of a cave in Sicily. I can hardly believe it. It will make my ancient Britons quite modern if man is carried back in England to the days when Elephants, Rhinoceroses, Hippopotamuses and Tigers were also inhabitants of the country."[1] At Abbeville the hardly credible was demonstrated as fact; "the flat axes and implements found among the beds of gravel", wrote Evans, were "evidently deposited at the same time with them—in fact the remains of a race of men who existed at the time when the deluge or whatever was the origin of these gravel beds took place".[2]

On returning to England Prestwich read a paper to the Royal Society on May 26, 1859, entitled: *On the Occurrence of Flint Implements, associated with the Remains of Animals of Extinct Species in beds of a late Geological Period at Amiens and Abbeville and in England at Hoxne*. Prestwich now demonstrated the importance of John Frere's hitherto forgotten discoveries at Hoxne, and showed how the work of Pengelly in Devonshire and Boucher de Perthes in north France had convinced him of the great antiquity of man. "It was not", he said "until I had myself witnessed the conditions under which these flint implements had been found at Brixham that I became fully impressed with the validity of the doubts thrown upon the previously prevailing opinions with respect to such remains in caves." After Prestwich's paper, which was attended by Lyell, Murchison, Huxley, Faraday

[1] Quoted from Joan Evans, *Time and Chance*, 100.
[2] *Ibid.*, 101.

and Wheatstone, John Evans spoke of the flint implements; on June 2 he read a paper on them to the Society of Antiquaries in which he said: "This much appears to be established beyond doubt, that in a period of antiquity remote beyond any of which we have hitherto found traces, this portion of the globe was peopled by man." Both papers were well received: "generally believed in" wrote Evans in his journal after the Antiquaries meeting. And in the meeting of the British Association at Aberdeen in 1859 Sir Charles Lyell, giving the presidential address to Section C, declared that he was "fully prepared to corroborate the conclusions . . . recently laid before the Royal Society by Mr Prestwich". The extent of the general acceptance is shown by Professor Ramsay's article in the *Athenaeum* for July 16, 1859, where he wrote: "For more than twenty years, like others of my craft, I have daily handled stones, whether fashioned by nature or art; and the flint hatchets of Amiens and Abbeville seem to me as clearly works of art as any Sheffield whittle."

In 1857, two years before these solemn pronouncements were being made in London and Aberdeen, the long bones and skull-cap of a manlike being were discovered in a limestone cave in the small ravine of Neanderthal on the River Düssel, in Rhenish Prussia. Schaaffhausen, who first described these remains at Bonn, noted the large size, the low forehead, and enormous brow-ridges of the skull-cap—the features we now list as typical of Neanderthal man. His view was that the Neanderthal skeleton belonged "to a barbarous and savage race" and he regarded it "as the most ancient memorial of the early inhabitants of Europe".[1] Dr Fuhlrott, who had assisted in the recovery of some of the bones, agreed with Schaaffhausen. Virchow, however, declared the remains those of a pathological idiot, while Broca insisted the remains were undiseased. Huxley accepted and confirmed the views of Schaaffhausen and Fuhlrott, recognising the Neanderthal find as the remains of the most apelike human being yet found. He placed it below the Australian aborigines in physical type and declared it "more nearly allied to the higher apes than the latter are to the lower".[2]

[1] Schaaffhausen, translated by Busk, *Nature History Review*, April 1861.

[2] *Man's Place in Nature*, iii, 156–171. See also Lyell, *Antiquity of Man*, 75, and Boyd Dawkins, *Cave Hunting*, 240–241.

Boucher de Perthes was not satisfied with finding only the artifacts of early man in the Somme gravels. It was his ambition to find also the bones of the makers of these early tools. His first finds of human bones from the Moulin-Quignon pit were declared by anatomists and geologists to be too badly preserved for certain diagnosis. Undeterred by this first failure, Boucher de Perthes offered a reward of two hundred francs to the finder of the fossil remains of man. Very shortly the reward was claimed: a complete jawbone and some teeth were found, together with hand-axes, in the gravels of the pit in March 1863. Quatrefages read a paper to the Institut accepting the Moulin-Quignon jaw. Lyell accepted its authenticity: "In 1863 de Perthes clinched his view by discovering near Abbeville, in a Pleistocene deposit, a human jaw associated with worked flints," he wrote. "The certainty of the find was absolute," declared de Perthes; but this was not so. For some while de Perthes's workmen had been forging flint implements and salting the gravel pit with them. John Evans visited the pit and wrote: "I doubt the whole affair." Prestwich and Evans found de Perthes honestly persuaded of the authenticity of these finds; they were equally persuaded they were spurious. Boucher de Perthes permitted Keeping, who had dug with Prestwich and Pengelly at Brixham, to make an independent investigation at Moulin-Quignon. After a most careful investigation Keeping found that Boucher de Perthes had been "swindled by his workmen and that the axes were false". Evans wrote in the *Athenaeum* for July 4, 1863, that the Moulin-Quignon finds were fraudulent, but vindicated Boucher from any imputation of fraud; he had merely been the victim of his own over-enthusiasm, and the cupidity and skill of his workmen. "The implements and jaw in the blackband at Moulin-Quignon are recent manufactures," wrote Evans, who, following his exposure of this unfortunate forgery, was described by Lartet as "Inspector-General of all forgeries on both sides of the Channel"!

2. *Prehistory and Evolution*

Pengelly often declared that the apathy and scepticism with which the discoveries of early man had been received before his researches at Brixham and Kent's Cavern, and the recognition by English geologists of the authenticity of Boucher de Perthes's work, was due not so much to the alleged improbability of these finds, but to doubts regarding the trustworthiness of the evidence given. Certainly his own work in Devon and its sponsoring by the Geological Society and the British Association, and the championship of de Perthes by Prestwich, Evans and Lyell, guaranteed the trustworthiness of the evidence, as F. S. Ellis writes in Pengelly's biography, "beyond all danger of refutation and out of the pale of reasonable controversy". But there was more to it than merely the authentication of well-attested excavations. The discoveries in Devon and on the Somme were announced to a world which was now prepared to accept them. The old battle between Diluvialists and Fluvialists was gradually ending in favour of the latter. The influence of Lyell's work was tremendous. Geology was becoming fashionable; crowds flocked to hear scientific lectures on geology whether they were given by Lyell in King's College, London, or by Pengelly to the Torquay Mechanics' Institute and Natural History Society. Harriet Martineau declared that in the period following the Waverley Novels "the general middle-class public purchased five copies of an expensive work on geology to one of the most popular novels of the time", and R. H. Murray notes that "the young lady who figures in *Pride and Prejudice* as a student of literature reappears in *Sybil* as a student of astronomy". Nevertheless the facts of the antiquity of man were very startling and difficult to assimilate. Pitt-Rivers, when addressing a meeting of the Archaeological Institute in Salisbury in 1887, recalled the first meeting of the Institute there thirty-eight years previously. "No individual amongst those who assembled here in 1849", he declared, "had the least idea that beneath his very feet were to be found relics of man's workmanship at a time when he was contemporary with the elephant and other extinct animals."

Lyell had discussed in his *Principles of Geology* the idea of the development of organic forms from one another, an idea which he referred to as transmutation. This idea of the transmutation or transformation of species had often been discussed by philosophers and naturalists in the preceding two hundred years, and the general philosophic doctrine of evolution, that is to say that the world attained its present form by a slow process through the ages and not by a single creative act, had been propounded by Greek and medieval philosophers. The general theory of the modification of species was discussed by Buffon (1707–88), who thought that apes were degraded men, by Charles Darwin's grandfather, Erasmus Darwin (1731–1802), who wrote in his *Zoonomia* (1794–96) that "animals undergo perpetual transformations which are in part produced by their own exertions . . . and many of these acquired forms or propensities are transmitted to their posterity"; by Lamarck (1744–1829), who believed that there were no frontiers between species, which changed due to variations in the environment, and remained constant only so long as the environment was unchanged, and, of course, by Robert Chambers, whose anonymously published *Vestiges of Creation* (1844) introduced Lamarckianism to the English reading public of the Chambers's publications, and had a very great vogue; it was in fact, for a while, a national sensation. And Herbert Spencer was preaching a fully developed doctrine of evolution in the years preceding the publication of the *Origin of Species* in 1859.

It was Lyell who first used the philosophy of evolution in its relation to the development of organic forms as revealed in the record of the rocks—the Palaeontological Record, to use the phrase he invented. It was the reading of Lyell's *Principles* that suggested to Darwin the general theory of evolution, just as it was the reading of Malthus's *Essay on Population* that suggested to him the ideas of the Struggle for Existence and the Survival of the Fittest. By a curious chance it was also the reading of Malthus's book that made Wallace, in Ternate, sit down and in three days write his famous paper, the reception of which in manuscript by Darwin precipitated his publication of the theories he had been working on for many years. Darwin and Wallace published their statements of the evolutionary theory separately in 1858 in the same volume of the *Proceedings* of the Linnaean Society, and in 1859 Darwin's case was stated fully in his *Origin of Species by Means of Natural Selection or the Preservation of Favoured Races in the Struggle for Life*.

What Darwin did was, by his advocacy, to win general acceptance for the general theory of evolution by showing how it could happen through natural selection "without the inference of Paley's super-watchmaker", to quote Esmé Wingfield-Stratford. He suggested a simple and apparently universal biological mechanism producing changes of form, and presented the struggle of living forms as natural selection by the survival of the fittest.

Darwin at first expressed no opinion on the effect of his theory on man's ancestry, nor did he in the *Origin of Species* comment on the oft-repeated anatomical likenesses between man and the apes except to say "much light will be thrown on the origin of man and his history". The extension of Darwinism to man was due to T. H. Huxley (1825–95), "Darwin's bulldog" as he styled himself, whose *Man's Place in Nature* was published in 1863. In this widely read work Huxley stated that in body and in brain man differed from some apes less than apes differed among themselves, a demonstration which Darwin accepted as "conclusive" in his *Descent of Man* (1871) and his *Expression of the Emotions in Man and the Animals* (1872). In these works Darwin expounds the extension to man of the theory of evolution. It is worth noting in passing that Wallace in his *Natural Selection* kept man quite apart from his general argument.

The publication of the *Origin of Species* projected a battle far more violent than that between Diluvialists and Fluvialists. The publication of *Essays and Reviews* in 1859 marked the beginning of that battle. To many, as Dampier has said, "the effect seemed . . . to be devastating, to overwhelm the philosophic and religious landmarks of the human race". Nowadays, when the belief in the mutability of species and the gradual development of organic life over long periods of time from simple to more developed forms is a part of the accepted thought of most people, and when natural selection is only one of several evolutionary hypotheses, the mid-nineteenth-century battles of the evolutionists and the anti-evolutionists seem very far away, and Huxley's clash with "Soapy Sam" Wilberforce at the 1860 British Association meeting at Oxford. In 1864 in a speech Disraeli asked the question, "Is man an ape or an angel?" and answered it with his personal affirmation, "I am on the side of the angels."

Very gradually the scientific world, and more slowly the informed public, became converted alike to uniformitarianism and Darwinism. Hooker, Huxley, Asa Gray, Lubbock and Carpenter were easily converted. Lyell announced his conversion at the Royal Society Dinner in 1864. But it was a slow process. Mivart called Darwinism "a puerile hypothesis"; as late as 1849 a pupil of Cuvier's was insisting on 27 successive creations, and Elie de Beaumont in 1868 still believed in the sudden formation of the organic world and of mountain chains. In 1857 Philip Henry

Gosse, in his *Omphalos: an Attempt to untie the Geological Knot*, argued that while the fossils discovered by the palaeontologist appeared to show organic evolution, as Lyell and Darwin were arguing, God might have so arranged them at the creation in order to damn nineteenth-century scientists, much as He gave Adam a navel to tempt men into the sin of sensible reasoning! [1] To this there is really no answer.

Very slowly the climate of thought of the scientific world of the second half of the nineteenth century was being formed. It was a climate disposed to scientific studies, and dominated by the twin doctrines of uniformitarianism and evolution. The Industrial Revolution, with its consequential excavations for canals and railways, had given a great fillip to the study of field geology and archaeology by providing large ready-cut sections to be studied. It created a new class of wealthy industrialists, some of whom had leisure to devote to the study of nature and early man. It called into being the consultant geologist: Prestwich was such a one and John Evans often worked in this capacity. The industrialists and consultant geologists began to take the place of the country squires and landed gentry, to whom in the nineteenth century field antiquarianism had almost been one of their field sports. It was in this new social and cultural environment that prehistoric archaeology came into being.

This new way of scientific thinking, with its emphasis on uniformitarianism and evolution, enabled the discoveries of Pengelly and Boucher de Perthes to be accepted readily, whereas only a generation before, when the immutability of species and catastrophist diluvianism were the orders of thought, the discoveries of Schmerling and MacEnery had passed unnoticed or been rejected with scorn. The doctrine of evolution not only made people more ready to believe in the antiquity of man; it made the roughly chipped artifacts from Devon and the Somme not only credible, but essential. If man had gradually evolved from a prehuman ancestor with no culture to the cultured animal of Egypt and Greece, then there *must* be evidence of his primitive culture in the most recent geological levels. Evolutionary beliefs not only made Boucher de Perthes's hand-axes easy to believe in, they made it necessary that more evidences of early human

[1] This is how a hasty Press interpreted Gosse's theory: actually his argument was not quite so crude. *Vide* Edmund Gosse, *Father and Son* (1907), chapter v.

culture should be found, and that traces should also be found of other stages of culture leading from these simple tools to the complex equipment and buildings of the known early historic civilisations.

The doctrine of evolution undermined the Mosaic theory of the fixity of species; it demanded a very long time for the development of the species including man, and it suggested that man was descended from a common ancestor with the apes. Clough said that now the First Cause would turn out to be "a smudgy person with a sub-intelligent look about the eyes". The Neanderthal man would have fitted this description. Huxley wrote of the *Origin of Species* that, "It did the immense service of freeing us for ever from the dilemma—Refuse to accept the Creation hypothesis, and what have you to propose that can be accepted by any cautious reasoner?" The geologists and archaeologists were producing a sequence of gradually evolving stages of material culture which they invited the cautious reasoner to accept.

Here then, in the discoveries of artifacts in south Devon and north France, and of a human skeleton in Prussia, and the recognition of these discoveries as human, is the beginning of prehistoric archaeology. Prehistory could only be ancient history, a subject dealing with the Greeks, the Celts, the Ancient Britons and Druids, the shadowy figures of early history, until its scope was clearly shown. Kent's Cavern, the Brixham Cave, the Somme gravels and Neanderthal man demonstrated this scope. Archaeology began, as we have seen, as an antiquarian study arising out of interest in nature, the landscape and ancient history. But it was geology, by demonstrating the antiquity of man and his artifacts, and by setting limits far back in the past before the shadowy beginnings of written history, and before the conventionally accepted date of 4004 B.C., that defined the limits and set the problems of prehistoric archaeology. If the teachings of stratigraphical geology were correct, man had existed as a cultured animal for countless centuries. What had been his culture during these centuries? How had it developed since the crude hand-axes of the Somme gravels? How long had that development taken? The discovery of this story and of techniques to unravel this story has been the central task of archaeology for the last hundred or so years.

3. *The Development of Near-Eastern Archaeology*

It has already been mentioned how Napoleon's expedition to Egypt began the interest of the West in the prehistoric and protohistoric antiquities of Egypt. It was during the French occupation, and quite by chance, that the famous Rosetta Stone was found. In 1799 one of Napoleon's officers, by name Boussard, or Bouchard, found in the excavations for a fort at Rashid, near Alexandria, a black basalt stone—the stone now famous as the Rosetta Stone—bearing inscriptions in Greek, demotic and hieroglyphics. The decipherment of the demotic and hieroglyphic inscriptions on the Rosetta Stone, and on other monuments, including an obelisk discovered on the island of Philae in 1822, was the key to the early records of Egyptian civilisation. The work of decipherment was carried out by De Sacy, Akerblad, Dr Thomas Young (1773–1829), whose results were printed in his article on Egypt in the 1818 edition of the *Encyclopædia Britannica*, and by Jean François Champollion (1790–1832), whose work was published in 1822 and who perhaps deserves the main credit, although he used the work of Akerblad and Young.

A second great survey of Egyptian antiquities was made in 1828 by Rosellini, assisted by Champollion. This survey extended southwards to the first cataract at Aswan. In 1840 Lepsius made a survey of Nubian antiquities as far south as Khartoum. He also excavated several sites in the neighbourhood of Memphis and elsewhere, and discovered and published inscriptions of Egyptian copper miners in Sinai.

By 1850 the major surface antiquities of ancient Egypt had been listed, and the Egyptian script had been deciphered. Ancient Egypt was now ready to take its place among the great civilisations on the verge of history *sensu stricto*. Books began to appear popularising the Egyptian discoveries. Among them were John Kenrick's *Ancient Egypt under the Pharaohs* (1850) and Sir John Gardner Wilkinson's *Manners and Customs of the Ancient Egyptians*.[1] And from this time Egypt begins to assume that primacy in claimants for the origin of civilisation which reached its oddest form in the Egyptocentric hyper-diffusionist doctrines of the Elliot Smith school many years later. "Egyptian archae-

[1] First series (3 vols.), 1837; second series (3 vols.), 1841; both series in 5 vols., 1847.

ology and history have undergone a complete revolution since the commencement of the present century, and especially since the discovery of the hieroglyphical character," wrote Kenrick in 1850. "There is no difficulty in fixing on the country from which Ancient History must begin. The monuments of Egypt, its records and its literature, surpass those of India and China in antiquity by many centuries." [1]

Excavation soon followed the description of monuments and the collection of portable antiquities. Among the most colourful and extraordinary people to commence excavations in Egypt during the early nineteenth century was Belzoni. His methods and techniques—or lack of techniques—are discussed in a later chapter. Belzoni's work in Egypt was accomplished in 1817–19 and published by Murray in the *Narrative of the Operations and Recent Discoveries within the Pyramids, Temples, Tombs, and Excavations in Egypt and Nubia*, in 1820. The real beginnings of Egyptian excavation are not, however, with tomb robbers like Belzoni and Drouetti, but with Mariette.

Mariette was sent out to Egypt in 1850 by the Louvre to search for Coptic manuscripts. He became at once more interested in the historic monuments of ancient Egypt, and excavated the Serapeum at Memphis, the great temple of Osiris-Apis, with its cemetery of sacred Apis bulls, in that year. He did not return to his post as assistant in the Egyptian Department of the Louvre but stayed on in Egypt. In 1858 he was appointed chief of the newly created Egyptian Service of Antiquities, an appointment which he retained until his death in 1881. In the thirty years of his reign in Egypt he excavated over thirty major sites of importance, including the temple of the Sphinx at Gizeh and the cemeteries of Sakkarah, as well as clearing the great temples of Abydos, Medinet et Habu, Der el-Bahri and Edfu. He was the father and founder of Egyptian archaeology. He organised the Egyptian antiquities for the Paris Exposition of 1867, which was the first time that any collection of ancient Egyptian art had been properly displayed in Europe. His work for the organisation of Egyptian archaeology and the creation of an Egyptian National Museum are described below (Chapter V).

The beginnings of Mesopotamian archaeology date from

[1] *Ancient Egypt under the Pharaohs* (1850), 1–2. For his chronology Kenrick refers to Lepsius, *Chronologie der Aegypter*.

roughly the same time as the beginning of Egyptology.[1] The work of Botta, Layard and Loftus is contemporary with the beginnings of Mariette's work. The two large tells near Hillah in Babylonia and near Mosul in Assyria were always pointed to in Jewish and Arab tradition as the sites of Babylon and Nineveh, and these sites were visited by European travellers from the sixteenth century onwards. These travellers were interested in the brickbats, potsherds and fragments of tablets covered with a curious writing like that in which certain old Persian monuments were inscribed. But it was not until the first half of the nineteenth century that Mesopotamian field antiquities were fully described, the first excavations undertaken, and the key to Mesopotamian history obtained by the decipherment of cuneiform. In 1765 the Danish scholar Karsten Niebuhr had visited the ruins of Persepolis and made copies of many cuneiform inscriptions, noting that there appeared to be three kinds of inscriptions, those that were later deciphered as Old Persian, Susian or Elamite, and Babylonian. The Abbé de Beauchamp, a Frenchman, who became the Pope's Vicar-General in Babylonia in 1780, described bricks inscribed in cuneiform which he had seen at Babylon. A few years later the East India Company was sufficiently interested to ask their representative in Basrah to send them back specimens of these inscribed bricks. At the turn of the century G. F. Grötefend was working on Niebuhr's copyings of the trilingual inscriptions from Persepolis. In 1802 he had deciphered three royal names in the simplest of the three scripts, the old Persian, and later he managed to decipher correctly about a third of the letters in this language. Grötefend was not an Oriental scholar and was unable to take his pioneer researches further. He submitted a dissertation embodying his discoveries to the Göttingen Academy, but it was refused publication. It was not in fact published until 1893, when it was of purely historical interest.

Field archaeology really began in Mesopotamia with the appointment of Claudius James Rich (1787–1820) as British Resident in Baghdad in 1808. Rich employed his leisure in visiting the sites of ancient Mesopotamian cities, and in collecting antiquities and manuscripts. He first visited Babylon in 1811, and

[1] In this section, and throughout this book where Mesopotamian archaeology is discussed, I have drawn extensively on the two recently published and excellent accounts of the subject, namely Seton Lloyd, *Foundations in the Dust* (1947), and André Parrot, *Archéologie Mésopotamienne : Les Étapes* (Paris, 1946).

made a thorough survey and examination of the site, publishing the result of his investigations first in the Viennese journal *Mines d'Orient*, and then reprinted separately in London in 1815 under the title of *Memoir on the Ruins of Babylon.* This account was revised and enlarged after a second visit to Babylon, in his *Second Memoir on Babylon* (1818), which, says Seton Lloyd, "virtually exhausted the possibilities of inference without excavation". Rich's later travels were published in his *Narrative of a Residence in Koordistan and on the site of Ancient Nineveh, with Journal of a Voyage down the Tigris to Baghdad, and an account of a Visit to Shiraz and Persepolis* (London, 1836). This was a posthumous work: Rich died of cholera at Shiraz in 1820. After his death his collections were bought by the British Museum, where they arrived in 1825.

The first excavations in Mesopotamia were those of Paul-Emile Botta at Nineveh in 1842 and Khorsabad in 1843. Botta was French consul at Mosul, and his appointment was largely due to the interest taken in France, especially among French orientalists, in Mesopotamian antiquities following the publication of Rich's *Memoirs* and *Narrative.* Nineveh was the third capital of Assyria, the first two being Ashur, whose ruins lie near the modern Sharqat, and Nimrud (the biblical Calah). Ashur is some thirty miles south of Mosul, Nimrud twenty miles south-east. Nineveh lies across the Tigris from Mosul and consists to-day of a large roughly rectangular collection of mounds, among which are two palace mounds, Kuyunjik, the main mound, and Nebi Yunus, to the south of it. In 1842 Botta proposed to begin excavations at Nebi Yunus, but opposition from Moslems, whose shrine crowned the palace mound, made him transfer to the northern palace mound of Kuyunjik. While excavating here late in 1842 and early in 1843 he learnt of sculptured stones found in the mound of Khorsabad, fourteen miles to the north. He therefore abandoned his excavations at Nineveh and began work at Khorsabad. Within a week he had discovered the remains of a huge Assyrian palace with large sculptured slabs and cuneiform inscriptions. Botta now believed Rich's identification of Kuyunjik–Nebi Yunus as Nineveh to be incorrect; he believed Khorsabad to be the correct site and signalled to Paris: "Ninève est retrouvé." As we now know, Khorsabad is in reality Dur Sharrukin, the city of one of the greatest Assyrian kings,

Sargon II (721–705 B.C.), and it was his palace that Botta had discovered.

Botta had hitherto been financing his excavations himself. The news of his discoveries at Khorsabad so excited French orientalists that they persuaded the French Government to grant funds for the continuance of his work and sent out M. E. Flandin, a skilled artist, to record the finds and draw the sculptures. Botta and Flandin returned to France, and the Khorsabad discoveries were published in their *Monument du Ninève* (Paris, 1849–50), a large work of five volumes, the first of text, and the other four consisting of Flandin's sketches. In 1846 many of the Khorsabad sculptures were sent to Paris, where they are now to be seen in the Louvre.

Meanwhile (Sir) Austen Henry Layard (1817–94) had begun excavations at Nimrud. His excavations lasted from late in 1845 to mid 1847, at first financed by himself and Stratford Canning, the British Ambassador to the Sublime Porte, but later by the British Museum. At Nimrud he discovered the palaces subsequently identified with the Assyrian kings Ashur-nasir-pal (883–859 B.C.), Esarhaddon (680–669 B.C.) and Shalmaneser III (858–824 B.C.). Layard also excavated for a short while at Kuyunjik and at Ashur. Many of his finds were sent to the British Museum, which they reached in 1848, having rested for a while on the quays of Bombay, where the cases were opened, some of the antiquities stolen, and even lectures given on the remains! Despite these surprising occurrences, the priceless treasures which eventually reached the British Museum included the huge winged bulls, the Black Obelisk of Shalmaneser III, and the sculptures of Ashur-nasir-pal, which are among the Museum's most valued possessions.

The British Museum were unable to get Treasury sanction for their proposal to spend £4,000 on the publication of Layard's finds in a manner similar to the sumptuous volumes of Botta and Flandin which the French Government had subsidised. A volume of drawings, *The Monuments of Nineveh*, was published in 1849 privately by John Murray, as also a popular account of Layard's excavations, *Nineveh and its Remains* (1848–49). This popular account—one of the earliest and most successful of archaeological best-sellers—was widely read, and great interest was aroused in the Nimrud sculptures when they were exhibited in the British Museum. Layard himself found that he was now a famous figure; he was given an honorary D.C.L. by the University of Oxford in 1848 at the early age of thirty-one.

Layard carried out a second expedition in Mesopotamia from 1849–51 at the instigation of, and financed by, the British Museum. He dug at Kuyunjik and Nebi Yunus, at Nimrud again, at Tell Billah, at Ashur, and at many other sites in Assyria and Babylonia, including Babylon and Nippur. His main discovery was the palace of Sennacherib at Kuyunjik, with its great library of cuneiform tablets. Layard's main criterion of the success of his excavations was the finding of portable antiquities and works of art. He was disappointed by his finds at Ashur and the Babylonian sites, and concentrated on the Assyrian palaces. On his return to England in 1851 he found himself more famous than ever; he was made a freeman of the City of London in 1853, and Lord Rector of Aberdeen University in 1855. In 1853 he published a second folio of drawings, *A Second Series of Monuments of Nineveh*, and a new popular account of his work, *Discoveries in the Ruins of Nineveh and Babylon.*

Botta had claimed that Khorsabad was Nineveh; Layard's famous *Nineveh and its Remains* assumed, as he had all through his first season of excavations, that Nimrud was Nineveh. By the time of his second expedition it was possible to prove that neither Khorsabad nor Nimrud was Nineveh, but, as Rich had said, the large site opposite Mosul including the mounds of Kuyunjik and Nebi Yunus. This was because cuneiform inscriptions could now be read, largely due to the work of Rawlinson. The work of Grötefend remained unpublished and unknown until the end of the nineteenth century, as we have said. Sir Henry Creswicke Rawlinson (1810–95) worked without any knowledge of Grötefend's work, but with a knowledge of Oriental languages which Grötefend had lacked: first on two short trilingual inscriptions from near Hamadan and then on the famous trilingual inscriptions, engraved in 516 B.C., at the instruction of Darius Hystaspes (521–485 B.C.), on the great rock of Behistun or Bisotun, twenty-two miles east of Kermanshah. Many have already written the remarkable tale of Rawlinson's copying of the famous Behistun inscriptions. They are 400 feet from the ground on the face of a rock-mass which rises 1,700 feet from the plain. Rawlinson began copying the Old Persian and

Elamite inscriptions in 1835, and by 1837 had accomplished much. He returned to the task in 1844, and in 1847, with the assistance of a wild Kurdish boy, who performed the most remarkable feats, hanging on to a cleft in the rock-face with his toes and fingers, swinging himself across gaps by ropes, and taking paper squeezes from a painter's swinging cradle, the task was completed and the Babylonian inscription recorded.

By the end of 1837 Rawlinson had succeeded in translating the first two paragraphs of the cuneiform inscription in Old Persian, and his results were published in papers in the *Journal of the Royal Asiatic Society* for 1837 and 1839. In 1846 the Royal Asiatic Society published in two volumes his *The Persian Cuneiform Inscription at Behistun*, which was a complete translation with notes and grammatical analysis of the Old Persian text. In the same year Dr Edward Hincks published an independent translation in the *Transactions of the Royal Irish Academy*. Rawlinson, Hincks, Oppert, de Saulcy and Talbot, among others, now began to work at the Babylonian inscription, and soon that too was translated, and the key to Babylonian and Assyrian obtained. Rawlinson in 1857 translated for the British Museum a cylinder of Tiglath Pileser I. Before publication, Hincks, Fox Talbot and Oppert were asked to translate the inscription independently. These four separate translations were sent sealed to the President of the Royal Asiatic Society, who had them examined by a committee consisting of Grote, Milman, Gardner, Wilkinson and others. The committee reported that the translations were so alike that there could be no longer any doubt that the true key had been found.

Rawlinson found himself as famous as was Layard, and he, too, was given an honorary D.C.L. by Oxford; he was knighted in 1856. There was no doubt of the popularity and interest of the findings of archaeologists in Mesopotamia in the middle of the nineteenth century. In 1847 the *Morning Post* published dispatches from its correspondent who visited Layard's excavations at Nimrud. Layard's *Nineveh and its Remains* was an instant success. In a letter to Mitford, Layard mentions that eight thousand copies had sold in one year, "which", he added, "will place it side by side with *Mrs Rundell's Cookery*".[1] In 1851 an abridgement of *Nineveh and its Remains*, under the title of *A*

[1] Layard, *Autobiography and Letters*, ii, 191.

Popular Account of Discoveries at Nineveh, was published specially for the railway bookstalls, forerunner of many later popularisations of archaeology, and ample witness to the interest in the subject.

In 1851 Victor Place was appointed successor to Botta and provided with funds for the resumption of excavations at Khorsabad, where, in two years, he recovered the plan of the surviving buildings of Sargon's palace. In the same year Layard decided against taking any further part in Mesopotamian excavations; actually he had been engaged on such work for no longer than five and a half years. His work was continued by Hormuzd Rassam, who had been trained by Layard and worked as his assistant. He was, though a Moslawi, an English national. In 1852–53 Rassam dug at Kuyunjik, Nimrud and other mounds, and in 1853 found the palace of Ashur-bani-pal, with its hall decorated with sculptures of a lion hunt, and its library of clay tablets. Rassam returned to England in 1853 and his work at Kuyunjik was continued for a short while by Loftus.

W. K. Loftus had already worked in the south of Mesopotamia. In 1849 he had visited several mounds in this region which, he said, "from our childhood we have been led to regard as the cradle of the human race". In 1850 and again in 1853–54 he excavated Warka (the site of the biblical Erech and the home of the mythical Sumerian hero Gilgamesh), finding a section of walling decorated with coloured mosaics of terracotta cones, and some cuneiform tablets. Loftus also dug at Senkera, Medina and Tell Sifr, at the first of which he found terraces of kiln-baked brick, clay tablets and barrel cylinders. Rawlinson, who examined all Loftus's inscribed material, was able to identify Senkera as the site of the ancient city of Larsa (the biblical Ellarsar) and the terraces of kiln-baked brick as part of the temple and ziggurat dedicated to Shamash, the sun-god.

In addition to sending out Place to succeed Botta, the French had provided money for "a scientific and artistic expedition to Mesopotamia and Media". Three Frenchmen—Fresnel, Oppert and Félix Thomas—constituted this expedition, which excavated in various south Mesopotamian sites, such as Kish and Babylon, with but little success, during the period 1851–53. In 1854–55 the British Vice-Consul at Basra, J. E. Taylor, excavated at Tell Mukayyar, a mound preserving a fine ziggurat. Here he found inscribed cylinders which enabled Rawlinson to identify the site as that of Ur-of-the-Chaldees, the home of Abraham. Another group of mounds at Tell-Abu-Shahrein south of Ur was excavated by Taylor, who found material enabling Rawlinson to identify it as the biblical Eridu. The mounds at Mukayyar and Abu Shahrein had been explored but not identified by Loftus. Rawlinson himself discovered at Birs Nimrod inscribed cylinders showing it to be Borsippa. The excavations of Loftus and Taylor, important as we now know them to be in their discovery of early Sumerian buildings, attracted little interest at the time: they did not produce spectacular finds of sculpture like those of Assyria.

In 1855 the country boats and rafts which were carrying downstream all the finds made by Oppert, Fresnel and Thomas in south Mesopotamia, and two hundred and forty cases of material from Khorsabad and from Ashur-bani-pal's palace at Nineveh, were maliciously capsized by Arab brigands at Kurnah, at the head of the Shatt el-Arab. This was a great disaster for archaeology, and especially for the European museums which were waiting for the material to adorn their galleries. But the European museums were already filling with Mesopotamian material. So full was the British Museum that a special Assyrian Room was arranged in the Crystal Palace; and when Bouvet, Place's successor, asked for more money to carry out excavations he was told: "Non . . . les fouilles sont finies, on a trop dépensé." Apart from this attitude, the Crimean War in 1855 put a stop to Mesopotamian excavation for a while. There was, in fact, a lull in operations for nearly twenty years.

The real significance to prehistoric archaeology of the linguistic decipherments of Rawlinson, Hincks and Norris was briefly this. Not only were they able to show that the Behistun inscription had been carved by Darius the Great to record his genealogy and victories, but they were able to show that the three languages in cuneiform at Behistun were related to each other, that Babylonian was the oldest and most complicated, and that the other two—Persian and Elamite—were derived from it. The Babylonian language was revealed as a Semitic language akin to Hebrew and Arabic. Now the Assyrian inscriptions found by Botta and Layard were in a language and writing almost identical with Babylonian, and they could thus be read. But more than this; the reading itself excited the general public because it abounded in biblical characters. The Assyrian inscriptions had names like

Sennacherib, Tiglath-Pileser, and kings of Israel and Judah like Jehu, Omri and Hezekiah. The linguistic decipherments were themselves a tremendous archaeological discovery, but by unlocking the Assyrian inscriptions they brought a public enthusiastic for Near-Eastern archaeology.

Edward Hincks pointed out with great acumen that the Semitic-speaking Babylonians could not have been the originators of a cuneiform writing, which he said must have been borrowed by them from an earlier people. In 1869 Jules Oppert identified these non-Semitic pre-Babylonian people as the Sumerians. The finds of Loftus and Taylor were of these Sumerians, but the Sumerians did not become a reality to people until de Sarzec's excavations at Telloh. Oppert's theory that the Sumerians had been in Iraq before the Babylonians and Assyrians was not widely accepted, and indeed there was nothing to show that the finds at Ur, Eridu and elsewhere were much older, if older at all, than the palaces which Layard and Botta were excavating. Yet the inferences of Hincks and Oppert on linguistic grounds alone were later brilliantly vindicated in one of the most splendid chapters in the history of archaeological exploration in the Near East.

4. *The Spread of the Three-Age System*

It has been argued that the great advance in prehistoric archaeology made in the first half of the nineteenth century was the formulation by the Danish archaeologists of the three-age system. It was, according to Worsaae, "the first clear ray . . . shed across the universal prehistoric gloom of the North and the world in general".[1] And these are not unduly extravagant words. The system had been designed by Thomsen as a museum classification and as a reasonable analysis of the numerous finds of heathen times. Worsaae had, however, hinted clearly the importance of studying the find spots of these museum objects. "In many instances", he wrote in his *Primeval Antiquities*, "antiquities have a value with reference to the spot in which they are found. . . . It is . . . indispensably necessary to examine and compare with care the places in which antiquities are usually found: otherwise many most important collateral points can either not be explained at all, or at least in a very unsatisfactory

[1] Worsaae, *The Prehistory of the North*, p. xxiv.

manner."[1] In fact, Worsaae hints that the three-age concept would not have originated or been widely accepted without some stratigraphical demonstration of its validity: "We should scarcely have been able to refer . . . the antiquities to three successive periods, if experience had not taught us that objects which belong to different periods are usually found by themselves."[2]

However that may be, Worsaae himself demonstrated the validity of the three-age system by stratigraphical researches in the Danish bogs. He was also able to demonstrate a succession of vegetation types in the Danish bogs and peat-mosses, beginning with a layer where thinning aspen forests give way to Scotch fir, a tree no longer growing in Denmark, and succeeded by a layer with oak, alder and birch, and then thirdly succeeded by a layer in which beech, the commonest tree in modern Denmark, appears. Only stone implements were found in the lowest or fir level, they persist into the oak-alder-birch level where bronze implements were found; iron implements were for the most part found only in the beech level.

This demonstration by stratigraphical and associational evidence of the validity of the three ages, first devised on typological and ethnological grounds, was one of the great services which were rendered to archaeology by Worsaae about the middle of the nineteenth century. At the same time he was engaged in extensive travels in Germany, France, England and Ireland, where he popularised the early Danish researches and taught the doctrine of the three ages, and himself studied the collections in the countries he visited and was thus able to begin the comparative study of archaeology. Worsaae visited Ireland in 1846, admired the collections of the Academy, and addressed the Academy on "being requested to give an account of the formation of the Museum of Antiquities in Copenhagen". After a visit to England he wrote: "the same division of the antiquities into three classes—those belonging to the periods of Stone, Bronze and Iron—which has been adopted in the arrangement of the Danish primeval monuments, will apply to the British remains".

Fortified by his extensive travels, and the stratigraphical demonstration of the validity of the three-age system, Worsaae proceeded to subdivide the stages still further, distinguishing two

[1] *Primeval Antiquities*, 156, 76.
[2] *Ibid.*, 76.

stone ages, two bronze ages, and three iron ages. He thus extended the simple tripartite system of Vedel-Simonsen and Thomsen to a more complicated sevenfold system, and so began the process which was carried to its logical conclusion by Gabriel de Mortillet and his disciples. He further published accounts of the northern antiquities, organised on the three-age system, which were a model of their kind. His *Afbildninger fra det Kongelige Museum for Nordiske Oldsager i Kjöbenhavn* was published in Copenhagen in 1854, and his *Atlas de l'Archéologie du Nord* a few years later (1857, text in 1860).

In Switzerland the Danish tripartite system was widely popular, largely due to the influence of Morlot, the Professor of Geology at Lausanne Academy. Morlot published in 1860 his *Etudes Géologico-Archéologiques en Danemark et en Suisse*, which had a wide circulation and influence.[1] In 1848 Lord Ellesmere translated the Copenhagen Museum guide under the title of *A Guide to Northern Antiquities*, the following year W. J. Thoms published a translation of Worsaae's *Danmarks Oldtid* as *The Primeval Antiquities of Denmark*, and in 1866 Avebury (then Lubbock) translated part of Nilsson's *Skandinaviska Nordens Urinvanåre* under the title of *The Primitive Inhabitants of Scandinavia*. Lubbock himself produced in 1865 his *Prehistoric Times*, which adopted the Danish system. This book was popular —it went into seven editions between 1865 and 1913—and was largely responsible for the adoption in England of the three-age system.

The spread of the system in England was slow. We may take as typical of British archaeology at the middle of the century three works: Akerman's *Archaeological Index*, Boutell's *Manual* and Vaux's *Handbook*. All reveal, on the whole, an attitude little different from that of Colt Hoare and Cunnington, and emphasise that, until the Danish antiquarian revolution had been assimilated, English antiquarianism had come to a dead end.

Akerman's *Archaeological Index to Remains of Antiquity of the Celtic, Romano-British and Anglo-Saxon Periods* was published in 1847. Akerman wrote of the first three periods of British history, but these were not the three prehistoric ages of the Danish prehistorians, but the Celtic, Romano-British and Anglo-Saxon

[1] This work forms vol. xlvi of the *Bulletin de la Société vaudoise des sciences naturelles*, and was translated into English under the title, *General Views on Archaeology* (1861).

periods of his title. He complained that many antiquaries had confused together relics of these three periods, and prided himself on the attempts he had made to separate them, declaring that it was not difficult except for some remains of the transitional periods between the Celtic and the Romano-British and the late Roman and early Pagan Saxon periods. Beyond this, Akerman makes no effort at chronological distinction; everything pre-Roman is Celtic and is lumped together. He does discuss the view that barrows should be divided on the basis of their grave goods into three groups, first those with no pottery, secondly those in which are found "urns or implements of flint or stone", and third "those containing metal weapons and personal adornments". He admits that this classification "appears to be based on rational supposition", but thinks the difference described may be due to the rank of those buried and not to age.

Akerman classifies the remains of the Celtic period—*i.e.* all pre-Roman antiquities—into the following nine categories: (i) tumuli or barrows and cairns, (ii) menhirs or peaulvans, (iii) dolmens, triliths and cromlechs or lichvaens, (iv) sepulchral caves, (v) rocking stones or logan stones, (vi) stone circles and avenues, (vii) colossal figures cut in the chalk hills, (viii) forts, camps and beacons, and (ix) objects such as urns, stone celts, bronze daggers and coins. He correctly ascribes the Uffington White Horse to the pre-Roman Celts, but also ascribes the Cerne Abbas Giant to pre-Roman times, and will not allow that there were any coins in Britain before the Romans. He is from time to time frankly puzzled as to methods whereby more information about pre-Roman times may be gleaned. "Who will afford us a rational account of these huge monuments of a people who had no written history?" he asks despairingly when writing of Avebury, Stonehenge and Carnac.

Together with Akerman's *Archaeological Index*, we may take as typical of British archaeology in the middle of the nineteenth century Boutell's *Manual* and Vaux's *Handbook to the Antiquities in the British Museum*. In a book of 360 pages Boutell finds room for only two brief sections on pre-Roman antiquities, a brief classification of pre-Roman sepulchral monuments, and three or four paragraphs on "British, Roman, and Saxon Earthworks and Encampments", in which he writes [1]:

[1] *Manual of British Archaeology* (1858), 360–361.

"The camps and hillforts of the *Britons* are circular in their outline. . . . British camps abound in the south and west of England. . . . These camps continually disclose relics of the races who formed and occupied them. . . . Similar relics are also found in barrows, in addition to weapons and personal ornaments. Thus, various *Celts*, evidently intended for peaceful occupations, have been discovered; they comprise chisels and gouges of many forms and sizes. With these may be associated a long series of other remains of the same general character, such as *querns*, or stone flour mills, pails, different vessels, mirrors, and other articles for personal use, etc., etc."

This was in 1858, ten years after Lord Ellesmere's translation of the *Ledetraad* had been published.

Vaux was an assistant in the Department of Antiquities in the British Museum; his *Handbook* was published in 1851 with the purpose of providing "some instruction with an hour's passing amusement among the numerous and valuable collections of the British Museum". It was published as one of their Handbooks by Murrays, who had published Fellows's *First and Second Excursions in Asia Minor*, Hamilton's *Researches*, Dennis's *Etruria*, and Layard's *Nineveh*. Despite its title it contained nothing about British antiquities. It was carefully sub-titled: "A description of the Remains of Greek, Assyrian, Egyptian, and Etruscan Art preserved there", and Vaux explains in his preface that he deliberately omits the collections "known by the names of British or Anglo-Roman antiquities, together with the ancient coins preserved in the Medal Room; the former being as yet too insufficiently arranged to admit of classification and description, and the latter embracing too wide a compass". Akerman, Boutell and Vaux present a depressing picture. It is clear that, with a few exceptions, British antiquaries were not aware of, or not impressed by, the great impetus to research already provided by the Danish prehistorians.

In 1759, when the British Museum was first opened to the public, it consisted of three departments only, Printed Books, Manuscripts, and Natural History, each under the care of an under-librarian. The presentation by George III of Egyptian antiquities, and the purchase of the Hamilton and Townley antiquities made the creation of a new department necessary.

This was called the Department of Antiquities of Art, which included the Prints and Drawings as well as Medals and Coins. The Elgin Marbles in 1816 made this department very important. In 1837 Prints and Drawings were separated from Antiquities, and in 1860 Antiquities was split into three departments. By 1871, when *A Guide to the Exhibition Rooms of the Departments of Natural History and Antiquities* was published—it was the first guide since Vaux's *Handbook*—there were departments of Oriental Antiquities, Greek and Roman Antiquities, Coins and Medals, and "British and Mediaeval Antiquities and Ethnography". Despite this, the whole organisation of the Department of Antiquities was still on the basis of the archaeology of art—a direct inheritance from the classical archaeology of the eighteenth century; the collections were divided into two series—Sculpture (including Inscriptions and Architectural Remains) on the ground floor, and on the first floor "the smaller remains, of whatever nation or period, such as Vases and Terracottas, Bronzes, Coins, and Medals and articles of personal and domestic use".[1]

The British Collection was now arranged by Franks, who in 1866 had become the First Keeper of the newly created Department of British and Medieval Antiquities. The pre-Roman antiquities were set out in forty-two cases and on the basis of the Danish tripartite system. Franks writes in the *Guide to the Exhibition Rooms*: "The remains of the inhabitants of the British islands, previous to the Roman invasion, embrace the *Stone*, *Bronze*, and a portion of the *Iron* period of Northern Antiquaries. They have, for convenience, been classed according to their materials, and in the order corresponding to that of the supposed introduction of such materials into this country." The tone of this note indicates clearly the reluctant acceptance of the system of the northern antiquities.

The spread of the Danish tripartite system did not take place, as might be expected, without some considerable opposition. It was the existence of a Bronze Age that was especially attacked. Nilsson himself, while a strong protagonist of the Stone Age, had had doubts about the Bronze Age. From 1860 to 1875 Christian Hostmann and Ludwig Lindenschmidt, the Director

[1] The Exhibition Rooms at this time included a Lycian Gallery, a Mausoleum Room, the Elgin Room, the Kuyunjik Room, etc. At this time the Christy Collection, presented in 1866, was on view at 103 Victoria Street, Westminster.

of the Mainz Museum, severely criticised the Danish idea of the Bronze Age, while Hostmann even declared that no Stone Age had existed either. Hostmann and Lindenschmidt argued that the finds ascribed to a pre-Roman Bronze Age were really those of the immediately pre-Roman and Roman Iron Age.[1]

In England, John Kemble did not accept the three-age system. In his address to the Royal Irish Academy in 1857 he confessed to embarrassment at addressing them so soon after Worsaae, when he could not accept Worsaae's views regarding the three ages of man's prehistoric development, and indeed was forced to regard men like Worsaae and Lisch as likely "to betray us into grave historical errors", and leading "into an historical *reductio ad absurdum*". Kemble did not deny that there was convenience in the three-age system, and that it had "some foundation in historical truth", and admitted that he was "perfectly aware of its value in the co-ordination and arrangement of a museum". James Fergusson, in his *Rude Stone Monuments* (1872), refused to accept the idea of a pre-Roman Bronze Age. Thomas Wright was perhaps the strongest English opponent of the three-age system, which he characterised as "specious and attractive in appearance but without foundation in truth". He described the "vain attempt" which was being made to introduce the system into Britain, "a system which I, in common with antiquaries of some eminence in their science, reject altogether and look upon as a mere delusion". Wright argued that stone, bronze, and iron implements were all used together, and that where they appeared segregated in archaeological contexts this was due to impoverishment; the stone-using communities of Britain being no more than the backward savages of pre-Roman Britain.

There is more in Wright's criticism of the Danish three-age system than mere refusal to accept a new idea. He conceived the whole system as the mistaken application of geology to man's past. He admits that until the middle of the nineteenth century antiquaries "limited their knowledge of the remains of human industry in this part of the world to a few generations, at most, before the date when we are acquainted with its inhabitants by the

[1] Hostmann, "Zur Geschichte und Kritik des nordischen Systemes der drei Kulturperioden," *Archiv. für Anthrop.*, III (1875): republished in 1890 as *Studien zur vorgeschichtlichen Archaeologie*, with a foreword by Lindenschmidt.

Roman historians, and everybody was satisfied with the biblical account that mankind had existed upon this earth somewhat more than six thousand years", and that geology has revealed the long extent of man's past and the inaccuracy of the Mosaic chronology. He agrees that archaeology and geology should work in alliance but complains that hitherto geology has had the main share in the partnership. "There is something, we may perhaps say poetical, certainly imaginative, in talking of an age of stone, or an age of bronze, or an age of iron," he writes, "but such divisions have no meaning in history, which cannot be treated as a physical science, and its objects arranged in genera and species. We have to do with races of mankind and we can only arrange the objects which come under our examination according to the peoples to whom they belonged and as they illustrate their manners and history." [1] Wright had no use for stratigraphy, and insisted that the method of archaeology must be historical: "We must enter upon the study of the remote period of archaeology of which we have no practical knowledge, with a very profound knowledge of the subsequent historic period . . . too much of prehistoric archaeology, as it has been hitherto presented to us, rests only upon a want of knowledge of what is historic." By the historic method, Wright meant tracing the waves of population, of which the two principal were the Celts and Teutons or Germans, from the east to their new homes in western Europe. His major contentions and his historic method are, of course, worthless, but it is interesting to see in his criticisms of the three-age system the same suspicion of the geological treatment of prehistory which many were to voice later.

As the three-age system spread to other countries of Europe it was modified slightly, and the antiquities of these countries fitted in to the Scandinavian sequence. The main modification related to the Stone Age. It gradually became clear that the Scandinavian Stone Age was really only the later part of the Stone Age, and that the implements of chipped flint, such as those found by Conyers near Gray's Inn Lane and John Frere at Hoxne, and by MacEnery and Schmerling in their cave explorations, belonged to an earlier Stone Age, or an earlier part of the Stone Age, unrepresented in Scandinavia, and therefore not in Thomsen's original scheme.

[1] All these quotations are from the third (1875) edition of Wright's *The Celt, the Roman and the Saxon.*

But this realisation depended first, of course, on the acceptance of the authenticity of these early chipped flints.[1]

5. *Palaeolithic and Neolithic*

The early nineteenth-century Danish archaeologists had, by typology and comparative ethnology, introduced some system into prehistory—the system of the three ages of stone, bronze and iron. The antiquity of man as proved by the finds in north France and south Devon posed a new question to archaeologists. Did the sequence of the three ages, worked out in Denmark, apply all over Europe? And how were the chipped hand-axes of the Somme to be fitted into the scheme?

John Evans had hinted at the answer in 1859 when the authenticity of the finds from the Somme was being acclaimed. In a letter read after Prestwich's paper to the Royal Society he says, "there is for the most part a marked difference between the worked flints from the drift and those of the ordinary stone period", and three years later, when writing to Pengelly, he describes a flint implement which has been sent to him as "not of the Drift period, but rather an unfinished or unground celt of the so-called Stone period". It was clear that the Stone Age must be divided into two parts, an earlier comprising the antiquities from the drift and caves of western Europe, and a later comprising the finds from settlements and barrows of northern and western Europe.

It was French archaeologists who first made clear that there were two ages of stone, distinguishing in the Stone Age the *période de la pierre taillée*, and the *période de la pierre polie*. Avebury, in his *Prehistoric Times*, published in 1865, accepts this division, and distinguishes two ages of stone: first the Palaeolithic—he toyed for a while with the name Archaeolithic—"that of the Drift, when man shared the possession of Europe with the Mammoth, the Cave Bear, the Woolly-haired rhinoceros, and other extinct animals", and the Neolithic or New Stone Age—"the later or polished stone age; a period characterised by beautiful weapons and instruments of flint and other kinds of stone, in which, however, we find no traces of the knowledge of any metal excepting gold, which seems to have been sometimes used for

[1] For a visual presentation of the three-age system as it was understood by the northern antiquaries in the middle of the nineteenth century see Worsaae, *The Prehistory of the North* (1886), diagram opposite title-page.

ornament". Avebury had in reality expanded the Danish three-age system into a four-age scheme. His scheme was no more than the formulation and christening of ideas current in the late fifties and early sixties of the century; it was soon widely accepted, and this fourfold scheme of the four ages of Prehistoric man became the framework into which all archaeological discoveries were fitted.

There was difficulty and uncertainty about the dovetailing of these archaeologically defined ages with the geological ages. In the tenth edition (1868) of his *Principles of Geology*, Lyell adopted Avebury's Palaeolithic and Neolithic, though he there speaks of a Reindeer period as between the two, and refers also to Glacial and post-Glacial periods. Lyell himself had changed his mind regarding the nomenclature of post-Pliocene times, at first proposing Pleistocene, then rejecting it in favour of the cumbrous "post-Pliocene division of the post-Tertiary formation", and eventually agreeing with Boyd Dawkins and reverting to Pleistocene. But where in this welter of Pleistocenes and Pliocenes, post-Pliocene, Recent, Glacial and post-Glacial were the Palaeolithic and Neolithic to be fitted? In a letter to Pengelly, dated 1867, Lyell confessed: "I am aware that, if asked what I mean by 'Recent' I may not be able to give a very clear answer." [1]

French geologists and prehistorians referred to post-Pliocene times as Quaternary and Recent, and Pengelly used the term Cainozoic to embrace both Tertiaries and Quaternaries. To the French the Quaternary was the Pleistocene, the period of the Old Stone Age or Palaeolithic, and the Recent included the Neolithic, Bronze and Iron ages. But there was no general agreement on the use of these terms as there was none at first about the term prehistory.

Daniel Wilson seems to be one of the first persons to use the term prehistory, in the title of his book *The Archaeology and Prehistoric Annals of Scotland*. This book was first published in 1851; in the preface to the second edition, published twelve years later, Wilson says "the application of the term prehistoric introduced—if I mistake not—for the first time in this work". Tylor used prehistory in his *Primitive Culture* (1871), and gradually the word came into general parlance and into respectable usage. The *O.E.D.* chronicles the stages in this access of

[1] Quoted in Pengelly, *William Pengelly*, 178.

respectability: Mr Gladstone used the word in 1878, *The Times* in 1888 and *Nature* in 1902. But the word had varying meanings.

To de Mortillet, prehistory meant the Stone and Bronze ages, protohistory was the Iron Age, and history began with the Romans. To Boyd Dawkins prehistory was the Neolithic, Bronze and Early Iron ages; history began with the Later Iron Age; and the Palaeolithic, which coincided with the Pleistocene, was a matter of geology. And Worsaae's *Prehistory of the North* dealt with everything from the Early Stone Age to the Vikings. There was, however, general agreement that the word prehistory was better than the alternative sometimes then used, which was antehistory. At the Spezzia meeting of 1865, when the Congrès international d'anthropologie et d'archéologie préhistoriques was founded, the word palaeo-ethnology was proposed as an alternative for prehistory and this was abbreviated by the Italians to palethnology, but these words, though taken up for a while, did not survive very long, except in Italy.

The Danish archaeologists, while accepting the extension of the Stone Age of Thomsen to include a Palaeolithic as well as a Neolithic, and realising that the greater part of their Stone Age was Neolithic, were yet puzzled where to fit in their own kitchen middens. These kitchen middens, or kjökkenmöddinger, had been objects of interest since they were first described by the zoologist Japetus Steenstrup in 1837. These had, by some, been regarded as natural beach formations dating from a time when the sea-level in Denmark was many feet higher than at present. Steenstrup argued that they were middens, and on his initiative the Royal Academy of Copenhagen set up, in 1848, a committee to study these sites. The committee consisted of the geologist Forchhammer, the archaeologist Worsaae, and Steenstrup himself.

In 1850, after field work on these kitchen middens, Worsaae wrote in his notebook: "One might almost think these heaps were the places where the people of the neighbourhood, in that far-off time, took their meals, as witness, for example, the potsherds, charcoal, bones of animals and stone implements. This is, of course, mere conjecture, and should be treated as such." Further excavations proved the conjecture of Worsaae and Steenstrup to be correct. In 1851 Steenstrup announced the conclusions of the committee to the Academy of Sciences and Worsaae to the Society of Antiquaries, and the investigations of the committee were fully published by Steenstrup in the *Proceedings of the Copenhagen Academy* for 1848–55.

The kjökkenmöddinger were then middens of shell-fish like oyster, cockle, *Mytilus edulis*, *Littorina littorea*, *Nassa reticulata*, bones of fish like sole and herring, birds such as duck, goose and sea-gull, and land animals like stag, *Sus*, *Bos primigenius*, bear and beaver. The investigations proved that the oldest culture represented in the middens was contemporary with the fir and pine, and with the appearance of oak. All the animals represented in the middens were "recent" animals, though none of them, with the exception perhaps of dog, were domesticated. None of the many implements found at that time in the middens were ground and polished.

Steenstrup argued that the middens belonged to the Neolithic—the original Stone Age of the north—but Worsaae held they belonged to the Old Stone Age—that they were the representatives in northern Europe of the last phase of the pre-Neolithic Stone Age being studied in western Europe. In 1862 Worsaae sets out the problem of correlating the Danish and European finds in a letter to John Evans. "I have also found", wrote Worsaae, "that very rude implements of stone and bone . . . have been discovered in caves and on the coasts of France, and even of England (*e.g.* Kent's Hole, Torquay), and I should now wish to know how far the other antiquaries and naturalists would agree with me in my conclusions:

> that the antiquities from the gravel pits in England and France which also show the rudest and simplest forms must have belonged to some peculiar race the existence of which in other countries is yet to be proved; that *after* this people, other hunting and fishing tribes have been spread over the coasts of Europe where they lived, in the North, on small islands and on the coasts of the lakes and bays, and in the West and South of Europe frequently in caves along the seashore, the borders of rivers and lakes; and that at last a higher civilisation with domestic animals, with agriculture and with better formed implements had been introduced, perhaps by new invasions. In every case now the interior parts of Europe were peopled

(like the habitations of Switzerland) and the transition to the Bronze Age prepared."[1]

The controversy about the place of the kitchen middens in the prehistoric sequence raged for some while. Avebury, to effect a compromise, suggested the kitchen middens should be relegated to a special "Early Neolithic" period, and here they remained for long.[2]

6. *Lake Dwellings, Crannogs and Terremare*

During the very dry winter of 1853–54 the low lake-levels of Lake Zurich revealed to the inhabitants of Obermeilen, in the bay between Obermeilen and Dollikon, the remains of wooden piles, as well as stone axes, horn implements, pottery and charred wood. The local schoolmaster, Aeppli, got Dr Ferdinand Keller of Zurich to examine these finds, which he did, diagnosing them as the remains of a lake dwelling. Previous reports had been made of similar finds at various times: in 1832 a Captain Pillichordy had dredged up a canoe and two bronze swords at Concise, on Lake Neuchâtel, and fishermen had reported "submerged forests" in several lakes, but it was not until Keller made his systematic investigations on Lake Zurich that the now famous Swiss lake villages were known to archaeology. Following the discovery at Obermeilen, other lake villages were found in other Swiss lakes, notably at Morges—"le grand cité de Morges"—on Lake Geneva, by Morlot and Troyon, at Cortaillod, Auvernier, Concise and Corcelettes, on Lake Neuchâtel, on Lake Bienne by Colonel Schwab—particularly the Steinberg at Nidau, at Robenhausen on Lake Pfaffikon, and on Moseedorf by Jahn, Uhlmann and Morlot. In 1863 Colonel Schwab published a list of 46 lake-side sites on Lake Neuchâtel, and by 1875 it was possible to list over 200 sites in Switzerland as a whole.

Keller published his findings in five memoirs presented between 1854 and 1863 to the Anthropological Society of Zurich. These were translated, with additions, into English by J. E. Lee, and published in 1866 under the title of *The Lake Dwellings of Switzerland and other Parts of Europe*. This translation included memoirs by Dr Rutimeyer on the fauna and Dr Heer on the flora

[1] Quoted in Evans, *Time and Chance*, 105–106.

[2] *Natural History Review*, i, 489–504 (1861). *Prehistoric Times* (1865), 171–197.

of the Swiss lake dwellings. Morlot, in his *Leçon d'Ouverture d'un cours sur la haute Antiquité fait à l'Académie de Lausanne*, and Troyon, in his *Habitations Lacustres des Temps Anciens et Modernes*, both published in 1860, gave general summaries of the new Swiss discoveries, and they were summarised for the English reading public in Lubbock's article on "The Swiss Lake Dwellings" in the *Natural History Review* for 1862 and in his *Prehistoric Times*.[1] Other notable memoirs on individual lake dwellings include Desor's *Les Palafittes ou Constructions Lacustres du Lac de Neuchâtel* (1865)—it was Desor who invented the phrase "le bel Age du Bronze".

It was found that similar or analogous structures existed in west France, south-west Germany and north Italy, and the discoveries were correlated with the *terremare* being found at this time in the south of Italy, and with the crannogs of Ireland. The *terremare* had been noted in the provinces of Parma, Reggio and Modena for a long time, but it was not until 1861 that Strobel and Pigorini suggested that these deposits of thick black earth were in fact the remains of pile dwellings. Desor and de Mortillet visited Lombardy in 1863 in search of lake dwellings. These searches for lake dwellings and the recognition of the *terremare* as types of lake dwellings brought into being a great interest in archaeology in Italy. A publication of Gastaldi's was translated into English under the title of *Lake Habitations and Prehistoric Remains in the Turbaries and Marl Beds of Northern and Central Italy*, in 1865. The International Congress of Prehistoric Anthropology and Archaeology, in its 1871 meeting at Bologna, was much concerned with lake dwellings and *terremare*, and as a result of the development of prehistoric archaeology in Italy the *Bullettino Paletnologia Italiana* was established in 1875, under the editorship of Strobel, Pigorini and Chierici.

The Irish crannogs had been known of since 1839. In that year (Sir) W. R. Wilde and George Petrie began exploring the Lagore crannog near Dunshaughlin, in County Meath. Wilde published his results in a paper on "The Animal Remains and Antiquities recently found at Dunshaughlin" in the *Proceedings of the Royal Irish Academy* for 1840. By 1857 no less than forty-six crannogs had been found. Reports of lake dwellings, crannogs

[1] The best summary of the discoveries in Switzerland is provided by Munro, *The Lake Dwellings of Europe* (1890).

and allied structures were made from various parts of northern Europe. Keller himself found it necessary to distinguish between the *Pfahlbauten*, or pile dwellings, and the *Packwerkbauten*, or crannogs, and it soon became evident that all these structures were not of the same age and type. In fact, there was not a generic type of prehistoric antiquity—the lake dwelling—which could be studied all over Europe in the way that megalithic monuments were being studied by Lukis and Bonstetten; lake dwellings and crannogs were a method of constructing settlements—some of which were prehistoric, others historic. Even in Switzerland it was clear that the lake villages did not all belong to one period. Troyon divided the Swiss lake dwellings into three periods, corresponding to the three ages of Stone, Bronze and Iron, and he argued that the Stone Age lake dwellings and the Bronze Age lake dwellings were brought to an end by the invasion of fresh people who destroyed by fire the earlier settlements. He further equated the Stone Age lake dwellers with the Finns or Iberians, whom he brought out of Asia "several thousand years before our era", the Bronze Age lake dwellers with the Celts, whom he likewise derived from Asia, and the Iron Age lake dwellers with the Helvetii. Troyon based his analysis of Swiss prehistory on the evidence, stratigraphical and otherwise, at many of the Swiss lake dwellings, and on the geographical distribution of various finds. He argued that the Bronze Age finds were mainly restricted to western Switzerland. Keller and others could not accept Troyon's thesis, while they did accept the facts that the Swiss lake dwellings were not all of one period, and that they did show a development from a Stone Age to an Iron Age. Keller especially denied the cataclysmic part of Troyon's thesis, with its destructive invaders at the beginning of the Bronze and Iron ages, and argued for transition periods.

The great value of the discoveries and researches in the Swiss lake dwellings between 1850 and 1875 to the development of prehistoric archaeology was twofold. In the first place, the excavations showed the truth of the Danish three-age system. It must be remembered that, by the middle of the nineteenth century, the system was still regarded by many archaeologists as no more than a hypothesis, and by many as an incorrect hypothesis. Although it was over thirty years between the opening to the public of the Copenhagen Museum, arranged on Thomsen's system, and the discoveries at Obermeilen, the Danish system had not yet attained general currency. The stratigraphical observations of Worsaae in the Danish bogs had given the first proof of the thesis. The second proof was given by the Swiss lake dwellings. Munro's view on this point is interesting: "Though the famous three ages of Stone, Bronze and Iron had been established as a method of classification before lacustrine treasures became known," he said in his 1888 Rhind Lectures, "I question if there is in the whole range of prehistoric archaeology any class of antiquities that gives greater support to this remarkable chronological sequence . . . than those collected from the early lake dwellings." The Swiss lake dwellings not only taught the truth of the three-age system: they taught the Swiss prehistorians the value of careful stratigraphical observation. In disputes such as those between Keller and Troyon on the nature of the lake dwelling sequence, it was only careful stratigraphical observation that could provide new facts of decisive value. The Swiss prehistorians were soon regarding the lake dwellings not as single period antiquities, but as sites occupied over a long period of time. The value of stratigraphy and the temporal sequence in prehistoric archaeology was made clear in Switzerland long before the excavations of tells and tepes in the Near East demonstrated it more dramatically.

The second great value of the Swiss lake dwelling researches was its demonstration of the potential detail which could be learnt about early man. Hitherto the remains of early man from Europe which had been thought to be the raw material of the archaeologist's researches were stone and bronze and iron tools, pottery, stone tombs, hut circles and the like—the almost indestructible remains of the past. Now it appeared that, sometimes, seemingly perishable things could survive from prehistory. The finds, particularly the tree coffins, from the Danish bogs would show this even more dramatically, but the carbonised apples and pears, the remains of wheat and barley and of cakes, and the pieces of flax fibres and mats of bast from the Swiss lake dwellings showed that archaeology would not be confined to stone and metal survivals from prehistoric time. Equally important were the reports of Rutimeyer and Heer on the fauna and flora from the Swiss lake dwellings. They showed the value to prehistoric archaeology of detailed specialist analyses of the materials found in prehistoric sites, and were the pioneers of the many specialist scientific analyses of flora, fauna, petrology and metallurgy carried out in the twentieth century.

7. *Upper Palaeolithic Man*

The discovery of Upper Palaeolithic man in the third quarter of the nineteenth century will always most properly be associated with the name of Edouard Lartet (1801–71), a magistrate in the district of Gers, who abandoned the study of law for that of palaeontology. Already in 1837, when the discoveries of Tournal, de Christol, Schmerling and MacEnery were attracting little attention, he had admitted the existence of Quaternary Man. His excavations in the Miocene deposits at Sansan yielded *Pliopithecus* in 1836 and *Dryopithecus* in 1850. In 1845 he had declared that Sansan might well yield the ancestor of modern man as well as the ancestors of the modern apes. Lartet came to the study of prehistoric archaeology fresh from the study of human palaeontology. In 1852 a roadmender of Aurignac in the Haute Garonne put his hand into a rabbit-hole and drew out a human bone. Interested in this discovery he dug down, found a great slab of rock closing the mouth of a rock shelter and behind it, in the cavity, some seventeen human skeletons, together with the remains of extinct animals, engravings on bones, and flint and ivory tools. The human skeletons were reburied in the Christian cemetery near by, and no interest evinced in the whole discovery until Lartet, who lived not far away, learnt of it and re-examined the cave. At first he considered the skeletons were a Neolithic collective burial, and that the bones were the remains of funeral feasts that had accompanied the Neolithic burials. Later, however, he changed his views and declared the flint and ivory tools, the engravings and hearths which he found under the Neolithic burials to be all pre-Neolithic and entirely unconnected in time with the burials. At another time he claimed that the burials themselves were pre-Neolithic. His changes of view, as well as the fact that he was examining the cave eight years after its first discovery, disposed some scholars at the time, not unnaturally, to doubt the authenticity of Lartet's conclusions.

Lartet went on to explore other Pyrenean caves. In 1860 he found, in a cave at Massat (Ariège), hearths with reindeer bones and chipped flints, barbed harpoons of stagshorn, bone needles and a bear's head engraved on the point of a broken stagshorn tine.

This discovery was published next year by Lartet in the *Annales des Sciences naturelles, Zool.*, vol. 15, together with an engraving of two deer on a reindeer bone which had been found somewhere between 1834 and 1845 by Brouillet in the cave of Chaffaud, Sevigné (Vienne). Brouillet and others had supposed this engraving to be "Celtic" in style, but Lartet recognised it as much earlier, and his appreciation of the significance and true date of the finds from Chaffaud and Massat was the first revelation of Franco-Cantabrian Upper Palaeolithic art.

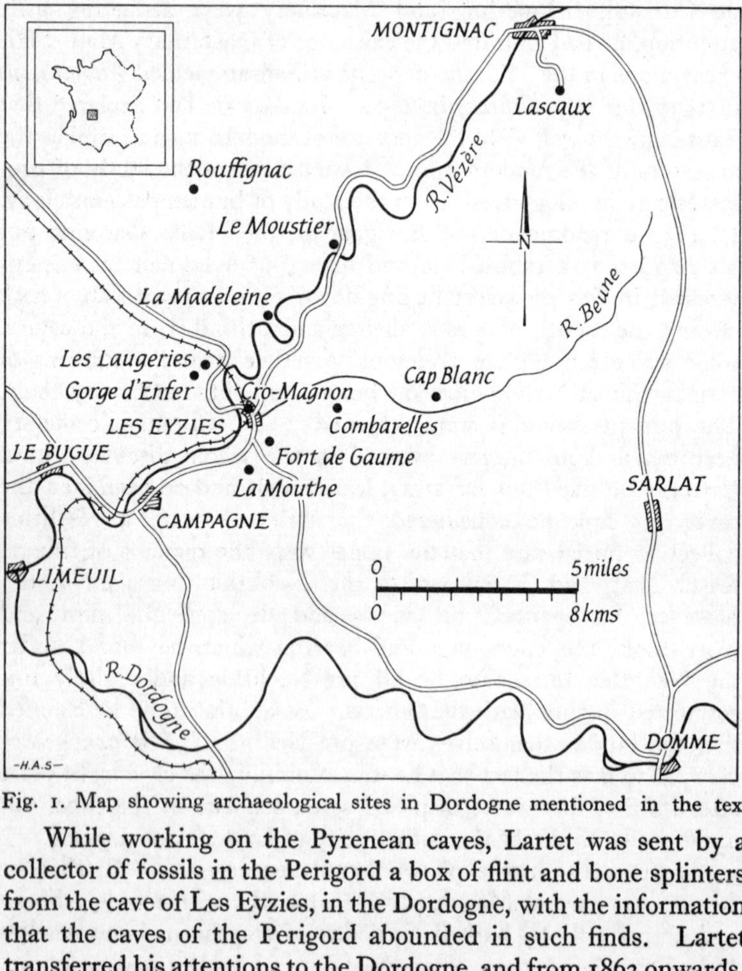

Fig. 1. Map showing archaeological sites in Dordogne mentioned in the text

While working on the Pyrenean caves, Lartet was sent by a collector of fossils in the Perigord a box of flint and bone splinters from the cave of Les Eyzies, in the Dordogne, with the information that the caves of the Perigord abounded in such finds. Lartet transferred his attentions to the Dordogne, and from 1863 onwards, helped financially and otherwise by an English banker friend, Henry Christy, began a series of excavations at sites in the valley of the Vézère, such as Gorge d'Enfer, Laugerie Haute, La Madeleine, Le Moustier and Les Eyzies—all names now famous in the annals of prehistoric archaeology. The results of their collaboration were published in articles in 1864—notably that on the "Caverns of Perigord" in the *Revue Archéologique* for that year—and later. A larger and complete work on the aborigines of Perigord was planned, but was delayed for many reasons: Christy died in 1865, "carried off", says the Prefatory Note to *Reliquiae Aquitanicae*, "in the midst of his self-imposed and well-directed work by acute illness brought on by over-exertion on a visit to the Belgian bone caves". Lartet continued the work alone, but the Franco-Prussian war upset him further, and he died in 1871. The full publication was edited by Professor Rupert Jones, assisted by John Evans, under the title of *Reliquiae Aquitanicae; being contributions to the Archaeology and Palaeontology of Perigord and the adjoining provinces of southern France.* This great work, which combined a full publication of the finds with general papers by several hands, was issued serially, over a period of ten years, being completed in 1875.

Many other names should be associated with Lartet and Christy in the work of cave exploration and excavation in south France at this time. The Marquis de Vibraye excavated in the Dordogne at the same time, and in many of the same sites, as did Lartet and Christy, the Vicomte de Lastic-Saint-Jal and Victor Brun at Bruniquel (Tarn-et-Garonne), Garrigou and Martin at Lourdes, Lalande and Massénat in the Corrèze and the Dordogne, and Ferry and Arcelin at Solutré (Saône-et-Loire). At the same time as all this activity was taking place in the south of France, Dupont was excavating caves in Belgium, and Delgado caves in the neighbourhood of Lisbon, and Boyd Dawkins and others were excavating various caves in England and Wales, from Wookey Hole in the Mendips to the St Asaph Caves in North Wales and Victoria Cave, Settle, in Yorkshire—and of course Pengelly went on working at Kent's Cavern until 1883. Dupont's researches were published in 1872 under the title of *Les Temps antéhistoriques en Belgique: L'Homme pendant les Ages de la Pierre dans les Environs de Dinant-sur-Meuse*,[1] and Boyd Dawkins summarised his own

[1] Brussels, 1872.

and all other cave explorations to 1874 in his *Cave-Hunting: Researches on the Evidences of Caves respecting the Early Inhabitants of Europe*,[1] a remarkably fine, learned and sober survey.

Lartet and Christy argued that their work in the Dordogne caves showed that the Stone Age was not a single and simple phase of human culture but rather a succession of phases; we shall deal with this aspect of their work later in this chapter. Lartet's importance to the development of prehistoric archaeology is threefold: he not only discovered the Upper Palaeolithic as a period of the Stone Age different from that of the diluvial axes of north France, and proposed the first classification of the Stone Age; he also was responsible for the discovery of Palaeolithic art—the first artistic manifestations of man. Lartet showed that the early men who had lived in the south French caves were not merely craftsmen but artists.

The acceptance of the authenticity of Palaeolithic art after the famous paper of Lartet and Christy in 1864 was not immediate nor universal. The case for the authenticity of the art had been damaged by a work published in Poitiers in 1864 under the title of *Époques Antédiluvienne et Celtique du Poitou.* It was written by Brouillet (son of the discoverer of the Chaffaud decorated bone) and Meillet, and included, among genuine examples of Palaeolithic art, fraudulent and absurd drawings as well as pieces of Sanskrit. Three years later Léon Fallue argued, in a pamphlet, *De l'Art récemment qualifié antédiluvien*, that the so-called Quaternary art was the work of Gallo-Roman forgers or of the same pre-Roman Ancient Gauls who had engraved serpents on the walls of their megaliths. But gradually the authenticity of Palaeolithic art was recognised. In 1869 Worsaae, at the Copenhagen International Congress of Anthropology, accepted the authenticity of the Chaffaud drawings.

But Palaeolithic man was not only an artist; he had also ideas about life and death. In 1868 contractors, clearing away material from the hillsides to construct the railway through Les Eyzies, uncovered in the rock shelter of Cro-Magnon chipped flints, animal bones and human remains. Edouard Lartet's son, Louis, excavated the shelter, and at the back of it found the remains of five people, together with ornaments, including pierced sea-shells. These were not only the first recognised human remains from the

[1] London, 1874.

Upper Palaeolithic,[1] they were clearly deliberate burials. Four years later Massénat found at Laugerie Basse a skeleton also accompanied by sea-shells, and Louis Lartet and Chaplain-Duparc found at Duruthy, Sordes (Landes), another Upper Palaeolithic skeleton buried with engraved and pierced animal teeth. In 1872 Emile Rivière began excavating the nine caves of Grimaldi, or Baoussé-Roussé, near Mentone. In the fourth, the Grotte du Cavillon, he found a skeleton covered with powdered haematite. The skull was decorated with over two hundred perforated sea-shells and twenty-two perforated red-deer canine teeth. Just below the left knee were forty-one perforated sea-shells. Buried with the skeleton were two flint blades and a flint bone implement. In 1874 and 1875, in the cave afterwards named the Grotte des Enfants, Rivière found the skeletons of two children. Near by were some flint implements, and on both, from navel to hips, a belt of more than one thousand perforated sea-shells. At first many refused to accept the fact that the Palaeolithic inhabitants of the French caves could have practised careful burial. The burials at Cro-Magnon, declared Boyd Dawkins, were "*above* the strata accumulated by the Palaeolithic cave dwellers", and "of a later age".[2]

These remarkable discoveries, like the discoveries of Palaeolithic art, were pointing the lesson that early emerges from the study of the development of prehistoric archaeology—that the prehistorian is an historian, although at times the techniques of archaeology may appear to one trained in the literary techniques of the humanities to be more akin to the natural sciences. The discovery of Palaeolithic man not merely as maker of flints, but as artist, and as a man who had already some primitive philosophy—for the careful burials mean this if they do not necessarily mean a belief in the after-life—are discoveries of the most vital importance to our picture of man's early history. This lesson was not early learnt, and for a while prehistoric archaeologists were content to think of themselves as natural scientists rather than historians.

8. *Tertiary Man*

The problem of Tertiary man first arose in 1863, when J. Desnoyers found incised fossil bones in the sand and gravel beds

[1] Buckland's discoveries at Paviland (*see supra*, p. 37) were, of course, still regarded as Romano-British.

[2] *Cave Hunting*, 20.

of Saint-Prest, near Chartres (Eure-et-Loire).[1] These were Pliocene in date. Desnoyers claimed that the incisions were made by man, but, in the absence of associated flint implements, the general conclusion was that they had been made by "some extinct rodent of the beaver family". By 1867 the Abbé Bourgeois claimed to have found roughly chipped flint implements from these Pliocene beds at Saint-Prest, and also from Miocene beds at Thenay (Loir-et-Cher). He exhibited these at the 1867 Congrès d'Archéologie et d'Anthropologie in Paris, when there were three other claimants for Tertiary man: Delaunay, with some more alleged humanly incised bones from the Miocene beds of Pouance (Maine-et-Loire), Arthur Issel, with alleged human skeletons from the Pliocene of Savone (Liguria), and Professor W. P. Blake, Professor of Mineralogy and Geology in the University of California, with some alleged Pliocene stone implements from California.[2]

These and other alleged discoveries of Tertiary man were canvassed and denied during the next few years, and formed the basis of controversial communications in the meetings of the Congress of Archaeology and Anthropology at Paris in 1867, Brussels in 1872, and Budapest in 1876.[3] At the Brussels Congress a committee of fifteen was appointed to report on the Abbé Bourgeois's chipped flints. Nine members of this committee (de Quatrefages, d'Omalius, Cartailhac, Capellini, Worsaae, Valdemar Schmidt, the Marquis de Vibraye, Franks and Engelhardt) accepted some of the flints as being humanly manufactured, five (Steenstrup, Virchow, Neyrincx, Fraas and Desor) denied that any of them were chipped by man; while one, Von Beneden; could not make up his mind.

At the same Brussels Congress of 1872 Carlos Ribeiro presented a paper on chipped flints of Miocene and Pliocene date from Otta and other sites in the Tagus valley, near Lisbon, which he had first published in the previous year.[4] Franks and de Mortillet accepted the authenticity of many of the Otta chipped flints.

[1] Desnoyers, *Comptes rendus Acad. Sc.*, 1863, 1077, 1082 and 1199. *See also* Lyell, *The Antiquity of Man*, 1863. Appendix to third edition, p. 4.

[2] *Compte rendu du Congrès de Paris*, 1867, pp. 67, 101. Bourgeois, *Comptes rendus Acad. Sc.*, 1867, 47.

[3] For a full discussion of the early eolithic controversies see de Mortillet, *Le Préhistorique*, section entitled "Homme Tertiare."

[4] Ribeiro, *Descripcao de alguns silex e quartzites lascados encontrados nas camadas de terreno terciario* (1871); *C. R. Brussels*, 1872, 95.

Ribeiro displayed ninety-five of his Tagus flints at the 1878 Exposition Internationale in Paris; de Mortillet declared that he and Cartailhac and all the "paleoethnologues" to whom these finds were shown were convinced of the authenticity of twenty-two of them.[1]

At the same Exposition, B. Rames displayed allegedly chipped flints found at Puy Corny, near Aurillac (Cantal), between 1869 and 1877, in beds of Upper Miocene age.[2] De Mortillet, Cartailhac, Chantre, Capellini and de Quatrefages were convinced of the authenticity of these flints, and declared that, had they been found in Quaternary deposits, there would have been no doubts of their authenticity. Nevertheless, many prehistorians refused to accept these or any of the alleged Tertiary finds. De Mortillet was the most persistent protagonist of pre-Quaternary man. He argued, very cogently, that man of the type found at Neanderthal, Denise and Cannstadt must have a hominid or anthropian precursor. As he differed from modern man, so the Tertiary precursor of Quaternary man would differ even more. He argued, too, that the flints found in the Quaternary drift must have primitive ancestors; *ergo*, and this of course was his *non sequitur*, the finds from Thenay, Puy Corny and Otta must be authentic. He invented the name *Anthropopithecus* for this Tertiary precursor of man, and acclaimed his tools in the discoveries of the Abbé Bourgeois, Ribeiro and Rames.[3] Abel Hovelacque, in an amazingly irrelevant argument, supported *Anthropopithecus* on linguistic grounds.[4] De Mortillet went further, and although no skeletal remains had been found, proposed to distinguish three species of this creature whom he had invented: *Anthropopithecus Bourgeoisii*, the maker of the Thenay flints, *Anthropopithecus Ramesii*, the maker of the Puy Corny flints, and *Anthropopithecus Ribeiroii*, the maker of the Otta flints. All, he averred, belonged to the "eolithic" or dawn-stone period of man's past.

9. *The Classification of the Stone Age*

In the first article in *Reliquiae Aquitanicae*, Lartet declared that the three stations of Le Moustier, Laugerie Haute and La

[1] Mortillet, *Bull. Soc. d'Anthropologie*, 1878, 428; *Revue d'Anthropologie*, 1879, 116.

[2] Mortillet, *Revue d'Anthropologie*, 1879, 118.

[3] Mortillet, *Revue d'Anthropologie*, 1879, 117, and "Le Precurseur de l'Homme," in *Compte rendu Ass. Fr.*, Lyon, 1873, 607.

[4] Hovelacque, "La Linguistique et le Precurseur de l'Homme," *Compte rendu Ass. Fr.*, Lyon, 1873, 613, and *Notre Ancêtre.*

Madeleine, "although within the chronological divisions of the *age of simply worked stone without the accompaniment of domestic animals*, do not possess a uniformity in the products of human industry collected there". Christy proposed classifying prehistoric stone implements into three periods: (i) the oldest, those of the Drift or Diluvium, (ii) those found in the caves, and (iii) the youngest, those found on the surface, and he defined the cave period as "an age prior to the construction of habitations for the living or receptacles for the dead".

Lartet preferred a classification based entirely on palaeontology to that of Christy, which was based on the find-spots of implements. He proposed to distinguish four periods in the cave finds of south France as follows:

(4) the Aurochs or Bison period;
(3) the Reindeer period;
(2) the Woolly Mammoth and Rhinoceros period;
(1) the Cave Bear period.

To these four periods Garrigou prefaced a period of "warm" elephant (*Elephas antiquus*), "warm" rhinoceros (*Rhinoceros merckii*), and hippopotamus (*Hippopotamus amphibius*), which he thought preceded the Arctic fauna of the caves (*Ursus spelaeus*, *Elephas primigenius* and *Rhinoceros tichorhinus*).

Lartet did not really defend the sharp differentiation of these periods, and gradually realised that the Cave Bear and Mammoth/Rhinoceros periods could not be separated. The Lartet/Garrigou scheme for the classification of the Stone Age, then, really distinguished four periods as follows: (1) the Hippopotamus/Warm elephant period, (2) the Cave Bear/Mammoth period, (3) the Reindeer period, (4) the Aurochs period, or period of polished stone. The Hippopotamus period was the period of the Diluvial axes of Saint-Acheul and Abbeville, when man was living mainly in open sites, and was not represented in the caves of south France. The succeeding period of Cave Bear and Mammoth was one in which man lived partly in open sites and partly in caves: Lartet used the Le Moustier site as typical of this period. Apart from the Le Moustier site, which produced some forms approaching the Diluvial forms of Saint-Acheul and Abbeville, the majority of the cave finds belonged to the Reindeer Age of Lartet and Christy. They took Laugerie Basse and La Madeleine as typical of this

Reindeer Age. Both Lartet and Christy were anxious to define the position of their Reindeer Age with relation to the earlier finds from the Somme and later finds from the Danish kitchen middens and the Swiss lake dwellings. "Geologically a wide gulf separates it from the Drift period, though wider perhaps in the geological than in the palaeontological aspect," wrote Christy, "but on the other hand, it will seem, both from the palaeontological and archaeological bearings, to be of higher antiquity than the Kjökkenmöddings of Denmark and the Lacustrine Dwellings of Switzerland, and very certainly than the whole group of so-called Celtic and Cromlech remains." [1]

Lartet and Christy had produced a classification of the Palaeolithic entirely on zoological and palaeontological grounds, but at least it *was* a classification of the Palaeolithic. They must be remembered not only for their exploratory work in the south French caves, and their recognition of Palaeolithic art, but for their introduction of some scheme of relative chronology into the remains of the Old Stone Age. The Danish pioneers in the first half of the century had begun the process of sorting out man's material prehistoric remains into their relative chronological position, Lubbock had taken the scheme further by recognising that the Stone Age of northern Europe was very different from the Stone Age of the Somme gravels and by inventing the Palaeolithic and Neolithic. Now Lartet introduced three divisions of the Palaeolithic, which were sometimes referred to as Lower, Middle and Upper, but more often by the palaeontological designations Hippopotamus, Cave Bear and Mammoth, and Reindeer, ages.

But, in so doing, Lartet, while subdividing the Palaeolithic, had introduced a new principle—the classification of archaeological remains on the basis of non-archaeological data. It was, in its way, a most revolutionary suggestion, and one which twentieth-century archaeology is adopting increasingly—in fact it was an attempt at an absolute chronology in terms of palaeontology. But the time was not ripe for such a change. Then, as all through the nineteenth century, it was easier to classify archaeological material *in terms of that material.* Very soon de Mortillet reinterpreted Lartet's classification in archaeological terms. In any case, Lartet's palaeontological criteria did not really provide an objective chronological scheme. Boyd Dawkins and de Mortillet were

[1] *Reliquiae Aquitanicae*, 25.

quick to point out that Hippopotamus, Rhinoceros and Mammoth would be found more often on open sites and Cave Bear in cave sites. And the incidence of these animals might vary according to the part of Europe which was being investigated.[1]

Boyd Dawkins held that the difference between the contents of one Palaeolithic cave and another was probably due to the fact that man could more easily catch some animals than others, or to a personal preference for one kind of food. He argued that the abundance of reindeer in the so-called Reindeer Age was probably due to the fact that man could more easily catch some animals; and may reasonably be accounted for by the fact that reindeer were perhaps easier to catch than mammoth, woolly rhinoceros, cave bear, lion and hyena. He declared that Lartet's attempted palaeontological classification was quite useless, and would apply "neither to the caves of this country, of Belgium, nor of France".

The "Reindeer Age" part of the Lartet-Christy scheme won general acceptance except among critics such as Boyd Dawkins and Mortillet. As we have seen, Lyell accepted it, at first thinking it should be a separate Stone Age between Paleolithic and Neolithic, but later placing it as the Upper Palaeolithic or later Palaeolithic. *L'Age du Renne* is a common phrase in the prehistory of the late nineteenth century, even being used by Piette, who had himself invented a different classification in which the Reindeer Age became the Glyptic Age or Age des Beaux Arts.

But while the Reindeer Age won general acceptance, the main Lartet scheme was superseded in various ways. Dupont proposed to distinguish only two periods in the Palaeolithic, namely: the Mammoth/Cave Bear period, or period of extinct animals, and secondly the Reindeer Age, or period of migrated animals.[2] In 1867 a French palaeontologist, Paul Gervais, proposed a fresh classification of the Stone Age as follows:

(4) Epoque des habitations lacustres ou palafittes;
(3) Epoque du renne utilisé;
(2) Epoque de l'*Elephas primigenius*;
(1) Epoque de l'*Elephas meridionalis*.

This was, at first, a palaeontological classification, but in its two later stages it was an archaeological one. It foreshadowed de

[1] *Quarterly Journal Geology*, June 5, 1872, and *Cave Hunting*, 352.
[2] *Bull. Acad. Roy. de Belgique*, ser. 2, XXII, 1866; *Les Temps préhistoriques en Belgique*.

Mortillet's scheme, which was clearly influenced by it considerably. At first, in his essay on *L'Origine de la Navigation et de la Pêche* (Paris, 1867), de Mortillet seems to have used Dupont's classification, later devising one of his own under the influence of Gervais's scheme.

Gabriel de Mortillet (1821–98), a devoted pupil and admirer of Lartet, was nevertheless the most persistent critic of Lartet's classification of the Palaeolithic, and the one who proposed the alternative scheme which won general acceptance. De Mortillet assisted Lartet in arranging the prehistoric section of the Universal Exhibition in Paris in 1867. He was then Professor in the Ecole d'Anthropologie in Paris. He had, in 1864, founded the journal *Matériaux pour l'Histoire positive et philosophique de l'Homme*. From 1868 to 1885 he was second in command at the French National Museum at Saint-Germain-de-Laye, which had been founded in 1867. This museum had, as its nucleus, collections from other Paris museums, and received some of the collections from the Dordogne. De Mortillet set about arranging these and based his classification on a modification of Lartet's scheme as it was being reinterpreted by Gervais.

De Mortillet was convinced that a palaeontological classification was impossible. "Il faut donc renoncer à baser de bonnes divisions sur la faune," he declared to the Brussels conference in 1872. A classification of prehistory, he insisted, must be archaeological. Archaeology, he claimed, had been responsible for phrases like the Etruscan and Greek and Roman periods; we must then distinguish earlier phases of history by various types of artifacts and he thought his proposals were no more than a logical development of the ideas of Thomsen and Lubbock.

De Mortillet substituted archaeological titles for the palaeontological names of Lartet. Lartet's Hippopotamus Age became the Chellean, named after Chelles, a site near Paris, and a great deal of the Great Bear and Mammoth Age was classified by de Mortillet as Moustierien,[1] after the rock shelter of Le Moustier. He characterised the Moustierien by tools chipped entirely on flakes and by an absence of worked bones. Lartet had recognised that the Aurignac remains and those of the Gorge d'Enfer rock shelter, while placed in his Great Bear/Mammoth epoch, were late in this series, for here, worked bones and stagshorn were found together

[1] These spellings were later modified to Mousterien, or Mousterian.

with flaked flints. De Mortillet separated the period of Aurignac and Gorge d'Enfer from the Great Bear/Mammoth period, and called it the Aurignacian. The Reindeer Age of Lartet he divided into two levels on archaeological grounds, the earliest of which he named after Laugerie Haute, and which was characterised by extremely fine flintwork, and no worked bones, and the later, named after La Madeleine, characterised by simpler trimming of flints, the abundance of worked bones and by the great development of the arts of engraving and sculpture.

The finds made at Solutré in 1866 and the following years revealed, according to de Mortillet, a better example of the epoch represented at Laugerie Haute, and he therefore proposed to substitute Solutré for Laugerie Haute as the type-site of this epoch. In 1869 de Mortillet read a paper entitled *Essai de Classification des Cavernes et des Stations sous Abri, fondée sur les produits de l'industrie humaine*, to the Académie des Sciences,[1] and in this paper he proposed the following classification of the Palaeolithic from the south French caves:

(4) Epoque de la Madeleine;
(3) Epoque d'Aurignac;
(2) Epoque de Solutré;
(1) Epoque du Moustier.

In 1872, at the International Congress in Brussels, he further explained his classification in detail in his paper *Classification des diverses Periodes de l'Age de la Pierre.*[2] The Aurignac period had now been dropped, and the Palaeolithic grouped into two periods: (i) the Lower, comprising only implements of chipped flint, into which he put the Chellean, Mousterian and Solutrean, and (ii) the Upper, consisting of the Magdalenian, and characterised by bone and horn implements as well as those of chipped flint.

In addition to his four periods of the Old Stone Age de Mortillet proposed to bring the Neolithic into line, and call it the Robenhausien, after the Swiss site of Robenhausen. He also characterised the Robenhausien specifically by six things, namely polished stone axes, barbed and tanged flint arrowheads, dolmens and menhirs, pottery, domesticated animals and agriculture. The

[1] *Comptes rendus de l'Académie des Sciences*, 1869; *Matériaux*, V, 187, 1867, 191; 1868, 458; 1869, 172.

[2] *Comptes rendu du Congrès International d'Anth. et d'Arch. préhist.*, Brussels, 1872, 432 ff.; *Revue d'Anthropologie*, 1874; *Matériaux*, 1872, 464.

Neolithic was so short, according to de Mortillet, and so homogeneous, that it should not be subdivided. In taking a site from the Swiss lake dwellings as typical of his Robenhausien he was following the suggestion of Gervais, whose fourth phase of the Stone Age had been *L'Epoque des Habitations lacustres.*[1]

De Mortillet further proposed an Eolithic period or the epoch of the Thenaisien, to comprise the eoliths we have already discussed, so that his classification of the Stone Age at the end of the quarter century we are here studying was as follows:

(6) Robenhausien;
(5) Magdalenian;
(4) Solutrean;
(3) Mousterian;
(2) Chellean;
(1) Thenaisian.

It was on this basis that we find the Stone Age divided in the first (1883) edition of his textbook *Le Préhistorique.*[2]

It was obvious that de Mortillet was not certain where to put the Aurignac epoch in his schemes of classification. At first, in 1867, he followed Lartet's suggestion and placed it before the Solutré-Laugerie Haute epoch, later he placed it after Solutré and before La Madeleine, while in his standard 1872 classification the Aurignac epoch disappears altogether. In 1872 Sir John Evans published *The Ancient Stone Implements, Weapons and Ornaments of Great Britain*, a critical analysis of Palaeolithic and Neolithic research to date. He discussed the various classifications of Lartet, Dupont and de Mortillet, and himself proposed a classification of the Old Stone Age into five periods, which corresponded generally to de Mortillet's 1869 scheme; first the River Gravel stage, which was the same as de Mortillet's Chellean, secondly the Le Moustier stage, the same as de Mortillet's Mousterian, then the Laugerie Haute stage, corresponding to de Mortillet's Solutrean, the Cro-Magnon stage, corresponding to de Mortillet's Aurignac epoch, and finally the La Madeleine stage, corresponding to de Mortillet's Magdalenian.

William Pengelly in his definitive statements on Kent's

[1] De Mortillet was at first inclined to call the Neolithic the Peurichardien, after the camp of Peu Richard, near Saintes (Charente Maritime).

[2] For the development of de Mortillet's classification see also the *Tableau archéologique de la Gaule*, 1876.

Cavern used a broad classification in many ways foreshadowing the twentieth-century grouping of Palaeolithic industries. He distinguished in the Palaeolithic deposits at Kent's Cavern, first, the Ursine deposits which yielded only nodule tools, and secondly, the Hyennine deposits which yielded only flake tools. "In the hyennine deposits", he writes, "were found flake tools, but the men of the ursine period did not strike off flakes from flint nodules and form the flakes into tools, but they took the nodules of flint and chipped *them* into useful shapes."[1] Here was the basis of a more archaeological classification of prehistory than that of de Mortillet, for all his protestations that his scheme was archaeological. Hamy, in his *Précis de Paléontologie humaine* (1870), accepted with many modifications the schemes of Lartet and de Mortillet. He insisted that cave bear and mammoth were contemporary, restored the Aurignac level to a time immediately following the Moustier epoch, and held that the Solutrean and Magdalenian were contemporary.

The evolution of Stone Age classification is set out graphically in the accompanying figure (fig. 2). The schemes of Lartet and de Mortillet provided a great fillip to the development of Palaeolithic studies. De Mortillet was of course the first to give to associations of archaeological types, names derived from type-sites, but it is to be emphasised here that his divisions, though named after Chelles, Le Moustier, Solutré and La Madeleine, were not cultures, but periods of time. The idea in the mind of Lartet and de Mortillet, though the forms taken were respectively zoological and archaeological, was essentially the same — the idea was foremost a chronological one. The objects cited as typical of the Chellean, Mousterian, or Robenhausien were thought of as zone fossils of a period of time. Nevertheless, although to this extent inaccurate, the scheme of de Mortillet remained the basis of Palaeolithic classification until well into the twentieth century. There were of course modifications, as we shall see, but they were modifications to a unilateral sequence of periods characterised by zone fossils.

The scheme itself became an accepted canon of prehistory, as accepted as the three-age scheme of the Danish prehistorians. "It commended itself", writes Breuil, "by its clarity, simplicity and logic, the latter indeed too pronounced to be true, for reality

[1] *The Antiquity of Cave Man.*

Lubbock	Worsaae	Lartet/Garrigou	Gervais	de Mortillet (1867–83)
Neolithic or New Stone Age. Age de la pierre polie	Later Stone Age	Aurochs Age	Lake-dwelling Age	Robenhausien
Palaeolithic (formerly Archaeolithic) or Old Stone Age. Age de la Pierre Taillée	The Older Stone Age comprising: (2) Kjökken-möddings and Coast Finds			
	(1) Stone Implements of the Drift and Caves	Reindeer Age	Age of utilised Reindeer Bones	Magdalenian
		Cave Bear/ Mammoth Age	Age of *E. primigenius*	Solutrean
		Hippopotamus Age	Age of *E. meridionalis*	Mousterian
				Chellean
				Thenasian

FIG. 2. Comparative Table of Classifications of the Stone Age.

is always more complex than our ideas about it."[1] It was easy for Breuil to say this in 1941; three-quarters of a century previously his predecessors in French archaeology did not conceive that the realities of prehistory were more complex. They were geologists and palaeontologists, and came to the problem of excavating caves and gravel pits by a geological approach. They were not historians and anthropologists, and were content to see man's story in the rigid terms of a geological succession. Indeed de Mortillet was at great pains on several occasions to insist that this scheme of his was entirely an extension of geology. Describing the evolution of his ideas in his *Le Préhistorique* (1883) he wrote: "Suivant d'une excellente méthode adoptée en géologie—il ne faut pas oublier que la paléoethnologie découle directement de la géologie—j'ai donné à chaque époque le nom d'une localité bien typique, parfaitement connue et étudiée; seulement, au lieu de dire: époque de Chelles, époque du Moustier, époque de Solutre et époque de la Madeleine; pour simplifier, en supprimant l'article, j'ai transformé en adjectif le nom de la localité, le terminant par d'une consonance uniforme. C'est encore là un procédé emprunté à la géologie."[2] Thus was born one of the basic methods of archaeological nomenclature.

Boyd Dawkins had been critical of Lartet's classification. He was equally critical of de Mortillet's scheme. It was, he declared, quite unsatisfactory, "for there is no greater difference in the implements of any two of the Palaeolithic caves than is to be observed between those of two different tribes of Eskimos".[3] He attacks the principle of typology, and in a remarkable passage in his *Cave Hunting* foreshadows the criticism of the de Mortillet sequence which was made in the twentieth century. "The principle of classification by relative rudeness", he wrote, "assumes that the ruder implements are therefore the older. The difference, however, may have been due to different tribes or families having coexisted without intercourse with each other, as is now generally the case with savage communities, or to the supply of flint, chert and other materials for cutting instruments being greater in one region than in another."[4] This was written in 1874; in these criticisms Boyd Dawkins was fifty years ahead of his time, but it must be said that he did not follow up his brilliant and

[1] *The Discovery of the Antiquity of Man*, Huxley Memorial Lecture for 1941.
[2] *Le Préhistorique : Antiquité de l'Homme*, first edition (1883), 20.
[3] *Cave Hunting*, 353.
[4] *Ibid.*

penetrating criticisms with a fresh and detailed analysis of prehistoric cultures. The de Mortillet system with its geological background—for all its archaeological form—became the orthodox system of prehistory until well into the twentieth century.

10. *Hallstatt and La Tène: Celts, Etruscans, Scythians*

Archaeological material belonging to the pre-Roman Iron Age in Europe was recognised as such even before Thomsen and his successors had defined the Iron Age, but was of course variously labelled British or Gaulish or Teutonic. Thus Colt Hoare had described the bridle-bits, iron tires and axle-mounts from Hampden Hill as British. In 1849 a disordered heap of iron weapons, horse-harness, parts of chariots, Celtic coins and pottery were found at Tiefenau, near Berne, and these were described by the Baron de Bonstetten as Alemannic of the third or fourth century A.D. The site of La Tène on Lake Neuchâtel was first excavated by Colonel Schwab in 1858. These excavations, which were continued for many years, brought to light, among other things, a splendid series of iron swords. Keller studied the swords and other finds from La Tène and proclaimed them neither Roman nor belonging to the Bronze Age, or what he called the "Celtic" period, but to the Iron Age, which he thought of as the "Helvetic" phase of Swiss prehistory. Meanwhile in 1846 excavations had begun at Hallstatt, under Ramsauer, on behalf of the Vienna Museum. These excavations were continued until 1864; the results of nearly twenty years' digging were summarised in Baron von Sacken's *Das Grabfeld von Hallstatt* (1868): 993 sepultures had been uncovered in these excavations at Hallstatt, 525 of them were inhumations, 455 were complete cremations, and 13 partial cremations. The Hallstatt cemetery appeared to demonstrate the transition from the Bronze to the Iron Age in Europe.

The remarkable antiquities from Hallstatt were first published by Gaisberger in his *Die Grüber bei Hallstatt im österreichischen Salzkammergute* (Linz, 1848) and by Friedrich Simony in *Die Alterthümer vom Hallstätter Salzburg* (Vienna, 1857).

The real understanding of the pre-Roman Iron Age in Europe came in the late fifties and early sixties, as de Navarro has pointed out.[1] It began with the work of Thurnam, Franks and Lindenschmitt, and this formative period might be said to come to an

[1] *Proc. Brit. Acad.*, XXII. (Rhŷs Lecture.)

end with Hildebrand's proposal, in 1872, to divide the Iron Age into an earlier or Hallstatt phase and a later or La Tène phase. Thurnam, in the *Crania Britannica* (1857), grouped together many isolated Iron Age finds from Britain, classifying them as "Late British" and assigning them to a "bronze and iron transition period". In his famous address to the Royal Irish Academy on February 9, 1857, John Kemble drew attention to a group of objects ornamented in the La Tène style which were being studied in the British Museum by Franks. Franks himself, in arranging and describing the plates which had been intended by Kemble to illustrate his *Horae Ferales*, and which were published after Kemble's death in 1863, devoted a large proportion of the plates to these objects, which he "ventured to term Late Celtic". He justified his allocation of a fourth of the plates to these La Tène objects "not only on account of their archaeological and national importance, but because the remains are comparatively unknown both to English and foreign antiquaries". Franks assigned these objects to a period dating from 200 to 100 years B.C. and ending "not much later than the first century after Christ, when Roman domination in the country was firmly established". Franks studied the British material in relation to the Continental, and very deliberately used the linguistic label "Celtic" for the finds he was studying, because their distribution appeared to coincide with that of Celtic occupation, and because their ornamental patterns coincided with those of Early Christian art in Ireland and differed from those of the Danish, Saxon and Roman antiquities in England.

Lindenschmitt, in his *Die Altertümer unserer heidnischen Vorzeit* (1858–62, 1870, and 1881), grouped together objects of La Tène type on the Continent, but regarded them not as the native work of the transalpine barbarians, but exports of the Etruscans, a view supported by Genthe in his *Über den etruskischen Tauschhandel nach dem Norden* (1874). Other workers, like Lohde, regarded La Tène art as Teutonic.

The first reliable evidence for the date of La Tène art was provided by the excavations at Mont Auxois (Alesia) and Mont Réa at Alise Ste Reine in Burgundy, carried on from 1861 to 1865 by order of Napoleon III. In the ditches of the Roman camp at Mont Réa were found iron swords and spears with Roman and Gaulish coins, none of the former being later than 54 B.C., which seemed to date the La Tène objects as pre-Roman and at least to the middle of the first century B.C. This discovery enabled Desor and Keller in Switzerland, and de Baye, Foudrignier and other French archaeologists, to assign finds and graves to the pre-Roman Iron Age. At the same time the extent of the La Tène phase of the Iron Age was being appreciated. In 1870 de Mortillet noted the identity of objects from graves at Marzabotto near Bologna with La Tène objects from graves in the Marne, and was thus the first to identify the La Tène Celtic invaders in Italy.

In addition to the Celts, two other protohistoric peoples of Europe began to have archaeological existence at the time of which we write—the Etruscans and the Scyths. The Etruscans had been studied in the early nineteenth century by Micali, Inghirami and Gerhard. The richly coloured mural paintings of Corneto were discovered in 1827; other grottoes with murals and tombs were later opened at Chiusi, Veii, at Cerveteri and Orvieto. The Etruscan remains were made known to English readers by George Dennis's *Cities and Cemeteries of Etruria* (1848), a delightfully written and widely read work. Dennis was persuaded of the extreme importance of the Etruscans in spreading Mediterranean civilisation to northern and north-western Europe: "antiquarians are now generally agreed", he wrote in his book—as if such a thing ever happened!—"that all the ancient bronzes found in various kinds north of the Alps from Switzerland to Denmark, and from Ireland to Hungary and Wallachia, are of Etruscan origin".

The Scythians had been described by Herodotus. The earliest discoveries of the Scyths by modern archaeologists were those of Paul Delrux at Kul Oba, near Kertch, in 1830. Later work was described in the *Antiquités de la Scythie d'Hérodote, 1866–73*, published by the Imperial Archaeological Commission of St. Petersburg.[1]

11. *Prehistoric Archaeology in 1870*

Let us now, at the conclusion of this long chapter describing the many important discoveries and changes that took place between 1840 and 1870, consider briefly what was the state of prehistoric archaeology in 1870, the date roughly selected for its coming of age. The first significant fact is that in 1870 prehistoric

[1] See also Kondaloff, Tolstoi and Reinach's *Antiquités de la Russie méridionale* (1891–92); E. H. Minns, *Scythians and Greeks*, 1913; M. I. Rostovtsev, *Iranians and Greeks in South Russia*, 1922.

archaeology existed, whereas in 1840 it can hardly be said to have existed anywhere except in Denmark and Sweden. The thirty years from 1840 to 1870 not only saw the discoveries and deductions which have been summarised in this chapter, but at the same time a widespread recognition of prehistoric studies. This widespread interest showed itself in the publication and sale of general books and magazine articles, the large audiences that flocked to lectures on geology and prehistory, and the formation of national and international organisations and societies for prehistoric archaeology.

We have already referred to the large sales of books like Layard's *Nineveh* and the popularity of works like Dennis's *Cities and Cemeteries*. Similar heavy sales were the good fortune of Lubbock's *Prehistoric Times* and Lyell's *Antiquity of Man*. This latter book—"a trilogy on the antiquity of Man, ice, and Darwin", as a reviewer in the *Saturday Review* called it—was first published in February 1863; a second edition was called for in the following April, and a third in the succeeding November. As Pengelly wrote, with obvious and justified satisfaction, "three editions of a bulky scientific work in less than a few months". Articles of archaeological interest were appearing more frequently in the *Spectator*, the *Gentleman's Magazine*, and the *Athenaeum*. We have noted John Mitford's policy of filling the *Gentleman's Magazine* with antiquarian and archaeological information and correspondence; especially notable were the Antiquarian Notes edited for the *Magazine* by Roach Smith.

W. J. Thoms, who had translated into English Worsaae's *The Primeval Antiquities of Denmark*, began in 1846 a series of articles on antiquities in the *Athenaeum* under the pseudonym of Ambrose Merton. He gave to these articles the title "Folklore" for he said "it was more a lore than a literature". These articles were so popular and caused such an amount of correspondence that Wentworth Dilke, editor and part proprietor of the paper, suggested to Thoms that he should start a special journal to deal popularly with the study of antiquities. The result was *Notes and Queries*, the first number of which appeared in November 1849. The public *were* interested in prehistory, whether their interest sprang from natural science and geology or from the romantic excavations in the Near East. Wherever Pengelly lectured, whether to the Mechanics' Institute at Torquay or to the Sciences Lectures Association in Glasgow, and on whatever subject—

Kent's Cavern, the discoveries on the Somme, the caves at Mentone—his audiences were large and enthusiastic.

In 1870 J. H. Parker, the Keeper of the Ashmolean, gave a lecture to the Oxford Architectural and Historical Society on *The Ashmolean Museum: its History, Present State and Prospects*, in which he said: "When Archaeology is made part of the system of Education in Oxford, as I trust it will be, with the help of this Museum, any educated man will feel it a disgrace to be ignorant of it. . . . The ladies are already taking the lead in this matter. Architecture or Archaeology is now part of the course of study in the education of young ladies, and I have frequently observed in society that to find out whether a young lady knows anything of Archaeology or not is a test whether she has been highly educated or not. The daughters of our higher nobility, who have generally had the best education that can be obtained, are almost always well acquainted with Archaeology. Some of my most favourite pupils have been young ladies of this class, our future Duchesses or Countesses."

In 1851 the British Association at its Ipswich meeting admitted Ethnology as a distinct section, and throughout the thirty years 1840–70 contributions on prehistoric archaeology appeared in the Geology and Ethnology sections. De Mortillet started *Matériaux* in 1864, and the next ten years saw the commencement of some of the most famous international journals, such as the Brunswick *Archiv für Anthropologie* in 1866, the Berlin *Zeitschrift für Ethnologie* in 1869, and the *Journal of the Anthropological Institute*, the *Mittheilungen der Anthropologischen Gesellschaft in Wien*, and the *Archivo per l'Anthropologia e la Etnologia*, all in 1871.

In 1865, at a special meeting in Spezzia of the Société Italienne des Sciences naturelles, de Mortillet proposed the creation of an International Congress of Palae-ethnology or of Archaeology and Prehistoric Anthropology. This proposal was warmly supported by Cornalia, Capellini and Stopani, and the first *Congrès international d'Anthropologie et d'Archéologie préhistoriques* was held in Neuchâtel in 1866. A meeting was held in Paris in 1867, in Norwich the following year, and in Copenhagen in 1869. We have seen how all the main issues of prehistoric archaeology were discussed at these sessions.

The same period of thirty years saw the great growth of local societies. The Cambrian Archaeological Association was founded in 1846, and three years later the Kilkenny Archaeological Society —it changed its name to the Royal Historical and Archaeological Association of Ireland in 1896, and to the Royal Society of Antiquaries of Ireland in 1890. The Wiltshire Archaeological Society was founded in 1853. Ten years previously, in 1843, Charles Roach Smith and Thomas Wright formed the Archaeological Association. The Society of Antiquaries, with its Royal Charter, and its apartments in London, was the product of the late seventeenth-century interest in natural science and antiquaries. The Archaeological Association first met in Canterbury; its schismatic successors, the British Archaeological Association and the Royal Archaeological Institute, held their first meetings in 1845 in Winchester. Archaeology was now not a specialist subject for scholars and eccentrics: it had become a subject of wide general interest. It is no exaggeration to say that field archaeology was a national pastime in early Victorian times.

We may take the first field meeting of the British Archaeological Association as typical of these mid-nineteenth-century archaeological parties. The Association had been founded in 1843. "The study of our national antiquities has been continually increasing in popularity," wrote Thoms in that year. "And it was evident that some great movement was necessary. The object of the Association is to unite and concentrate the whole antiquarian force of the kingdom, and thus to increase its efficiency and consequent utility." The first meeting was held in Canterbury in 1844, and was acclaimed a great success, rarely, it was claimed, have "so large a number of persons passed a week with such entire satisfaction". The meeting went to a pattern familiar to all who have ever attended the field meeting of any archaeological society in Britain or France. It opened with "a judicious speech by the zealous and active president . . . Lord Albert Conyngham", and lasted a week: there were sectional meetings— "evening conversaziones in Barnes's Rooms . . . many interesting papers were read and discussed; and on the whole, an impression was made both on the visitors and the visited which it will take years to wear off".

The Canterbury meeting was organised in four sections: a medieval section, an architectural section, an historical section, and a first section "devoted to the *primeval antiquities* of our island, under which title were included all monuments (British,

Roman and Saxon) of a date anterior to the conversion of the Anglo-Saxons to Christianity". In this section papers were read on barrows in general, on barrows near Bakewell (by T. Bateman, jun.), on Kimmeridge coal-money, on the place of Caesar's landing in Britain; and on a gold Saxon fibula dug up in Hampshire; and "on the Friday evening after the last meeting, and previous to the opening of an Egyptian mummy in the theatre, Mr Pettigrew read a very able and interesting paper on the subject of the embalmment of the dead among the ancient Egyptians which elicited much applause". Excursions were made to Reculver, Richborough, Dover and to Saxon barrows on the downs; and, under the superintendence of Lord Albert Conyngham, a number of these barrows were excavated—the day's excavations ending with a party, "the archaeologists partook of the hospitality of their noble and learned President, who had prepared a plentiful repast in his fine old mansion".[1]

Few felt compelled to justify their interest in field archaeology; Akerman was one: "To the reflecting mind", he declared piously, "the fact that Providence has veiled from us the future, and given us the past for retrospect and experience, is alone sufficient to justify the occupation of a portion of our leisure in the examination and elucidation of the remains of Antiquity."[2]

The Great Exhibition of 1851 contained no prehistory. Sixteen years later the Exposition at Paris did. Of course the purpose of the Great Exhibition was only to summarise the material advances made during the first half of the nineteenth century, and illustrate the possibilities of future progress. But by 1867 the French planners of the Exposition envisaged a broader background to the story of development, and it is an index of the growth of archaeology that they did. The Prehistoric Collections at the Exposition were arranged by a Commission presided over by Lartet, and including Alexander Betrand, Desnoyers, and the Marquis de Vibraye, with Gabriel de Mortillet as secretary. In response to repeated requests from readers of *Matériaux*, de Mortillet wrote a guide to the collections under the title of *Promenades préhistoriques à l'Éxposition Universelle* (1867). Most of the prehistoric archaeological collections were set out in the main *Galerie de l'Histoire du Travail.* The French collections

[1] These extracts are from Thomas Wright, *The Archaeological Album*, pp. 1–3. See also below, p. 154.

[2] *Archaeological Index* (1847), preface.

contained material from Aurignac lent by Lartet, the Laugerie Haute finds lent by de Vibraye, a case of rock-shelter art, material from Grand Pressigny, and from the megaliths of the Paris Basin (*e.g.* Meudon) and Brittany (*e.g.* Mané-er-Hroeck), and from the Count Costa de Beauregard's collection of material from the Lac du Bourget lake villages. It was split into two parts: *La Gaule avant l'emploi des Métaux* and *Les Epoques celtiques, gauloise et gallo-romaine.* There were also collections from all over Europe, the British collection being arranged by Woollaston Franks.

If one had to choose any one special year for the coming of age of archaeology it would be this one of 1867—the year of the Exposition Universelle and the meeting of the Congress in Paris. It was indeed a triumph for archaeology. As de Mortillet claimed in his *Promenades*, it was "la première fois que les temps préhistoriques se manifestent d'une manière solennelle et générale. Eh bien, cette première manifestation a été pour eux un triomphe complet". Its triumph was so complete because archaeology seemed to prove once and for all, and in an entirely unexpected way, the widely held doctrine of progress. The evidence of the geological and archaeological sequences seemed to show that evolution and progress were facts not theories, and that man's story on the earth had been one of gradual progress from the primitive chipped flints of Chelles—perhaps even from the more primitive flints of Puy Corny, Thenay and Otta—to the ancient civilisations of Egypt, Assyria, Greece and Rome. "Impossible", declared de Mortillet, after conducting his tour around the Exposition, "de mettre en doute la grande loi du progrès de l'humanité." And this progress was clearly revealed in the archaeological stages: "Pierre taillée à éclats, pierre polie, bronze, fer, sont autant de grandes étapes qu'a traversé l'humanité entière pour arriver à notre civilisation."

Some archaeologists were prepared to recognise the possibility of retrogression: indeed Pengelly very wisely pointed to the post-Roman period in Britain, and asked whether it was not likely that similar periods of cultural retrogression had occurred in man's prehistoric past. But for the most part the story was conceived of as one of progress—progress revealed clearly in the succession of archaeological stages. Even Pengelly, despite his reservations on retrogression, wrote: that for northern Europe at least "all present and probable requirements would be met by the terms

Iron Age, Bronze Age, Neolithic Age, Palaeolithic Age, Glacial Age, Newer Pliocene, etc."

Gradually the great dispute between the evolutionists and the creationists was being fought out and won by the former, and the doctrine of evolution was erected into a sort of rigid creed. In Darwin's modest mind he had conceived of evolution as a scientific theory perhaps partly explained by the hypothesis of natural selection. Herbert Spencer, who, as we have already said, was putting out evolutionary ideas long before the publication of the *Origin of Species*, assumed that progress was the universal law of being. In 1850 he wrote in his *Social Studies*: "Progress is not an accident but a necessity. It is part of nature. . . . Evil tends perpetually to disappear. . . . Civilisation, instead of being artificial, is a part of nature; all of a piece with the development of the embryo or the unfolding of a flower." Evolution and progress became a panacea, which Darwin, who provided it with its biological credentials, had never intended—a national creed translated into verse by Tennyson in *In Memoriam*. Prehistoric archaeology in part reflected this climate of thought, dominated by progress and evolution; in part it seemed to sustain it.

It had taken such an effort to assimilate the doctrines of evolution, and the proofs of the antiquity of man, that for the most part archaeologists were ready to believe complacently that they had discovered the whole story of man's prehistoric past. This story was a succession of archaeological periods. The Chellean and the Robenhausien, the Hallstatt and the La Tène were conceived of as stages in the temporal development of man; the objects labelled Chellean or La Tène were conceived of as zone fossils. Lartet's scheme for the objective description of Palaeolithic remains in terms of palaeontology was forgotten, or derided as unsuitable: Boyd Dawkins, who refused to believe in the extension of the zone fossil idea to the cultural remains of man, was a lone voice. Of course by 1875 few were prepared to argue that the stages represented a natural development which took place uniformly all over the world, even if at varying rates in different localities. Most prehistorians were already arguing for a number of invasions to account for the more sudden cultural changes. There was fairly general acceptance of a Neolithic invasion, a Bronze Age invasion, and an Iron Age invasion to account for the beginning of each of these three phases. It will be remembered that Worsaae had argued for an invasion to account for the Danish kjökkenmöddings, but prehistorians were as yet conservative in the number of invasions they would allow.

There was no agreement on where these invasions came from, and no clear attempt to derive them from the civilisations of Egypt and the Near East, whose outlines were being sketched in by the discoveries of Mariette and Layard. There was perhaps a tendency to derive the invaders of Europe vaguely from Asia, or just "the East", or sometimes from India, and the Near East and Egyptian civilisations, while appreciated, were perhaps thought of still as ancient history—something behind Greece and Rome—but all much later than the prehistory of the archaeologists. There was as yet no integration of the results of archaeology everywhere into the general early history of man. It is to be noted that Lubbock's *Prehistoric Times* did not touch upon the discoveries in Egypt or Assyria.

Even if the prehistorians of this time did not seem anxious to link up their truly prehistoric discoveries with the protohistoric discoveries in the Near East, they were anxious to make two equations with the more normal conventions of history. They wanted to give names to their invasions, and they wanted to produce some sort of absolute chronology for their periods. The labels Celtic, Teutonic, Hyperborean, Aryan were confidently attached to the prehistoric invasions, and so developed one of the most false byways that has for the last hundred years beset prehistoric speculation.

The need for some kind of absolute chronology was a more reasonable speculation. Hitherto the biblical chronology had been accepted, but now two things made it seem impossible to crowd man's past as revealed archaeologically into a mere six thousand years. The decipherment of the Egyptian documents suggested that the civilisation of Egypt most go back at least to before 2000 B.C. Surely the prehistoric record could not be crowded into the time from 4004 B.C. to 2000 B.C.? In the second place, the succession of artifacts, the thickness of the deposits in which they were found, and the changes in the associated fauna in the French caves and gravels must imply a very long period of time. But how long? Could a figure be estimated for the first appearance of man, for the beginning of the Chellean? It was, as Prestwich said, "a curious and interesting problem".

Lyell estimated 100,000 years; de Mortillet 230,000 to 240,000 years. Worsaae found Lyell's figure hard to accept, and few paid much attention to de Mortillet's date.

But if it was not possible to calculate the remote date when man first appeared, surely, many archaeologists of this time argued, it would be possible to calculate the duration of the post-Palaeolithic cultures? Many attempts were made and many methods tried. The methods were based on the thickness of deposits, the rate of formation of deltas and river gravels, the rate of movement of glaciers, the rate of formation of stalagmite. These were entirely geological methods; as might be expected from the geological origins of Palaeolithic studies, and the reluctance to study Egyptian and Near East archaeology in direct relation to that of Europe, the synchronological technique was not yet used. Hinted at by the northern archaeologists before 1850, it awaited Montelius for its full development. But this did not prevent estimates from being made on geological bases only. Gilleron calculated, from the rate of formation of deposits in the Swiss lakes, that the first pile dwellings dated from 5000 to 4000 B.C. Morlot, with a different set of calculations from the same Swiss lakes, dated the Swiss Bronze Age as beginning from 3000 to 4000 B.C. and the Swiss New Stone Age 5000 to 7000 B.C. Troyon, with yet another set of calculations, fixed the beginning of the Swiss Bronze Age at 3300 B.C. Pengelly thought that the Scotch fir period at the base of the Danish bogs could be estimated at 5000 years B.C.

But whatever the precise dates accepted it was widely realised that prehistoric archaeology had no use for the Mosaic chronology of Archbishop Ussher, and assailed what Gladstone called the impregnable rock of Holy Scripture. Indeed archaeology provided the fourth nail in the coffin of the fundamentalists. To the Tübingen critics like Baur, to Lyell's *Principles*, to Darwin and evolution, was now added the sequence of prehistoric cultures which must have taken a long time even if the geological proofs of the antiquity of the Lower Palaeolithic were not accepted. Apart from an awareness of this, little attention was paid, either then or later in the nineteenth century, to the philosophical implications of prehistory—except perhaps in so far as prehistoric archaeology was held to prove the doctrines of progress and cultural evolution. At the end of his *Promenades* de Mortillet summarises the three main facts which, according to him, emerged from prehistoric scholarship. They were—he printed them in capitals as the last words in his book:

LOI DU PROGRÈS DE L'HUMANITÉ.
LOI DU DÉVELOPPEMENT SIMILAIRE.
HAUTE ANTIQUITÉ DE L'HOMME.

It would have been impossible for archaeology, any more than any other branch of knowledge first explored in the second half of the nineteenth century, to grow up uninfluenced by the theories of progress and evolution which dominated nineteenth-century thought; "History is evolution" declared General Pitt-Rivers in 1874, and it is clear that, while they admitted diffusion, the early archaeologists thought of the overall picture of prehistory as one of evolutionary progress. Archaeology owed much of its evolutionary outlook to the Darwinian popularisation of organic evolution, to the evolutionary philosophy of Spencer which so dominated English thought, and to the evolutionary study of institutions begun by McLennan and Maine. But archaeology also contributed in no small measure to this evolutionary outlook. Much of the concern with cultural evolution in all fields of thought in the later nineteenth century owes a great deal to the demonstration of technological development which archaeology now represented as early human history. It was so easy to make the illogical inference that this demonstration, which few denied, apparently *proved* that all aspects of culture were the result of gradual evolution from the simple to the complex—from forms of culture not now observed in western Europe to the form now observed there, where the most complicated technology existed. This lesson was not pointed out in the Great Exhibition of 1851; we were then content to admire our technical efficiency and skill, as Macaulay was content to admire the improved condition of the people in all material matters. By 1867 the planners of the Exposition Universelle in Paris were pointing out this moral by several backward glances. The palaces of the Exposition and the Crystal Palace of 1851 were now to be seen at the end of a great sequence of evolutionary progress starting with the rude chipped flints of the Somme gravels. The interval between 1851 and 1867 was a significant one; it showed not only the acceptance of the proofs of man's antiquity by Boucher de Perthes in north

France and Pengelly in south Devon, and the publication of the *Origin of Species*, but the popularisation of the Danish tripartite system, and its development in France into a complicated sequence of man's prehistory. It may be true to say that Darwin and evolution proved the doctrine of progress. Darwin's was an organic and philosophical proof. It was the technological sequences of the archaeologists that, apparently, proved the reality of cultural progress. Thereafter, once this proof was widely understood, archaeology became part of the general study of man and his culture, not merely an antiquarian hobby. As Tylor wrote in his *Primitive Culture* in 1871: "The history and prehistory of man take their proper places in the general scheme of knowledge."

CHAPTER FOUR

ARCHAEOLOGY COMES OF AGE: 1870–1900

1. *The Classification of the Stone Age*

DE MORTILLET'S classic division of the Palaeolithic proposed four divisions: the Chellean, the Mousterian, the Solutrean and the Magdalenian. It remained the framework for Palaeolithic studies, particularly in France, during the last quarter of the nineteenth century, although it was criticised and various alternative schemes proposed. One modification was accepted by de Mortillet himself—the insertion of an Acheulian between the Chellean and the Mousterian. A mixed industry had been found lying over deposits containing the typical Chellean hand-axes: this mixed industry had smaller axes as well as flake tools similar to those characterising the Mousterian. For this mixed industry between the Chellean and the Mousterian, D'Acy and D'Ault de Mesnil introduced in 1895 the term Acheulian. Others proposed the term Chelleo-Mousterian for this industry, but it was canonised into de Mortillet's sequence as Acheulian. In the third (1903) edition of *Le Préhistorique* the Palaeolithic is divided into the Lower Palaeolithic consisting of the Chellean, a Transition period (being the Acheulian), the Middle Palaeolithic consisting of the Mousterian, and the Upper Palaeolithic comprising the Solutrean and the Magdalenian.

John Evans, who in the first (1872) edition of his *Ancient Stone Implements* had proposed a different classification from de Mortillet, accepted de Mortillet's scheme in his second edition published in 1897, a quarter of a century later. It was a measure of the success which de Mortillet's scheme had attained generally in western Europe. Other schemes were, however, proposed towards the end of the nineteenth century: those which gained sufficient currency to be noted here are those of Salmon, Piette, Rutot and Schiattarella.

Salmon distinguished only three industrial phases in the

Palaeolithic; these were the Chellean, the Mousterian and the Magdalenian, and they corresponded to the three stages, Lower Quaternary, Middle Quaternary and Upper Quaternary, distinguished by d'Ault du Mesnil.[1] Salmon's Chellean and Magdalenian coincided with those periods in de Mortillet's scheme; his Mousterian really consisted of the Acheulian (or Chelleo-Mousterian), the Mousterian proper and the Solutrean, but he labelled the first and third of these as periods of transition and insisted that they did not constitute epochs.[2]

Piette divided the Palaeolithic into three periods, which he labelled Amygdalithic, Niphetic and Glyptic. The Amygdalithic was characterised by hand-axes, the "grands instruments amygdaloides taillés à éclats sur les deux faces", as he called them, and comprised the Chellean and Acheulian. The Niphetic, which was the Mousterian of de Mortillet, while still having some hand-axes, was characterised by scrapers and points on flakes. The Glyptic or "Age des Beaux Arts" was characterised by the presence of art and by "petits instruments en silex, de formes très variées, appropriées aux usages auxquels ils sont destinés"; it was subdivided by Piette into three stages, first the Papalian or Eburnian, characterised by sculpture in relief and in the round, second the Gordanian, characterised by drawings engraved but still belonging to a time when animals now extinct existed, and thirdly the Lorthetian, also characterised by engraved drawings, particularly on reindeer bone, but not associated with any extinct fauna. Piette invented the names Gordanian and Lorthetian after the two rock shelters of Gordan and Lorthet which he excavated in the Hautes-Pyrénées. Déchelette very properly complains of the way in which the divisions and nomenclature of Piette's system varies between his many papers and books.[3]

Rutot, working in Belgium, adopted at first a scheme for the Palaeolithic which was little more than the de Mortillet scheme with Belgian names. He distinguished four stages, namely the Moséen, the Campinien, the Hesbayen and the Flandrien. The Moséen, named after the Meuse, corresponded to the Chellean, the Campinien (after Campine) to the Acheulian and Mousterian, the Hesbayen (after Hesbaye) to the Solutrean, and the Flandrien

[1] *La Société, l'Ecole et le Laboratoire d'Anthropologie à l'Exposition universelle de Paris en 1889.*

[2] Salmon, *Age de la Pierre*, Paris 1891; *Bull. de la Société dauphinoise d'Ethn.*, 1894.

[3] *Manuel*, i, 113.

(after Flanders) to the Magdalenian.[1] Later, following Dupont, Rutot adopted a fresh classification of post-Mousterian or post-Campinian times, distinguishing the Eburnian and the Tarandian. The Eburnian was divided into the Montaiglian, the Magritian and the Goyetian, while only one division of the Tarandian was recognised, namely the Chaleuxian. The Montaiglian corresponded to the pre-Solutrean upper Palaeolithic, soon to be known as the Aurignacian, the Magritian to the Lower Solutrean, the Goyetian and the Chaleuxian both corresponded to the Magdalenian.[2]

In Italy, Enrico Morselli adopted the de Mortillet scheme, while observing that Italian prehistory might not correspond exactly with the stages distinguished in France and Central Europe.[3] In the south of Italy Schiattarella also adopted the de Mortillet scheme, but modified it as Rutot had done, substituting Italian names for the French sites. Thus the Chellean and Acheulian became the Perugina phase, the Mousterian the Vibratiana phase, the Solutrean the Ventimiglian, and the Magdalenian the Fanian.[4]

This recital of the variant classifications proposed towards the end of the nineteenth century has more than an academic interest to the historian of prehistoric archaeology. It showed that de Mortillet's scheme was not entirely satisfactory, and that it was being found unsatisfactory for two reasons. In the first place, it was designed as a classification of French antiquities, but de Mortillet had tended to think that it was more than this, that he had in fact discovered stages of universal validity in the human past of man. Yet as his scheme was used to classify the antiquities of areas outside France there were already difficulties. These difficulties were at first met when local names were substituted for the French names; this was the essence of the schemes proposed by Rutot and Schiattarella. But Morselli had observed that these French classifications might not coincide exactly with the Italian sequence. It is clear that Morselli in his remarkable lectures was thinking of the Stone Age as providing different

[1] A. Rutot, *Conditions d'Existence de l'Homme*, 1897.

[2] Rutot, *Le Préhist. dans l'Europe centrale*, 1904. This classification is also summarised in G. Engerrand, *Six Leçons de Préhistoire*, 1905, 151.

[3] Morselli, *Antropologia generale. Lezioni su l'uomo secondo la teoria dell' evoluzione*, 292.

[4] On Schiattarella's classification see Pinsero, *La Psicologia dell' uomo preistorico*, 1895.

sequences in different areas. And the problem was really posed by the adoption in Italy and Belgium of separate names. Did the Hesbayen and the Ventimiglian coincide with the Solutrean?—and what did this coincidence mean? This was the second difficulty which serious prehistorians began to face toward the end of the nineteenth century: what exactly were the "divisions" of the Stone Age invented by de Mortillet? Were they periods of time or were they in fact merely local assemblages of artefacts?

Gabriel de Mortillet had no doubt of the answer to this question. The whole problem was one of periods of time to him, and in his classifications he distinguished between *Times*, *Ages*, *Periods* and *Epochs*. By *Time* he meant divisions such as Tertiary, Quaternary, Recent, Prehistory, Protohistory and History; by *Ages* he meant the Tripartite Danish system of the Ages of Stone, Bronze and Iron; by *Periods* he meant the Eolithic, Palaeolithic and Neolithic, which he conceived of as periods of time comparable with the terms Roman and Merovingian; and his smaller divisions, such as the Chellean, Acheulian and Magdalenian, were *Epochs*. These epochs were, to de Mortillet, most certainly periods of time, and for all his protestations that he was applying an archaeological method, as distinct from the Palaeontological method of Lartet, he was still in the grip of his geological training. He had diligently applied the geological method to the subdivision of the Danish Tripartite system. And Piette's schemes were also carefully drawn up on a geological time basis; his epochs or stages, such as the Lorthetian and Acheulian, were grouped into ages or sections, such as the Niphetic and Glyptic, these into periods or systems, and these into Times or Sub-Groups, which were the Pleistocene and Recent, the whole forming part of the Anthropique or Quaternary Era or Group.

Boyd Dawkins, it will be remembered, had criticised de Mortillet's scheme when first published on the grounds that it merely recognised vertical changes in the archaeological record, not horizontal changes. The extension of the French scheme to central Europe and Italy began to show that horizontal differences would have to be recognised. If this were done then the epochs of de Mortillet and Piette would no longer be epochs, but assemblages of artefacts. De Mortillet had arranged the collections in the Saint-Germain Museum according to his carefully graded subdivisions. He was infuriated because the curator of the

Museum, Alexander Bertrand, changed the word Epoch on the labels in every case to Type. Adrien de Mortillet characterised this action as a craven compromise with the opponents of prehistory.[1] But Bertrand was wiser than the de Mortillets and Piettes of late nineteenth-century prehistory; indeed wiser than he himself at the time knew. For in changing the labels he had been right: the "epochs" were assemblages of "types". But it took many years before this lesson was widely learnt.

The problems of the classification of prehistoric man were further thrown into relief by discoveries in the last quarter of the nineteenth century relating to the Neolithic, and the period between the end of the Palaeolithic and Neolithic. The original Danish tripartite system had envisaged a sharp break between the Palaeolithic and the Neolithic, and this had become an article of faith in the schemes of Lartet and de Mortillet. The Magdalenian hunters were supposed to have followed the retreating reindeer northwards, and the Neolithic civilisation with its polished axes, domestic animals, crops and pottery was brought from Asia by invaders spreading over a completely depopulated Europe. The gap or hiatus between Palaeolithic and Neolithic was thought to be complete, and French prehistorians pointed to sterile layers that, in some caves and rock shelters, lay between Magdalenian and Neolithic as geological proof of this *Ancien Hiatus*. Discoveries at various sites in France between 1875 and 1900, however, produced artefacts that were post-Magdalenian, yet not typical of the Robenhausian Neolithic.

The first of these discoveries was made in the south of France. Edouard Piette had for many years been excavating caves and rock shelters in the south of France. In 1887 he began excavating at Mas d'Azil (Ariège) in the foothills of the Pyrenees, some forty miles south-west of Toulouse. Here the River Arise tunnels through the rock for over a quarter of a mile, and in this great tunnel, on both banks of the river, Piette excavated two rock shelters and found, above a rich Magdalenian deposit, a thick deposit containing flat harpoons of stagshorn and pebbles painted with red ochre associated with bones of red deer and wild boar. To this post-Magdalenian industry Piette gave the name Azilian, from its type-site. It was also referred to as the Arisian.[2] In

[1] *Le Préhistorique*, 1900, 240. [2] Cartailhac, "La Grotte du Mas d'Azil," *L'Anth.*, 1891, 143; Piette, *L'Anth.*, 1895, 276; 1896, 386.

1891 Chamaison and Darbas excavated the rock shelter of La Tourasse at Saint-Martory (Haute Garonne),[1] which also had an Azilian industry. De Mortillet republished the finds from La Tourasse and at a meeting of the Anthropological Society of Paris in 1894 proposed the name Tourassian for the industry as a whole. He retained this name in the third (1900) edition of *Le Préhistorique*, but the name Azilian gained currency over either Tourassian or Arisian.

In 1879 Judge Edmond Vielle discovered and began excavating a site in the park of the Château de Fère at Fère-en-Tardenois (Aisne). This site was characterised by small geometric flint implements, including triangular and trapezoidal forms, among them arrowheads with transverse edges. The Fère-en-Tardenois site was fully described by Vielle in 1890,[2] and in 1896 Gabriel de Mortillet described similar geometric microlithic flints elsewhere in France, in Belgium, England, Portugal, Spain, Italy, Germany, Russia, Algiers, Tunis, Egypt, Syria and India, calling them all part of a Tardenoisian period.

In 1886 Philippe Salmon described the site of Campigny, about a mile north-west of the village of Blangy-sur-Bresle, not far from Bouillancourt-en-Sery (Seine-Inférieure) [3]. It consisted of *fonds de cabanes*, or pit dwellings, and the industry was characterised by the Campignian axe and pick, transverse arrowheads, rough awls and scrapers associated with ox, horse and stag bones, and charcoal from oak-trees and ash-trees. Polished stone tools were found in the humus overlying the infilling of these pit dwellings. The site was fully excavated and described by Salmon, Capitan and d'Ault du Mesnil.[4] Salmon postulated a Campignian epoch, and attributed to it many other sites from the north of France.

The recognition of the Azilian (or Arisian or Tourassian), the Tardenoisian and the Campignian posed the difficult problem of where these assemblages of artefacts, or epochs, as their discoverers preferred to call them, were to be fitted into the scheme of prehistory. It was the same problem as had exercised

[1] Chamaison and Darbas, *L'Anth.*, 1892, 121.

[2] Vielle, "Pointes de Flêches typiques de Fère-en-Tardenois (Aisne)," *Bull. Soc. Anthrop. Paris*, ser. 4., vol. 1 (1890), 959–964.

[3] P. Salmon. *Dictionnaire des Sciences anthropologiques* (Paris, 1886), *s.v.* Néolithique.

[4] Salmon, du Mesnil and Capitan, *Rev. de l'Ecole d'Anth. de Paris*, 1898, 365–408.

Steenstrup and Worsaae when they had disputed the position of the Danish kjökkenmöddings, Steenstrup attributing them to the true Neolithic, and Worsaae to a late phase of the Palaeolithic. Lubbock had then attempted a compromise by placing the kitchen middens in a special "Early Neolithic period". In 1892 Allen Brown suggested that an intermediate period should be recognised between the Palaeolithic and Neolithic and that it should be called the Mesolithic,[1] but Boyd Dawkins disapproved of this suggestion,[2] and there was no general acceptance of a special period to include the post-Magdalenian and pre-true-Neolithic industries. De Mortillet and Piette were content to dispute the place of these epochs in relation to the Palaeolithic and Neolithic just as Worsaae and Steenstrup had done.

De Mortillet classified the Azilian (under the name he proferred, namely Tourassian) as Final Palaeolithic, and subtitled it "Ancien Hiatus", and the Tardenoisian as the first stage of the Neolithic, the second being the Robenhausien. The various sites claimed by Salmon as belonging to a Campignian epoch were placed by de Mortillet at the base of the Neolithic proper, *i.e.* the Robenhausien. As early as 1873 he had noted the similarity between some of the artefacts claimed as typical of the Campignian and finds from the Danish kitchen middens.[3] Piette created a special age between his Glyptique and the Neolithic; this he termed the Metabatic Age, or Age of Transition, characterised by the Azilian (which he spelt Asylienne), and he placed in the Neolithic an epoch before the full Neolithic of the Robenhausien with its polished stone axes: this he called the Etage Coquillière, or the Epoch Arisienne.[4] Despite the difficulties which de Mortillet and Piette had in fitting the assemblages of artefacts we know now as the Mesolithic cultures into their schemes, there was at least one thing on which they were agreed, namely that the hiatus was a myth and that there were in fact transitional "epochs" between Magdalenian and Robenhausien.

So impressed was Philippe Salmon by the transitional nature of these new epochs that he suggested in his *Age de la Pierre*,

[1] J. A. Brown, *J.R.A.I.*, xxii, 66–98.

[2] Boyd Dawkins, *J.R.A.I.*, xxiii, 242–250.

[3] *Matériax*, 1883, 455. Flouest in his *Notice sur le Camp de Chassey* Châlons, 1869, 24, had also made this comparison.

[4] Piette's Arisien is not to be confused with the Azilian, also sometimes called by this name. Piette's Arisiens were grain-growers.

published in Paris in 1891, that the division of the Stone Age into Palaeolithic and Neolithic ought to be abandoned. He conceived of a single Stone Age divided into six stages, with transitions between them. We have already spoken of his division of the Palaeolithic into Chellean, Mousterian and Magdalenian. These were the first three of his six divisions of the Stone Age; the second three, corresponding roughly to the Neolithic, were first the Campignian, secondly the Chasseo-Robenhausienne, and thirdly the Carnacian. His second period took the sites of Camp de Chassey, the Camp Barbet, and the Camp de Catenoy in north France, as well as Robenhausen, for types, and his third period was characterised by megalithic monuments.

Gross and Heierli made a detailed study of the Swiss lake dwellings and proposed to distinguish three stages in the Swiss Neolithic.[1] These were called after sites, the Chavannes period, the Moosseedorf period and the Vinelz period. The Chavannes period was transitional from Palaeolithic cultures, the Moosseedorf was the full Neolithic—the Robenhausen of de Mortillet—while the Vinelz was a sort of copper age or transition from the Neolithic to the Bronze Age.

At about the same time Montelius devised a fourfold classification of the Neolithic in northern Europe,[2] and distinguished, in post-kitchen-midden times, first a period characterised by pointed polished axes and no megalithic tombs, secondly a period characterised by thin-butted polished axes and "dolmens", by which Montelius meant single rectangular or polygonal megalithic tombs, a third period characterised by thick-butted polished axes and passage graves—megalithic tombs with approaching passages, and the fourth final period characterised by long stone cists. Montelius did not give names to his periods, as had been the tradition since Lartet and de Mortillet began experimenting with subdivisions of the Stone Age. He was content to name his periods I, II, III and IV, but this change in methodology meant that, instead of convenient labels like Robenhausien or Chellean, his periods could only be referred to as Montelius Neolithic Period III—a cumbersome form, but one which gradually superseded the older named epochs for two reasons—such a system did not appear to be tied to type-sites in one country, and secondly

[1] V. Gross, *Protohelvètes*, 1883; Heierli, *Urgeschichte der Schweiz*, 1901.
[2] *Temps Préhistorique en Suède*, 1895.

it appeared more "scientific". But Montelius's numbered periods of the Neolithic were still only a change of form: his classification was still a division into successive periods.

And this was true of all the many and varied attempts at subdivision of the Stone Age attempted between 1875 and 1900, and which we have been briefly reviewing in this chapter. They were all still basically classifications: man was still an animal whose development could be studied by his artifacts, the fossils of the various stages of his development. The main task of the prehistoric archaeologist was conceived of as the distinction of these several stages. It was realised that each stage did not develop out of the previous one in all cases—most archaeologists allowed at least one invasion to account for the origin of the true Neolithic, and it was realised that all stages, at least of the Neolithic, were not exactly contemporary all over Europe, but there was as yet no concept that the assemblages of artifacts, thought of as characterising periods of time, did in fact characterise the material culture of groups of people, and that such groups could coexist. Archaeologists were still congratulating themselves on being scientists instead of antiquaries, and would have considered suggestions that the Mousterian and Acheulian might be contemporary, or the Azilian and Tardenoisian flourishing at the same time, as absurd as if it had been suggested that the Eocene and Oligocene were contemporary. Two factors contributed to the strength of this "epochal" conception of prehistory. The first was the strength of the geological background out of which prehistoric archaeology had in part grown. The second was the widespread conviction that evolution was the way of all things, whether it be the flesh of the animal world, or the artifacts—the extra-corporeal limbs, as Crawford has called them—of the human world.

2. *The Discovery of Cave Art*

More important than the disputes about the classification of the Palaeolithic in the last quarter of the nineteenth century was the discovery of Upper Palaeolithic cave art. In 1875 the Marquis de Sautuola began excavating in the cave of Altamira, near Santander, and found black paintings on the back wall of the cave: these he claimed to be of the same age as the Palaeolithic deposits in the cave. Four years later his small daughter wandered into a part of the great cave so low that no grown-up person had yet penetrated there, and found on the roof the now famous polychrome paintings of animals. In 1880 the Marquis de Sautuola published the Altamira paintings in his *Breves apuntes sobre algunos objetos prehistoricos de la provincia de Santander* (Santander, 1880), claiming they were Palaeolithic in date. Meanwhile, in 1878, Chiron had found drawings on the walls of the cave of Chabot (Ardèche).

These discoveries and claims precipitated a great dispute among prehistorians. In 1877 de Mortillet had accepted the authenticity of the Cave Art, declaring: "C'est l'enfance de l'art, ce n'est pas l'art de l'enfant." Vilanova y Piera, Professor of Palaeontology at Madrid, supported Sautuola and declared himself satisfied with the authenticity of the paintings. Others refused to accept the paintings, declaring that the Marquis was a fraud and an impostor, and had hired an artist from Madrid to make them. Edouard Harlé, an engineer who visited Altamira, was fierce in his denunciation of the paintings. In 1882 the paintings from Altamira were discussed at the Berlin Anthropological Society, and Vilanova and Harlé disputed their authenticity at the Congrès of the Association Française.

In general the Altamira and Chiron discoveries were disbelieved in, or thrust aside as inconvenient, except among some of the foremost prehistorians. Piette in 1887 claimed that the Altamira paintings were Magdalenian in date, and their authenticity was accepted in his *Équidès de la Période quaternaire d'après les Gravures de ce Temps*, and Chauvet's *Les Débuts de la Gravure et de la Sculpture*, both published in that year. Piette continued his championship of Palaeolithic art, but Cartailhac in his *La France Préhistorique*, and Salomon Reinach in his *Alluvions et Cavernes*, both published in 1889, are full of doubts and reservations about it.

Meanwhile fresh discoveries of Palaeolithic home or mobiliary art had been made, notably the broken ivory statuette of a woman —first described as "La Poire"—from Brassempouy. This was in 1892. Two years later Piette and de Laportière excavated more completely at Brassempouy and several ivory figurines were found.

In 1895 E. and G. Bertoumeyrou discovered some drawings on the walls of the rock shelter of La Mouthe, Tayac (Dordogne). The next year Emile Rivière excavated La Mouthe fully, and discovered more paintings and engravings. Deposits of Palaeolithic and Neolithic date completely blocked the entrance to this cave before the excavations were undertaken. Rivière was convinced of the authenticity of the La Mouthe Cave Art, and this conviction, together with the proof supplied by the La Mouthe deposits, also included the disputed Altamira paintings, with which Piette at once linked the La Mouthe engravings on stylistic grounds. In the same year Dumas discovered the silhouette of a mammoth on the walls of the Chabot cave. The following year Daleau published animal drawings on the walls of the cave of Pair-non-Pair (Gironde), which he had been excavating and studying since 1883. In 1897 Regnault and Jammes discovered the paintings and engravings in the Marsoulas (Haute Garonne) have.

Gradually the authenticity of Palaeolithic Cave Art was accepted, especially after the spectacular discovery in 1901 by Breuil, Capitan and Peyrony of paintings and engravings at Combarelles and Font-de-Gaume, both in the Dordogne. In the following year Cartailhac published an article in *L'Anthropologie*, entitled "Les Cavernes ornées de dessins: La grotte d'Altamira. Mea culpa d'un sceptique", in which he recounted his conversion to the authenticity of Cave Art. And Palaeolithic Art, both from home sites and from caves, now begins to be treated as it should be, as the first artistic manifestation of man in Europe, not merely as a curious feature of ancient man. It is the first chapter in a long story of artistic achievement, and as such it is treated by Hoernes in his *Urgeschichte der bildenden Kunst in Europa* (1898).

3. *Near-Eastern Archaeology*

Interest in Mesopotamian archaeology was revived in the early seventies of the nineteenth century after a period of no activity since the outbreak of the Crimean War. George Smith, a minor official in the Assyrian Department of the British Museum, published in 1871 *The History of Ashur-bani-pal translated from the Cuneiform Inscriptions.* The following year, while engaged in sorting, assembling and translating the broken clay tablets from the Nineveh libraries, he discovered a fragment of a tablet which contained "the statement that the ship rested on the mountains of Nizur, followed by the account of the sending forth of the dove, and its finding no resting place and returning". "I saw at once", he wrote, "that I had discovered a portion at least of the Chaldean account of the Deluge." He later discovered further fragments of the same tablet and fragments of a duplicate text. From these he could complete a large amount of the Babylonian flood story, which he read to the Society of Biblical Archaeology in December 1872. The interest created by this discovery was tremendous. A portion of the Deluge tablet was still missing and the *Daily Telegraph* offered £1,000 to equip an expedition led by Smith to look for the missing fragment. Smith began work at Kuyunjik in 1873, and by an amazing stroke of luck found the missing fragment on the fifth day of his work. Smith carried out further excavation work on behalf of the British Museum in the next few years, but died at Aleppo in 1877 as he was returning from his third season's work. He published general accounts of his work in his *Assyrian Discoveries* and his *The Chaldean Account of Genesis*, which, like Layard's *Nineveh*, became a best-seller.

Smith's place in the late nineteenth-century Mesopotamian excavations organised by the British Museum was taken by Hormuzd Rassam, who returned after an absence of many years. His final campaigns of excavation were from 1878 to 1882. He ranged over the whole of Mesopotamia to the frontiers of Syria and the shores of Lake Van, digging into as many mounds as he could in the search for works of art and inscriptions for the British Museum. In 1878 he discovered at Tell Balawat the famous bronze gates of Shalmaneser II. In 1880 he began work at Abu Habbah, in south Mesopotamia, the site of the biblical Sepharvaim. Here he found an inscription which identified the site as Sippar, and as a temple dedicated to the Sun-god Shamash. He excavated here for eighteen months and discovered a very large collection of inscribed cylinders and tablets, one of which recorded how Nabonidus, the last king of Babylon, had himself excavated in the foundations of the temple of Shamash to discover who had first built it, and how he had found, eighteen cubits beneath the pavement, a foundation stone laid by Naram-Sin, son of Sargon of Akkad, "which for 3,200 years no previous king had seen". This invaluable chronological document was also the record, as we have earlier said, of the first archaeological activities known in human history.

Gradually archaeologists were becoming aware of the early civilisation of Mesopotamia which we designate the Sumerian, and from which the Assyrian and Babylonian civilisations were derived. Traces of these Sumerians had been found by Loftus at Warka, by Taylor at Ur and Eridu, by Rawlinson at Borsippa, and again by Rassam at Sippar. In 1869 Oppert had postulated the existence of a non-Semitic pre-Babylonian people, and in his famous paper on the Deluge tablets George Smith stated that the Assyrian text in Ashur-bani-pal's Library was copied from some earlier source, the language of which he assumed to have been Akkadian, or Sumerian, and the earliest account he hazarded to have been written at Eridu. The Sumerians did not, however, become a reality to the archaeological world in general until the excavations at Telloh.

In 1874 some Arabs informed the new French consul at Basra, Ernest de Sarzec, that stone statuettes were to be found in a place called Telloh. De Sarzec began excavating there in 1877, continuing his work intermittently, and under the auspices of the Louvre, until 1900. His finds showed the site to be the Sumerian city of Lagash, and included many archaic sculptures of the late third millennium, including the famous portrait statues of Gudea, seventh governor of Lagash. The discoveries of de Sarzec created similar sensations as had those of Botta and Layard. Oppert told the International Congress of Orientalists in Berlin that "since the discovery of Nineveh . . . no discovery has been made which compares in importance with the recent excavations in Chaldea", and the Louvre Catalogue of 1901 described the city of Lagash as "the Pompeii of early Babylonian antiquity". Certainly it is to de Sarzec's excavations at Telloh that we owe our great familiarity with the art, history and language of the Sumerians. One might almost say with de Genouillac: "C'est Telloh qui nous a revelé les Sumeriens."[1]

In 1884 the first American expedition to Mesopotamia took place. It was from the University of Pennsylvania and was a reconnaissance. Three years later excavations began at Nippur, under Peters and Hilprecht. The first season ended disastrously in the sack of the excavators' camp by tribesmen. The excavations recommenced in 1890 and were continued until 1900. The Temple of the Wind-god was found, holiest centre of pilgrimage

[1] *Fouilles de Telloh* (1934).

in ancient Sumer. A very large number of tablets were found —over 50,000—mostly in the Sumerian language and extending over a thousand years. They included a large proportion of all the Sumerian literary texts which have been found up to the present, as well as historical records of enormous value.

In Egypt, Mariette had died in 1880, and been succeeded by (Sir) Gaston Maspero, whose Directorship of Archaeology in Egypt began with the opening of the pyramid of Unas at Sakkarah and the discovery of the famous "Pyramid Texts". The Cairo Museum still reserved the right to retain any objects excavated in Egypt, but permission was now granted for excavations to be undertaken by representatives of other countries. The Egypt Exploration Fund (later the Egypt Exploration Society) was founded in London in 1883. The French Mission Archéologique was founded in Cairo about the same time, and later expeditions and institutions were organised by the Germans, the Swiss and the Americans. The work of the Egypt Exploration Fund was directed in the field by (Sir) W. M. Flinders Petrie. In 1883 he wrote to Miss Edwards, the secretary of the Fund: "The prospect of excavating in Egypt is a most fascinating one to me, and I hope the results may justify my undertaking such a work." This hope was brilliantly realised. Petrie began at Tanis in 1885, and thereafter there were annual excavations, followed by publications and exhibitions in London, many of them in the Egyptian Hall in Piccadilly where Belzoni had exhibited. In 1892 Petrie was able to publish his *Ten Years' Digging*; among the most remarkable of his finds were the Tell el-Amarna correspondence and the numerous relics of Tell el-Amarna itself, the discoveries of Mycenaean and pre-Mycenaean pottery at Gurob and Kahun, and the discovery of the predynastic Egyptian civilisation. We discuss elsewhere in this book Petrie's discoveries of Aegean pottery: here was one of the great foundations of comparative archaeology.[1] Our knowledge of predynastic Egypt comes first from Petrie's work at Naqada and Ballas in 1894–95 and at Diospolis Parva (Hu) in 1898–99. Naqada was revealed as a prehistoric cemetery of over 2,000 graves, and has given its name to the Naqada Period. The British Museum declined Petrie's offer of the type series from this cemetery on the ground that they were advised it was "unhistoric rather than prehistoric", so the

[1] See p. 144 *infra*.

collection went to the Ashmolean instead. In his memoir on *Diospolis Parva*, published in 1901, Petrie arranged the predynastic Egyptian material systematically for the first time, inventing the technique of sequence-dating, which he further described in his *Methods and Aims in Archaeology* (1904). These advances in techniques and method, which are discussed further elsewhere,[1] as well as the actual discoveries of dynastic and predynastic Egypt, make the last quarter of the nineteenth century truly the Heroic Age of Egyptian archaeology.

4. *Schliemann and the Prehistory of the Aegean*

The story of our knowledge of prehistoric Greece and the Aegean is always associated with the name of Heinrich Schliemann, and this is very proper since he was, in Walter Leaf's phrase, "the creator of prehistoric Greek archaeology"; but some isolated discoveries had been made before he began digging in Troy in 1871. In 1826 the German geologist Fiedler had published some graves in the Cyclades containing copper tools and marble statuettes. In 1841 Ross recorded barbaric seal-stones from the Greek islands. In 1862 a Greek antiquary, Pappadopoulos, excavated tombs in Syros, but thought they were the graves of Roman convicts, and in the same year Fouqué excavated at Santorin painted pottery—the *type de Thera*—and fresco-covered walls from old houses beneath twenty-six foot of pumice belonging to the great eruption that divided the original island into Thera and Therasia. The geologists dated the Santorin eruption at about 2000 B.C., and although it is archaeology rather than geology that must provide an accurate date for this event, even an approximate geological date of this kind suggested great antiquity for the finds of Fouqué. In 1866 Salzmann and Biliotti excavated at Camirus and Ialysus in Rhodes, and were able to distinguish stylistically between the Hellenic pottery of the first site and the Mycenaean of the second. The British Museum was presented by John Ruskin with the Ialysus pottery from Rhodes in 1870, and labelled them vaguely as Greco-Phoenician, which, though non-committal, was a little better than the fate of Mycenaean vases from Melos at Sèvres and from Cephalonia at Neuchâtel, which were regarded as unplaceable. In 1869 George Finlay published, in Greek,

[1] See pp. 175–177 *infra*.

Observations on Prehistoric Archaeology in Switzerland and Greece, in which he argued from the discoveries of Swiss lake dwellings, the account of Herodotus, and his own small collection of stone implements that there should be lake dwellings in the marshes of Boeotia and Thessaly.

Schliemann had been excited by the Homeric sagas since his childhood in Germany, and a picture of Troy in flames, printed in a copy of Jerrer's *Universal History*, which his father gave him as a Christmas present, ever remained in his memory and fortified his belief in the reality of the events described by Homer, during a long business career in Holland, Russia and America. Having amassed a great fortune, he retired from business at the age of forty-six and prepared to devote himself to the study of prehistoric archaeology, especially to the problem of finding the remains of Troy. To this end he travelled extensively and studied archaeology in Paris. In 1868 he visited sites in Greece and Asia Minor; the following year he dug in Ithaca and published *Ithaka, the Peloponnese and Troy*, in which he argued that the graves of Agamemnon and Clytemnestra were not the Treasuries outside the citadel at Mycenae but were in the citadel itself, and that the city of Troy was not a myth, nor situated in a mountain fastness near Bunarbashi on the Balidagh, but at Hissarlik, on the site of the historic Ilion. Two years later he began excavating at Hissarlik.

Schliemann had four periods of excavation at Hissarlik, the first from 1871–73, the second in 1879, the third from 1882–83 and the fourth from 1889 until his death in 1890. In his first campaign he worked alone with his young Greek wife, Sophie. In 1879 he was assisted by Burnouf, a classical archaeological scholar, and by Virchow, founder of the German Society for Anthropology, Ethnology and Prehistory, and organiser of the German survey of antiquities and physical anthropology, and the Berlin Museum für Völkerkunde. In the last two seasons he had the expert assistance of Dörpfeld, who continued the fourth campaign after Schliemann's death, working on at Troy until 1894. Between the first and second campaigns of excavation at Hissarlik Schliemann dug at Mycenae and Ithaka, in 1874–76. In 1880, following his second Hissarlik campaign, he excavated the Treasury of Minyas at Orchomenos. Between his third and fourth campaigns he dug the palace at Tiryns in 1884–85. With his strong aptitude for and training in businesslike methods Schliemann was assiduous in immediately publishing his results. His *Trojan Antiquities* appeared in 1874, *Mycenae* in 1876—it was written in eight weeks and was a kind of diary of his excavations—*Ilios* in 1880, *Troja* in 1884, and *Orchomenos* in 1887.

These works of Schliemann first appeared in German, but were soon translated into French and English. The English translation of *Mycenae* in 1877 had a preface by W. E. Gladstone, Homeric scholar as well as statesman. There is no doubt that, even among scholars who disbelieved his conclusions, Schliemann's excavations aroused a tremendous interest. The world was really excited by his work. It has justly been said that "every person of culture and education lived through the drama of discovering Troy".[1] When he discovered what he took to be the graves of Agamemnon and his family, at Mycenae, Schliemann sent off telegrams to the King of Greece, to the Prime Minister, to the editor of *The Times* and the Emperor of Brazil, and throughout the Mycenae excavations he sent almost daily reports and articles to the London *Times*. These were the first great excavations followed with interest by an informed public everywhere. A popular summary of Schliemann's work was given by Schuchhardt in his *Schliemann's Ausgrabungen* (1890), translated into English in 1892, and universally known as "Schuchhardt's *Schliemann*", and an authoritative survey of the whole problem by Dörpfeld and others in *Troja und Ilion* (1901) and in A. Schmidt's *Heinrich Schliemann's Sammlung Trojanischer Altertümer* (Berlin, 1902).

Schliemann proved that Hissarlik was a prehistoric settlement of great antiquity that had been heavily fortified. He distinguished seven cities, identifying the second as Homeric Troy—"the citadel of Priam". On the day before he closed the 1873 season of digging there he discovered a magnificent collection of gold treasures dating from the second city, which he smuggled out of Turkey and claimed to be Priam's Treasure. Three years after Schliemann's death Dörpfeld identified the sixth city as Homeric Troy. The object of Schliemann's excavations at Hissarlik had been to prove by archaeology the truth of Homer. Although he himself first made the wrong identification of the Homeric Troy, he achieved his general purpose. But from the point of view of the history of archaeology he achieved much more: he discovered

[1] A. T. White, *Lost Worlds* (1947), 27.

as well as Homeric Troy, long centuries of the pre-Homeric and prehistoric occupation of the site, and a non-Greek, "barbaric" civilisation. The prehistoric city of Troy (Troy II), with its fortress walls, its traces of violent capture, its trade in gold, silver, ivory, amber and jade, was only succeeded by the sixth Mycenaean city after its total destruction by fire and after an interval filled archaeologically by three small villages (Troy III, IV and V). This interval must have been a long one; whatever date was given to the prehistoric city of Troy II it must be well before the traditional first date for Greek history when Schliemann began digging, namely the first Olympiad in 776 B.C.

At Mycenae, Schliemann hoped to find, and believed he did find, the tombs of Agamemnon and Clytemnestra. He dug in the circle of stones inside the Lion Gate and there found the graves he was looking for—the now famous Shaft Graves. He interpreted Pausanias as listing only five graves here, and having found five graves he stopped digging. Actually Pausanias listed six graves, and the sixth was found a year after Schliemann had left. The contents of the graves at Mycenae were sensational and spectacular—vases of gold and silver, inlaid swords of gold and silver and copper and bronze, finger rings and bracelets, thin gold ornaments for the clothing of the dead, and gold face-masks. Here was treasure far greater than "Priam's Treasure" from Troy: it was, in Hall's words, "one of the most important discoveries of past human civilisation that has ever been made".[1] Schliemann also excavated at Mycenae the two great beehive tombs, or tholoi, the Treasury of Atreus (or Agamemnon), and the Treasury of Clytemnestra. In 1880 at Orchomenos he excavated a similar monument, the Treasury of Minyas. Schliemann believed that the civilisation he had found in the shaft graves of Mycenae, the tholoi of Mycenae and Orchomenos, and the palace of Tiryns, was that of the Homeric Greeks. The Greeks themselves had always regarded Mycenae and Tiryns as belonging to the Mycenaean Heroic Age of Homer. The world of scholarship was deeply divided over Schliemann's finds. Some, including Gladstone, accepted his claims. Others argued that his finds were Byzantine in date, or the work of Celts, Goths, Avars, Huns, or just "Orientals". Curtius even declared that one of the gold masks from Mycenae was a portrait of Christ dating from the Byzantine

[1] H. R. Hall, *Aegean Archaeology* (1914), 12.

period. Many German scholars, however, were certain that the Mycenaean civilisation was not Homeric but pre-Homeric, and this we know now to be true. Schliemann had in fact discovered in Greece, as he had in western Anatolia, a great prehistoric civilisation.

This was Schliemann's great contribution to the development of prehistoric archaeology: the discovery of the pre-Hellenic civilisations of the East Mediterranean—the Mycenaean civilisation of Greece, and the pre-Mycenaean Anatolian civilisation of Troy II. He had set out to prove the historical truth of Homer, and had done so, but he had also discovered the prehistory of the Aegean and shown the limitations of all written and literary history. He intended to show that Homer was history, was in fact the earliest Greek history; instead he proved that he was the latest prehistory. Schliemann showed that the stories of Homer have a solid foundation in fact; he revealed to archaeologists the magnificent Greek Bronze Age, which was hitherto unknown and which is, in part at least, reflected in the Homeric stories; and he suggested that there must be antecedents to this Bronze Age civilisation to be sought perhaps outside Greece.

Of his technique as an archaeologist we write elsewhere in this book. Here we must recognise his great discoveries and the widespread effect they had on European thought. It would not be too much to say that Schliemann's excavations really put prehistoric archaeology "on the map", and demonstrated dramatically to the world the potentialities of the modern reconstruction of ancient history by excavation and the study of non-literary sources. The work of archaeologists in Mesopotamia and Egypt had, as we know, enormously excited public interest, but these were dealing with civilisations known historically—particularly from the Bible. The prehistoric discoveries in the Danish bogs and the Swiss lake dwellings, in the French gravels and the south Devon caves had stirred the minds of many scholars. But it was the Trojan and Mycenaean finds that stirred the minds of the masses, from Gladstone and Walter Leaf down to the ordinary reader of *The Times* and the *Telegraph*. It was not only the classical associations of these excavations and the richness of the finds that excited interest; it was the sudden humanity of the finds that, with their jewellery and gold-masks, seemed nearer to modern times than the stone axes and pottery of the Danish and

Swiss archaeologists, and the romance and excitement of Schliemann's successful quest that touched and enlivened the imagination of the world. Schliemann's biographer, Emil Ludwig, has described him as a man with a "monomaniacal and perhaps also a mythomaniacal nature which at times overstepped the limits of normal", but, in a kinder phrase, as "a great and thoughtful dilettante of genius". This is what touched the readers of Schliemann's dispatches and books; the enthusiasm of the amateur archaeologist who was lucky beyond all belief in finding what he had been looking for—proof of Homer, and treasure of gold buried in the earth. But it was not only the general reading public that he fired. A generation of archaeological scholars was inspired by his work. Sir John Myres has put this well when he writes that at the news of Schliemann's death it seemed to him that "the spring had gone out of the year".[1]

Schliemann's work, like all great archaeological discoveries, had posed as many problems as it had solved. He had discovered two hitherto unknown prehistoric civilisations. What were their interrelations, their origins, their dates? Dumont, who died in 1884, published posthumously his *Céramiques de la Grèce propre* (1888), in which he correctly appreciated the significance of the various finds made before Schliemann and classed Fouqué's *type de Thera* between Hissarlik and Ialysus, and recognised the pottery from Mycenae as the "résultat d'une longue pratique", and the "époque de décadence d'une population ancienne, commerçante, et industrielle". Similar views were expressed by Furtwängler and Loeschcke in their *Mykenische Thongefässe* (1879) and *Mykenische Vasen* (1886). Meanwhile the early stages of the civilisation thought to be in its decadence at Mycenae, and traces of a pre-Mycenaean civilisation, were being discovered in the Cyclades and in Cyprus.

Excavations in the Cyclades, and especially in the islands of Amorgos, Antiparos and Syra, revealed primitive tombs—cists of large stones—containing contracted inhumations, together with weapons of stone and copper and pottery of simple form comparable in a general way with Troy II. Bent dug tombs in Antiparos in 1884 and also found an obsidian workers' factory of this period: in 1888 he excavated similar tombs on the Carian coast of Asia Minor. Dümmler in 1886 excavated cemeteries on Amorgos.

[1] *The Cretan Labyrinth*, 272.

Mackenzie, Edgar and Myres, by field work and excavation in the Cyclades, enlarged the picture of prehistory there and distinguished three principal types of pottery and periods in the islands. In 1894–95 the British School at Athens, under Sir Cecil Smith of the British Museum, excavated at Phylakopi on the eastern coast of Melos. This was a stratified site, and revealed first an open village comparable archaeologically with the finds from the Cycladic cist graves, secondly a fortified site when copper and bronze were in use, obsidian and local marble were traded to the Greek mainland and the pottery resembled that of Troy II and the earliest shaft graves, and thirdly a settlement of mainland Greek type with a little Mycenaean palace. Phylakopi was the first stratified site to be excavated in the east Mediterranean after Hissarlik. It provided a relative sequence for the development of the pre-Mycenaean or, as it now began to be called, the Cycladic civilisation, but the finds were not fully published until 1904, by which time discoveries in Crete had re-defined the pre-Mycenaean, emphasising the Cretan rather than the Cycladic element.

There had been sporadic excavations in Cyprus from about 1865 made by various people, among them General Louis Palma di Cesnola and Alexander di Cesnola and a young Austrian artist, Max Ohnefalsch-Richter. The greater part of these excavations was unscientific and unrelated to a research policy. The results were summarised by Reinach in 1885, and by Dümmler in 1886, who, with his knowledge of the Cycladic material, was able to see at once that the Cyprus material showed an Early Bronze Age civilisation comparable with that of Troy II but developing in a different way, a colonial equivalent of Mycenae intruding into the Late Bronze Age development of the native Cyprus Bronze Age, and a total absence of Phoenician elements from both these phases of the Cyprus Bronze Age. In 1894 Sir John Myres carried out some excavations in Cyprus "to settle some crucial points of tomb chronology", as he himself puts it, and, together with Ohnefalsch-Richter, arranged and catalogued the Cyprus Museum. The *Cyprus Museum Catalogue* by Myres and Ohnefalsch-Richter appeared in 1899. Meanwhile the British Museum began a series of excavations in Cyprus, the results of which were published by Murray, Smith and Walters in *Excavations in Cyprus* (1900). The most important of these sites were Enkomi and Hala Sultan Tekke, near Larnaka, and they revealed tombs rich in gold work, and, though not as rich as Mycenae, richer than the shaft graves in Egyptian and Syrian imports.

The antecedents and development of the Mycenaean civilisation were being studied in Greece itself, as well as in the Cyclades and Cyprus. Actually, before Schliemann's discoveries at Mycenae and Orchomenos, a beehive tomb, or tholos, had been excavated at Menidi (Acharnai), in Attica, by Köhler. It was described by Köhler in his *Das Kuppelgrab von Menidi*: the chamber contained late Mycenaean objects, and the *dromos*, pottery of Geometric and later styles. During the eighties many beehive tombs were excavated, including Dimini in Thessaly and Vaphio in Lakonia. Vaphio was dug by Tsountas for the Greek Archaeological Society in 1889, and it was here that were found the famous gold cups with their repoussé designs of men capturing bulls. In 1890 and 1891 Tsountas dug the beehive tombs at Thorikos in Attica and at Kampos in Messenia. The Greek Archaeological Society continued excavation at Mycenae during the period 1886–93; they found more beehive tombs, a palace like that found by Schliemann at Tiryns, and Mycenaean houses—the first Bronze Age Greek town. The society also dug several new tholoi and rock-cut tombs. On the Acropolis of Athens were found traces of another palace like those of Tiryns and Mycenae. These excavations revealed clearly the extent of the Mycenaean civilisation in Greece, and these discoveries were summarised in the works of Furtwängler and Loeschcke, and Schuchhardt, already cited, and in Perrot and Chipiez's *La Grèce Primitive* (1895) and Gardner's *New Chapters in Greek History* (1893).

Various dates for the Mycenaean civilisation had been suggested going backwards from 800 B.C. Actually the answer to the question of date had been given before Schliemann began excavating at Mycenae. The excavations of Salzmann and Biliotti in Rhodes in 1866 had produced at Ialysus a scarab of Amenhotep III with Mycenaean pottery in a tomb, which meant that the tomb could not have been built before 1400 B.C. In the Treasury of Minyas, at Orchomenos, Schliemann found in 1886 a stone roof-slab carved with spirals, lotus-flowers and rosettes such as decorate Egyptian tomb ceilings of Amenhotep III. In 1889 Flinders Petrie found at Gurob, in Egypt, Mycenaean pottery mixed up with remains of the end of the XVIIIth dynasty, as well as what he called proto-Greek or Aegean pottery. In the following year, at Kahun, Flinders Petrie found painted Aegean or proto-Greek pottery mixed with that of the XIIth dynasty. It is important to realise that no pottery of this "proto-Greek" kind had hitherto been found in the Aegean. Petrie's diagnosis was skilled guess-work: he was not content to leave the pottery just as "foreign" ware; he unhesitatingly and with great prescience diagnosed it as Aegean.

In 1891 Petrie visited Mycenae to test there the dating of the Gurob and Kahun sites. He was helped by Ernest Gardner, Petrie's former pupil and companion in Egypt, then Head of the British School in Athens. Petrie recognised examples of Egyptian influence and actual imports of Egyptian objects in Mycenae, all of about the same XVIIIth dynasty period. Petrie had thus established two synchronisms, one between the Aegean or "proto-Greek" ware and the XIIth dynasty, and the second between Mycenaean and the XVIIIth dynasty. On the basis of these synchronisms and his own work at Mycenae, he declared that the Aegean civilisation had come into being about 2500 B.C. and that the dates of the late Mycenaean civilisation were between 1500 and 1000 B.C. He actually dated the treasuries between 1400 and 1200 B.C., the Vaphio cups at about 1200 B.C. and the shaft graves 1150 B.C. It was a most remarkably fine piece of cross-dating and one of the first demonstrations of this method; Gardner declared that Petrie had "done more in a week than the Germans had done in ten years to clear up the matter from an Egyptian basis", and writing in 1931, and looking back on his early conclusions on Greek chronology, Petrie said "there seems little to alter in the outline reached then, though forty years have since passed".

The Egyptian objects found in the tombs excavated in Cyprus by the British Museum were of the late XVIIIth and the XIXth dynasty. In 1899 Petrie found at Tell el-Amarna, and dating from the reign of Akhenaten (1380–60), fragments of Mycenaean pottery. The year before J. L. Myres had found near the Cretan village of Kamarais, on Mount Ida, pottery identical with the Aegean or proto-Greek ware of Petrie.

Dörpfeld in his *Troja und Ilion* (1902) set out a chronology of Troy which served as the basis of European dating for the first thirty years of the twentieth century. It was as follows:

Troy I	3000–2500 B.C.
Troy II	2500–2000 B.C.
Troy III-V	2000–1500 B.C.
Troy VI (the Homeric City)	1500–1000 B.C.
Troy VII	1000–700 B.C.
Troy VIII	700–0 B.C.
Troy IX	A.D. 0–500

This was the accepted state of knowledge of Anatolian chronology at the end of the nineteenth century, and the whole state of our knowledge at that time of the prehistoric Aegean and Troy may be seen not only from Dörpfeld's book already cited, and from Schuchhardt's *Schliemann*, but also from Tsountas's work, translated into English by Manatt as *The Mycenaean Age* (1897), Ridgeway's *Early Age of Greece* (1896) and Hall's *Oldest Civilisation of Greece* (1901).

5. *The Bronze and Iron Ages*

During the last thirty years of the nineteenth century research on the Bronze and Iron ages in Europe was at first, and for the greater part, concerned with the subdivision of these "ages" into "epochs" or "periods", in much the same way as the Palaeolithic and Neolithic had been subdivided. As early as 1859, in his *Nordiske Oldsager*, Worsaae argued that at least in N. Germany, England and Scandinavia the Bronze Age could be divided into two phases, first, an older phase characterised by inhumation and a vigour and freshness in the design and decoration of bronze tools and weapons, and secondly, a later phase characterised by cremation, and in which the bronze tools and weapons show decadence in form and decoration. This argument was set out again by Worsaae in his paper on "La Colonisation de la Russie du nord Scandinavie" in 1873.[1] At about the same time, in 1875, Gabriel de Mortillet set out a classification of the French Bronze Age into two phases, which he christened the Morgien, after the site of Les Roseaux at Morges, on the Lake of Geneva, and the Larnaudian, after the hoard from Larnaud in the Jura. The Morgien was characterised, according to de Mortillet, by flat axes and short swords, the Larnaudian by winged and socketed axes and by long swords.[2] This classification was used by the two

[1] *Mémoires de la Société des Antiquaires du Nord*, 1873–74.
[2] *Matériaux*, 1875.

de Mortillets as a basis for their description of the Bronze Age in the *Musée préhistorique* (first published in 1881), in their revised second edition of this standard work in 1903, by Adrien de Mortillet in his *Classification palethnologique* (Paris, 1908), and it was employed by him in his courses in the Ecole d'Anthropologie in Paris up to 1925.

Italian archaeologists found this classification of the Bronze Age into two phases impracticable for the proper study of their material from Italy, and proposed an "Eneolithic" period between the end of the Stone Age and the beginning of the Bronze Age. This Eneolithic phase figures in the writings of archaeologists like Pigorini, Colini and Orsi in the last quarter of the nineteenth century. Similar difficulties were experienced in analysing the archaeological material in Hungary, and at the International Congress at Budapest in 1876 François von Pulszky proposed the recognition of a Copper Age between Stone Age and Bronze Age, and his views were further set out in his *Die Kupferzeit in Ungarn* (Budapest, 1884). Sir William Wilde, in his *Catalogue of the Antiquities in the Museum of the Royal Irish Academy* (Dublin, 1863), had distinguished between a copper industry and a bronze industry, and in 1886, in his *Die Kupferzeit in Europa und ihr Verhältniss zur Kultur der Indogermanen*, Much noted the wide distribution of copper tools over Europe. In 1885, in his *L'Age du cuivre dans les Cévennes*, Jeanjean argued for a Copper Age in the south of France, and proposed calling it the Durfortian, after the Grotte des Morts at Durfort (Gard), described by Cazalis de Fondouce and Ollier de Marichard. The researches of Saint-Venant and Raymond, in the south of France, and of du Chatellier, in Brittany, confirmed the existence of this Copper Age, or Durfortian. Chantre, who in 1871 and 1872 had been publishing papers proposing a threefold division of the Bronze Age, published in 1875–76 his *L'Age du Bronze*, in which he regarded the Bronze Age as a unitary phase of human culture preceded by a Copper Age. He further proposed changing the name Durfortian to Cébénnian.

It looked, then, in the late nineteenth century, as though the Danish three-age system might now be extended by the addition of a Copper Age or Eneolithic period between the Neolithic and the Bronze Age. That this development was not widely followed was due to the writings and influence of Oscar

Montelius. After extensive comparative archaeological studies all over Europe and the east Mediterranean Montelius proposed a detailed subdivision of the Bronze Age into numbered periods, the first of which, though in reality the Copper Age of Wilde and von Pulszky and the Eneolithic of the Italians, he proposed to call Bronze Age I. Montelius's scheme was first set out in his paper 'Sur la Chronologie de l'Age du Bronze, spécialement dans la Scandinavie," in *Matériaux* for 1885, and then developed in three famous works: the *Die Chronologie der ältesten Bronzezeit in Nord-Deutschland und Skandinavien* (Brunswick, 1900), *La Civilisation primitive en Italie depuis l'introduction des métaux* (Stockholm, 1895 and 1904), and *Les Temps préhistoriques en Suède et dans les autres Pays Scandinaves* (Paris, 1895).

Montelius recognised five phases in the Bronze Age of northern Europe, and these he numbered from I to V. In adapting his scheme to Italy he distinguished only periods I to IV, splitting period I into I.1, the Copper Age, and I.2, the Bronze Age proper. Montelius's first contribution to prehistoric archaeology was the use of numbers to distinguish his postulated periods. While his typological sequences have not stood the test of time in their detailed applications, his whole scheme of numbered periods got away from the French named "epochs". As we shall see, the French system of "epochs" like the Acheulian, the Azilian, or the Cébénnian was, in a way, a step towards the recognition of cultural groups, although being incompletely realised it distinguished neither cultural nor chronological groups. Montelius provided in the Bronze Age, as he had tried to do in the Neolithic, an objective scheme of classification which was primarily techno-typological. His second great contribution was the attempt to give absolute dates to his techno-typological periods. Worsaae had attempted to give general dates for the Neolithic and Bronze ages in northern Europe on the basis of synchronisms with the archaeology of the east Mediterranean. Now the comparative archaeological researches of Petrie and others in the east Mediterranean had tied the Aegean and Mycenaean chronology with that of Egypt by a pioneer effort of cross-dating. Montelius attempted to extend this system of tied finds across Europe to Scandinavia and the British Isles. He extended his scheme to cover the British Isles in a paper in *Archaeologia* published in 1909: he had expounded his views in Britain before this. He envisaged the

British Bronze Age as covering 1700 years, from 2500 to 800 B.C., and split it up into five periods as follows: I, the Copper Age from 2500–2000 B.C.; II, the first period of the Bronze Age proper, from 2000–1650 B.C.; III, from 1650–1400 B.C.; IV, 1400–1150 B.C.; and V, from 1150 to 800 B.C. One is amazed to-day at the confidence with which Montelius proposed to refine his dates to half-centuries, such as 1650 and 1150 B.C., but his scheme did provide an objective framework for studying relics of the Bronze Age, and it did demonstrate for the first time the possibilities and value of the synchronological technique of cross-dating.

Similar schemes were devised during the last quarter of the nineteenth century for subdividing the Iron Age. In 1872 Hildebrand proposed the division of the pre-Roman Iron Age into an earlier and later phase, to which he gave the names Hallstatt and La Tène. In 1875 de Mortillet adopted the same dual division of the Iron Age, but called the second phase the Gaulish or Marnian Iron Age. Later he split the second phase into two and proposed a threefold division of the Iron Age, into Hallstattian, Marnian and Beuvraysian (after the pre-Roman French town of Mont Beuvray). In 1885 Otto Tischler applied Montelius's techno-typological ideas to the La Tène period (the Marnian and Beuvraysian of de Mortillet) and, following a detailed examination of the material in France, divided it into three phases, which he named Early, Middle and Late. He dated the beginning of the La Tène period at about 400 B.C.

To a certain extent, then, the study of the Bronze and Iron ages in Europe in the last quarter of the nineteenth century merely carried on the traditions laid down by the French archaeologists in the third quarter of the century, the traditions of minutely subdividing the three ages into epochs. But during this period archaeologists began to realise that this "epochal subdivision" was an insufficient end in prehistoric archaeology and was in any case open to many objections. The most important difficulty was the regional one — the problem of making any classification applicable to Europe as a whole. As early as 1858 Worsaae had suggested that Europe in the Bronze Age would have to be studied on the basis of different geographical groups, and in 1873–74 he set out this idea again, and in his *L'Age du Bronze* Chantre distinguished three "provinces" in the European Bronze Age, which he called the Uralian, comprising Siberia, Russia and

Finland; the Danubian, comprising Hungary, Scandinavia and the British Isles, and the Mediterranean, comprising the Graeco-Italian and Franco-Swiss groups.

These geographical provinces and groups were a first realisation that the study of the Bronze and Iron ages could not be pursued merely by the subdivision of the three ages. The problem of prehistoric classification was thrown into relief by the discoveries in Greece and the Aegean. In the first place, the archaeological finds from the east Mediterranean had not been classified by means of subdivisions of the Bronze and Iron ages. Schliemann's classification of the remains at Hissarlik was an objective one based on the stratigraphy there, and, as we have seen, the tendency was to refer east Mediterranean finds to the Mycenaean, the pre-Mycenaean, or other named periods, which were not necessarily related to the Bronze and Iron ages. In the second place, this development of archaeological nomenclature in the east Mediterranean not only provided a new way of labelling and studying antiquities, it posed a difficult question: was the prehistory of Europe to be studied on a dual basis, the east Mediterranean basis of named civilisations or cultures, and the European basis of named epochal subdivisions of the three-age framework?

At the end of the nineteenth century there seemed to be three possible answers to this question. The first, championed by Montelius, was the extension of the three-age system, with its minute subdivisions, all over the east Mediterranean and the ancient civilisations of the Near East. The second, implicit in the geographical distinctions being drawn by Worsaae and Chantre, suggested that the solution was to extend the methods of east Mediterranean archaeology all over Europe. The third was the application of historical names to archaeological groups in Europe, whether geographical or epochal. This had already been a problem for the early Danish archaeologists, who had spent much of their time arguing whether the Stone Age was the work of the Lapps, the Bronze Age that of the Finns or Phoenicians and the Iron Age the work of Celts or Goths. The development of east Mediterranean archaeology, from the first dig of Schliemann at Hissarlik, while it had provided an archaeological classification based on archaeological names like Mycenaean, Aegean, Cycladic and so forth, had of course not escaped that bane of the prehistorian's existence—the desire to give historical names to prehistorical groups. And so the various archaeological phenomena distinguished in the east Mediterranean were variously labelled Graeco-Phoenician, Phoenician, Trojan, Carian, Phrygian, Thraco-Phrygian, Aryan, Dorian, Achaean. Fortunately there was in east Mediterranean archaeology an objective archaeological grouping and the beginnings of an objective archaeological nomenclature, so that disputes over linguistic and historical labelling could be pursued independently of the development of knowledge about the Mycenaeans and the pre-Mycenaeans. But the disputes about this labelling infused archaeologists outside the east Mediterranean with a fresh desire to label the groups and types, distinguished archaeologically in northern and western Europe, with names which had an historical or linguistic connotation. The Bronze and Iron ages began to be loaded with tendentious names like Phoenician, Ligurian, Iberian, Celtic and Teutonic, and archaeologists began to add to their already difficult problems the gratuitous difficulty of saying what language had been spoken by the people of their groups and epochs. In Britain, Sir John Rhŷs suggested that the Neolithic was introduced by Iberians, the Bronze Age by Q-Celts or Goidels, and the Iron Age by the P-Celts or Brythons.

This third solution, the adoption of linguistic and historical names, is, as we know now, a delusion, but it gave to many archaeological summaries produced at the end of the century, such as those of Anderson's articles in *Chambers's Encyclopedia* of 1904, Windle's *Remains of the Prehistoric Age in England* (1904) and Rice Holmes's *Ancient Britain and the Invasions of Julius Caesar* (1907), a clarity and definiteness which the material available then or now has never justified. The three-age system had taken a long time to be accepted in England; once accepted it was adopted universally and regarded with a kind of religious sanctity. The great problem of early twentieth-century prehistoric archaeology has been how to modify the three-age system to the increasing complexity of the archaeological record. The late nineteenth-century archaeologists were not prepared to face this problem, challengingly as it was set for them by the development of east Mediterranean archaeology.

Another challenge had been provided by British archaeologists nearer home. In 1890 Sir Arthur Evans published in *Archaeologia* his finds of the "Late Celtic" urnfield at Aylesford, in Kent, a paper which de Navarro has described as "one of the outstanding contributions to La Tène studies". But this paper is outstanding not only for its clear analysis of the elements in La Tène art. Sir Arthur Evans identified the Aylesford people with the Belgic invaders of south-east Britain, and in so doing recognised a group of invaders within the framework of the Iron Age. It was a challenge to the idea of the three invasions of the Neolithic, Bronze and Iron ages as constituting British prehistory, but a challenge which, for the time, passed unheeded.

CHAPTER FIVE

THE DEVELOPMENT OF TECHNIQUE AND METHOD BEFORE 1900

1. *The Beginnings of Excavation*

THE half-century from 1850 to 1900 not only saw the birth of archaeology from antiquarianism, history and geology, the discovery of the proofs of man's antiquity and of the ancient civilisations of Egypt, Assyria and Sumeria, and the creation of a complicated "sequence" of man's prehistoric cultures based on subdivisions of the Danish tripartite system: it also saw, slowly and with difficulty, the beginnings of systematic archaeological techniques of excavation, field survey, conservation and protection. It also saw, even more slowly and uncertainly, what Seton Lloyd has aptly called "The Birth of a Conscience",[1] regarding the expropriation of antiquities from other countries.

In the first half of the nineteenth century, and for a long while afterwards, excavation was principally concerned with the quick discovery of what was hidden in a barrow, tell, or pyramid, and with the acquisition of works of art to adorn the museums and private collections of Europe. Layard himself described his object of excavating at Nimrud as "to obtain the largest possible number of well-preserved objects of art at the least possible outlay of time and money", and Loftus frankly admitted in much the same words that in excavating at Warka he was actuated by "a nervous desire to find important large museum pieces at the least possible outlay of time and money".

In these confessions, Layard and Loftus are merely carrying on the old traditions of the west European collector begun in the sixteenth century by the Popes, and by men such as Lord Arundel, who had frankly admitted that his purpose was "to transplant old Greece to England". The English travellers in Greece in the eighteenth and early nineteenth century had no scruples about carrying away to England the antiquities of the Near East and

[1] *Foundations in the Dust*, Chapter XII, *passim*.

Aegean peoples, who were regarded as effete and unworthy possessors of such works of art. "Inscriptions we copied as they fell in our way," wrote Robert Wood in his *Ruins of Palmyra*, "and carried off the marbles wherever it was possible, for the avarice and superstition of the inhabitants made the task difficult and sometimes impracticable." The Cambridge don E. D. Clarke discovered the tomb of one Euclid—not the mathematician—in Athens, and wrote: "How interesting . . . such an antiquity must be for the University of Cambridge, where the name of Euclid is so particularly revered." And Clarke's account of the removal of the colossal Cistophoros of Eleusis, now in the Fitzwilliam Museum, is a fascinating revelation of archaeological methods at the time. "I found the goddess in a dunghill," he writes, "buried to her ears. The Eleusinian peasants, at the very mention of moving it, regarded me as one who would bring the moon from her orbit. What would become of their corn, they said, if the old lady with the basket were removed? I went to Athens and made an application to the Pasha, aiding my request by letting an English telescope glide between his fingers. The business was done." [1]

In excavation, no less than in collection, methods were such as we to-day find strange. The early eighteenth-century excavations at Herculaneum and Pompeii were conducted over many years with small groups of workmen—four, eight, or at most thirty. Houses were exposed and looted, paintings were sawn off, and the robbed houses left to decay away.[2] Right at the end of the eighteenth century and at the beginning of the nineteenth, due to the keen and generous interest taken by the Napoleonic kings of Naples, carefully planned excavations of Pompeii took place—the first large planned excavations in history. The plan was due to a scholar of Naples, Michele Arditi, and enough money was forthcoming to employ at times six hundred men at this work.

This premature birth of organised and conscientious excavation had no counterpart in England, where the old methods of the early antiquaries continued for a long while. We have already

[1] Otter, *Life of Clarke*, 505.

[2] Herculaneum was first excavated in 1711, after which excavation was forbidden, until undertaken by the Government from 1738 to 1766. The excavations were abandoned in 1766 because of insurmountable difficulties occasioned by thick layers of hardened ashes and pumice-stone. The ruins of Pompeii were accidentally discovered in 1748; it was easier to excavate, and it soon took the place of Herculaneum.

referred to the first meeting of the British Archaeological Association at Canterbury in 1844. During this meeting several barrows were excavated in the course of one day's expedition. The account of this excavation, only too typical of mid-nineteenth-century barrow digging, is worth quoting here. The barrows "were excavated to within about a foot of the bottom, before the arrival of the visitors, in order that the deposits might be uncovered in their presence. . . . The archaeologists assembled at Breach Down between nine and ten o'clock . . . and eight barrows were successively opened for their inspection. The only interruption arose from a heavy shower of rain, which was so far from damping the zeal of the visitors, that many, both ladies and gentlemen, raised their umbrellas (if they had any) and stood patiently looking at the operations of the excavators, whilst others sought a temporary covering in a windmill which stood in the middle of the scene. The barrows . . . were less productive than was anticipated. All however contained human remains, and in some were found different articles, which appeared to indicate the character of the person interred in them. . . . From Breach Down the party proceeded to Bourne Park . . . where two barrows were excavated which proved much richer than those at Breach Down." After the excavation of these ten barrows the party "partook of . . . a plentiful repast".[1]

Nearly a quarter of a century after this, in 1866, a party of archaeologists of international reputation went off to excavate at Hallstatt. The party included John Evans, Lubbock, Lartet, Morlot and Franks. Evans describes their activities in letters to his wife. "We arranged with the Bergmeister to set some men at work digging and are going up there early to-morrow morning to see the result: it may be that we shall stop there all day," he writes; and then next day: "We found our diggings too pleasant for us to be able to tear ourselves away from them. Lubbock and I breakfasted soon after 6 and about half past 7 were up at the cemetery . . . and found the men had already discovered a bronze bracelet and a broken fibula. I subsequently found in one of our trenches and dug out with my own hands one of the iron socketed celts with a part of the handle remaining in it and having on one part the impression of a fine twilled cloth against which it had lain. . . . I hope to be able to arrange in Vienna for our friend the

[1] Wright, *The Archaeological Museum*, 6–8.

Bergmeister Stapf to carry on some further excavations for us." [1]

Exciting though the excavations in Mesopotamia were in the middle of the nineteenth century, and remarkable though the discoveries were, made by pioneers like Botta, Layard and Rassam, they can hardly be acclaimed the originators of scientific excavation. The excavation methods of Botta and Place at Khorsabad consisted of tunnelling along the face of the walls and getting light by occasional vertical shafts to the surface. Even after years of work in Mesopotamia, Rassam was incapable of recognising sun-dried brickwork. And nowhere was there much attempt at conservation of monuments or artifacts. Layard visited Khorsabad some time after Botta had finished his excavations and wrote: "Since M. Botta's departure, the chambers had been partly filled up by the falling in of the trenches; the sculptures were rapidly perishing; and shortly, little will remain of this remarkable monument." But Layard himself did little for the preservation of his own finds. *Nineveh and its Remains* abounds in the phrase reminiscent of the earlier barrow diggers in England, and the early nineteenth-century excavators of Egyptian mummies: "entire when first exposed to view, it crumbled into dust as soon as touched". Thus copper helmets, iron armour, copper vessels, painted frescoes, ivories, all "fell to pieces almost immediately on exposure to the air". Rassam found, sixty feet to the north-west of the famous Shalmaneser II gates at Balawat, a second pair of gates, but "as soon as they were exposed to the air, they crumbled to pieces", he wrote.

There had also arrived in Egypt by the middle of the century that villain in archaeology, the tomb robber—under the guise of scientific enquirer—in the person of Giovanni Belzoni, surely one of the most eccentric characters in the history of archaeology—that long calendar of bizarre characters. Belzoni was a native of Padua, who made a living in England by performing prodigious feats of strength at circuses, went to Egypt to sell hydraulic machinery for irrigation purposes, and stayed on to rob tombs. He began his search for Pharaohs in 1817 at Thebes. He broke into one tomb, crashing his way through antiquities; "every step I took I crushed a mummy in some part or other," he declares. "When my weight bore on the body of an Egyptian it crushed like a band-box. I sank altogether among the broken mummies

[1] Joan Evans, *Time and Chance*, 123.

with a crash of bones, rags and wooden cases. . . . I could not avoid being covered with bones, legs, arms and heads rolling from above." Small wonder that Belzoni fainted frequently during these outrageous escapades, and that he was so overcome after one tomb exploration that he wandered about for three weeks in a trance. Small wonder, too, that the modern Egyptologist when he reads about the doings of Belzoni becomes, as Magoffin and Davis write, "a human chameleon", turning "green with envy, then red with shame, and then white with rage".[1]

The robbing of tombs and mounds and the private sale of antiquities and art treasures was typical of Egypt and Mesopotamia during much of the nineteenth century, and was, of course, a great hindrance to serious archaeology. In 1859 Mariette's workmen found near Thebes the gilded sarcophagus of Queen Aahhotep. Before Mariette could arrange for it to be sent to Cairo, a local potentate, the Mudir of Keneh, stole it, opened it in his harem, and set off by boat with the jewellery to present to the Khedive as an offering from himself. Mariette pursued the Mudir in a steamboat, caught up with him and boarded his boat, forcing him by physical violence to give up the jewellery, which he then took safely to Cairo. Rassam left his excavations unsupervised, and tablets from them found their way on to the market both before and after he completed his excavations. Budge, in 1888, was able to recover hundreds of these tablets from Baghdad dealers, though his own methods of getting the tablets out of the country were, to say the least, unusual—Seton Lloyd describes them as a "very blatant piece of sharp practice"[2] and his outspoken comments on the leakages from Rassam's digs involved him in an action for slander brought by Rassam.

For some while the rivalry between excavators in the Near East made the search for antiquities nothing short of piracy. The archaeological pirates were none the better even when working on behalf of the British Museum or the Louvre. "Those were the great days of excavating," declared Howard Carter. "Anything to which a fancy was taken, from a scarab to an obelisk, was just appropriated, and if there was a difference with a brother excavator, one laid for him with a gun."[3] On one occasion, Belzoni, who had been working on behalf of the British Consul-General in

[1] *The Romance of Archaeology*, 50
[2] *Foundations in the Dust*, 193.
[3] *The Tomb of Tut-ankh-Amen*, i, 68

Egypt as well as on his own account, had a remarkable encounter with the agents of Drouetti, who had been working on behalf of the French Consul. Belzoni had secured the Philae Obelisk and was returning to Luxor when, as he writes, "I saw a group of people running towards us; they were about thirty Arabs, headed by two Europeans, agents of Mr Drouetti. On their approaching, Mr Lebulo was first, and the renegade Rossignano second, both Piedmontese and countrymen of Mr Drouetti. Lebulo began . . . by asking what business I had to take away an obelisk that did not belong to me; and that I had done so many things of this kind to him, that I should not do any more. Meanwhile he seized the bridle of my donkey with one hand, and with the other laid hold of my waistcoat and stopped me from proceeding any farther: he had also a large stick hung to his wrist by a string. . . . At the same moment the renegade Rossignano reached within four yards of me, and with all the rage of a ruffian levelled a double-barrelled gun at my breast, loading me with all the imprecations that a villain could invent; by this time my servant was disarmed and overpowered by numbers. . . . The two gallant knights before me, I mean Lebulo and Rossignano, escorted by the two other Arabian servants of Mr Drouetti, both armed with pistols, and many others armed with sticks, continued their clamorous imprecations against me, and the brave Rossignano, still keeping the gun pointed at my breast, said it was time that I should pay for all I had done to them. The courageous Lebulo said . . . that he was to have one-third of the profit derived from the selling of the obelisk when in Europe, according to a promise from Mr Drouetti, had I not stolen it from the island of Philae. . . . I have no doubt that if I had attempted to dismount, the cowards would have despatched me on the ground, and said they did it in defence of their lives, as I had been the aggressor." [1]

This encounter between Belzoni and the agents of Drouetti is very typical of the picturesque methods of archaeological reconnaissance and excavation in the early nineteenth century. It is worth remembering, as Baikie has pointed out,[2] that these methods represent not the worst but the best of Near Eastern excavations at the time. Much of Belzoni's work has been praised by later workers, and it was certainly due to the unprincipled

[1] Belzoni, *Narrative of the . . . Recent Discoveries in Egypt and Nubia* [1821] 366–367.

[2] *The Glamour of Near East Excavation*, 42

depredations of Belzoni, Drouetti and their kind that representations of Egyptian art appeared in London, Paris and Turin, just as many of the British Museum's Assyrian treasures owe their existence to the surprising methods of Rassam.

Rouet, who replaced Botta as French consul at Mosul, sent agents hurriedly around the countryside opening mounds at random to stake a claim and prevent Layard from digging in them; and Layard himself was compelled to do much the same thing. At one moment, the French, disbelieving Layard's claim to have had permission to dig at Nineveh, were digging little pits while Layard was excavating elsewhere in the same mound. Rassam engaged himself in what can only be described, in Seton Lloyd's words, as "an undignified scramble for archaeological loot". Using Mosul as his base he examined mounds over an area of two hundred miles, leaving groups of his workmen digging away, often without any supervision, in a frantic attempt to get out of the ground whatever treasures there might be, before the mounds were claimed by agents or archaeologists of another nation. And at times Rassam unashamedly excavated mounds already conceded to other missions. His discovery of Ashur-bani-pal's library was due to a blatant act of piracy. Kuyunjik had, with the permission of Rawlinson, been divided into a northern or French area, and a southern or British area, and in 1853 Place's men and Rassam's men were both excavating there. Rassam was alarmed to see Place's men, while still working within their conceded areas, getting towards what he thought the most promising area at Kuyunjik. At the risk, as he said, "of getting into hot water with M. Place", Rassam excavated at night in the French area and discovered Ashur-bani-pal's palace with its library and lion-hunt gallery. Rassam described this episode as "using strategy": and says that Place accepted his act of piracy with equanimity, even congratulating Rassam on his "good fortune" at the time. But when Place came to write his *Ninive et L'Assyrie* he found himself unable to give Rassam credit for the discovery, claiming it for Loftus and his artist Boutcher.

Rassam was not so successful in his piratical attempts at Telloh. De Sarzec had excavated there in 1877 and 1878 and, while he was out of the country on a visit to France in 1878, Rassam decided to excavate there on his own. He collected a gang of Arab workmen who began fighting among themselves after three days, and thus thwarted his plans. Rassam was annoyed. "From what I have seen of the place of M. de Sarzec's discoveries," he wrote, "I am certain that if I had continued my researches there one day longer, I should have come upon the nest of black statues which were discovered in the highest mound."

It is very easy at the present day to be critical of the methods and achievements of the mid-nineteenth-century archaeologists. Every generation of archaeologists is likely to be critical of the methods of its predecessors. So far it is almost only Pitt Rivers among nineteenth-century British excavators whose reputation survives entirely unscathed. Layard, Rassam, Belzoni and their contemporaries have all been adversely criticised. Yet they were all excavating according to their lights. Very few archaeologists, either then or now, genuinely feel that they and their contemporaries are not technically equipped to undertake a complicated excavation and that it should be left to a later generation. It was, from our present point of view, perhaps unfortunate that many of the great discoveries were made in Egypt and Mesopotamia when they were. We may regret this, but we cannot convict the discoverers of any greater villainy than that they were not well ahead of their times. And we must remember that without their work the beginnings of Near Eastern archaeology would never have been made, nor an interest in archaeology fostered in mid-nineteenth-century England and France. Nor can we blame them unduly for the removal of antiquities and art treasures from Mesopotamia and Egypt to Europe. Botta, Layard, Belzoni and Drouetti were merely carrying on the traditions started in Greek lands by the agents of Charles I, the Earl of Arundel and the Duke of Buckingham in the seventeenth century, and maintained by Stuart and Revett, Hamilton, Robert Wood, E. D. Clarke and others in the eighteenth century. It should be remembered that only some forty years separate the arrival of the Elgin Marbles in London and the Kurnah disaster, but very gradually, towards the end of the nineteenth century, some standards of archaeological excavations were beginning to be recognised and established, and serious thought entertained on the propriety of removing to the museums of Europe the ancient treasures of the Near East. Traditions of excavation were beginning in western Europe as well as in the Near East. Greenwell wrote to John Evans in 1867 saying:

"That scoundrel Mortimer has been spreading calumnious reports to the effect that I am destroying all the Wold barrows and missing half the interments, in fact, doing the work in a thoroughly bad way. This is with a view to stopping my getting leave. His conduct . . . has been that of a rascal. . . . I may possibly have to get you to give me a testimonial as to my mode of barrow opening."[1] Censure of excavation methods became rife in the Near East, although perhaps it was not untouched with national sympathies and antipathies. Fossey, a Frenchman, described Rassam's campaign of 1879–82 as resembling "plus à un pillage qu'à une fouille scientifique". Breasted, an American, criticised British methods at Kuyunjik as "unscientific". Hilprecht, another American, expressed disapproval of all Mesopotamian excavations before those at Nippur in which he took part. Budge, an Englishman, disparaged the work of Rassam and de Sarzec, and wrote of the technique of the Americans—Hilprecht included—at Nippur: "More travellers than one who have seen the site of the American excavations at Nippur have failed to see there any exhibition of scientific digging."[2]

This critical awareness of the need for standards in archaeological technique is in itself an indication of the gradual development of new techniques of scientific archaeology. Excavations in England, the continent of Europe, in classical lands, in Egypt and in Mesopotamia all contributed to this development. Credit has been variously apportioned. Many names stand out as those of the great pioneers of the new archaeology of scientific excavation —Mariette, Conze, Newton, Curtius, Schliemann, Petrie and Pitt-Rivers. We shall discuss the contribution of these in the remaining sections of this chapter. But here we should especially remember the work of the Danes in their bogs, and of the Swiss archaeologists in their lake dwellings. The foundations of the stratigraphical principles of excavation were devised in Denmark and Switzerland. And it was the Swiss lake-dwelling excavations that revealed the extent to which apparently perishable material could, under special conditions, survive, and could, under very special conditions of excavation, be preserved. Earlier discoveries of tree coffins had also demonstrated this.

In July 1834 a barrow at Gristhorpe, between Scarborough and

[1] Quoted in Joan Evans, *Time and Chance*, 123.
[2] *The Rise and Progress of Assyriology*, 144.

Filey, was excavated by Mr Beswick, its owner, and a Mr Alexander of Halifax. They found an oak-tree coffin containing the perfect skeleton of "an Ancient Briton" wrapped in the skin of a sheep or goat. The bones were stained an ebony colour—a fact satisfactorily explained by Dean Buckland in a letter to the *Literary Gazette* as due to the tannin and gallic acid of the oak. In the coffin, with the skeleton, were also found "the flint head of a small javelin . . . two rude arrowheads of flint . . . the head of a spear or javelin formed of brass or some other composition of copper . . . a pin, and a beautifully formed ornament of either horn or the bone of some of the larger cetaceous tribe of fishes . . . an instrument of wood resembling in form the knife used by the Egyptian embalmers . . . fragments of a ring of horn . . . a wickerwork basket" and "a quantity of vegetable substance" described as the leaves and berries of the mistletoe—"they were however very tender and soon crumbled to dust".[1]

Gristhorpe and the other tree-coffin finds taught an important lesson to archaeologists, namely that it might be possible to recover a very detailed picture of early man, and that archaeology would not be a discipline like geology, dealing only with the fossils of man, but would deal with material survivals of a far less tangible form. It would be a long time before archaeological technique permitted the study of material objects like Queen Shub-ad's harp and the spear from Palestine which had left only their "ghosts" behind, but the tree coffins made a point which was hammered home by the finds from the Swiss lake dwellings—that archaeology had to develop a technique of excavation and preservation all its own, and that careful excavation of specially preserved sites would yield the most detailed knowledge of the way of life of early man. It is indeed a long way from Stukeley's "garden of the Druids" to the list of plants and animals recovered from the Swiss lake dwellings, but it is the measure of the change that was taking place in the early nineteenth century in the awareness and practice of archaeological technique.

2. *Mariette*

Mariette's own methods of excavation and research have frequently been decried. He himself excavated over thirty

[1] This find is described in a pamphlet published in 1834 by W. Williamson, and by W. J. Thoms in his introduction to his translation of Worsaae's *Primeval Antiquities of Denmark* (1849), from which these quotations are taken.

important sites in as many years. He was mainly concerned with obtaining splendid results, and was always after precious and imposing finds and historic monuments, rather than the common things of everyday life. Petrie describes how Mariette made excavations near the Sphinx and had blasted away with dynamite the fallen ruins of a temple. "Nothing was done", wrote Petrie sadly in 1883, two years after Mariette's death, "with any uniform plan; work is begun and left unfinished; no regard is paid to future requirements of exploration and no civilised or labour-saving appliances are used. It is sickening to see the rate at which everything is being destroyed, and the little regard paid to preservation." Mariette certainly never published his results adequately; some of his excavations were not published at all. He was content with gathering together a vast mass of material without recording the details of its provenance or assessing its historical significance.

Yet, with all these limitations, he was a pioneer of new methods in archaeology. Even if his own methods were, in the judgement of subsequent archaeologists, still primitive, at least he saw that no one practised even more primitive methods. As Director of the Egyptian Service of Antiquities he forbade any excavations in Egypt except those which he himself conducted. Thus, for a while, by the high-handed institution of a personal monopoly in excavation, he stopped the undignified and regrettable scramble for antiquities such as was taking place at the time in Mesopotamia, and, for a while, he rid Egypt of tomb robbers and art collection touts masquerading as archaeologists. Mariette regularised and systematised the various works undertaken in Egypt, providing for the first time a proper control of excavation and research.

This in itself was a great service to the development of a new outlook in archaeology. But Mariette did more than this; he devoted himself strenuously to prevent the exportation of Egyptian antiquities to Europe. He wanted the remains of Ancient Egypt properly housed in modern Egypt, and, to this end, bent all his efforts to prohibit the removal of antiquities from Egypt and to the creation of a National Museum of Egyptian Antiquities. He felt that, once there was such a museum in Egypt, it would no longer be possible for the agents of European missions to justify their removal of treasures from Egypt on the grounds that the Egyptians were not fit to look after their own antiquities.

In pursuance of his aims he had first to convince Said Pasha, the Khedive, that Egyptian antiquities mattered at all. The creation of the Egyptian Service of Antiquities and Mariette's appointment as Director were largely due to the machinations of de Lesseps and Napoleon III, rather than to the interest of the Khedive who, as Maspero wrote, reluctantly "came to the conclusion that he would be more acceptable to the Emperor if he made some show of taking pity on the Pharaohs". Mariette had a difficult task turning this diplomatic demonstration of pity into real interest. He could never secure a regular and permanent grant from the Egyptian Government but had to apply for *ad hoc* grants direct from the Khedive. These applications were refused or granted according to the whim of the moment; several of Mariette's digs had to be stopped owing to the cessation of funds by Said Pasha in a moment of bad temper. Mariette collected all he could from every excavation in the hope that the size of his collection would eventually shock the Khedive into providing a museum. We must not therefore censure too sharply his preoccupation with large and dramatic finds.

At first his scheme bore no fruit. To house his treasures he was first allocated "a deserted mosque which was falling into ruin, some filthy sheds, and a dwelling-house alive with vermin in which he lived himself".[1] He turned this unpromising site into the first Egyptian Museum, and continued collecting, and importuning the Khedive for a real museum. It was Queen Aahhotep's jewellery that eventually moved Said Pasha. We have already described how the Mudir of Keneh stole this jewellery and how Mariette boarded the Mudir's boat and forced him to return it. The Khedive was amused by this incident, kept a gold chain for one of his wives, a scarab for himself, and ordained that the rest of the jewellery should go into a specially built museum. The gold and jewellery had produced at once the effect which the large historic monuments had failed to do. In 1859 a special museum was built at Boulak.

Even so, Mariette had to maintain the greatest watchfulness over the new museum, which he filled with fresh treasures after each year's excavations. The Khedive would often have liked

[1] Baikie, *A Century of Excavation in the Land of the Pharaohs*, 26.

to give away exhibits from the Boulak Museum to his friends, and on occasion suggested that the whole collection should be pawned as security for a loan. The Empress Eugénie was so delighted by the Egyptian jewellery exhibited in the Exposition at Paris in 1867 that she informed the Khedive Ismail that she would be graciously pleased to receive the whole collection as a present. It was a great moment in the history of archaeology when the Khedive, surprised by this request, yet anxious to please France, and short of money, still made his consent conditional on Mariette's agreement. "There is someone at Boulak more powerful than I," he said to the Empress's agent, "and you must address yourself to him." Mariette firmly refused, and the collection of Egyptian antiquities returned safely from Paris to Boulak. What strength of character and fixity of purpose is revealed in that refusal of Mariette, made to the highest in his native land, in the interests of what he thought right for archaeology and Egypt. It cost him the support of France and, for a short while, the favour of the Khedive. But after 1870 he was again in favour and from then until his death in 1881 his schemes prospered. Ismail even had grand plans for the extension of the museum buildings at Boulak, but these never came to anything, and on one occasion during this period the proposal for raising a loan on the collections was again mooted, and again defeated by Mariette. When he died he could look back on three magnificent achievements—the creation of the first National Museum in the Near East, the creation of the first National Service of Antiquities, and the birth of a conscience about the expropriation of antiquities.[1]

3. *The Development of Classical Archaeology*

Up to the sixties and seventies of the nineteenth century, classical excavations, apart from Pompeii, had been confined to the recovery of single objects or single structures. There had been little attempt at complete excavation, and no idea of recovering a succession of occupations. From 1870 onwards a new archaeovogical method was developed in classical excavations which became the pattern of all subsequent excavational technique elery where. This development was largely due to the Austrian

[1] In 1889 the museum was moved from Boulak to a disused palace at Gizeh. In 1902 the collections were moved again to the present museum in Cairo, in the Qasr-el-Nil.

and German excavators in the Aegean, especially Conze, Curtius and Dörpfeld. Its aims have been summarised by Michaelis, himself a friend and fellow-pupil of Conze, as follows: "To ascertain the original form both of the general plan and of its separate parts, to follow the successive alterations that have come in the course of time, to assign to each detail its place in the development, and thus to make the excavation a reconstruction of the lost whole, is the distinguishing mark of the new method." [1]

The names of two archaeologists must be mentioned who, working in classical lands before the Germans, yet showed the beginnings of scientific technique. These were Fiorelli and Newton. Giuseppe Fiorelli took over the excavation of Pompeii in 1860. Hitherto complete excavation of houses had rarely if ever been done; the upper storey had been dug and collapsed into the trenches, burying the lower levels. Now, Fiorelli uncovered whole insulae and dug them carefully stratum by stratum, preserving any features of interest *in situ*. He founded a "Scuola di Pompei", where foreigners as well as Italians could learn archaeological technique, and himself made a special study of the materials and technique of building at Pompeii. Michaelis calls Fiorelli "a thoroughly scientific man": he was certainly one of the pioneers of stratigraphical analysis.

This is what Gaston Bossier wrote in summing up the new methods initiated by Fiorelli in 1863 at Pompeii: "He declared and repeated in his reports that the centre of interest in the Pompeian excavations was Pompeii itself; that the discovery of works of art was a matter of secondary importance; that efforts were directed, above all, to reviving a Roman city that would depict for us the life of bygone ages; that it was necessary to see the city in its entirety and in its minutest details in order that the lesson it taught might be complete, that knowledge was sought not only of the houses of the wealthy but also of the dwellings of the poor, with their common household utensils and crude wall decoration. With that end in view, everything became important, and nothing could legitimately be overlooked." Here was a manifesto which might still be used as a statement of the essential aims of excavations in a settlement.

Charles Thomas Newton was an official of the British Museum who arranged to be sent by the Foreign Office for seven years of

[1] *A Century of Archaeological Discoveries*, p. 158.

diplomatic service in the Levant, and to combine his consular duties with collecting material for the British Museum. In 1852 he was vice-consul at Mytilene, later acting as consul at Rhodes and Rome, returning in 1861 to the British Museum to take charge of the department of Greek and Roman Antiquities there. Newton had been excited by reliefs sent to the British Museum in 1846 by Sir Stratford Canning, who had taken them from the Turkish fortress of Budrum. Newton suspected these fragments were from the Mausoleum of Halicarnassos. He succeeded in identifying the site of this wonder of the world, and in assembling in the British Museum all that was left of it, including fragments that had been taken to Genoa, Constantinople and Rhodes. In 1858–59 he went to Cnidos and discovered the plan of the Greek city there; this was the first time that an old city plan had been carefully and accurately recovered. Newton made extensive use of photography in his work.

Alexander Conze dug in Samothrace in 1873. He had two architects working with him and a photographer, as well as a man-of-war placed at his disposal by the Austrian Government. His second Samothrace expedition was in 1875. A complete record was published of these excavations; it is the first "modern" excavation report in existence. All the plans were beautifully drawn in detail by the architects, and the reports were illustrated by photographs. This was the first time that photography had been used to illustrate archaeological reports. While Newton had used photography on his excavations, he had had lithographs made from the photographs to illustrate his reports.

The German Archaeological Institute became a Prussian Government institution in 1871, and an Imperial institution in 1874. A branch was set up in Athens and in 1875 excavations were begun at Olympia under the energetic and skilful direction of Ernst Curtius, assisted by the architect Friedrich Adler. This work occupied the six winters of 1875–80. The German Empire spent £30,000 on the work, and the expenses of the last winter were borne personally by the Emperor William. As the Greek Government prohibited the export of antiquities the German Government renounced all claims except in the case of duplicates being found. Everything that was discovered at Olympia was preserved, and a small museum built on the spot to house the finds. The stratigraphy of the sites was carefully and completely studied. The architectural work at Olympia was undertaken first by Richard Bohn and later by Dörpfeld, who became the moving spirit in the new methods of preservation and excavation.

The great work of Conze at Samothrace and Curtius at Olympia initiated a period of thirty years of great classical excavations, and classical lands became a school for the method and technique of excavation. The French at Delos and Delphi, the Greeks themselves in Athens, and the American Archaeological Institute under Bacon and Clarke at Assos, on the south coast of the Troad, and at Neandreia, north of Assos, carried on the traditions which the Germans had established. These traditions were transmitted by Dörpfeld to a perhaps unwilling Schliemann.

In assessing the work of the Germans and Austrians in Greece at this time we must especially mention the work of Adolf Furtwängler, who, as Albright has recently insisted, developed to the highest degree the chronological value of pottery, more especially painted pottery.[1] It was also Furtwängler who with Löschcke issued, in their *Mykenische Vasen* (1886), a complete publication of all Mycenaean vases and potsherds found in all the islands of the Aegean as far east as Cyprus. This was the beginning of that essential of modern archaeology—the corpus of finds.

4. *Schliemann*

Schliemann's contribution to the development of archaeological technique and method has been vigorously disputed. To some he was the first modern archaeologist and much of modern methods derives from his excavations. To others he was a plundering, blundering robber whose reputation was made by the astonishing value and interest of his finds. Casson, for example, claims Schliemann as the founder of scientific method in archaeology, declaring that he laid "the solid foundations of a proper archaeological method which could be followed in any land", and that his methods "constituted an innovation of the first order of importance in the study of the antiquity of man by archaeological methods".[2] Michaelis, on the other hand, said Schliemann was "a complete stranger to every scientific method of treatment of his subject and had no idea that a method and a well-defined technique existed".[3] Karo, less enthusiastic than Casson

[1] *From the Stone Age to Christianity*, 1946, 20. [2] *The Discovery of Man*, 221.
[3] *A Century of Archaeological Discoveries*, 217.

but more charitable than Michaelis, gives this verdict on Schliemann's work: "No one with archaeological experience will refuse to acknowledge a great debt to Schliemann and his young wife for their achievements; without any training in technique and method, and without any of the resources that are available to-day, they brought thousands of objects to light."

On one point there can be no dispute. Schliemann's excavation at Hissarlik was the first excavation of a tell: "the first large-scale dissection of a dryland settlement unguided by the remains of great monuments such as simplified the task in Babylon and Nineveh", as Myres has put it. In this Schliemann was the precursor of a long line of excavators in the Near East. He cut right through the mound, distinguishing seven occupation levels: it was a great moment in the application of stratigraphical principles to archaeology. The principles of stratigraphy in their general application to archaeology were already appreciated and the work of the Danish archaeologists in their peat bogs, of Keller and others in the Swiss lakes, and of Gastaldi and Stroebel in the *etrremare* mounds of Piedmont and Lombardy had been ample demonstration of geological superposition as a key to relative chronology in prehistoric archaeology. Schliemann demonstrated the applicability of these principles to the excavation of a great mound. But it would be only fair to say that the stratigraphy of Hissarlik only gradually forced its way into his understanding. He puzzled his way slowly and laboriously to an appreciation of what he was uncovering; at one moment he thought the whole mound covered remains of Priam's Troy, and the widespread occurrence of stone tools was confusing: "I cannot understand", he wrote, "how it is that I am unearthing stone implements throughout the length of my excavations."

We should distinguish two periods in Schliemann's digging: the earlier period from 1870 to 1882, and the second from 1882 until his death, when he was assisted by Dörpfeld. In his first season at Troy, from 1871–73, Schliemann was alone with his young and gifted Greek wife. At Mycenae, from 1874–76, he had Greek colleagues, but they suspected him, and were most uncooperative. In 1879, in his second season at Troy, he was assisted by, and learnt much from, Virchow and Burnouf. From 1882 onwards, for his third and last season at Troy, he was assisted by Dörpfeld, who, as we have said, was a practical architect and had worked under Curtius at Olympia. Dörpfeld brought to the Schliemann digs the new system and efficiency of the German classical archaeologists. Perhaps "assisted" is not the right word to use in describing the relations of Dörpfeld to Schliemann at Troy. Myres calls Schliemann in his last season "a constitutional sovereign among expert ministers", and Ludwig calls him "a captive king". Whatever were the human relations, Dörpfeld was able to expose the stratigraphy more clearly than previously; he revolutionised Schliemann's technique, changing it, as Myres says, "from digging to dissection".

But it would be wrong to suppose that all that was good in Schliemann's methods came from his half-reluctant adoption of the methods of Curtius and the Germans in Greece. Long before Dörpfeld joined him he was working on certain principles basic to good excavation. He preserved everything he found; although he was driven on by the desire to recover the treasures that were buried in the earth, he preserved all his finds, realising the importance of ordinary things in providing a true picture of the past. He recorded carefully the level at which all finds were made, and he had every important find drawn or photographed as soon as possible. And he was prompt in publishing his results as fully as possible. In fact, Schliemann was applying to his excavations the business methods which he had learnt in his long career as a merchant, and we may consider the great success of the excavations he made at Troy as the result of the happy combination of his own business methods and acumen with the methods and training brought by Dörpfeld.

5. *Pitt-Rivers*

General Pitt-Rivers made two great contributions to the method of prehistoric archaeology. The first related to the analysis of artifacts, the second to the technique of excavation. Pitt-Rivers was professionally concerned in the Army with investigations into the use and improvement of the rifle between 1851 and 1857 at Woolwich, Enfield, Malta and Hythe. He was virtually the originator of the Hythe School of Musketry. Pitt-Rivers had great talents for organisation and for experimental research. In studying the development of firearms he found himself arranging collections of types in developing or evolutionary sequences. He was also interested in the evolutionary ideas which at that time were informing biological knowledge. From his own detailed study of British firearms, and the Darwinian concept of evolution, he formulated the idea that all material objects developed in an evolutionary way and could be arranged in typological sequences. In this he was developing the idea of the early Danish and Swedish antiquaries who had discussed typological sequences, and was working parallel to John Evans who was busy classifying and arranging prehistoric flint and bronze implements in categories and in sequences. But he was not consciously indebted to the northern antiquaries or to Evans; his work on the material culture of primitive peoples and of prehistoric man was a direct offshoot of his work on firearms and his interest in biology. It was essentially from the study of firearms that "he was led to believe that the same principles must probably govern the development of the other arts, appliances and ideas of mankind".[1]

To prove this thesis and to illustrate its truth he began collecting everything he could lay his hands on—first weapons and then boats, looms, dress, musical instruments, magical and religious symbols. Soon his house was filled from cellar to attic with these ethnographical and prehistorical collections, and in 1851 his collections were lent to the museum at Bethnal Green. Later the collection was moved to South Kensington, and finally to Oxford, where a special annexe of the University Museum was designed for it. The Pitt-Rivers collections were specially interesting for two reasons: in the first place they were arranged typologically and not geographically. Hitherto ethnographical and prehistoric collections had been set out by sites or countries. Pitt-Rivers disregarded find spots and arranged the material on a taxonomic and typologic basis. He thus performed an enormous service to comparative archaeology, and also demonstrated the values of the comparative ethnographic method in archaeology. This method had been hinted at by Nilsson; Pitt-Rivers showed how it could best be used, and how a comparison of prehistoric artefacts with contemporary ethnographical material made one the better able to appreciate the function and importance of prehistoric artefacts. Secondly, Pitt-Rivers began what may justly be called a sociological approach to artefacts, whether contemporary or prehistoric. He stressed that his collection

[1] Balfour, in (ed. J. L. Myres) *The Evolution of Culture*, v.

was "not for the purpose of surprising anyone, either by the beauty or value of the objects exhibited, but solely with a view to instruction. For this purpose ordinary and typical specimens rather than rare objects have been selected and arranged in sequence". He was stressing the point made later by Petrie in Egypt—the importance of the ordinary artifact, and the necessity of collecting complete collections of the material culture of contemporary or prehistoric societies. Pitt-Rivers and Petrie were the leaders of the revolution in archaeology which led it away from the contemplation of *art* objects to the contemplation of *all* objects. Archaeology as a study of art treasures was a nineteenth-century legacy from the late eighteenth-century study of classical antiquities. It survived to the Egyptian tomb robbers and in the persons of Botta and Layard, and it survived into the arrangement of the British Museum as late as the seventies of the nineteenth century. Pitt-Rivers and Petrie were mainly responsible for the transformation of the archaeological outlook from one of curiosity to one which was frankly sociological.

Pitt-Rivers explained his point of view in several lectures and papers, notably his lectures on *The Principles of Classification* to the Anthropological Institute in 1874, on *The Evolution of Culture* to the Royal Institution in 1875, his three lectures on *Primitive Warfare* to the United Services Institution in 1867, 1868, 1869, and his lecture on *Early Modes of Navigation* to the Anthropological Institute in 1874.[1] He urged everywhere the study of *all* material objects of human culture, and their arrangement in typological sequences. His general principle for the arrangement of all these sequences was that the "seemingly more primitive and generalised forms were the nearest natural forms". He was not, however, a slave to this principle; he recognised the existence of periods of degeneration. He was startled by the achievements of Upper Palaeolithic Art, compared with the degeneration in art that succeeded it, and by Mariette's discovery that the most faithful and true sculptures in Egypt were the work of the IIIrd dynasty. He appreciated the work of Sir John Evans on British coins, and also Schliemann's Trojan finds illustrating the devolution of the human-face motive. He stressed, moreover, that formal

[1] These lectures, together with an extract from Balfour's address to the British Association in 1914 on Pitt-Rivers, were reissued under the editorship of J. L. Myres as *The Evolution of Culture and other Essays* (Oxford, 1906).

identities between objects were not enough, and taught a lesson begun by Nilsson, that before identity could be proclaimed, functional as well as formal identity must be proved. Pitt-Rivers believed implicitly in progress. He arranged his artifacts in this belief, and was sure that they demonstrated the truth of progress. But he remained uncertain of the possibility of forecasting the course of progress. "Progress is like a game of dominoes," he declared in the closing words of his 1874 lecture on *The Principles of Classification.* "Like fits on to like. In neither case can we tell beforehand what will be the ultimate figure produced by the cohesions: all we know is that the fundamental rule of the game is sequence."

As Colonel Lane-Fox, Pitt-Rivers carried out many excavations in various parts of England and Wales, and in some of these he worked with Canon Greenwell. After 1880, when he inherited the Rivers estates, comprising over 29,000 acres of land, including much of Cranborne Chase, he began a remarkable campaign of excavation which comprised camps, villages, cemeteries, barrows and ditches. Among the most famous of these excavations between 1880 and 1900 were the now classic settlements of Woodcuts and Rotherley, Woodyates, Wor Barrow, Bokerly Dyke and Wansdyke.[1] Unlimited by considerations of finance, time, or labour, Pitt-Rivers was able to make these excavations a model of scientific excavations. He indulged to the full his talent for organisation and research, and his experience gained during a long career of soldiering and administration. His excavations were well organised and thoroughly carried out. He demanded and obtained the highest standard of accuracy and care from his assistants and workmen. All his excavations were on a grand scale, and in most of the sites he studied he examined them comprehensively and completely down to the bedrock. For the technique of the mid-nineteenth century, which consisted of digging a hole in a barrow to find the primary interment and any associated grave goods, Pitt-Rivers substituted the *total* excavation of sites. He stressed the importance of stratigraphical

[1] Pitt-Rivers was one of the first archaeologists to concentrate on dwelling places rather than barrows. Casson has cited the excavation of an Iron Age village at Standlake, Oxon, by Stone in the eighteen-fifties as the first example of a non-barrow dig in England. Of course settlement sites were more difficult to excavate than barrows, less rewarding, but more fruitful in common things.

observation, and of the necessity of recording the position of everything found. He caused accurate plans and sections and detailed drawings and descriptions to be made of all his excavations, and constructed models of all the main sites.

Pitt-Rivers carried into prehistoric archaeology the insistence on the importance of common things which had marked his collections of ethnographical and prehistoric objects. "Common things are of more importance than particular things, because they are more prevalent," he wrote in 1898. "I have always remembered a remark of Professor Huxley's in one of his addresses: 'The word *importance*', he says, 'ought to be struck out of scientific dictionaries; that which is important is that which is persistent.' Common things vary in form, as the idea of them passes from place to place, and the date of them and of the places in which they are found may sometimes be determined by gradual variations in form. There is no knowing what may hereafter be found to be most interesting. Things are apt to be of the greatest value in tracing the distribution of forms. This will be admitted when it is recognised that distribution is a necessary prelude to generalisation." [1]

Pitt-Rivers believed in, and practised, the prompt and complete publication of all his excavations. In four privately printed sumptuous volumes produced between 1887 and 1898, under the title of *Excavations in Cranborne Chase*, he set and achieved the highest standard of archaeological publication.[2] From his publications, and the models in the Farnham Museum, it is possible at the present day to re-create every stage of his excavations. In every way his work was of the highest standard; in fifteen years he transformed excavation from the pleasant hobby of barrow digging to an arduous scientific pursuit. He was at the time far in advance of his contemporaries; indeed Collingwood has suggested that in many ways he was in advance of modern archaeological technique, and many a modern excavator must envy his resources and the way in which he was able to carry out his excavations with the precision, thoroughness and discipline of a military operation.

Pitt-Rivers has been claimed as the father of scientific

[1] *Excavations in Cranborne Chase*, iv (1898), 27.

[2] Volume i (1887), ii (1888), iii (1892), iv (1898), and an Index by St George Gray (1905).

excavation. He himself said in 1875 that "science is organised common sense", but his excavations were not only organised common sense—they had, too, an element of genius, and it is this that makes him stand out in nineteenth-century English archaeology. We must not consider Pitt-Rivers's techniques of excavation in isolation—as something completely new that developed suddenly between 1880 and 1900. His is the development of the techniques at which Cunnington and Colt Hoare were aiming at the beginning of the century, and Canon Greenwell is the link between the early nineteenth-century antiquaries and Pitt-Rivers.[1] To this tradition Pitt-Rivers brought his own flair for efficiency and administration and his own particular genius.

Pitt-Rivers was regarded at the time by many as an eccentric and his standards of excavation and publication impracticable and even undesirable. He was, in many ways, eccentric, with his Gypsy School, and his Larmer Tree grounds, where llamas and yaks roamed wild, and public concerts were given free on Sundays. But all this was a part of a deliberate policy to interest the ordinary person in prehistory and ethnography. He wanted to give prehistory a place in the general framework of everyday education. He built a museum at Farnham, which contained the finds from his Cranborne Chase digs as well as the models of the excavations, a second collection of ethnographical objects which he began assembling as soon as his first collection was set up at Oxford, and the nucleus of a folk museum. He sensed the gradual shift of power to the educated masses and insisted they must be educated aright. "What they lack is history," he said. "They must learn the links between the past and present."

6. *Petrie*

Petrie, although his name will always primarily be associated with excavations in Egypt and Palestine, began as a British archaeologist, visiting and surveying prehistoric monuments in southern Britain. A work on *Stonehenge* published in 1880 is among his earliest publications. When he transferred his attention to Egypt in 1881 and the following years he took with him a thorough training as a surveyor, as well as the strongest beliefs in

[1] Randall (*History in the Open Air*, 11) rightly emphasises the part played by Cunnington and Greenwell in the building up of the tradition of English field archaeology.

archaeological excavation as a painstaking and laborious research not to be undertaken lightly or hurriedly. In his autobiography he claims that when he was eight he was horrified at the description of how a Roman villa had been unearthed in the Isle of Wight: "I was horrified", he wrote, "at hearing of the rough shovelling out of the contents and protested that the earth ought to be pared away inch by inch to see all that was in it, and how it lay."[1] However true it be that, even as a child, he was, as he claimed, "in archaeology by nature", it is certainly true that he was one of the main founders of archaeological method as we now understand and practise it.

When he first went to Egypt, Petrie was full of criticism for Mariette, whom he describes as having "most rascally blasted to pieces all the fallen parts of the granite temple by a large gang of soldiers", as only visiting his excavations once in a few weeks, and being completely hoodwinked by his *reises*, or overseers, who salted his sites with *antikas* bought in Cairo to keep up his interest in the sites![2]

Petrie at first had little assistance from anyone. His techniques were self-devised. He complained that he got no training or criticism from the Egypt Exploration Fund and wrote in 1885 that his work was "in fact a case of breaking new ground in archaeology". His method was based on the following principles: First, care for the monuments being excavated, and respect for future visitors and excavators; Second, meticulous care in excavation and the collecting and description of everything found; Third, the accurate planning of all monuments and excavations; Fourth, the full publication of all excavations as soon as possible. These were principles that Petrie was formulating consciously as the basis of his method in 1889. They were an enormous advance on anything that had existed before in Egypt. It was only after these principles had been carried out, argued Petrie, that the archaeologist could begin to write history; then he would see the importance "of everything found" and in setting out his story would use "all materials of inscriptions, objects, positions and probabilities".

Furtwängler had appreciated the value of painted and decorated pottery as an archaeological chronometer. It was Petrie who first showed how unpainted pottery could be used in the same way,

[1] *Seventy Years in Archaeology*, 8.

[2] See also p. 162 *supra*.

if studied in detail. He had begun to appreciate this fact in the eighties when working at Naucratis, but it was his excavation of a Palestinian tell, Tell el-Hesi, in 1890, that drove home the lesson to him. Here he had to deal with sixty feet of occupation debris. The debris was clearly divided into occupation levels each characterised by pottery types, although, as Petrie also realised, the pottery types and the levels did not coincide exactly. Petrie was able to synchronise some of the Tell el-Hesi levels with Egyptian dynasties and so build up an absolute chronology of the whole sixty feet of occupation. Here was a model of the study of a stratified occupation site—a model far in advance of the work at Troy.

In addition to the definition of general method, Petrie made three specific contributions to the development of prehistoric archaeology. The first, the extension of comparative archaeology by cross-dating Egyptian and Greek remains, we have already discussed. The second was the scientific study of the materials used by prehistoric and protohistoric man. The archaeologist, he declared, must study "all details of material, colour, fabric and mechanical questions of tools". He laid down the basis of artifact analysis in archaeology, a method which has yielded such interesting results in the twentieth century. In the third place, Petrie invented the idea of sequence-dating. His work at Naqada, Ballas, Diospolis Parva and elsewhere forced him to study material that dated before the Ist dynasty. How was this to be given an absolute chronology? It would have been possible to give guesses in years assisted by dead reckoning from the thickness of deposits. In Europe prehistoric material had been arranged in typological sequences, and had been classified according to its place in the subdivisions of the three-age system. Petrie had little respect for the system of prehistory built up by subdivisions of the three-age system with its illusory appearance of exact chronology. "Such a piecemeal plan is well enough for a beginning," he wrote in 1904, "but it is not capable of exact definition: it is cumbersome, and it does not express the relation of one period to another."[1] He therefore devised a system of sequence dates which he applied to the typological sequence of prehistoric pottery worked out at Diospolis Parva. He started his sequence with S.D. 30, supposing very rightly that he had not as yet discovered the earliest prehistoric

[1] *Methods and Aims in Archaeology*, 127.

material in Egypt, and carried on to dynastic times at S.D. 80. For each of the fifty numbers in his series he used the contents of twenty graves.

This system of sequence-dating was first set out in *Diospolis Parva* and in *Methods and Aims in Archaeology*. Petrie regarded it as one of his main contributions to prehistory and wrote of it: "This system enables us to deal with material which is entirely undated otherwise; and the larger the quantity of it the more accurate are the results. There is no reason now why prehistoric ages, from which there are groups of remains, should not be dealt with as surely and clearly as the historic ages with recorded dates." [1] This was too optimistic a hope. Actually Petrie's system has not been adopted widely outside Egypt, and for a very good reason. Although it appeared to be something very new, it was merely a restatement of a typological method of dating in a new guise. But it was objective in the sense that, although it, too, was not in terms of absolute chronology, it did set out a relative chronological sequence in terms of numbers and not in terms of ambiguous phrases like "Early Bronze Age" or "Mycenaean". It was a system that answered no questions of absolute chronology, but it begged no questions, which is after all the first requirement of an objective chronology.

It is difficult to overestimate the contribution made to archaeological method in the last quarter of the nineteenth century by Schliemann, Pitt-Rivers and Petrie. It would be no exaggeration to say that, with the experience of the Danes and the Swiss behind them, they forged the essential technique of archaeology. The remarkable thing is that these giants were not really contemporaries, Both Schliemann and Pitt-Rivers were nineteenth-century figures. but Petrie was only forty-seven years old when Pitt-Rivers died, and lived to complete over seventy years of archaeological work, and to be the mentor and inspiration of many archaeologists who are still young to-day. It is, then, interesting to recollect now that Pitt-Rivers visited Petrie's excavations in Egypt, and so did Schliemann. Schliemann came in 1888 with Virchow, and Petrie described him as "dogmatic, but always ready for facts".

[1] *Methods and Aims in Archaeology*, 129.

7. *Prehistoric Archaeology in 1900*

The changes in prehistoric archaeology between 1870 and 1900 had been very many. They had been due to the discoveries described in the previous chapter, and to the changes in technique which have been discussed in the present chapter. The result was that by the end of the century prehistoric archaeology was in a more assured position. But recognition was still slow, and the appreciation of the existence of ancient civilisations was gradual. Petrie has recorded a meeting of the Board of Studies in History of the University of London in 1901 when the teaching of the history of art was discussed: "The scope of ideas on the Board may be seen by the proposal that the history should begin at A.D. 1500. I remarked that we had done nothing but copy since then: dead silence. Then someone proposed 1400."[1] In the early eighties there were rumours and discussions about the establishment of a Professorship of Archaeology in Oxford; Sir Arthur Evans was being advised to stand until he learnt that it was to be confined to classical archaeology. In a letter to Freeman in 1883 he said "to confine a Professorship of Archaeology to classical times seems to me as reasonable as to create a chair of 'Insular Geography' or 'Mesozoic Geology'".[2]

But although recognition in universities was slow, the subject was by now thoroughly established, and a broad picture of man's prehistory was available to be repeated in textbooks and encyclopaedia articles. This picture was well summarised by Arthur Evans in his inaugural lecture at the Ashmolean in 1884. Prehistoric archaeology, he declared, in words often to be borrowed, "has drawn aside the curtain and revealed the dawn. It has dispelled, like the unsubstantial phantoms of a dream, those preconceived notions as to the origin of human arts and institutions at which Epicurus and Lucretius already laughed, before the days of biblical chronology. It has taught us that, at a time when Britain formed still a part of the continent of Europe with an arctic climate and another fauna . . . Man was already in existence here, fashioning his flint weapons to aid him in his struggle against the sabre-toothed tiger, or the woolly-haired Rhinoceros. It has tracked him onwards to his cavern homes, and dragged into the light his bone harpoons, and the flint scrapers wherewith he

[1] *Seventy Years in Archaeology*, 179.
[2] Quoted in Joan Evans, *Time and Chance*.

cleaned the shaggy hides that served for his apparel; it has unearthed in the grottoes of the Dordogne the earliest known relics of other than the purest utilitarian art; it has followed him through the later periods of the Age of Stone in Europe, whetting and polishing his tomahawks, or delicately flaking out his arrow-heads and lanceheads. It has dived to the lake bottoms, and reconstructed his pile dwellings; it has fished out the very clothes he wore, the spindle whorls that spun their threads, the cereals that he had learnt to cultivate—nay the very cakes he ate, and the caraway and poppy seeds wherewith he flavoured them. It has shown us the beginnings of metallurgy characterised in this quarter of the globe by the use of implements of Bronze; and by the discovery of great prehistoric cemeteries like that of Hallstatt, in Upper Austria, it has revealed to us that at the close of this first Age of Metal, ancient lines of commerce were already bringing the Mediterranean shores into direct connexion with the Baltic lands of fur and amber." [1]

This passage has been quoted *in extenso* because it represents so well the picture of prehistoric Europe current in the late nineteenth century. Underlying it is no clear statement as to whether the cultural changes described in Europe were the result of spontaneous development in Europe or of "influence" from outside Europe. The absence of this clear statement is in its way characteristic, because in the late nineteenth century many prehistorians were content to describe the archaeological record in their own area without following out the implications of their interpretations. This is not to say that prehistory was not already being interpreted in terms either of independent invention or diffusion; it was, and indeed had been since the days of Worsaae and Nilsson. But the disputes in prehistory were not yet consciously in terms of independent invention or diffusion. It would take the development of ethnological theory, and particularly the hyperdiffusionist excesses of Elliot Smith and his followers, to do this. Meanwhile, the issues were disputed on specific grounds, and often enough, as in the typical passage quoted from Evans's inaugural lecture at the Ashmolean, were not regarded as of vital importance. The late nineteenth-century archaeologists were so excited by the discoveries they were making about man's early past that they spent little time in explaining their interrelations.

[1] Quoted in Joan Evans, *Time and Chance*, 270–271.

The discoveries in the Aegean brought into being a local controversy regarding the origin of the prehistoric cultures in terms of independent invention and discovery. To some the Mycenaean civilisation was the work of Aryan invaders from the north: Schuchhardt, Furtwängler and Leaf identified these with the Achaeans and thought they developed their splendid civilisation on the Greek mainland. Leaf's *Companion to the Iliad* (1892) is typical of this viewpoint. To others the Mycenaean civilisation was the work of invaders from outside Greece—the Phoenicians according to Meyer and Busolt, the Carians according to Köhler.

Reinach, Sergi, Evans and Montelius saw the disputes about the origin of the Mycenaeans as part of a larger dispute about the origin of European prehistoric culture in general. Salomon Reinach attacked the theory of *ex oriente lux* in his *Le Mirage Oriental* (1893) and his paper on "Les Déesses nues" published in the *Revue Archéologique* for 1895, declaring that European prehistorians had for long overrated the "eastern" elements, whether they were labelled Phoenician, Semitic, Aryan, or Carian, and that the Mycenaean civilisation, like other European prehistoric civilisations, was native. Montelius was a strong exponent of *ex oriente lux* and in his *Orient und Europa* (1899) argued forcibly for the derivation of all European culture from the ancient East. "At a time when the peoples of Europe were, so to speak, without any civilisation whatsoever," he wrote, "the Orient and particularly the Euphrates region and the Nile valley were already in enjoyment of a flourishing culture. The civilisation which gradually dawned on our continent was for long only a pale reflection of Oriental culture."

Arthur Evans and Myres saw that the theories of Reinach and Montelius were not mutually exclusive. In 1895 Sergi published his *La Stirpe Mediterranea*: it was translated into German two years later and published in England in 1901. Sergi argued for a Mediterranean race with its centre in North Africa, which spread all over the Mediterranean region. Arthur Evans's *Eastern Question in Anthropology* (1895) accepted this, and distinguished a great Anatolo-Danubian province within which Aegean civilisation was a local manifestation, owing something both to the ancient East and to Europe. In his *Prehistoric Man in the Eastern Mediterranean* (1895) Sir John Myres developed the same basic thesis. In his own words, written much later: "To recognise adequately the eastern background of European origins is no *Mirage Oriental.* The 'independent European element' is not extinguished by its own capacity for assimilation." [1]

In the thirty years from 1840–70 archaeologists had been naturally imbued with the prevailing doctrines of evolution and progress. They saw in the prehistoric sequence both a mirror and a proof of evolutionary progress. Some, like Pengelly, as we have noted, had doubts about the universality of progress. These doubts were shared by other archaeologists in the last quarter of the nineteenth century, themselves affected by current doubts of progress.

> "Evolution ever climbing after some ideal good
> And Reversion ever dragging Evolution in the mud,"

wrote Tennyson in *Locksley Hall Sixty Years After* (1886). The late nineteenth-century archaeologist began to wonder whether, in presenting his picture of technological progress, he was making objective observations confirming the general Victorian belief in progress or whether he was merely projecting into prehistory his own belief in evolutionary progress. The question which the late nineteenth-century prehistorian began to face was this: Did archaeology really prove the cultural progress of man, or was it merely being used to demonstrate that cultural progress?

The archaeological reason which impelled prehistorians and others to reconsider their views of history as a single progressive development was the discovery of civilisations which had perished. Work in Egypt and Mesopotamia was revealing the extent of the ancient civilisations there and giving suggestions of a civilisation —that of the Sumerians—even earlier than the Babylonians of history; Schliemann had revealed behind classical Greece the barbaric splendours of Mycenaean civilisation and of Troy II. Petrie had revealed the predynastic civilisation behind dynastic Egypt. Perhaps the most startling archaeological discoveries were those of Upper Palaeolithic Cave Art. At first this art was disregarded, but as soon as its authenticity and age were accepted

[1] *The Cretan Labyrinth*, 284. "Ex Oriente Lux" became the motto of a group of German archaeologists at the end of the nineteenth century. It was the title of a series edited by Hugo Winckler, published at Leipzig, and is the text of Fick's *Vorgriechische Ortsnamen* (1905).

it raised a great problem with regard to human history. Here was a remarkably naturalistic and competent art which flourished in south France and north Spain at least ten and probably twenty thousand years ago—and which came to an end. The Upper Palaeolithic artists had no successors and their artistic impetus died out. This was surely a tremendous example of retrogression or degeneration even more dramatic than the decay of the Egyptian, Mesopotamian and Aegean civilisations, or the decay of British civilisation in post-Roman times which Pengelly had noted. Even Pitt Rivers, for so long a staunch supporter of evolutionary progress, began to have doubts whether progressive evolution was the fact that emerged out of the archaeologists' study of man's earliest past. We have already quoted him as saying "that the fundamental rule of the game is sequence". Sequence was very different from evolution. Evolution meant progress—gradual but persistent improvement, a change always in the complexity of technical equipment and the mastery of man over the environment. Sequence meant developments that might retrogress as well as progress. This was the essential difference between late and early Victorian thought in so far as it related to early man. We see the same change in Victorian anthropologists. At first they were dominated by evolution, but later they began to admit doubts as to its universality as an explanation of culture. In his *Primitive Culture* (1871) Sir E. B. Tylor described his aim as "to sketch a theoretical course of civilisation among mankind" which he calls "a progression-theory of civilisation", but he also admitted that "culture gained by progression may be lost by degradation".

The last quarter of the nineteenth century saw the prehistoric archaeologists entertaining not only doubts as to the story told by prehistory, but also as to whether archaeology was the only source for information of man's earliest past. The claims of the physical anthropologist, the philologist and linguistic palaeontologist, and the student of survivals had been made earlier in the century, but were being given a most serious hearing in the last few decades. Classifications of races had been formulated since the pioneer work of Linnaeus and Blumenbach. The second half of the nineteenth century saw new classifications by de Quatrefages, Broca, Virchow, Sergi, Ripley and Deniker. Ripley's *The Races of Europe: A Sociological Study*, and Deniker's *The Races of Man: an Outline of Anthropology and Ethnography* were both published in 1900, and are good examples of the way in which classifications and deductions valid in physical anthropology were being used as sources in prehistoric archaeology. We have already mentioned how Evans and Myres used Sergi's Mediterranean race in formulating their theories of prehistoric origins in the Mediterranean. Dr John Beddoe's pioneer studies in British anthropology had involved equations between prehistory and physical anthropology. In his excavations in Wiltshire Dr John Thurnam had been impressed by the seeming co-ordination between long barrows and long skulls, and round barrows with round skulls. He published these conclusions in papers in *Archaeologia* and the *Memoirs of the Anthropological Society* between 1860 and 1870, concerning what he termed "the two principal forms of ancient British and Gaulish skulls". His ideas were set out more fully in the great work *Crania Britannica* produced jointly by Davis and Thurnam in 1865.

The comparative study of languages as a key to the early human past goes back to the now famous Presidential Address delivered by Sir William Jones to the Asiatic Society of Bengal in 1788, in which he pointed out similarities between Sanskrit, Greek, Latin, Celtic and German languages and suggested they all were to be derived from a common mother tongue. Bopp confirmed this suggestion in his *Vergleichende Grammatik* (1833–35) using the term Indo-Germanic for the whole group of languages, a term first suggested by Klaproth in 1823. Max Müller suggested the term Aryan as an alternative and this superseded Indo-Germanic as the label for this group of languages. In 1847 Baron Bunsen read a paper to the British Association in which he attempted a classification of mankind as a whole on the basis of language. "At that date", writes Haddon, "it was taken for granted that the study of comparative philology would be in future the only safe foundation for the study of anthropology."[1] It was also put forward as a safe foundation for the study of prehistory, and a whole edifice of supposed fact about prehistoric man was created on linguistic deduction. The prehistory of Europe was seen in terms of the movements of Finno-Ugrians and Aryans. A typical summary of this linguistic prehistory is to be found in Isaac Taylor's *The Origin of the Aryans: An Account*

[1] *History of Anthropology*, 96.

of the Prehistoric Ethnology and Civilisation of Europe (1890) and Huxley's essay on *The Aryan Question and Prehistoric Man*, first published in the same year.

Equations were made not only between race and prehistory, and between language and prehistory, but also between race and language. The Aryans became Nordics not only in the minds of "blond-beast" theorists like Boulainvilliers and Gobineau but to serious scholars. Many deplored this confusion. Max Müller wrote: "To me an ethnologist who speaks of Aryan race, Aryan blood, Aryan eyes and hair is as great a sinner as a linguist who speaks of a dolichocephalic dictionary or a brachycephalic grammar." [1] There were plenty of sinners among anthropologists and archaeologists at the end of the nineteenth century. Max Müller might write firmly that "there ought to be no compromise between ethnological and phonological science" [2]; but it was very characteristic of the writings of the turn of the century to attempt a compromise between the data derived from language, physical anthropology and archaeology, and to deny the primacy of archaeology as a source for prehistory.

In the works of the great Welsh scholar, Sir John Rhŷs, we have an excellent example of the attempt to unravel the early history and prehistory of a country by means other than archaeological ones. Rhŷs's *Celtic Britain* was first published in 1882; *The Welsh People*, which he wrote with D. Brynmor Jones, in 1900. Both works had a most considerable influence in and outside Wales; they entirely neglected archaeological sources, and set out an interpretation of the prehistory of Wales entirely in terms of three "peoples" distinguished on linguistic and literary grounds, the Iberians, the Goidels and the Brythons.[3]

The idea of studying survivals in modern culture from ancient civilisations and from man's barbaric prehistoric past was first put forward by Tylor in his *Primitive Culture* in 1871. In studying survivals we must distinguish two kinds—the fossils and the functioning survivals. The study of "folklore" as the study of survivals was initiated by W. J. Thoms, who invented the

[1] *Biographies of Words and the Homes of the Aryans* (1888), 120.
[2] *Report of the British Association* (1891), 787.
[3] In Sir John Edward Lloyd's *History of Wales* (1910) we see the first recognition of archaeological sources. Lloyd tries to marry the archaeological and non-archaeological sources, and equate the three ages of the archaeologists with the peoples of Rhŷs and Brynmor Jones.

word in 1846, and whose articles in the *Athenaeum* and *Notes and Queries* have already been referred to. The great exponent of survivals in folklore as a source of information about the past was Sir G. Laurence Gomme, whose *Folklore as an Historical Science* was published in 1908. Otis T. Mason in his *The Origins of Invention* (1895) and *Woman's Share in Primitive Culture* (1895) studied survivals in material culture. Field systems, villages, tribal organisations and primitive law as they exist at present, or existed in the historic past, were also studied as survivals from prehistoric times and as sources of light on man's prehistoric past. Sir Henry Maine's *Ancient Law* (1861) and his *Village Communities in the East and West* (1872), Fustel de Coulanges's *La Cité antique* (1872) and *The Origin of Property in Land* (1891), de Laveleye's *Primitive Property* (1874), Gomme's *The Village Community* (1890), Seebohm's *The English Village Community* (1883), *Tribal Custom in Anglo-Saxon Law* (1902) and *The Tribal System in Wales* (1904) are good examples of this approach, also evident in the writings of Maitland, Vinogradoff and Arbois de Jubainville.[1] The subtitle of Maine's *Ancient Law* is significant: it is "its connection with the early history of society and its relation to modern ideas".

This is what so many were hoping to get at the end of the nineteenth century—the early history of society. Archaeology provided the technological development of man, but historians of man as a whole wanted more than this; they wanted the story of the development of man's society, and his mental and moral ideas, as well as the tale of the development of his tools. This is why they turned so avidly to the conclusions of physical anthropology, linguistics and survivals, and why they sought an answer in the study of modern primitive peoples. The early Danish archaeologists, such as Worsaae and Nilsson, had stressed the value of comparative ethnography to the archaeologists, and this cannot be disputed—the archaeologist cannot understand the uses of artefacts except by reference to modern primitive usages. It is of course possible to point to similarities in form and function between prehistoric and modern artifacts. Intoxicated by these appropriate material parallels, and thwarted by their inability to speak of prehistoric man's social and spiritual culture from the

[1] For an admirable critique of these studies see Peake, *The Study of Prehistoric Times*, 10–11.

archaeological record, some archaeologists and anthropologists fell into what may be termed the comparative ethnographic fallacy, namely the belief that identity between the material culture of prehistoric people and that of modern primitives implies an identity of social and spiritual culture. The acceptance of this fallacious equation is implicit in the writings of Lubbock. Some went even further, and accepted as facts the evolutionary sequences of social and spiritual culture which ethnologists had produced, and treated them as objective facts with which the facts of archaeology must be equated.

The nineteenth century was full of classifications of man's past based on the supposed sequence of economies. Coleridge had declared that "the progress from savagery to civilisation is evidently first from the hunting to the pastoral stage",[1] and, as we have seen, Sven Nilsson distinguished four stages in the human past, the savage state, when man was a hunter, fisher and collector, secondly the herdsman or nomad stage, thirdly the agricultural stage, and fourthly civilisation, which he defined in terms of coined money, writing and a well-organised state of society, with labour divided among different professions. These four stages of the evolution of society were first published in Sweden in 1838, and became widely known in England after 1867, when Lubbock translated them and edited them in *The Primitive Inhabitants of Scandinavia*.

Sir Edward Tylor recognised the Danish system of the three ages, and agreed that the Stone Age was the beginning of man's prehistoric development, but proposed to distinguish in the human past three different stages of Savagery, Barbarism and Civilisation. In his *Anthropology: An Introduction to the Study of Man and Civilisation*, first published in 1881, Tylor defines barbarism as beginning with agriculture, and civilisation with writing. These terms were more exactly defined by Lewis H. Morgan, the American anthropologist, in his *Ancient Society: or, Researches in the Lines of Human Progress from Savagery through Barbarism to Civilisation* (1877). Morgan thought the system of the three ages "extremely useful for certain purposes, and will remain so for the classification of objects of ancient art", but he thought that methods of subsistence provided better lines of division: "the great epochs of human progress have been identified more or less directly", he

[1] *Lit. Rem.*, ii, 327 (1836).

wrote, "with the enlargement of the sources of subsistence". He proposed to distinguish seven ethnic periods, as he called them, as follows:

1. Lower Savagery, from the emergence of man to the discovery of fire.
2. Middle Savagery, from the discovery of fire to the discovery of the bow and arrow.
3. Upper Savagery, from the discovery of the bow and arrow to the discovery of pottery.
4. Lower Barbarism. This stage began with the discovery of pottery which, to Morgan, was the line between Savagery and Barbarism, and ended with the domestication of animals.[1]
5. Middle Barbarism, from the domestication of animals to the smelting of iron ore.[1]
6. Upper Barbarism, from the discovery of iron to the invention of a phonetic alphabet.
7. Civilisation, from writing and the alphabet onwards. Morgan distinguished the Ancient Civilisations of Egypt, south-west Asia, and classical lands, and the Modern Civilisation of which he himself was a product.

Morgan envisaged these seven ethnic periods as providing a progressive sequence of man's cultural evolution, and he thought that this sequence developed naturally in different regions. All showed, he believed, "the unity of the origin of mankind, the similarity of human wants in the same stage of advancement, and the uniformity of the operations of the human mind in similar conditions of society". "Mankind", he declared, "commenced their career at the bottom of the scale and worked their way up from savagery to civilisation through the slow accumulations of experimental knowledge." While Morgan believed in the natural nature of progress, he realised the seven ethnic periods were homotaxial and not contemporary all over the world. "The *condition*", he wrote, "is the material fact, the *time* being immaterial."

We are not concerned here with a critique of Morgan but with

[1] These distinctions relate to the Old World. Morgan had slightly different criteria for his periods in the Americas.

realising the nature of his classification. It was based primarily not on archaeological evidence but on the comparative study of modern primitive peoples, the arrangement of these existing economies and societies into an evolutionary sequence, and the projection of this hypothetical sequence into the prehistoric past. Morgan's scheme was not securely anchored to the analysis of artifacts and ancient remains. Nevertheless it fitted in tolerably well with the archaeological record, and achieved popularity because it was used by Engels in his *Origin of the Family* (1884), where he declared: "Morgan is the first man who with expert knowledge has attempted to introduce a definite order into human prehistory." This claim of Engels cannot for a moment be sustained, but it is interesting because Morgan's method had, by the use of his projection of hypothetical periods, appeared to surmount the apparent limitations of archaeology—that it could speak only of man's material culture in the early human past.

This seems one of the main reasons why in the latter part of the nineteenth century scholars were turning to sources like physical anthropology, linguistic palaeontology, the study of survivals and comparative ethnology as prime sources for the early human past. They were disappointed that archaeology did not provide them at once with the early history of all aspects of society. A second reason was that prehistoric archaeology was still young and had not yet established its paramountcy among other sources for information about the prehistoric past.

But if they were sensing its limitations, and searching the possibilities of other sources, the late Victorians had few doubts as to the nature of archaeology. It was science, one of the newest of the new sciences which were, they thought, the peculiar triumph of Victorian knowledge. Boyd Dawkins declared triumphantly in 1874 that "Archaeology, by the use of strictly inductive methods, has grown from a mere antiquarian speculation into a science",[1] and Joseph Anderson defined archaeology at the turn of the century as "the science which deduces a knowledge of past times from the study of existing remains".[2] Charles Boutell in his *Manual of British Archaeology* had declared

[1] *Cave Hunting*, viii.

[2] The first words of Petrie's *Methods and Aims* were: "Archaeology is the latest born of the sciences."

archaeology to be history, and Tylor spoke of prehistory and history taking their proper place in the general scheme of knowledge. But to Joseph Anderson the story that the archaeological record revealed "is not history. History deals with events and incidents as manifestations of human motive and action; archaeology deals with types and systems as expressions of human culture and civilisation",[1] and the views of Anderson and Boyd Dawkins were most representative of late Victorian thought.

The late nineteenth century did not effect a synthesis of the facts of prehistoric archaeology with history itself. The late Victorians still talked of archaeology *and* history. They had created archaeology—out of history, out of antiquarian studies, and out of geology, but it was this last element that remained the strongest. The historical component was largely forgotten, and we should remember that in any case these were the days when history itself was being claimed as a science. There yawned at the end of the nineteenth century a gulf between the archaeologists who looked to geology and natural science, and thought themselves scientists, and those who looked to history and art, and thought themselves students of the humanities. It is this gulf which, as Taylor has recently insisted,[2] caused prehistoric archaeology, and the archaeology of the "classical" and other protohistoric civilisations, to develop separately.[3]

There was much excuse for this state of affairs. The methods of archaeology—excavation, museum analysis, field work—seemed to take it away from the humanities. Then so many of the great nineteenth-century archaeologists were in the first instance geologists and natural scientists. It is, then, quite understandable that, although in its origins archaeology had owed most to historians and antiquarians, throughout the nineteenth century it became more and more allied with science. It was left to the early twentieth century to right this balance, to effect a synthesis of prehistory and written history, to create what Elliot Smith called "human history"—the full story of man, the cultured animal.

[1] *Chambers's Encyclopædia* (1922), *s.v.* Archaeology.
[2] W. W. Taylor, *A Study of Archaeology*.
[3] It is the gulf which still yawns in the prehistoric scholarship of many countries—France, for example.

CHAPTER SIX

THE DISCOVERY OF THE NEAR-EASTERN CIVILISATIONS: 1900–50

1. *Crete and the Aegean*

THE great discoveries of Schliemann and his successors in the last thirty years of the nineteenth century had brought to light a great civilisation, the Mycenaean, but had also posed a great problem: what was the origin of the Mycenaean civilisation? Was it indigenous to Greece, or was it brought into Greece from outside, and if so, from where? Was it Asia Minor?—or was it Crete? Schliemann, pursuing the study of legends which led him to Troy, noted that Knossos in Crete was the home of the Minotaur, of King Minos and the Labyrinth. In 1878 a Greek of Candia called Minos Kalokairinos had found at Kephala, the site of Knossos, pottery comparable with some of the best wares from Mycenae. In 1880 an American journalist, Stillman, excited and inspired by the discoveries of Schliemann, got a permit to dig in Crete. In 1883 the German scholar Milchhöfer noted that there were to be found in Crete peculiar types of carved seal-stones bearing symbols resembling a kind of primitive writing. Milchhöfer affirmed, as had his countryman Hoeck many years before, that Crete would prove to be one of the oldest homes of Greek civilisation and art. Milchhöfer's views, set out in his *Anfänge der Kunst in Griechenland* (1883), seem to have inspired both Arthur Evans and Halbherr.

The same year in which Milchhöfer wrote his book Schliemann applied for and obtained permission from the Governor of Crete to dig at Kephala. At first he could not find time to take up his permit, but later he was unprepared to pay the large sums demanded by the owner of the site for permission to excavate, and was still negotiating with him at the time of his death in 1890. For a while excavation in Crete was out of the question because of the disturbed political condition of the country, but in 1891 Orsi dug a cupola-tomb on the Mesara plain. Meanwhile Sir Arthur

Evans was elaborating Milchhöfer's ideas and in 1894 published his *Cretan Pictographs*. In 1896, in the Presidential Address to the Anthropological Section of the British Association at Liverpool, he referred to his ideas of the Cretan origin of Mycenaean civilisation, and his hopes of Cretan independence, in these words: "To Crete the earliest Greek tradition looks back as the home of divinely inspired legislation and the first centre of maritime dominion. Inhabited since the days of the first Greek settlement by the same race, speaking the same language, and moved by the same independent impulses, Crete stands forth again to-day as the champion of the European spirit against the yoke of Asia." In 1898 Crete declared herself independent of Turkey, and the following year Sir Arthur Evans began excavations at Kephala.

The excavations were immediately successful; in nine weeks of digging more than two acres of a vast prehistoric building had been uncovered, which Evans identified as the palace of Minos. Evans continued these excavations year after year for over a quarter of a century, but the pattern of the story he had found was established early in his work. His work revealed a completely new civilisation hitherto entirely unknown. It was moreover a civilisation which lay behind the Mycenaean, and which came to an end as the Mycenaean civilisation was beginning. It was unquestionably not only earlier than the Mycenaean civilisation but the parent of that civilisation. Evans discovered not only the palace of Minos but a smaller palace before that, and earlier pre-palatial phases of culture. Behind the Bronze Age civilisation of Crete he found an earlier Neolithic civilisation, which at Knossos itself formed a tell six and a half metres thick beneath the oldest levels of the Bronze Age civilisation. Evans's discoveries not only revealed, as Hall has said, "a new Mycenae, and far more than a new Mycenae"[1]; they put the Mycenaean discoveries into an historical perspective which led back to the Neolithic levels of absolute prehistory. They constitute, as Casson has claimed, one of archaeology's greatest achievements.[2]

The great discoveries at Knossos were published first by Evans in an article in 1901 in the *Monthly Review*. They created an immediate sensation, but this time, unlike the discoveries of Schliemann, there were few doubters. Evans came to his discoveries after a lifetime of scholarship and archaeology. As

[1] *Aegean Archaeology*, 30.

[2] *The Discovery of Man.*

fresh discoveries appeared—the "Cup-bearer" fresco, the bull-leaping frescoes of boys and girls, the long lines of magazines with their *pithoi*, the walls covered with the double-axe emblem, the faience snake-goddesses—the public imagination was captured as it had not been since Schliemann sent his famous telegram to the King of the Hellenes telling him he had discovered the tomb of Agamemnon. But here in Crete it appeared that Evans had discovered King Minos, the Labyrinth and the Minotaur. An authoritative but popular account of the discoveries was provided in 1907 by R. M. Burrows's *The Discoveries in Crete and their bearing on the history of Ancient Civilisation*, and in 1908 by Père M. J. Lagrange's *La Crète ancienne* (1908), while Duncan Mackenzie, Sir Arthur Evans's second in command at Knossos, produced *Cretan Vase Painting* in 1906 and *Cretan Palaces* in 1904; and Angelo Mosso's *Dawn of Mediterranean Civilisation* was published in 1910 and Dussaud's *Les Civilizations Préhelleniques dans le bassin de la mer Égée* in 1910–14. Sir Arthur Evans's own definitive publication of his work, *The Palace of Minos at Knossos*, was published in four volumes between 1921 and 1935.

To the great Bronze Age civilisation which he discovered in Crete, Sir Arthur Evans gave the name Minoan, after the great traditional Cretan lawgiver and thalassocrat. He suggested this name in his address to the British Association at Cambridge in 1904. In the following year he developed these ideas at the Prehellenic Section of the Archaeological Congress at Athens, dividing the Minoan civilisation into three main sections—Early, Middle and Late, each with three sub-periods. As Sir Arthur Evans pointed out himself, with justifiable warmth, the *Comptes rendus* of the Athens Congress published his scheme mutilated and with the order of the periods inverted; he therefore published in 1906 a corrected version of his scheme in *Essai de Classification des Époques de la Civilisation Minoenne*. Sir William Ridgeway protested against the use of the name Minoan, arguing that Minos was the destroyer rather than the creator of the Cretan Bronze Age; while Professor Reisch and Dr Dörpfeld argued that it was absurd to describe periods stretching over two and a half thousand years by the name of one historical or legendary character. Other names were suggested, such as Knossian, Cretan, or Aegean, but Evans's system was adopted by other excavators in other sites in Crete and gradually won acceptance generally.

For the spectacular discoveries at Knossos soon gave rise to other excavations in Crete. An Italian mission under Halbherr excavated the palace at Phaestos and the great chamber-tomb of Hagia Triada, which contained over 250 bodies; the Phaestos excavations have now been published in full by Pernier and others in *Il Palazzo Minoico di Festos* (1935). The Germans did not follow up their successes in Greece by turning their attention to Crete. French archaeologists worked at Goulas, but with little success. The British School at Athens excavated, under Professor R. C. Bosanquet and R. M. Dawkins, Praisos and Palaikastro. Americans under Miss Harriet Boyd (later Mrs Boyd-Hawes) and R. B. Seager excavated completely, in 1903, the little Bronze Age town of Gournia, and smaller settlements on the islands of Pseria and Mochlos, formerly part of the isthmus of Hierapetra.[1] Cretans themselves took a part in this great archaeological activity; Joseph Hatzidakis dug a Minoan palace at Tylissos, and Stephanos Xanthoudides dug chamber-tombs at Koumasa in the Mesara. Xanthoudides's results were made available to English readers in Droop's translation, *The Vaulted Tombs of the Mesara.* All these developments of Cretan archaeology have been summarised by Finmen in his *Die Kretisch-Mykenische Kultur* (1921) and by J. D. S. Pendlebury in his *Archaeology of Crete* (1939)—and in Glotz's *Aegean Civilisation.* Later, French archaeologists successfully excavated the palace at Mallia, published by Chapouthier in his *Fouilles exécutées à Mallia* (1928) and by Chapouthier, Charbonneaux and others in *Études Crétoises* (*Mallia*).

From objects found at Knossos that were evidently imported from Egypt, checked by a few Minoan vases in Egyptian tombs and depicted on their walls, Sir Arthur Evans was able to synchronise most of his nine periods with corresponding Egyptian dynasties. At first Evans put forward a scheme of dates based on Brugsch's Egyptian chronology, but later adopted Meyer's scheme as modified by Breasted, and suggested 3400 to 2100 for the Early Minoan period, 2100 to 1550 for the Middle Minoan period and 1550 to 1100 for the Late Minoan period. Allowing three feet for every millennium before the beginning of the Early Minoan civilisation, Evans first thought that the Neolithic of Crete began

[1] Hawes, Williams, Seager and Hall, *Gournia, Vasiliki, and other particular sites on the Isthmus of Hierapetra (Crete).* Philadelphia: American Exploration Society, 1908.

between 12,000 and 10,000 B.C. In the light of modern research on the Neolithic these dates seem very highly inflated, and indeed the date of the beginning of the Minoan civilisation itself should probably now be scaled down. The Minoan synchronisms before 1700 are very incomplete, and the revision of Egyptian and Mesopotamian chronologies, in any case, requires a shortening of the Minoan dates. After an examination of the Early Minoan material Reisner would date the Early Minoan period from 2700 to 2100, Pendlebury would scale the beginning of E.M.I down no further than 3100, while Hutchinson, in his *Notes on Minoan Chronology*,[1] argues for a date between Reisner and Pendlebury, *i.e.* between 3100 and 2700. There is general agreement that the Middle Minoan period commenced round about 2000 B.C., and the Cretan Neolithic not much before 4000 B.C.

Two attempts have been made to upset the ninefold division into periods set out by Evans. Franchet, in his introduction to Hazzidakis's *Tylissos, Villas Minoennes*, proposes a new system of Cretan chronology based on that of prehistoric provincial France. Åberg in his *Bronzezeitliche und Früheisenzeitliche Chronologie* (1930–35) argues that there is little true stratification at Knossos and that the nine periods are based on a fallacious analysis of pottery types. He proposes a fresh analysis and divides Knossos into three periods only: pre-Palatial (E.M.I to M.M.I*a*), Kamarais (M.M.I*b* to M.M.III*b* pre-earthquake) and Late Minoan. Åberg's criticisms are analysed carefully by Pendlebury, in *The Archaeology of Crete*, who insists on the validity of Evans's nine periods and reaffirms the stratigraphy of Knossos, while accepting the fact that the periods are not absolute divisions of time applicable for the whole island. "Because L.M.I*a* begins at Knossos at a particular date, that is not to say that provincial towns, such as those of Kastellos above Tzermiadha in Lasithi, discarded all their M.M.III*b* vessels on the same day," writes Pendlebury.[2] In the archaeology of Crete, as elsewhere, we must remember that "periods," based on stratigraphy or typology are only homotaxial stages, not absolutes in time.

One of the main attractions of Cretan archaeology for Arthur Evans had been the writing. In 1909 he produced volume one of his *Scripta Minoa*, containing the hieroglyphics and the two

[1] *Antiquity*, 1948, 61 ff.
[2] *The Archaeology of Crete*, xxiv.

linear scripts resulting from a simplification of the Cretan pictorial writing. Evans, of course, hoped to produce another volume in which these scripts were deciphered, but neither he nor anyone else has yet succeeded in deciphering either the Minoan script or the Cretan syllabary. We can only continue to hope for a bilingual inscription—perhaps a bill of lading in Egyptian and Minoan, as Pendlebury has suggested. While a strong case has been made out for the post-Minoan Eteo-cretan language being Indo-European, it seems likely that the language of the Minoans was Anatolian, perhaps allied to Cilician or Carian or Lykian. The origin of the Minoan civilisation, while disputed, is perhaps more easily susceptible of archaeological solution. Evans stressed the Egyptian and Libyan affinities of the early Minoans, but it now seems more likely that the closest contacts of early Minoan culture were with Anatolia and north Syria.

The excavations at Phylakopi on Melos (centre of the Stone Age obsidian trade) had taken place before Knossos, but were not published until 1904.[1] In 1907 Sir Arthur Evans analysed the Phylakopi material, as well as material found from tombs and settlements in the other Cycladic islands of Antiparos and Amorgos, Siphnos and Syros, and divided it into three periods, which he termed Early, Middle and Late Cycladic, and equated with his three main Minoan periods.

2. *Egypt*

Up to 1900 the British, at first through the Egypt Exploration Fund, and later through Petrie's Egyptian Research Account, and the French, through their Institut and as members of the Egyptian Antiquities Service, had a monopoly of archaeological work in Egypt. From 1900 onwards the work of the British and French continued, but in addition there have been expeditions from America, Germany, Italy, Belgium and Poland, while the Department of Antiquities and the Cairo University have carried out on behalf of the Egyptian Government excavations financed and manned by Egyptians. Sir Flinders Petrie, the doyen of modern Egyptian archaeology, who had already by 1900 done more than an average man in a lifetime of Egyptian excavation—his *Ten Years' Digging* had been published in 1892—continued his work

[1] *Excavations at Phylakopi in Melos*, Society for Promotion of Hellenic Studies, Supplementary Volume IV, 1904.

in Egypt for the first quarter of the twentieth century, until in 1926, after forty years' excavation in Egypt, he transferred his attentions to Palestine. Among his historic discoveries in the twentieth century was the treasury of Lahun (1914). The cessation of excavation due to the 1914–18 War enabled Petrie to publish general works of synthesis which he had wanted to do for some while. His *Arts and Crafts of Ancient Egypt* (1909) had been published before the war; during the war years he produced his *Scarabs and Cylinders* (1915), *Tools and Weapons* (1916), the *Corpus of Prehistoric Pottery* (1918), and his *Prehistoric Egypt illustrated by over 1000 Objects in University College, London* (1920).

But the great discoveries of the twentieth century in Egyptian archaeology—Tell el-Amarna, the tombs of Yuaa and Tuiu, the tomb of Tutankhamen, the Badarian and Tasian civilisations—fell to hands other than Petrie's. Tell el-Amarna had been visited by Wilkinson, and engravings of scenes from some of the tombs were made for the Denkmäler of Lepsius. Between 1883 and 1893 Maspero and the French mission cleared the tombs of debris. It was in 1887 that a peasant woman digging for brick-dust manure found, in what is now known as the "Place of the Correspondence of Pharaoh", the famous Amarna letters, tablets of baked clay written in cuneiform in the diplomatic Babylonian of the period. These tablets, at first neglected and then proclaimed as forgeries, were eventually recognised as important, although by then half of them were lost. The tablets were fully published by Winckler and Knudtzon, and the site excavated, first by Bouriant, Barsanti and Grebaut, then by Petrie in 1891–92, and then from 1907 onwards by the Deutsche Orient-Gesellschaft. During the war the German concession lapsed and in 1921 the Egypt Exploration Society took over the work, which continued for many years, being directed successively by T. E. Peet, C. L. Woolley, F. G. Newton, Llewelyn Griffith, Frankfort and Pendlebury. These latest excavations, summarised briefly in Pendlebury's *Tell el-Amarna*, have produced a most detailed picture of life in the fourteenth century B.C. in this remarkable and short-lived city under Akhenaten, in the years following the destruction of Knossos and the Minoan Empire.

The work at Tell el-Amarna, and the excavation of Tutankhamen's tomb in 1923 by Howard Carter, Mace and Lord

Carnarvon [1] belong properly to the story of protohistoric Egyptian archaeology, but they must be mentioned here because of the very great effect they had on the maintenance and stimulation of popular interest in archaeology.

Meanwhile discoveries of far-reaching importance were being made regarding the beginnings of Egyptian civilisation. In Lower Egypt the settlement of Merimde-Beni-Salame was excavated by Junker, Menghin and Scharff and claimed by them as Neolithic, and the prehistoric cultures of the Fayum depression were studied by Miss Caton-Thompson and Miss E. W. Gardner during the years 1924–28. On physiographical and typological grounds two cultures were distinguished in the Fayum: Fayum A, associated with the 10 metre lake of the Fayum and characterised by flaked and polished axes and adzes, sickles and crude pottery, and Fayum B, associated with the 4–2 metre lake, a much poorer industry and containing no pottery. Miss Caton-Thompson dated Fayum A to about 5000 B.C. and Fayum B to 4500 B.C., with a span of 800 years for the duration of both groups.[2] At Ma'adi, just south of Cairo, a site was excavated in 1930–31 by the Egyptian University under Menghin and Amer, which, at first classified as Neolithic, was later dated to Middle and Late predynastic times and equated with the Gerzean-Semainian horizon.[3]

In Upper and Middle Egypt the British School of Archaeology in Egypt excavated at and near Badari between 1922–25; Guy Brunton excavated cemeteries at Badari and Miss Caton-Thompson dug a settlement at Hemamieh, between Qau and Badari. Their results, published in 1928 in their joint work, *The Badarian Civilisation and Predynastic Remains near Badari*, established the Badarian as the immediate predecessor of the predynastic period in Upper Egypt. Later, in 1928 and 1929, Brunton, working on behalf of the British Museum Expedition to Middle Egypt, excavated at Deir Tasa, near Mostagedda, a cemetery and village, which he published in his *Mostagedda and the Tasian Culture* (1937), and which he claimed as the ancestor of the Badarian. Other excavations included those of Vignard at Naq' Hammadi and those

[1] Carter and Mace, *The Tomb of Tut-ankh-Amen*, vol. i (1923), vol. ii (1927), vol. iii (1933).

[2] Caton-Thompson and Gardner, *The Desert Fayum*, 1934 (London, Royal Anthropological Institute).

[3] Meghin and Amer, *The Excavations of the Egyptian University at Maadi* (Cairo, 1932, Publication 19 of Egyptian University; Faculty of Arts).

at Armant, published by Mond and Myres in their *Cemeteries of Armant I* (1937).

As this prehistoric material accumulated from Lower and Upper Egypt it became possible to arrange it in some kind of sequence and to hazard views on the origins of the prehistoric civilisation of Egypt. The predynastic cultures of Middle and Upper Egypt had been divided by Petrie into the three classic stages of Amratian, after al'Amrah, and occupying Sequence Dates 30 to 38; the Gerzean, after the Girzah cemeteries, and occupying S.D. 39 to 63; and the Semainian, after al-Semaynah, occupying S.D. 64 to 78.[1] These terms were used interchangeably with the terms Early, Middle and Late Predynastic. Petrie had very wisely begun his sequence at S.D. 30, and the Badarian and Tasian cultures were now fitted in before this, and a sequence described leading from Tasian to dynastic times, with Badarian, Amratian, Gerzean and Semainian as intermediate stages. Frankfort, Scharff and others emphasised the new cultural elements that appeared in the Gerzean which seemed to indicate influences from the East. Attempts were made to fit the early cultures of Lower Egypt into this sequence; such sequences can be seen in the recent summaries such as Childe's *New Light on the Most Ancient East* (1935) and Huzzayin's *The Place of Egypt in Prehistory* (1941).[2] Huzzayin sees the Fayum A and Merimde industries as comparable with the Tasian, and Fayum B with the Badarian/Amratian, while Miss Caton-Thompson at one time was disposed to regard the Neolithic cultures of Lower and Upper Egypt as both derived from the Kharga Oasis until her excavations there showed the Kharga Neolithic to be more allied to Fayum B.

In her *The Cultures of Prehistoric Egypt* (1947), a work of extraordinary importance, Elise J. Baumgärtel publishes the first results of her researches in the prehistoric material from Egypt. Her work is important for many reasons—her sharp dismissal of the term Neolithic in connection with any early cultures of hither Asia and Egypt, her insistence on studying the Egyptian cultures in close relation to those of south-west Asia, for example—but most of all for her cogent analysis of Petrie's material in relation to later work on predynastic and prehistoric Egypt. She considers that Petrie's own uncertainty over Naqada has made English

[1] Petrie, *Diospolis Parva* (1901) and *Prehistoric Egypt* (1920).
[2] *Mémoires présentées à l'Institut d'Egypte*, vol. 43.

writers obscure the importance of this site. Not so the French, who, following de Morgan's suggestions, called the whole predynastic period the Naqada period. Baumgärtel follows Scharff in dividing Naqada into two periods: Naqada I, which coincides with Amratian, and Naqada II, which coincides with the rest of the predynastic period. Naqada I she considers as the last stage in a development from the Tasian through the Badarian, but a development affected by external contacts, such as the arrival of people responsible for the white cross-lined painted pottery which she derives from Iran via Hormuz, the Straits of Aden and the Upper Course of the Nile. Naqada II, Baumgärtel considers as a new culture derived from a home not far from that of the Sumerians, and which came into Egypt, as Petrie first suggested, via the Wadi Hammamat. Most revolutionary are Baumgärtel's ideas regarding the dating of Fayum A and Merimde, hitherto regarded as the Neolithic beginnings of Egypt, but which she dates to Naqada II. The wider implications of Baumgärtel's views cannot be discussed here, but they form a fresh starting-point for a study of Egyptian prehistory.

3. *Mesopotamia*

The first few years of the twentieth century saw the beginnings of serious German excavations in Mesopotamia under the auspices of the Deutsche Orient Gesellschaft. Ten years after de Sarzec had started work at Telloh, a German expedition made a reconnaissance of several important Sumerian sites but did not excavate any of them completely. From 1899 until the war of 1914 the Germans, led by Koldewey and Andrae, excavated thoroughly two sites: Babylon and Ashur. The aim of these excavations was twofold: to excavate completely the buildings of a Babylonian town and to excavate completely through a tell to reveal the stratigraphical sequence. Neither of these things had been accomplished before the Deutsche Orient Gesellschaft began work[1]; indeed Budge complained that "no British excavator had yet laid bare the ruins of the buildings of any Assyrian or Babylonian town".[2] Koldewey's expedition worked at Babylon from 1899 to 1914, and some of the results are published in

[1] This Society was founded in Berlin in 1898 under the patronage of William II.

[2] *By Nile and Tigris*, vol. i, 126.

Koldewey's book, *The Excavations at Babylon* (1914). These excavations were dealing mainly with the neo-Babylonian period and remains of the sixth and seventh centuries B.C., but they were of great interest to the student of prehistoric archaeology because they were the first complete and scientifically conducted excavations of a large site in Mesopotamia. Ashur was excavated by Dr Walter Andrae between 1903–14. Here the Germans not only excavated with skill and care the Assyrian city, the first capital of the Assyrian nation, but also adopted for the first time in Mesopotamian excavation the sondage method. They cut through the Temple of Ishtar, and beneath it, through the remains of other temples, to an original archaic temple. This was not only an original experiment in the application of stratigraphical analysis to Mesopotamian sites, but it also provided detailed evidence of Sumerian religious ceremonies.

While these splendid German excavations were taking place some other smaller digs were made. In 1903 E. J. Banks, United States Consul at Baghdad, dug at Bismayah, the ancient Adab, near Nippur. His work, in which he adapted and copied the methods tried out by Koldewey and Andrae, was undertaken on behalf of the University of Chicago, and is summarised in his *Bismaya, or the Lost City of Adab* (1912). King was working for the British Museum at Kuyunjik at this time, and suspected a pre-Assyrian settlement; while de Genouillac was in charge of French excavations at Kish.

The 1914–18 War put an end to excavation in Mesopotamia for a while, but excavations were resumed immediately upon the cessation of hostilities. Even before the 1918 Armistice, R. Campbell Thompson began excavating, under the auspices of the British Museum, at Ur and at Eridu. On the strength of his finds the British Museum sent an expedition under H. R. Hall to dig at both these sites. Hall found Al'Ubaid, a new site four miles west of Ur, and here excavated a small temple platform, the prototype of the later Sumerian ziggurats, and contemporary with the archaic temple found by Andrae at Ashur. In 1922 a joint expedition of the British Museum and the University Museum of Pennsylvania, under the direction of Sir Leonard Woolley, carried on the work of Campbell Thompson and Hall. Woolley began work at Ur, then transferred his attentions to Al'Ubaid, returning to Ur again in 1926 and the following years. It was in

1926 that the great prehistoric cemetery at Ur, with its "Royal Tombs", was excavated. The discovery of these tombs, with their splendid treasures of gold and lapis lazuli, and their remarkable evidence of funerary ritual, caused a sensation comparable only with Schliemann's discoveries at Mycenae and those of Lord Carnarvon and Howard Carter of Tutankhamen's tomb. The joint expedition under Woolley not only inaugurated the brilliant revival of excavation in Mesopotamia that took place in the twenties and early thirties; it was also responsible for widespread popular interest in Mesopotamian origins. In 1900 few people had ever heard of the Sumerians, in 1930 the Sumerians had been added to the collection of prehistoric peoples of whom everyone knew something. This was due in part to the sensational nature of the Ur excavations, but also to the clear and helpful general accounts published by Woolley, notably his *The Sumerians* (1930), *Ur of the Chaldees* (1929) and *Abraham, Recent Discoveries and Hebrew Origins* (1936). The full account of the excavations at Al'Ubaid and Ur was published in six volumes between 1928 and 1938.[1]

At Al'Ubaid, Woolley completely excavated a Sumerian temple whose limestone foundation tablet bore the inscription: "A-anni-padda, king of Ur, son of Mes-anni-padda, has built a temple for Nin-Khursag." These kings were known from king lists and inscriptions found elsewhere; the temple was thus the first Sumerian building that could be associated with an historical figure. In another part of the mound at Al'Ubaid Woolley found remains of a settlement characterised by a fine hand-made pottery with designs painted in black on grey-green. Later, at Ur, Woolley sunk a shaft beneath the bottom of the forty-foot pit produced by excavating the great cemetery. Towards the bottom of this pit he found a layer of clean uniform clay eight foot thick, and beneath it pottery like the black on grey-green ware from the little settlement at Al'Ubaid.

The Ur excavations were only the most spectacular of several large expeditions at this time. In 1923 a second Anglo-American

[1] Preliminary reports were published in *The Antiquaries Journal* (1923–34); the full reports as follows: Vol. I, *Al-Ubaid* (Hall and Woolley), 1937; Vol. II, *The Royal Cemetery* (Woolley), 1934, 2 vols.; Vol. III, *Archaic Seal Impressions* (Legrain), 1936; Vol. IV, Texts, I, *Royal Inscriptions* (Gadd and Legrain), 1928, 2 vols.; Texts, II, *Archaic Texts* (Burrows), 1935; Vol. V, *The Ziggurat and its Surroundings* (Woolley), 1938.

expedition began work at Kish. It was directed by Professor Langdon on behalf of the University of Oxford and the Field Museum of Chicago. Kish is situated eight miles east of Babylon and consisted of two cities, Kish itself and Harsagkalamma, separated by the ancient bed of the River Euphrates. During the work of this expedition a low tell eighteen miles north-east of Kish was discovered at Jemdet Nasr. This site was excavated in 1926 and 1928, and was characterised by a new kind of polychrome pottery consisting of elaborate lattice-work or check patterns in black and yellow on red. The Kish excavations were later continued under the direction of Watelin, a Frenchman, who made a sondage right through the mound and found polychrome pottery of Jemdet Nasr type stratified below tombs of the Early Dynastic period.

In 1928 the Germans returned to field excavation in Mesopotamia under Dr Julius Norden and Dr Arnold Nöldeke on behalf of the Notgemeinschaft der Deutschen Wissenschaften, and excavated from then until 1939 at Warka, where the Germans had previously excavated in 1912–13. Here they made a sondage shaft right through the tell and found, above virgin soil, pottery of the black on grey-green Al'Ubaid ware, and above this a kind of pottery hitherto new to Mesopotamian excavations apart from a few isolated sherds at Ur. This was an unpainted burnished brick- or plum-red pottery now known as Uruk ware. Norden excavated the remains of three superimposed temples belonging to the time when this Uruk ware was used.

By 1931 the Eighteenth International Conference of Orientalists at Leiden discussed the various Mesopotamian finds made since 1918 and agreed to distinguish three predynastic periods in Mesopotamian prehistory: the earliest, the Al'Ubaid period, the second the Uruk period, and the third, and immediately predynastic period, that of Jemdet Nasr. This scheme provided a much-needed systematisation of Mesopotamian prehistory, and approximate dates for these three periods were given as Al'Ubaid, 4000 to 3500 B.C., Uruk, 3500 to 3200 B.C. and Jemdet Nasr, 3200 to 2800 B.C.

But although the Leiden conference had produced this systematisation, it was by no means certain that this scheme did accurately provide for the whole prehistory of Mesopotamia. Further north, in the eastern end of what Breasted called the

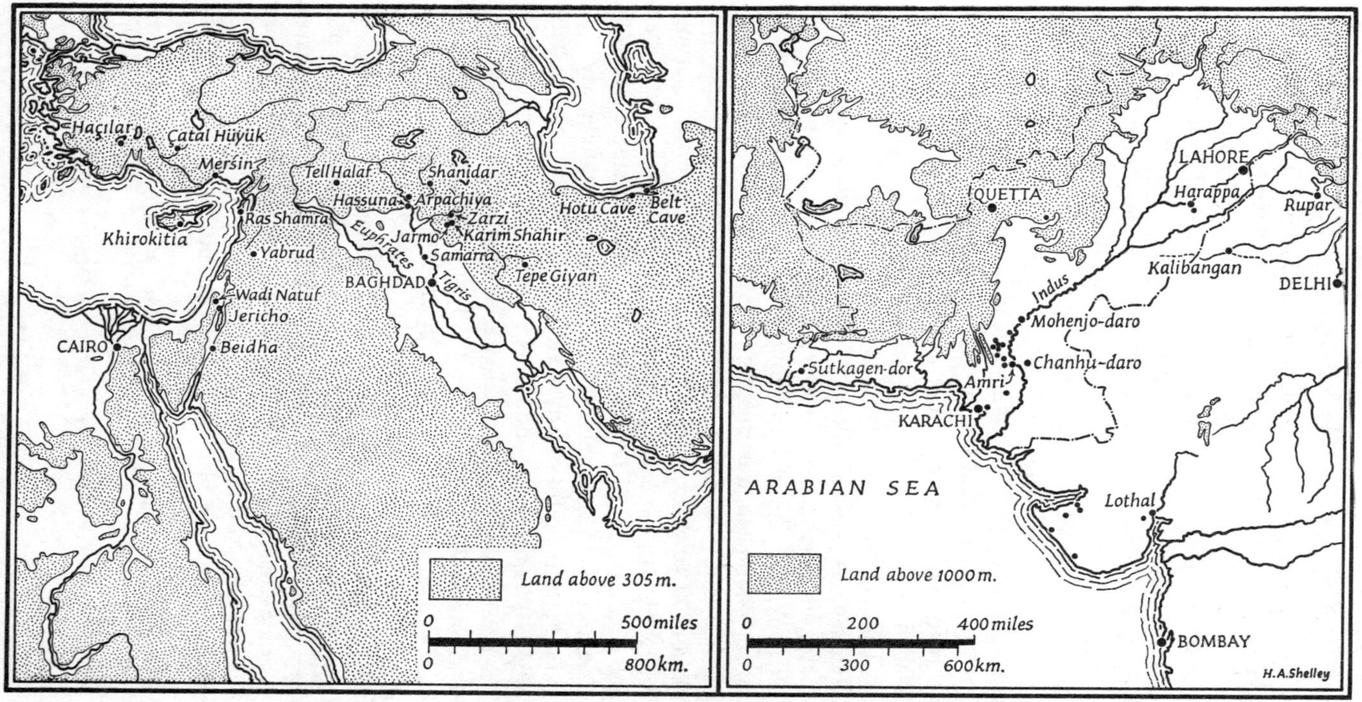

Fig. 3. Maps showing important sites in the Near East and in the Indus Valley.

Fertile Crescent, discoveries of great importance had been made. Tell Halaf, a mound near the source of the Khabur in the Mosul area, was excavated by the Baron Max von Oppenheim between 1911 and 1914. Excavations were resumed there in 1929 [1]; Tell Halaf revealed a chalcolithic culture characterised by a brilliant polychrome painted pottery. Comparable pottery had been found by Herzfeld in his excavations at Samarra in 1912–14, and the same sort of pottery and culture was found at other sites in the east of the Fertile Crescent, at Arpachiyah near Nineveh, excavated in 1933 by Mallowan on behalf of the British Museum,[2] and in Speiser's excavations for the University of Pennsylvania from 1930 onwards at Tepe Gawra and Tell Billa near Khorsabad.

At Tepe Gawra and Arpachiyah, the Tell Halaf culture or the Halafian, as it was called, could be accurately dated below Al'Ubaid, and seemed to take the prehistory of Mesopotamia yet further back, into the fifth millennium B.C. From 1931 onwards Campbell Thompson was digging at Kuyunjik on behalf of the British Museum; he cut a shaft down to virgin soil from the foundations of an Assyrian temple, and his sondage went through the following strata—Assyrian, Babylonian, Akkadian, Sumerian, Jemdet Nasr, Uruk, Al'Ubaid, Halafian—thus giving a complete cross-section of Mesopotamian prehistory and protohistory. At the very bottom of his shaft, seventy feet beneath the surface, Campbell Thompson found eleven potsherds decorated with curious scratched designs, which were formally classified as pre-Halafian or Neolithic. This was the first indication of the oldest stage of post-Palaeolithic archaeology in Mesopotamia. Speiser, collating the Mesopotamian material with other finds in the Near East, proposed to add two periods to the Leiden stages and distinguish the following five periods in Mesopotamian prehistory: 5, Jemdet Nasr; 4, Uruk; 3, Al'Ubaid; 2, Halaf-Samarra, and 1, Sakje-Geuzu or Neolithic.[3] This scheme of five prehistoric periods has been widely accepted.

Excavations were also continued in southern Mesopotamia.

[1] First published in Leipzig in 1931 as *Der Tell Halaf: eine neue Kultur im ältesten Mesopotamien*. English translation, 1933, as *Tell Halaf: A New Culture in Oldest Mesopotamia*.

[2] Mallowan and Rose, *Prehistoric Assyria: the excavations at Tell-Arpachiyah*, 1933.

[3] *Antiquity*, 1941, 173.

In 1929 J. H. Breasted's Oriental Institute of Chicago began work in Iraq by completing the work of Botta and Place at Khorsabad, and then the following year beginning at Tell Asmar (the ancient Eshunna) and Khafaje (the ancient Akshak). These excavations in the Diyala region east of Baghdad were continued until 1937, under the direction of Henri Frankfort and Conrad Preusser. Another Diyala site, Tell Agrab, was excavated by the Oriental Institute between 1934–36. The Sumerian temples at these Diyala sites yielded a great deal of sculpture comparable only in quantity and interest with the Gudea statues at Lagash found by de Sarzec. The French in 1929 resumed excavations at Telloh; these were directed first by the Abbé de Genouillac and later by André Parrot.

In 1933 a new Iraq law prevented the export of any antiquities from the country by foreign expeditions. The French and British field expeditions transferred their activities to Syria. Parrot began work in 1934 at Tell Hariri, in Syria, the ruins of the royal city of Mari, a remarkable outpost of Sumerian culture. Mallowan continued his work in the Khabur district, but excavated at Tell Chagar Bazar and Tell Brak in Syria, while Woolley transferred his attentions to Atchana in the plain of Antioch.

By 1939 the various foreign archaeological expeditions working in Mesopotamia had finished their work, but, unlike the 1914–18 War, the 1939–45 War did not mean a cessation in archaeological activities. By now the Antiquities Department of Iraq and the Iraq Museum, both created after the 1914–18 War, largely due to the initiative and drive of Gertrude Bell, were able to act on their own initiative. The first excavations undertaken directly by the Iraq Government were those in the Omayyid capital of Wasit and the Abbasid capital of Samarra. This was in 1936; four years later the Iraq Government undertook its first prehistoric excavation at Tell Uquair, fifty miles south of Baghdad, and discovered a fine temple of the Uruk period, its walls covered with painted frescoes. These excavations were conducted by Seton Lloyd, and in a note prefaced to Lloyd's published account of the excavations in 1943 Frankfort wrote: "scholars owe a debt of gratitude to the Iraq Government for its courage in undertaking and continuing the purely cultural enterprise of research notwithstanding the disturbed times through which the country has passed". The debt was to be increased by the discoveries at Tell Hassunah in 1943 and at Eridu from 1946 onwards. At Tell Hassunah, twenty miles south of Nineveh, the Iraq Department of Antiquities under Seton Lloyd and Sayyid Fuad Safar discovered a small settlement of pre-Halaf times with the same pottery as had been found at the bottom of the great shaft at Nineveh. With its full evidence this site completed the picture of the five prehistoric periods of Mesopotamia—pre-Halaf or Nineveh/Hassunah, Halafian, Al'Ubaid, Uruk and Jemdet Nasr. Excavations began at Eridu under Sayyid Fuad Safar in 1946. Hitherto the Al'Ubaid phase of Mesopotamian prehistory had been regarded as one of small villages like Al'Ubaid itself, but these excavations showed that Eridu was a city in Al'Ubaid times and had a temple. Perhaps Eridu, whose occupation as an urban community must date from very early in the fourth millennium, will turn out to be, as Seton Lloyd has suggested, the oldest city made by man. The bilingual version of the Babylonian legend of Creation says: "All the lands were sea; then Eridu was made."

However true this legend may be in regard to Eridu there can be no doubt that the excavations in Mesopotamia in the last twenty years have enabled us to appreciate the truth in the Creation and Flood legends preserved in Genesis and for long part of the cosmological background of all Christians. The reading of inscriptions showed that the biblical accounts were derived from Sumerian Creation and Flood stories. The Sumerian creation story, with its references to the land being created out of the waters, is surely a folk-memory of the first settlement of Mesopotamia, which did consist of villages like Al'Ubaid and cities like Eridu in the marshy delta, just as the Flood story is a folk-memory of the floods which are attested archaeologically in the sections at Warka, Farah, Kish and Ur. It is also now possible to see in the biblical story of Cain and Abel the antagonism between the steppe nomads of Arabia and the agriculturists and city dwellers of Sumeria, which played such a prominent part in the early history of Mesopotamia and which has been so rightly stressed by students of human geography.[1]

[1] On these points see Peake and Fleure, *The Corridors of Time*, passim, and Peake, *The Flood*.

The establishment of a prehistoric sequence of cultures in Mesopotamia at once raised the problem: Who were the Sumerians? It is the same problem which arose when the Mycenaeans and the Trojan sequence were discovered by Schliemann, and which persists as a diabolically fascinating preoccupation among many prehistorians. Frankfort argued that there was no real break in the Mesopotamian sequence from Al'Ubaid to dynastic times and that the Sumerians were the Obeidians. Jordan and Contenau argued that the Uruk people *were* the Sumerians and that they arrived in Mesopotamia and imposed themselves on the pre-Sumerian Obeidians. Speiser argued for a break in the sequence in Uruk B times, while others see no possibility of labelling any levels as Sumerian until early dynastic times. It is an age-old problem of prehistory and one which probably cannot be solved; it is doubtful how far the back-ascription of linguistic and historical labels is possible. As Mallowan says, the whole thing rests on "speculation rather than proof",[1] and we may agree with Speiser's wise words in 1941 that "to identify the individual ethnic elements which co-operated in producing the civilisation of pre-literate Mesopotamia is a more hopeless task to-day than it ever appeared to be".[2]

4. *Iran and Transcaspia*

In 1891 Jacques de Morgan visited the ruins of Susa in the Persian province of Khuzistan. Here he found four gigantic mounds, one of them a hundred feet in height, standing up out of the plain, and covering an area of 300 acres. Previous excavations had revealed remains of the fifth century B.C., but de Morgan picked up, from the skirts of the tells, flints and sherds of painted pottery. He persuaded the French Government that Susa was a site of the greatest importance archaeologically, and in 1897 the French Government purchased from the Shah of Persia the sole right to dig for antiquities in Persian soil; and in that year the *Délégation Française en Perse* went out, under de Morgan, to start work at Susa. The *Délégation* has been described as "probably the most important archaeological expedition that has ever left Europe".[3] The work begun by de Morgan was continued until the 1914–18 War, and afterwards resumed under the

[1] *Antiquity*, 1939, 163.

[2] *Ibid.*, 1941, 173.

[3] Carleton, *Buried Empires*, 34.

directorship of R. de Mecquenem. Its results have been published in a series of *Mémoires* by the *Délégation.* The finds from Susa were spectacular, notably the early painted pottery now in the Louvre. Herzfeld writes of the discovery at Susa of the oldest Elamite civilisation of painted potters that it "came as a great surprise to all students of the Ancient East. Neither Egypt nor Babylonia and Mesopotamia, nor Anatolia had at the time furnished anything comparable in artistic value to the oldest painted pottery from Susa".[1]

De Morgan distinguished two cultural phases at Susa, I and II, but it is now clear from subsequent excavations and comparative studies of the excavated material that he had only partly understood the stratigraphical sequence which the *Délégation* was revealing. McCown now proposes to distinguish four phases at Susa: A, being the earliest settlements and burials that have for long been known as Susa I, and which he regards as systadially equivalent to Al'Ubaid; B, equivalent to the Uruk phase; C, to the Jemdet Nasr phase, and D, the phase formerly known as Susa II, and systadially equivalent to the Early Dynastic period in Mesopotamia.

The *Délégation* has, in addition to Susa, worked at other sites in Khuzistan, such as Tepe Musyan, described by Gautier and Lampre in 1905,[2] and Tepe Duvaisyah, Tepe Jafarabad, Tepe Juwi, Tepe Band-i-Bal and Tepe Buhallan by de Mecquenem.[3] At all these sites painted pottery was found comparable with that at Susa I, or A.

While the excavations at Susa were in progress the American R. Pumpelly and the German archaeologist Dr Hubert Schmidt excavated, in 1904, two occupation mounds, the North and the South Kurgans, each 40 to 50 feet in height, at Anau, near Ashkabad, in Russian Turkestan or Transcaspia. Two culture levels, Anau I and II, were distinguished in the North Kurgan, and two later cultural levels, III and IV, in the South Kurgan, and these were fully published by Pumpelly, Schmidt and others in their *Explorations in Turkestan: Expedition of 1904: Prehistoric Civilisations of Anau: Origins, Growth and Influence of Environment.*[4] Recently McCown proposes to distinguish two

[1] *Iran in the Ancient East*, 1941.
[2] *Fouilles de Moussian. Délégation en Perse. Mémoires*, viii, 59–148. Paris.
[3] *L'Anthropologie*, XLV, 93–104, and XLVIII, 55–71.
[4] *Carnegie Institution of Washington*, Publication No. 73 (1908).

phases, A and B, in Anau I. Anau I A is a formally Neolithic culture with painted pottery and appears contemporary with Halaf. Anau I B is the phase in which pins and other objects of copper appear, and carries on the painted pottery tradition through Al'Ubaid and into Uruk times, being roughly contemporary with Susa A. The Neolithic/Chalcolithic villagers of Anau I lived in four-sided houses of dried-clay brick, cultivated wheat and barley, and had oxen, horse, pig and two breeds of sheep. Duerst of Zürich, who studied the animal bones, claimed that they showed a transition from a wild to a tame state for ox, sheep and pig, and Pumpelly claimed that this was also demonstrated stratigraphically and that Anau I provided rare archaeological evidence of the actual transition from an earlier agricultural stage to mixed farming.

Towards the end of Anau I B a grey ware appears, mixed with the painted pottery, and these continue side by side in Anau II although the red or grey monochrome ware is predominant. In addition to the characteristic Anau I painted pottery, which was in black on a red ground, there also appear in Anau II black on buff ware, and a polychrome ware. Pumpelly and Schmidt thought the tournette was in use in this phase, and noted the addition of dog, goat and camel to the list of domesticated animals. Anau III, the first phase of occupation in the South Kurgan, is what Schmidt characterised as "the brilliant epoch of the copper age in Transcaspia". Copper implements were numerous and sometimes include slight admixture of tin; the pottery is wheel-made and is mainly decorated by incision—painting is rare. Anau IV is an Iron Age culture.

For some while our knowledge of Iranian and Transcaspian prehistory depended on the discoveries of Susa and Anau, and fresh discoveries made in Mesopotamia, and even China and India, in the early twenties, were fitted in to the sequence of cultures distinguished by de Morgan and Pumpelly. In the thirties our knowledge of Middle Eastern prehistory was enormously increased by excavations at sites such as Tepe Hissar, Shah Tepe [1] and Turang Tepe,[2] in north Iran, Tepe Giyan and Tepe Sialk in north-west Iran, Tall-i-Bakun at Persepolis in Fars

[1] T. J. Arne, "The Swedish Archaeological Expedition to Iran 1932–33," *Acta Archaeologia*, VI, 1–48.

[2] F. R. Wulsin, "Excavations at Turang Tepe, near Asterabad," *Bulletin of the American Institute for Persian Art and Archaeology*, II.

province, and by the excavations and reconnaissances of Sir Aurel Stein mainly in east and south-east Iran.[1]

Of these the excavations at Tepe Sialk were the most important, because they provided a splendid stratigraphical sequence. Sialk is near Kashan, and was excavated in 1933, 1934 and 1937 by Roman Ghirshman, and was fully published in *Fouilles de Sialk* in 1938 (vol. i) and 1941 (vol. ii). Ghirshman dug two mounds at Sialk, and distinguished four successive cultural periods: I, represented by the four lowest occupation levels of the north mound, II, by the last three settlements on the north mound. Sialk I is characterised by *pisé* houses with contracted burials under the houses, generally without grave goods but covered in red ochre, and at least two kinds of painted pottery, a clear light ware and a rare black ware. The villagers of Sialk I had slings, stone maces, stone axes and adzes, as well as pins and needles of hammered copper. They bred sheep and cattle, and may have grown cereals, reaping them with sickles mounted in bone handles very like those of the Natufian, and grinding them in saddle querns. It is quite clear that the Sialk I villagers were hunters and collectors, as well as domesticators of animals and perhaps cultivators of grain. Indeed it may well be a transitional culture between food-gathering Mesolithic folk and the food-producing chalcolithic cultures well known in the Near and Middle East. Sialk I is formally Neolithic and is equated systadially with the pre-Halaf phase in Mesopotamian prehistory.

Sialk II, contemporary with the Halaf and Samarra cultures of Mesopotamia, is essentially a continuation of the village economy of Sialk I, but contains new features such as hand-made mud bricks, concave-based whorls, and a new repertoire of pottery designs, as well as imported objects from the Persian Gulf such as *Pterocera* shells, turquoise and cornelian. Food-gathering now seems to have occupied a less important part in the economy, and the pig and horse have been domesticated. There is a gap between Sialk II and III, which phase is represented by eight occupation levels running from early Ubaid to mid-Uruk periods. Sialk III is a full Chalcolithic culture with cast tools, including a shaft-hole adze, the potter's kiln and the

[1] Stein's work in Iran is to be found published mainly in *Innermost Asia*, iii, 1928; *An Archaeological Tour of the Ancient Persis, Iraq*, iii, 111 ff.; *Archaeological Reconnaissances in North-west India and South-eastern Iran*, 1937; and *Old Routes of Western Iran*, 1940.

construction of more complicated buildings with buttresses and recesses. A thick layer of ashes indicates the destruction of Sialk III at the end of its last occupation level, above which was built Sialk IV, a city of the Jemdet Nasr period with bichrome pottery and early inscribed tablets, presumably an outpost of the literate urban civilisation of the Elamites.

The site of Tall-i-Bakun, near Persepolis, was discovered in 1923, and excavations were begun in 1928 by Herzfeld, and continued in 1931–32 by the Oriental Institute of Chicago, under the direction of Langsdorff and McCown.[1] This site also consists of twin mounds like Anau and Sialk; of these, Bakun B is the earliest and consists of Bakun B I, a culture claimed by McCown and Herzfeld as Neolithic or epi-Neolithic, and contemporary with pre-Halaf and Sialk I, and Bakun B II, which has painted pottery and is contemporary with Halaf. The later mound, Bakun B, begins contemporary with early Ubaid times in Bakun A I and overlaps with Uruk in its latest phase Bakun A V.

Tepe Giyan, a large tell near Nihavend, was excavated in 1931 and 1932 by Georges Contenau and Roman Ghirshman. A succession of five cultural periods was distinguished: Giyan V, the earliest level, spanned from early Halaf (V A) to mid-Uruk times (V D). The second period at Giyan, Giyan IV, covered the time from early dynastic to Akkadian (3000 to 2300 B.C.) and has pottery similar to Susa D. The remaining three levels occupy from 2300 to 1000 B.C. and the appearance of iron.[2] Tepe Hissar, a tell near Damghan, was excavated in 1931 by E. F. Schmidt, who distinguished three main cultural periods[3]: Hissar I, lasting from early Ubaid to mid-Uruk; Hissar II, a transitional period in which the old painted pottery of Hissar I is superseded by a plain burnished black or grey ware—this new pottery and the appearance of new metal types such as double spiral-headed pins suggests the arrival of new folk in the time between mid-Uruk and the end of Jemdet Nasr. Hissar III reveals the new grey-ware people well established. McCown dates Hissar III as contemporary with Giyan IV, *i.e.* the early

[1] A. Langsdorff and D. E. McCown "Tall-i-Bakun A; Season of 1932," *Oriental Institute of Chicago University Publications*, LIX, 1942.

[2] Contenau and Ghirshman, "Fouilles de Tepé-Giyan," *Musée du Louvre. Serie archaeologique*, III. Paris, 1935. The levels at Giyan are lettered from the top downwards, V being the earliest.

[3] "Tepé Hissar Excavations 1931," *Pennsylvania University Museum Journal*, XXIII (1932–33), 318–483. Philadelphia, 1933.

dynastic period to Akkadian,[1] but Piggott argues that this phase cannot be before 2000 B.C.[2]

These various excavations have established in Iran the widespread existence of cultures characterised by painted pottery, cultures mainly Chalcolithic but occasionally, as at Sialk I and Bakun B I, formally Neolithic. At one time archaeologists referred to a "painted pottery culture", and the material from Anau I and Susa I was compared with that from Al'Ubaid and Halaf in Mesopotamia, from S. E. Europe, from China and India. Frankfort in his *Archaeology and the Sumerian Problem* (1932) proposed to distinguish two painted pottery cultures or civilisations in the Near East—a Syrian with Tell Halaf as a type site, and one centred in the Iranian Highlands, which he referred to as the Iranian, and others, like Childe and Carleton, have called the Highland culture. In 1942 D. E. McCown published his *The Comparative Stratigraphy of Early Iran*, in which he split the Iranian or Highland painted pottery civilisation into two separate painted pottery cultures, the first or red-ware group characterised by painting in black on red pottery, and seen mainly in N. E. Iran at Sialk (from period I to early III), Anau I, and Hissar I, and at another site, Chesmeh Ali, in the same region, and the second or buff-ware group, characterised by black on buff pottery and represented by Giyan V, Susa A, and Bakun. In his North Iranian Red Ware Culture McCown distinguishes three periods, which he describes as cultures, namely, first, the Sialk Culture, (Sialk I), second, the Chesmah Ali Culture (Sialk II, Chesmah Ali IA, Anau IA), and thirdly the Hissar Culture (Sialk III, Chesmah Ali IB, and Hissar I).

The absolute dating of the Iranian and Transcaspian cultures has varied greatly with the date, vagaries and methods of the archaeologists concerned. Pumpelly visited Egypt in 1906-7 and calculated the rate of occupational debris accumulation there to be 1·6 feet per century. On the basis of this he dated Anau II, 6000 to 5000 B.C., Anau III, 5000 to 2000, and put the beginnings of Anau I back in the tenth millennium B.C.[3] A similarly inflated chronology was proposed by de Morgan for Susa I. Dr Hubert Schmidt, however, proposed a quite different absolute chronology

[1] *The Comparative Stratigraphy of Early Iran*, 50–52.

[2] *Antiquity*, XVII, 1943, 169.

[3] Pumpelly even dated the domestication of *Bos nomadicus* as in the eighth millennium B.C.

for Anau. Schmidt was really responsible under Pumpelly for the archaeological aspects of the excavations there and his dates appear in the same volume as those of Pumpelly. He dated Anau I to the third millennium B.C., Anau II to 2000 to 1500 B.C., Anau III to 1500 to 1000 B.C. and Anau IV to 1000 to 500 B.C. Ghirshman calculated the date of the early occupation of Sialk on the basis of the accumulated debris. Before Sialk IV there were seventeen successive layers of mud or mud-brick huts, forming in all 28 metres of deposit. Allowing seventy-five years for each level, and to-day such huts last for at least a hundred years, and taking the date of Sialk IV as 3000 plus or minus 200 years, Ghirshman calculated 4300 B.C. plus/minus 200 for the first occupation of Sialk; dates which McCown calls "certainly too low".

5. *Anatolia*

Schliemann had distinguished seven superimposed prehistoric cities at Troy, and Dörpfeld had dated these from 3000 to 700 B.C. identifying VI, which he dated from 1500 to 1000 B.C., as the Homeric city. This chronology and the identification of the VIth city with the Homeric one was attacked by Åberg in his *Bronzezeitliche und Früheisenzeitliche Chronologie*, where he equated the second city with the shaft graves of Mycenae, giving a date for it of 1600–1450. From 1932 onwards an American expedition under C. W. Blegen began fresh excavations at Troy, with the intention of examining new areas and checking the earlier stratigraphy. No complete publication of these re-excavations has yet appeared, but interim reports in the *American Journal of Archaeology* and elsewhere suggest that the Homeric city, dated by imports from Mycenae to the early twelfth and late thirteenth centuries B.C., was Troy VIIA. Troy I is revealed as a little township, which Blegen, refusing Åberg's suggestions, dates before 2500 B.C. Troy II, a city which was to play so great a rôle in the development of European metallurgy, is dated by Blegen to between 2500 and 2300 B.C.; the settlements of Troy III, IV and V, formerly described as villages, appear to have been of greater importance, whereas Troy VI was a city destroyed by an earthquake.

The prehistoric archaeology of west Anatolia can now be supplemented by three sites: Kum Tepe, Yortan and Thermi. Kum Tepe, a site in the Troad excavated by the American expedition under Blegen, is claimed as earlier even than Troy I.[1] The cemetery of Yortan in Mysia was contemporary with Troy I. Miss Winifred Lamb's excavations at Thermi, published in 1928 in her *Excavations at Thermi in Lesbos*,[2] revealed a succession of five superimposed townships, of which towns I to IV are contemporary with Troy I, and Thermi V with Troy II.

Our further knowledge of Anatolian prehistory is bound up, not with the search for Greek prehistoric origins, but with interest in the Hittites. The beginning of our modern knowledge of the Hittites dates from 1736, when Jean Otter discovered the famous relief at Ibriz in south Cappadocia. In 1812 Burckhardt discovered one of the Hamath inscriptions. Other finds of the same kind, and of seals and seal inscriptions, were made during the early nineteenth century, but little interest was taken in them until the period 1860–75. In 1861 Georges Perrot, the art historian, was sent to investigate the monument of Augustus at Ankara, and went on from there to the Cappadocian hills east of the rivers Halys and Sangarius. Here, at a Turkish village called Boghaz Keui, about ninety miles east of Ankara within the bend of the Halys river, he found the remains of a vast fortified city, with sculptures quite unlike the then known ancient arts from Mesopotamia, Egypt, or the Aegean. In 1870 the Hamath inscription was rediscovered and several others found for the first time. In 1872 Richard Burton, in his *Unexplored Syria*, published a transcription of the Hamath inscription, and Dr W. Wright, an Irish missionary at Damascus, got the Hamath stones sent to the Constantinople Museum and two sets of plaster casts sent to the British Museum, which also secured at this time a number of inscriptions from Jerabis, the ancient Carchemish.

Richard Burton showed that the writing on the Hamath inscriptions was a hitherto unknown script. Perrot had recognised the art at Boghaz Keui as hitherto unknown. Now Wright suggested that the sculptures and the inscriptions were the work of the people known in the Bible as the Hittites, and in 1884 published his *Empire of the Hittites*, summarising all that was then known about them, including facsimiles of all the known inscriptions and an attempt at decipherment of the cuneiform script by A. H. Sayce, Professor of Assyriology at Oxford. Four years

[1] *American Journal of Archaeology*, 39, 33.
[2] *British School at Athens*, 30 and 31.

later Sayce himself published his *The Hittites: the Story of a Forgotten Empire*, in which he studied all the known remains and brilliantly inferred the forgotten empire of the Hittites.

In 1906–8 German and Turkish excavators under Professor Hugo Winckler excavated the site found by Perrot and revealed Boghaz Keui as the capital of the Hittites, the city of Hattosas. The excavations were brief and inadequate, but they brought to light a large deposit of official archives consisting of thousands of tablets forming a sort of library of Foreign Office documents organised in the period 1350 and 1300 B.C., and mentioning peoples like the Egyptians, the Babylonians, the Cypriots and Ahhiyava, a people described as settled on the southern coasts of Asia Minor and Cyprus and now identified with the Achaeans. In 1923 Macalister wrote, in the first volume of the *Cambridge Ancient History*, that "in spite of heroic attempts, the hieroglyphs of the Hittites have not yet been deciphered". The next year the translation of many of these Hittite texts was announced, largely as the result of the work of the Czech scholar Friedrich Hrozny, whose *Die Sprache der Hethiter* had appeared in 1917, and who had published the key to the translation of the Hittite documents in the *Mitteilungen der Deutschen Orient Gesellschaft* eight years before that.[1] Hrozny's initial work was followed up by a team of workers including Ehelof, Figulla, Forrer, Weber, Weidner and Gotze, and the Boghaz Keui correspondence began to be a part of our general knowledge of the most ancient East.

Meanwhile other sites in central and eastern Anatolia were being excavated, Hüyük (or Eyuk), near Aladja, some twenty miles north of Boghaz Keui, Kul Tepe, north of Kaisariyeh, Akalan, near Samsan, Senjirli (the ancient Samal), and Sakje-Geuzu, or Sakcagözü. Senjirli was excavated by the Germans under von Luschan. Hüyük and many other sites were visited by the expedition of the Liverpool University Institute of Archaeology, which started work in Anatolia in 1907 under John Garstang and which excavated Sakje-Geuzu the following year. This work has been continued by Professor Garstang for over forty years, culminating in the excavations of Mersin, and in his appointment as Director of the British School of Archaeology in Ankara in 1947. Our increased knowledge of the Hittites from these excavations and from the reading of the Boghaz Keui library was summarised

[1] No. 35 (1907).

in A. E. Cowley's *The Hittites* (1920), Contenau's *Éléments de Bibliographie Hittite* (Paris, 1922), and later by Garstang's *Hittites* (1929). Carchemish, in north Syria, a southern outpost of the Hittite civilisation, was excavated before the 1914–18 War by a British Museum expedition under Hogarth, Campbell Thompson, Lawrence and Woolley.[1]

But it was not only our knowledge of the Hittites that was improved by these excavations. Gradually earlier pre-Hittite civilisations and cultures were distinguished in central and eastern Anatolia comparable with those known from the early levels of Troy. In 1893 Chantre made archaeological explorations in Anatolia, which included a sondage through Orta Hüyük; his findings were published in his *Recherches Archéologiques dans l'Asie occidentale: Mission en Cappadoce*, in 1898, and included painted pottery. In 1903 J. L. Myres compared this Cappadocian painted pottery with the Bronze Age painted pottery from Cyprus and Sicily, and the then little-known Thessalian painted pottery, a comparison sustained by de Morgan in his *Préhistoire Orientale* (iii, 1927). In 1926 de Genouillac published the Anatolian painted pottery from the Louvre in his *Céramique Cappadocienne*, suggesting that it represented two distinct periods, including pottery painted in dark on a white slip resembling the painted wares from Thessaly and the Trans-Danube area. At Sakje-Geuzu, Garstang distinguished four occupations, which he labelled Early Neolithic, Later Neolithic, Early Painted and Later Painted.[2] The Neolithic pottery included a black ware sometimes decorated with a white incised pattern, which Garstang compared with similar wares from Troy and Crete, some of the early painted wares he compared with Susa and Anau rather than with Aegean painted wares.

What was now needed in Anatolian prehistory was an excavation in central or eastern Anatolia comparable with the great work of Schliemann and Dörpfeld at Troy. The German re-excavations at Boghaz Keui tied some of the Cappadocian painted wares into the historical Hittite sequence but were unable to provide a complete sequence of central Anatolian prehistory. This was the aim of the Oriental Institute of the University of Chicago, which in

[1] Woolley, Lawrence and Hogarth, *Carchemish: Report on the Excavations at Djerabis* (1914, 1921).

[2] *Liverpool Annals*, I (1908), 97 ff.; *The Land of the Hittites* (1910), 298–316.

the mid twenties planned a full investigation of Hittite civilisation by exploration, survey, and excavation. The explorations began in 1926, when, in one season, Von der Osten found over three hundred new sites in Anatolia, including no less than seventy in the Kuzul Irmak basin. The most promising of these was a hüyük near Alishar village, 128 miles south-east of Ankara. Alishar Hüyük, a mound over 100 feet high, was excavated by Von der Osten and E. F. Schmidt between 1927 and 1932. It was a complete excavation carried out with great thoroughness and efficiency, and the reports published in the *Communications* and *Publications* of the Oriental Institute constitute one of the most important contributions to archaeological scholarship made in the twentieth century.[1] Four principal levels were distinguished, as follows: Alishar A, a Chalcolithic culture (classified in some of the earlier reports as Neolithic), characterised by self-coloured black to red pottery and dated to the fourth millennium B.C.; Alishar B, a Copper Age culture (classified in the earlier reports as Alishar I), with five building levels occupying 11 metres of deposit, and dated from 3000 to 2400 B.C.; Alishar C, an early Bronze Age culture (classified in the earlier reports as Alishar III), characterised by the Cappadocian painted pottery and dated from 2400 B.C. to the rise of the first Hittite Empire *circa* 2000 B.C., which is represented by Alishar D (classified in the earlier reports as Alishar II).

Further knowledge of this Anatolian sequence was provided by excavations at Ahlatlibel, near Ankara, where Dr Hamit Zubeyr Kosay, Director of Antiquities and Museums in Turkey, found settlements and burials of the Copper Age comparable with Alishar B[2]; and at Alaca Hüyük. Alaca lies thirty-five miles north of Boghaz Keui and was excavated by Dr Kosay from 1935 onwards[3]; here he found a fourth-millennium Chalcolithic culture comparable with Alishar A, represented by four building levels and characterised by a coarse grey-and-pink ware with, in addition, about five per cent. of an unusual black slip ware with

[1] E. F. Schmidt, *Anatolia through the Ages; Discoveries at the Alishar Mound, 1927–29: Oriental Institute Communications*, No. 11 (Chicago, 1931); Von der Osten and Schmidt, *The Alishar Huyuk Excavations, 1927–32 ; Oriental Institute Publications*, 8 vols., 1930–37.

[2] Kosay, *Ahlatlibel Hafriyati* (*Türk Tarih Arkeologya ve Etnografya Dergisi*, II, 1934).

[3] R. O. Arik, "Les Fouilles d'Alaca Hoyuk . . . rapport préliminaire sur les travaux en 1935" (*Pub. de la Société d'Hist. Turque*, Ankara, 1937); Kosay, *Illustrated London News*, July 21, 1945, 78 ff.

geometrical designs in black paint and incised or dotted patterns, succeeded by a pre-Hittite culture which Kosay dates from 3000 to 2100 B.C., and calls Copper Age, and alternatively Old or Early Bronze Age, and equates with Alishar B and C. The Alaca Copper Age contained four building levels, and, among dwellings dated roughly to the middle of the third millennium B.C., Kosay found thirteen rich graves, which he describes as "those of thirteen members of a royal family whose bodies were placed inside jars"; accompanying the burials were metal sun-discs, idols and figures of bulls and stags, as well as ornaments, weapons and vessels, many of them gold. Kosay declares with some justice that, both in point of wealth and of craftsmanship, Alaca Hüyük bears comparison with the material from the so-called Royal Tombs at Ur.

In the last fifteen years important discoveries have been made at three sites in south-east Turkey—at Mersin, on the Cilician Plain, at Alalakh, near Aleppo, and at Karatepe, in the foothills of the Taurus mountains.

A preliminary study of remains in the Cilician plain by Gjerstad [1] was followed in 1936–37 by the Neilson Expedition, under Garstang, which listed over a hundred hüyüks in the small area studied, made preliminary excavations at Chaushli Hüyük, a few miles north-west of Mersin, and then carried out many seasons' work until the war at Yumuk Tepé, or Souk Su Hüyük, usually referred to as the Mersin Tell.[2] Here a succession of levels was revealed, of which levels XII to XVI were classified as Chalcolithic. Level XII, which underlay a gap in the sequence, was classified as Late Chalcolithic and dated to about 3000 B.C.; levels XIII and XIV were classified as Middle Mersin Chalcolithic ii, with Uruk wares in it; levels XV and XVA were classified as Middle Mersin Chalcolithic i, and contained wares resembling those of Arpachiyah and Al'Ubaid; while level XVI was classified as standard Mersin Chalcolithic, described as contemporary with Tell Halaf polychrome wares and dated to 3600 B.C. or earlier. Beneath this Halaf Chalcolithic were found, first, a culture with painted pottery recalling to some extent that of Ninevite I and II, which was considered to be pre-Halaf in date and classified as proto-Chalcolithic, and then a Neolithic culture with worked obsidian

[1] Gjerstad, "Cilician Studies," *Revue Archéologique*, III, 1934.

[2] Garstang, *Liverpool Annals of Archaeology and Anthropology*, 1937–40.

tools and black and brown burnished pottery and polished stone axes. The pre-Halaf industries at Mersin were specially studied by Burkitt, who claims the Neolithic there as one of the oldest post-Palaeolithic cultures in the Near East and dates it at least to 5500 B.C.: he compares the pottery with the lowest at Nineveh, with some of the incised wares in the lowest levels at Alishar, and with sites in Thessaly such as Lianokladi I, Rakhmani I and Tsani Maghala.[1] Seton Lloyd compares some of the early Mersin wares with those found by him at Hassunah.

Atchana-Alalakh was excavated by Woolley in 1946 and in 1947. It was revealed as the ancient Hittite capital of what is now the province of Hatay, in Turkey, which was destroyed in 1200 B.C. and which had nine periods of occupation going back from 1200 B.C. to the twentieth century B.C. Before this Woolley discovered a developed Copper Age culture with plain and painted pottery showing astonishingly little change for at least fifteen hundred years. Atchana-Alalakh itself had no occupation levels earlier than this Copper Age culture, but at Tayanat, near by, a Chicago expedition found Neolithic and Chalcolithic remains, and in 1947 Woolley excavated a low mound two miles west of Atchana which yielded plain and painted pottery, flints and obsidian tools, some seals and a fragment of copper. The Chalcolithic painted pottery at Tayanat and at the site west of Alalakh compares closely with that found at Mersin, while the burnished wares from Tayanat compare with the earlier unpainted wares of Anatolia.[2]

At Karatepe, in the foothills of the Taurus, where the Jeihan river forces its way into the plain of Adana, a neo-Hittite city was found in 1945 with sculptures showing Aegean influences and inscriptions of great value, some of which refer to the Danuna, Danauna, or Danau, who have long been identified with the Danaoi who fought on the side of the Achaeans at Troy.[3]

Sir John Myres described, as early as 1903, what he called the "endemic gourd ware of Anatolia" which appeared in Troy I, at Yortan and at Sakje-Geuzu, and on which he defined his Red-ware or Anatolian culture. He distinguished this culture as the source of new elements introduced into Anau II and into Susa,

[1] M. C. Burkitt, "The Earlier Cultures at Mersin," *Liverpool Annals*, 1939, 53 ff.

[2] *The Times* of London.

[3] *Ibid.*, April 24 1947.

and identified it as the probable source of the Danubian, taking its home area to be from north Palestine to the Hellespont and embracing all Anatolia to the Upper Euphrates. Myres distinguished an earlier Neolithic stage in which the clay was black and hand-burnished and a later Chalcolithic stage with brick-red pottery. It seems likely from the excavations at Alishar and Alaca that the earliest food-producing Anatolian culture should be classified as Chalcolithic (or Cuprolithic or Aeneolithic or Mixoneolithic—whichever term is favoured). Bittel [1] argues for a common Anatolian Chalcolithic culture, but Von der Osten sees two Chalcolithic cultures, a west Anatolian with Troy I as type site and closely connected with the Balkan cultures, and a central Anatolian with Alishar A as type site and closely connected with the Danubians and Black Earth cultures. Von der Osten sees the same duality in the succeeding Copper Age cultures of Anatolia, except that he considers the west Anatolian Copper Age of Thermi and Troy II developed out of the west Anatolian Chalcolithic culture, whereas the central and east Anatolian Copper Age culture of Alishar, Alaca and Ahlatlibel is new, and represents a break with the earlier central Anatolian Chalcolithic culture. At Alalakh and Tayanat, Woolley considers that the earlier "Late Neolithic" culture is an extension southwards of the Anatolian Chalcolithic but that the Copper Age culture was introduced by a westward expansion of Upper Mesopotamian people.

6. *Palestine, Syria and Cyprus*

The biblical settings in Syria and Palestine had given from an early date the archaeology of those areas an interest comparable with that in the archaeology of Mesopotamia and Egypt. Among early nineteenth-century travellers Burckhardt discovered Petra in 1809, Edward Robinson, an American Congregationalist missionary, published the results of surveys made from 1838 to 1852 in his *Biblical Researches in Palestine*, while in 1860 Renan made valuable surveys in Phoenicia. The Palestine Exploration Fund was founded in London in 1865, and embarked in 1870 on a survey of antiquities under the direction of Conder, Tyrwhit Drake and later a young sapper who ultimately became Lord Kitchener. Excavations began with Warren's work in and around Jerusalem in 1867–70 and the work of Petrie and Bliss at Tell

[1] "Praehistorische Forschungen in Kleinasien," *Istanbul Forschungen*, 1934.

el-Hesy in 1891–92. The site of Gezer was identified at Tell Jezer in the nineteenth century by Clermont-Ganneau and was excavated by R. A. S. Macalister for the Palestine Exploration Fund in 1902–8, where he found early Neolithic dwellers in caves, some natural and some artificial, while in the Early Bronze Age several of the caves were used for burials and a city grew up, forerunner of the historic Gezer, whose stone pillars have been interpreted by Macalister as a Canaanite high place and by Watzinger as memorial stones of kings of the city.[1]

Beth-shemesh, the modern Ain Shems, or Tell er-Rumeileh, lying south-east of Gezer, was excavated for the Palestine Exploration Fund by Dr Duncan Mackenzie in 1911–12, and re-excavated by Professor Elihu Grant, of Haverford College, from 1928 inwards; the excavations revealed a succession of cities from 2000 B.C. to its destruction by Nebuchadnezzar II about 600 B.C.[2] Megiddo, the modern Tell el-Mutesellim, was first excavated by Schumacher, of the Deutsche Orient Gesellschaft, who made a sondage through the mound in 1903–5 [3]; large-scale excavation of the site was begun by the Oriental Institute of Chicago in 1925, first under C. S. Fisher and later under P. L. O. Guy and Gordon Loud. Megiddo was revealed as a city in the Early Bronze Age with continuing occupations until near the end of the twelfth century, when the Canaanite city was destroyed, while the Israelite occupation began about half a century later. In 1937 Gordon Loud excavated the palaces of the princes who at Megiddo ruled on behalf of the Egyptian pharaohs.[4] Debir, the ancient Kiriath-sepher, was another site giving much the same story; it was identified with the mound of Tell Beit Mirsim, thirteen miles south-west of Hebron, and excavated by Kyle and Albright on behalf of the Pittsburgh Xenia Theological Seminary and the American School of Oriental Research in Jerusalem; above a Late Bronze Age city is a great burned layer, and above it Israelite remains of just after 1200 B.C.[5]

On the north coast of Syria, opposite Cyprus, the site of Ras

[1] Macalister, *The Excavations at Gezer*, 1912; and *Bible Side-Lights from the Mound of Gezer*, *1906*. Carl Watzinger, *Denkmäler Palästinas*, I (1933), 63 ff.

[2] E. Grant, *Beth Shemesh* (1929); *Ains Shems Excavations* (5 vols., 1931–39).

[3] Schumacher and Steuernagel, *Tell el-Mutesellim* (1908).

[4] Loud, *The Megiddo Ivories* (1939).

[5] M. G. Kyle, *Excavating Kirjath-Sepher's Ten Cities* (1934). Albright, *Annual of the American Schools of Oriental Research*, 12, 13, 17, 21–22.

Shamra (ancient Ugarit) was discovered almost by chance in 1929 and excavated during the ten years before the 1939 war by Schaeffer. Ras Shamra revealed a long succession of cultures going back to the Neolithic, where plain and incised pottery occurs which Schaeffer compares with the Neolithic of Mersin and others with the Neolithic of Nineveh and Tel Hassunah. A flourishing Chalcolithic city succeeded the Neolithic settlement and in the second millennium B.C. this city was mentioned as Ugarit in the Tell el-Amarna letters, in Hittite correspondence and in Egyptian inscriptions. Ugarit was destroyed by an earthquake in the middle of the fourteenth century, but was reconstructed, and finally destroyed by people from the north and the peoples of the sea at the end of the thirteenth and the beginning of the twelfth century B.C. Ugarit was a sort of international port and from the fifteenth to the twelfth centuries was under the influence of Egypt, the Hittites and the Mycenaeans. In a library at Ras Shamra between the two great temples of the city were found hundreds of clay tablets dating from the fifteenth and early fourteenth centuries. These bear texts in a cuneiform alphabet, the earliest known alphabet, in a language identified by Professor Bauer of Halle as Semitic, and finally deciphered by Bauer, and the French scholars Virolleaud and Dhorme. The language of Ugaritic is closely related to Phoenician and biblical Hebrew; the discovery of the Ras Shamra tablets and the relation of their material to the Bible has given rise to a large literature.[1]

While Schaeffer was working year after year at Ras Shamra, Garstang began at Jericho. Jericho had been first excavated by Professor Ernst Sellin, of the Deutsche Orient Gesellschaft, in 1907–9 [2]; Garstang's excavations were from 1930–36 and revealed a remarkable succession from Neolithic times through to its destruction, as described in Joshua vi. The Neolithic occupation at Jericho occupied levels IX to XVII; only in level IX was there pottery, levels X to XVII contained no pottery, but the inhabitants of Jericho were living in houses with walls of beaten earth, they practised agriculture, had cattle, sheep, goats and pigs, and a flint

[1] Schaeffer, in *Syria*, 1929–39, and *The Cuneiform Texts of Ras Shamra-Ugarit* (1939); and *Ugaritica, études relatives aux découvertes de Ras Shamra* (1939); J. W. Jack, *The Ras Shamra Tablets, their Bearing on the Old Testament* (1935); R. Dussaud, *Les Découvertes de Ras Shamra (Ugarit) et l'Ancien Testament* (1937).

[2] Sellin and Watzinger, *Jericho* (1913).

industry. Garstang and Ben Dor believed that the Jericho Neolithic pottery had been locally invented, but Droop does not agree with this view. The Jerichoan Neolithic pottery has been compared with the Nineveh Neolithic and the Hassunah pottery, and may well be partly intrusive and partly indigenous. Garstang divides the Stone Age in Jericho into a first Neolithic, which he dates from 4000 to 4500 B.C. (levels X to XVII), a second Neolithic (level IX), which he dates from 3500 to 4000 B.C. and equates with the Halafian, and a third Neolithic (level VIII), which is elsewhere labelled Chalcolithic or Jerichoan, and is dated 3000–3500 B.C. and made contemporary with the Ubaid and Jemdet Nasr periods of Mesopotamian prehistory. Jericho became a city in the Early Bronze Age at about 3000 B.C. and Garstang distinguished four cities between this date and its destruction as described in Joshua. This destruction is dated by Garstang to 1400 B.C., by Father Vincent to 1250 B.C., and by Professor Ernest Wright to somewhere between 1475–1300 B.C.[1]

An early Neolithic comparable with that of Jericho was studied by René Neuville at the site of El Khiam, excavated by him in 1930–34. El Khiam is an open station on the banks of the Wadi Kareitoum, south-west of Bethlehem. Neuville distinguished here three cultures, a Caspian, a Natufian, and later a culture which he called the Tahunian, after a site south of Palestine found by Père Buzy.[2] Neuville divides the Tahunian at El Khiam into two levels, Tahunian I, which he claims developed out of the Natufian IV, and Tahunian II, which has pottery developed out of Tahunian I.[3]

Another site excavated by Neuville is Teleilat Chassul, just north of the Dead Sea and not far from Jericho. Here was found a culture much advanced from the Neolithic Tahunian, with painted pottery, houses of mud brick, with walls plastered and decorated with mural paintings. To this Chalcolithic culture the name Ghassulian has been given.[4]

The site of Lachish was identified first at Umm Lakis and

[1] Garstang, *Liverpool Annals*, 1932–36; *Joshua–Judges, The Foundations of Bible History* (1931); J. Garstang and J. B. E. Garstang, *The Story of Jericho* (1940).

[2] D. Buzy, "Une Industrie mésolithique en Palestine," *Revue Biblique*, 1934.

[3] El Khiam is unpublished in detail but described in Neuville's "Le Préhistorique de Palestine," *Revue Biblique*, 1934.

[4] Mallon, Koeppel and Neuville, "Teleilat Ghassul I," *Compte Rendu des Fouilles de l'Institut Biblique Pontifical*, 1929–32.

later, by Petrie, et Tell el-Hesy, where he dug in 1891 [1]; in 1933 it was finally identified at Tell ed-Duweir, where excavations began under the Wellcome-Marston Archaeological Expedition in 1933. These were directed by J. L. Starkey, until his murder by brigands in January 1938, and, afterwards, by C. H. Inge and Lankester Harding. These excavations revealed a cave-dwelling settlement in the Early Bronze Age, giving way to a succession of cities. Among the important discoveries at Lachish were a bowl and a jar in a Late Bronze Age temple, on which were inscriptions written in an early type of Canaanite script found in a few other sites and forming a link between proto-Sinaitic and the earliest known Phoenician alphabets.[2] In 1933–34 Madame Judith Marquet-Krause excavated et-Tell (the ancient Ai), a site thirteen miles west-north-west of Jericho; here she found another important city of the Early Bronze Age, destroyed about 2200 B.C. and later occupied by a village settlement.[3]

These and other excavations in the last fifty years in Palestine and Syria have built up a picture of the culture succession there; first a Neolithic culture such as that of Jericho, Ras Shamra, El Khiam, and Djededieh,[4] and which Neuville calls Tahunian; secondly the Chalcolithic culture which has sometimes been called the Jerichoan; and thirdly the Canaanite Bronze Age with its great development of cities, many of them great trading centres with the Egyptians to the south, the Hittites to the north, the Mesopotamian city-states to the east, and the Mycenaeans on the west; and fourthly, the destruction of these Bronze Age cities round about the period 1400–1200 B.C. by invaders from the north, west and south, these latter in Palestine being the Israelites.

Interest in the archaeology of Cyprus began with the development of interest in Mycenaean civilisation outside Greece. Dümmler went to Cyprus and was able to relate some of the finds of Cretan archaeology with material already found in Greece and the Aegean. In 1865 General Louis Palma di Cesnola was appointed American consul in Cyprus. His collections went to

[1] Petrie, *Tell el-Hesy* (*Lachish*), 1891; F. J. Bliss, *A Mound of Many Cities* (1894).

[2] Tufnell, Inge and Harding, *Lachish II* (*Tell ed Duweir*): *The Fosse Temple* (1940).

[3] *American Journal of Archaeology*, 1936, 158.

[4] Djededieh is a site in Syria not yet published, but referred to in Braidwood's paper "Mounds in the Plain of Antioch," Chicago, 1937. Level XIV is the Neolithic culture.

the Metropolitan Museum of New York, of which he became Director, and the account of his work was published in his *Cyprus: its ancient Cities, Tombs and Temples* (1877). The Cyprus Museum was founded in 1883, four years after the island came into British occupation. J. L. Myres and Max Ohnefalsch-Richter catalogued and arranged the new museum; their *Cyprus Museum Catalogue* was published in 1899, and in 1915 Myres published his *Handbook of the Cesnola Collection.* The modern era in Cyprus archaeology begins in the twenties with the Swedish excavations under Gjerstad between 1927–31. These excavations laid a sure foundation of our knowledge of the Cyprus Bronze Age. The first Neolithic site in Cyprus, at Erimi near Limasol, was excavated by Dikaios in 1933.[1]

7. *The New Past*

We have traced in this chapter, very briefly, the development in the last fifty years of our archaeological knowledge regarding the prehistory and protohistory of the Near East. It is a splendid story stretching back into the late nineteenth century, to the heroic days of Petrie and Schliemann in Egypt and the Aegean, and leading us to the present very detailed knowledge of the early archaeology of a large area extending from Egypt and the Aegean to north-west India and Transcaspia. It is a story which can only for convenience sake be divided into approximate geographical or political areas as we have done here. Behind the details of excavations and the local records of work there emerges the tale of what Childe calls the Most Ancient East, the tale of the development of peasant village communities—whether these be formally Neolithic or Chalcolithic—in the sixth or seventh millennium B.C., and the development among these early peasant village communities of the great urban prehistoric or protohistoric civilisations of Egypt, Palestine and Syria, Anatolia, Mesopotamia, Iran and the Aegean. It is this great story which Breasted triumphantly described as "the New Past" of man.

This story is, of course, not only in the province of prehistoric archaeology, but is in the provinces of those specialist studies which have grown up to deal with all the sources of information

[1] Gjerstad, Lindros, Sjoqvist and Westholm, *The Swedish Cyprus Expeditions: 1927–31.* See also Gjerstad, "The Swedish Excavations in Cyprus," *Antiquity*, 1928, 189; and Casson, *Ancient Cyprus.*

—material and non-material—about the Near-Eastern civilisations. Egyptology was the earliest of these specialist studies to develop; beginning with Napoleon's savants and the decipherments of Young and Champollion, it came of age, as Glanville has recently said,[1] in the sixties of last century. The example of Egyptology must prepare us for the emergence, as Casson feared,[2] of Sumerology, Hittitology and Minology.

Behind these specialist studies of the early civilisations, prehistoric archaeology has been trying to answer the difficult questions of the ultimate origins of these civilisations. It was Egypt that was first thought of as the home of civilisation, once this problem had been thought of at all, and in terms other than those of migrations from Central Asia or the Hindu Kush. Lee, in his translation of Keller's *Lake Dwellings*, asserts confidently that Egypt was then generally considered the cradle of civilisation, while in 1907 George Massey, with equal confidence, called his book *Ancient Egypt: The Light of the World*—long before Elliot Smith accepted the Chair of Anatomy at Cairo.

The dethronement of Egypt by Mesopotamia as the home of civilisation began with the discovery of the Sumerians, was helped by the over-advocacy of Egypt as the cradle of all civilisation by Elliot Smith and Perry, and has continued as sites like Tell Hassunah have revealed the great antiquity of Mesopotamian prehistory, and as analyses like those of Mrs E. J. Baumgärtel have thrown doubts on the antiquity of the most ancient Egyptian "Neolithic" of Lower Egypt. Others, like Albright and Garstang, have emphasised the antiquity of the Palestinian Neolithic and Chalcolithic cultures, while Herzfeld has put in a claim for Iran as the home of the first food-producing economy. Attempts have been made to distinguish certain provinces among the first peasant village communities of the Near East. Myres distinguished his Red-Ware or Anatolian province as early as the first decade of the present century. Many have spoken of a painted-pottery culture or civilisation, but Frankfort demonstrated, as we have said, that this was an abstraction, and distinguished several styles and cultures within what he described as his Iranian or Highland culture. McCown, as we have seen, has made a subdivision of Frankfort's Highland culture into two groups, and

[1] *The Growth and Nature of Egyptology*, 1947, *passim*.
[2] *Archaeology*, 60.

it may be that detailed analysis on these and similar lines will eventually enable us to see the origins and growth of the peasant village communities in their proper perspectives. At present it remains true that we can still not give a complete picture of that great change in human history which Childe has described as the Neolithic Revolution.

But it does appear likely that some of the earliest peasant village sites may well be those in Syria, north Iraq and east Anatolia characterised by Neolithic burnished and incised wares, which Seton Williams has recently studied and mapped.[1] These Neolithic peasant villages were succeeded by the Chalcolithic cultures or civilisation, which with Frankfort we may classify into four groups: the Egyptian, the Anatolian-Transcaucasian (Myres's red-gourd ware group), the Syrian, and the Highland or Iranian,[2] and it is as part of these Chalcolithic economies that the city-states of the Near East came into being. With the city-states we move out of the zone of absolute prehistory and begin to deal with the literate civilisations of the Most Ancient East.

[1] M. V. Seton Williams, "Neolithic Burnished Wares in the Near East," *Iraq*, 1948, 34 ff.

[2] See Frankfort, *Archaeology and the Sumerian Problem* (Oriental Institute, Chicago, 1932); and *Studies in Early Pottery in the Near East* (Royal Anthropological Institute), 1924 and 1927.

CHAPTER SEVEN

EUROPEAN PREHISTORY: 1900–50

1. *Discovery*

THE first forty years of the twentieth century, from the point of view of European prehistory, is one of tremendous discovery and advance, and this despite the fact that the energies of most prehistorians and archaeologists were hampered or locked up in other pursuits during the war years of 1914–18 and 1939–45. The period was characterised, to use Georges Daux's phrase, by the "multiplication et extension des recherches".[1] A notable and brilliant attempt to summarise these researches early in the century was made by Joseph Déchelette in his great *Manuel d'Archéologie.* The first volume of this remarkable work, originally entitled *Manuel d'Archéologie Préhistorique, Celtique, et Gallo-romaine*, was published in 1908; it was the *préhistorique* part. Volume II, the *Celtique ou Protohistorique* part, came out in several volumes, the Bronze Age in 1910, Hallstatt in 1913 and the La Tène in 1915, with appendices in 1910 and 1913. Déchelette was killed early in the war in 1914, and his work completed by Albert Grenier. A more ambitious summary is the *Reallexikon der Vorgeschichte*, edited by Max Ebert, and published in Berlin between 1924–32 in fifteen volumes.

Another attempt to summarise the developments of European prehistory was begun after the 1914–18 War by Professor R. A. S. Macalister in his *Textbook of European Archaeology*, but this never got beyond the first volume, published in 1921, and dealing only with the Palaeolithic periods. No one has since attempted on the scale of Déchelette, or on the scale projected by Macalister, a summary and survey of European prehistory as a whole. Such a work is needed; indeed even general surveys of European prehistory are notably lacking. A number of surveys of the development of prehistoric archaeology to the beginning of the thirties

[1] *Les Étapes d'Archéologie*, chapter iv, *passim.*

was made under the auspices of the Römisch-Germanische Commission, among which that of Kendrick and Hawkes, republished in English as *Archaeology in England and Wales, 1914–31*, justly achieved great fame. We should also mention a survey of French archaeology published about the same time as part of the proceedings of the *Congrès Archéologique de France* in 1934, in which l'Abbé Breuil and R. Lantier summarised a century of archaeological work. After the 1939–45 War the Prehistoric Society of Great Britain has instituted a series of national surveys of archaeological progress. The nearest we get to general surveys of European archaeology are V. G. Childe's *Dawn of European Civilisation*, first published in 1925, and C. F. C. Hawkes's *Prehistoric Foundations of Europe* (1940). These two works cover mainly the period from the Mesolithic to the end of the second millennium B.C., but they give a remarkable indication of the extent and rapidity of prehistoric research when compared with, say, Déchelette, or, more properly, with de Mortillet's *Le Préhistorique* of 1903, and Rice Holmes's *Ancient Britain and the Invasion of Julius Caesar*—for Déchelette was in many things well ahead of his time.

While no general surveys of European prehistory exist, national surveys have been made which summarise our increased knowledge. In Spain there have been published three such summaries: Bosch-Gimpera's *Etnologia de la Peninsula Ibérica* (Barcelona, 1932), and the first volumes of the great histories of Spain edited by Pericot y Garcia and Ramon Menendez y Pidal.

In Denmark, Brøndsted's great *Danmarks Oldtid* (1938–40) is a monument of what is required in prehistoric archaeology, while in Britain we have been fortunate in several detailed surveys: for Scotland, Childe's *Prehistory of Scotland* (1935), for Ireland, Adolf Mahr's *New Aspects and Problems in Irish Prehistory*,[1] for Wales, R. E. M. Wheeler's *Prehistoric and Roman Wales* (1925) and Grimes's *Guide to the Collections illustrating the Prehistory of Wales* (1939), and for the British Isles, as a whole, Childe's *Prehistoric Communities of the British Isles* (1940). We should also mention here the German series of surveys, the *Handbuch der Urgeschichte Deutschlands*,[2] which have included Sprockhoff's *Die*

[1] *Proc. Preh. Soc.*, 1937, 261.

[2] Series edited by Ernst Sprockhoff and fourteen of the twenty to cover pre-Roman times.

nordische Megalithkultur (Berlin, 1938) and Buttler's *Der Donauländische und der Westische Kulturkreis der Jungeren Steinzeit* (1938).

We have already described the nineteenth-century disputes about Tertiary Man, which began with the St Prest discoveries of Desnoyers and the Abbé Bourgeois in the sixties and might be said to reach their height with de Mortillet's descriptions of *Anthropopithecus Bourgeoisii*, *Ramesii* and *Ribeiroii*—the makers of the eoliths. Claims and counterclaims of the authenticity of pre-Chellean artefacts punctuate the history of archaeology towards the end of the nineteenth century, and the eolithic controversy reached its height in the first two decades of the twentieth century. In 1894 Fritz Noetling discovered what he claimed as artefacts in Lower Pliocene beds at Yenang Yung in Burma. The most celebrated claims in the last quarter of the nineteenth century were, however, those of Benjamin Harrison, a village shopkeeper of Ightham in Kent, who, stimulated by Gilbert White's *Natural History of Selborne*, Lyell's *Principles of Geology* and Robert Chambers's *Vestiges of Creation*, and encouraged by Lubbock, Prestwich and Geikie, began to collect stone tools in Kent, especially in the plateau gravels. Here he found what are now referred to as Harrisonian eoliths. Rutot claimed these gravels as Pliocene; Prestwich and Wallace accepted the authenticity of the finds, and Geikie wrote to Harrison encouraging him in these words, that stone tools "will yet be found in such deposits and at such elevations as will cause the hairs of cautious archaeologists to rise on end". This is indeed what happened. Sir John Evans did not accept Harrison's finds; the eolithic controversy became like a repetition of the controversy over the authenticity of the finds of de Perthes and Pengelly. In 1895 Harrison gave an exhibition of his eoliths at the Royal Society; in a way it recalled the famous meeting in 1859.

But the acceptance of eoliths came more slowly than did that of Palaeolithic man. In 1907 de Munck and Rutot claimed to have found eoliths in Middle Oligocene beds at Boncelles, but a committee set up to study these claims rejected them and declared the Boncelles eoliths to be due to the pressure of overlying shifting strata. Many were much influenced in their views on the eolithic problem by the observations of Boule in *L'Anthropologie* for 1905. Laville, of the Paris School of Mines, drew the attention of Boule,

Cartailhac and Obermaier to the apparent "eoliths" made by cement-mixers at Mantes and he argued from this that all eoliths were natural, although Professor Verworn insisted that the Mantes pseudo-eoliths were quite different from those found *in situ* at Boncelles and by Harrison. Breuil, in another paper in *L'Anthropologie* in 1910, argued the natural origin of eoliths, and so did Hazzledine Warren in his paper in the *Quarterly Journal of the Geological Society* for 1921, in which he described naturally produced "eoliths" from the Eocene "Bull-head" bed at Grays, Essex.

The change in the general attitude to pre-Chellean man was brought about by the discoveries in East Anglia of pre-Crag man. In 1905 W. G. Clarke published artefacts from the Norwich Crag and the Red Crag of Suffolk, but the leading protagonist of pre-Crag man was J. Reid Moir, who worked at sites in the neighbourhood of Ipswich, and whose work is published in a wealth of papers, his *Pre-Palaeolithic Man* (Ipswich, 1919) and in his *Antiquity of Man in East Anglia* (1927). Sir E. Ray Lankester was a great protagonist of Moir's finds; he published in 1914 the test specimen of one of Moir's types, the so-called rostro-carinate, and said: "I am of the opinion that the probability that it was produced by human agency is so overwhelming as to constitute what is called 'certainty'."[1] At first, Boule and Breuil would not accept Moir's evidence, but in 1920 Breuil was convinced by the evidence at the Foxhall pit near Ipswich, and the following year, in the Congress at Liége, publicly accepted them. From that time pre-Crag man gradually won acceptance, and of Moir's work Kendrick has written: "it would be hard to name any one who has made such a memorable contribution to the study of English prehistory as that which is the fruit of his arduous and persistent labours".[2] This is not to mean that Moir's work has shown all eoliths to be humanly manufactured; he showed that *some* pre-Chellean tools undoubtedly can be recognised. It may well be that it will always be difficult to recognise the earliest humanly fashioned tools.

The first half of the twentieth century has seen the gradual elaboration of the simple succession of Palaeolithic cultures envisaged by de Mortillet. In this process of elaboration the

[1] *Royal Anthropological Institute Occasional Papers*, No. 4.
[2] Kendrick and Hawkes, *Archaeology in England and Wales*, 1914–31, p. 8.

name of the Abbé Breuil will always be associated, and it was his advocacy and authority that got the Chellean re-christened the Abbevillian. The Aurignacian had been reported by Lartet, but eventually left out of his and of de Mortillet's classifications. Dupont had felt the need of some such epoch to account for the material in the caves of Montaigle and Hastière in Belgium, and in 1912 Breuil, seconded by Cartailhac and Rutot, reintroduced the Aurignacian into the Palaeolithic succession. He also produced a complex subdivision of the Upper Palaeolithic which recognised three divisions of the Aurignacian and Solutrean and also six divisions of the Magdalenian. Meanwhile discoveries of Palaeolithic art have steadily increased. In the early years of the century there were still people who doubted the authenticity and antiquity of Palaeolithic art; as the discoveries continued, and were made available to the public, doubts began to disappear. The famous engravings and paintings of Combarelles and Font de Gaume were discovered in 1901 by Breuil, Capitan and Peyrony, and the story is one of continued discoveries leading to the truly great discovery of Lascaux in 1940 and the discoveries of Norbert Casteret and the Abbé Cathala in the Grotte de Fauzan in Hérault in 1948. Among the most famous discoveries in this long list are those of the Count Begouen and his sons at Tuc d'Audoubert in 1912 and at Trois Frères in 1914, and of Norbert Casteret at Montespan in 1923. Casteret's work, which has reached a wide public through his popular works such as *Ten Years under the Earth* (1934) and *My Caves* (1947), is an astonishing saga of ingenuity and endurance. Through the generosity of the Prince of Monaco, who founded the Institute of Human Palaeontology in Paris, a series of volumes has appeared describing the classic sites of the Cave Art of France and Spain. *La Caverne d'Altamira* was published in 1906–8 and *La Caverne de Font-de-Gaume* in 1910. Most of these works are chiefly due to Breuil.

Piette in 1895 had distinguished at Mas d'Azil two cultural horizons lying between the Magdalenian and Neolithic deposits, but for many years the recognition of these industries as neither Palaeolithic nor Neolithic but Mesolithic was confused by disputes regarding the *ancien hiatus*, and by suggestions of alternative names. Menghin wanted to group the Mesolithic industries with the Upper Palaeolithic industries and call them both Miolithic, while Obermaier proposed to distinguish the *epi-Palaeolithic*, in which he included the Azilian and the Tardenoisian, and the *proto-Neolithic*, which comprised the Campignian, Kitchen-Midden and Asturian cultures. The Mesolithic was clearly defined by Macalister in 1921 in his *Textbook of European Archaeology*, and was given definitive treatment by Grahame Clark in his two books, *The Mesolithic Age in Britain* (1932) and *The Mesolithic Cultures of Northern Europe* (1936). These books showed how far the knowledge of the Mesolithic had travelled since Piette's work at Mas d'Azil, or de Mortillet's recognition of the Tardenoisian in 1896, or Sarauw's excavations at Mullerup in 1900. The work of Schwantes and Rust completed the bridging of the *ancien hiatus*; in 1928 Schwantes recognised the significance of a flint industry found on surface sites at Ahrensburg, north-east of Hamburg, and in 1932 claimed a Hamburg culture contemporary with the late Magdalenian of France. Excavations such as those of Rust at Meiendorf and Stellmoor gave stratigraphical proof of the succession of these Mesolithic cultures.

Our knowledge of the Neolithic cultures of Europe by the beginning of the twentieth century was derived largely from the work in the Swiss lake dwellings, and in the bogs and megalithic tombs of northern Europe, and from the upward extension of Palaeolithic and Mesolithic studies in western Europe. A surer knowledge of Neolithic and Chalcolithic cultures began with the extension of excavation and comparative archaeology in south-east Europe. Tsountas excavated the stratified mound of Sesklo in Greece in 1901, and, two years later, the neighbouring mound of Dimini — a site already deserted when a Mycenaean tomb was constructed in the side of it. Tsountas's discoveries were published in his *Prehistoric Acropolis of Dimini and Sesklo* (1908). Other discoveries were being made in similar mounds; these, as well as the pioneer researches of Tsountas, were summarised for English readers in Wace and Thompson's book *Prehistoric Thessaly* (1912). The Neolithic cultures at Sesklo and Dimini were characterised by painted pottery; other painted-pottery cultures were being studied at the same time in Rumania and the Ukraine. As long ago as 1889 a Rumanian, by name Butureanu, had dug a painted-pottery Neolithic settlement at Cucuteni near Jassy; this was the first of many such sites to be studied, including Laszlo's work on Erosd, published in 1914. At the same time as these painted-pottery cultures of south-east Europe were being studied other work was revealing a non-painted-pottery Neolithic culture—that now known as the Danubian—between south-east Europe and the Rhine. In 1902 Vassits began work at a Danubian site at Jablaniča, in the Morava valley, and soon after began work on the classic Danubian site of Vinča, near Belgrade.

The comparative study of these sites developed as excavation proceeded. In 1903 Schmidt was able to study the painted-pottery cultures in general, though his own detailed publication of Cucuteni did not appear until 1932. The knowledge of these Neolithic cultures became available in Britain mainly through the writings of Gordon Childe, first in his study of the site of Schipenitz,[1] and then in his *Danube in Prehistory* and his *Dawn*. This knowledge has become intensified by the classic excavations of Danubian sites at the Goldberg and Koln-Lindenthal.

Our knowledge of Neolithic cultures in Atlantic Europe lagged behind the developments in south-eastern Europe, and was largely complicated by the collective tombs which have been interpreted in a wider variety of ways than have even most archaeological facts. Out of the welter of megalithic controversies, and due largely to stratigraphical analysis like that of Héléna at Narbonne, and Vouga in Switzerland, and to the painstaking regional surveys of collective tombs such as those of the Leisners in Iberia, Le Rouzic in Brittany and van Giffen in Holland, we are now beginning to distinguish the various cultural elements that made up the Neolithic/Chalcolithic cultures of western Europe. If we must put a date on these beginnings it should be 1913, when Schuchhardt distinguished his *beutelstil* or leathery pottery in western Europe [2]—the ceramic which Poisson called *le style de bourse*,[3] Peake bag-ware,[4] and is now generally known as Western Neolithic pottery. The second great step forward in our understanding of the Western cultures was the putting forward by Fleure, Peake and Forde in 1930 [5] of an alternative explanation of the Iberian megalithic tombs which linked the western Neolithic

[1] "Schipenitz: A Late Neolithic Station with painted pottery in Bukowina," *Journal of the Royal Anthropological Institute*, 1923, 263.

[2] *Westeuropa als alter Kulturkreis* (1913) and *Alteuropa in seiner Kultur und Stilentwicklung* (1919).

[3] Poisson, *Les Civilisations Néolithiques et Énéolithiques de la France* (1928).

[4] H. J. E. Peake, "Some problems of the New Stone Age," *Manchester Memoirs*, 1937, 37.

[5] Fleure and Peake, "Megaliths and Beakers," *Journal of the Royal Anthropological Institute*, 1930, 47; Forde, "Early Cultures of Atlantic Europe," *American Anthropologist*, 1930, 19.

cultures with those of the east Mediterranean in a way that was not possible according to the then orthodox typologies advocated by Cartailhac, Leeds and Bosch-Gimpera.

The Neolithic period in Britain remained until 1923, as Fox has said, "an ill-defined dumping ground for stone implements (other than Palaeolithic and Mesolithic) not known by clear-cut associations with datable grave deposits to be of the early metal age".[1] Light had been thrown on British Neolithic industries by Schuchhardt's recognition of the *beutelstil* in 1913. Menghin and Kendrick noted that there were two distinct ceramics in Neolithic Britain, only one of which was the *beutelstil*, which Menghin called Grimstonkeramik and Kendrick Wexcombe ware, and the other a coarser, heavily decorated fabric which was called Peterborough ware.[2] These distinctions were made clear by Leeds,[3] and the distinction was set out definitively in Piggott's *The Neolithic Pottery of the British Isles* in 1932.[4] As the relation of the Windmill Hill people to the megalithic tombs was studied it became clear that there was a third, Atlantic, element in the British Neolithic, and now we see that even the division into three cultural elements—a southern or Windmill Hill, an eastern or Peterborough, and a western Atlantic or Megalithic—is not sufficiently complicated. The Atlantic element probably consisted of at least four groups, the Carlingford group, the Boyne group, the Scilly group, and the Severn-Cotswold group[5] while the eastern group is complicated by rusticated and grooved-ware groups, and Piggott proposes to distinguish separate groups in the Windmill Hill culture. So that the Neolithic, from being an ill-defined "epoch", has become a series of roughly contemporary cultural patterns.

Northern European archaeologists have for long been content to interpret the Neolithic period there in terms of Montelius's four periods, except that doubts have been cast on the validity of his period I. The Montelian periods were rendered difficult to use because of their very close linkage in typology and name with the various classes of collective tombs. Recent work in northern

[1] *Cambridge Historical Journal*, 1947, p. 1.
[2] Kendrick, *The Axe Age* (1925); Menghin, appendix to third edition of M. Hoernes's *Urgeschichte der bildenden Kunst in Europa* (1925).
[3] E. T. Leeds, *Antiquaries' Journal*, 1927, 459.
[4] *Archaeological Journal*, 1932, 90.
[5] See Daniel, *The Prehistoric Chamber Tombs of England and Wales* (1950).

Europe, notably the excavation of settlement sites such as Trøldebjerg, Blandebjerg, Trelleborg, Bundsø and Lindø, has enabled a fresh evaluation of northern Neolithic cultures to be made into a framework of Early, Middle and Late Neolithic and the old bogy of the collective tombs in northern Europe to be laid at last.[1]

It would be impossible to chronicle here the immensely important discoveries of the Bronze Age and Early Iron Age made in Europe in the last fifty years. In England alone Abercromby's *Bronze Age Pottery of Great Britain and Ireland* (1912) began a new era in the study of our Bronze Age, which continued with the work of Fox on bronze implements and weapons and the distributional and comparative studies of Grimes, Crawford and Piggott. Among the many excavations which have added enormously to our knowledge of the pre-Roman Iron Age in Britain should be mentioned those of Bulleid and Gray at the Glastonbury and Meare lake villages, that of Wheeler at Maiden Castle, of Hawkes at Colchester, of the Cunningtons at All Cannings Cross, and of the Prehistoric Society under Dr Bersu at Little Woodbury.

2. *Interpretation*

We have seen that nineteenth-century archaeologists had been building up their discoveries into a picture which was essentially geological in outlook it treated artifacts as though they were zone fossils, and divided man's prehistoric past into epochs or ages characterised by assemblages of these zone fossils. It is often difficult, in reading the works of the late nineteenth-century archaeologists, or looking at tables such as those which de Mortillet printed with increasing complexity in the successive editions of *Le Préhistorique*, to understand clearly what they envisaged by these successions.[2] It is clear, however, that many did not bother to think at all, and were satisfied with the successions without attempting to understand them in terms of human development—and in this acquiescence the geological background must be remembered. When they were specific in trying to explain the prehistoric sequences, the late nineteenth-century

[1] For a summary of recent research in Northern Europe see Childe, *The Culture-Sequence in the Northern Stone Age*, Fourth Annual Report of Institute of Archaeology, University of London (1948).

[2] An example of one of de Mortillet's tables is given here (p. 237).

TEMPS		AGES	PÉRIODES	ÉPOQUES
Quaternaires actuels.	Historiques.	du Fer.	Mérovingienne.	Wabenienne. (*Waben, Pas-de-Calais.*)
			Romaine.	Champdolienne. (*Champdolent, Seine-et-Oise.*)
				Lugdunienne. (*Lyon, Rhône.*)
	Protohistoriques.		Galatienne.	Beuvraysienne. (*Mont-Beuvray, Nièvre.*)
				Marnienne. (*Département de la Marne.*)
				Hallstattienne. (*Hallstatt, haute Autriche.*)
		du Bronze.	Tsiganienne.	Larnaudienne. (*Larnaud, Jura.*)
				Morgienne. (*Morges, canton de Vaud, Suisse.*)
	Préhistoriques.	de la Pierre.	Néolithique.	Robenhausienne. (*Robenhausen, Zurich.*)
				Campignyenne. (*Campigny, Seine-Inférieure.*)
				Tardenoisienne (*Fère-en-Tardenois, Aisne.*)
Quaternaires anciens.			Paléolithique.	Tourassienne. (*La Tourasse, Haute-Garonne.*) Ancien Hiatus.
				Magdalénienne. (*La Madeleine, Dordogne.*)
				Solutréenne. (*Solutré, Saône-et-Loire.*)
				Moustérienne. (*Le Moustier, Dordogne.*)
				Acheuléenne. (*Saint-Acheul, Somme.*)
				Chelléenne. (*Chelles, Seine-et-Marne.*)
Tertiaires.			Éolithique.	Puycournienne. (*Puy-Courny, Cantal.*)
				Thenaysienne. (*Thenay, Loir-et-Cher.*)

Fig. 4. The Epochs of Prehistory according to G. de Mortillet. After *Formation de la Nation Française* (1897).

archaeologists adopted an evolutionary or a diffusionist point of view, or attempted to embrace them both.

The point of view which has unfortunately been called the evolutionary view of prehistory suggests that the archaeological sequences betoken parallel development throughout the world, that, in Peake's words, "most people had automatically passed through successive stages of culture, and that each had somehow learned the arts of agriculture, pot-making and metallurgy, as soon as their intellectual condition had fitted them to make use of these industries". This view, the view of the psychic unity of man, was a current one in anthropology and archaeology for a long time in the nineteenth century. It did seem at first sight to be the logical development of the holding of evolutionary views: man's cultural development was considered as an extension of man's physical development.

Against this point of view stood the "invasion" or "influence" archaeologists. With a more historical and less geological sense of man, they saw that changes in culture in historical times were often due to the arrival of new people, and postulated similar invasions and movements of people in prehistoric times to account for sudden changes in the archaeological record. They were frankly diffusionists. It has been argued that the doctrines of diffusion in prehistory are due to Schmidt and Elliot Smith, or to borrowings from anthropology. Nothing could be further from the truth. The early Scandinavian archaeologists like Thomsen, Worsaae and Nilsson were all, in their way, as we have said earlier, diffusionists, and thought of northern prehistory in terms of invasions from Asia. And of course the last decades of the nineteenth century were much concerned with the interrelations of western Europe and the Aegean area in terms of cultural origins and priorities. We have already mentioned the battle between the slogans "Ex Oriente Lux" and "Le Mirage Oriental"; the protagonists of both schools were diffusionists. What interests us here is not whether the Eastern or the Western school was right, but the implications of the acceptance of diffusion as the mechanics of culture change in prehistoric times. If man's culture had changed by the diffusion of trade, ideas, or people, then cultures apparently the same need not necessarily have flourished at the same time all over the world. Geology had got over this difficulty by describing geological sequences in different parts of the world as homotaxial, and, as, we have seen, Morgan tried to import the idea of homotaxy into prehistory.[1] It would not work; the time and the condition *are* material in prehistory and if the same conditions, to go on using Morgan's words, flourish at different times, then these conditions define not periods of time but varieties of human culture, and different varieties may coexist. In brief, the epochs of the late nineteenth-century archaeologists were not epochs, but local varieties in the development of man's culture. Boyd Dawkins, Morselli, Bertrand and others had already seen this, but most did not appear to realise that the acceptance of diffusion was in itself the negation of the epochal idea.

In the first half of the twentieth century four things contributed to the general realisation that the epochal idea was dead. The first was the demonstration, not the inference, of the contemporaneity of the alleged periods or epochs. The second was the extension of prehistoric research first to eastern Europe and Africa, and then, all over the world. The third was the new orientation which archaeological studies received in the early twentieth century from human geography and anthropology. And the fourth was the marrying together of Near-Eastern and Aegean archaeology with European prehistory.

In 1909 in the Grotte de Valle, near Gibaja (Santander), in North Spain, Breuil and Obermaier discovered a classic Azilian deposit together with microlithic flints of the typical geometric Tardenoisian form. "After this discovery", as Osborn said, "it could no longer be questioned that the Azilian and Tardenoisian were contemporary." What was true for the Mesolithic, namely the contemporaneity of several of the supposed "epochs", appeared also to be true as each of the other great "stages" of human culture was studied. In the Lower and Middle Palaeolithic detailed studies revealed many industries instead of the simple succession Chellean (or Abbevillian), Acheulian, Mousterian. Breuil's great paper of 1912[2] foreshadowed the break-up of the old epochal system of the Palaeolithic as described by de Mortillet, although it seemed at the same time to be the final elaboration of that scheme. Four years later Obermaier was

[1] On homotaxy, see Huxley's Anniversary Address to the Geological Society for 1862 and for 1870.

[2] "Les Subdivisions du Paléolithique supérieur et leur Signification," *Comptes Rendus du Congrès International d'Anthropologie et d'Archéologie préhistoriques*, Geneva, 1912; a second edition was produced in 1937.

distinguishing between flake and tool industries existing contemporaneously side by side in the Palaeolithic, and his ideas were taken up, notably by Baer and Menghin.[1] As Breuil extended his first-hand knowledge of the European palaeolithic industries to eastern Europe he was converted to the idea of contemporary groups rather than successive epochs; his paper *Voyage Paléolithique en L'Europe çentrale*[2] is a landmark in this process of conversion. His paper on Levallois flakes in *Man* for 1926 marks the complete conversion, as does Garrod's presidential address to the Prehistoric Society of East Anglia in 1928.[3] Five years later de Mortillet's ideas had disappeared from the English textbooks, and works like Burkitt's *Old Stone Age* and Leakey's *Adam's Ancestors* were speaking in terms of these new ideas, while Breuil was distinguishing three cultural groups among the Lower Palaeolithic flake industries: the Clactonian with the Languedocian (a prolonged Clactonian), the Levalloisian, and the Tayacian, or Tayo-Mousterian.[4] In the Upper Palaeolithic of France, instead of the simple succession Aurignacian, Solutrean and Magdalenian, similar contemporaneous industries have been distinguished. Peyrony, carrying on the work of Breuil, grouped the Lower and Upper Aurignacian together into the Perigordian, re-defining the Aurignacian as the old Middle Aurignacian, and arguing that Aurignacian *sensu novo* and Perigordian were contemporary in south France. Peyrony's thesis has been modified by Garrod, who distinguishes a Chatelperronian (old Lower Aurignacian) and a Gravettian (old Upper Aurignacian) in his Perigordian, while agreeing on the contemporaneity of certain phases of the old Aurignacian.[5]

In studying the Neolithic, Capitan distinguished five groups —the old European Neolithic, the Nordic, the Campignian, the Megalithic and the Lake Dwelling, and did not regard these as successive epochs but as roughly contemporary phases of culture. In northern Europe Sophus Müller distinguished several contemporaneous industries in the Neolithic instead of the four

[1] See Appendix to the third edition of Hoernes's *Urgeschichte der bildenden Kunst* (1925).

[2] *L'Anthropologie*, XXXIII and XXXIV.

[3] *Proc. Preh. Soc. East Anglia*, V, 260.

[4] "Les Industries à éclats du Paléolithique ancien," *Préhistoire*, 1932, 125.

[5] Garrod, "The Upper Palaeolithic in the Light of Recent Discovery," *Proc. Preh. Soc.*, 1938, 1; Peyrony, "Les Industries Aurignaciennes dans le Bassin de la Vézère," *Bulletin de la Société Préhistorique Française*, 1933.

successive phases of Montelius's sequence, and we have seen how different culture groups were distinguished in the British Neolithic.

The breakdown of the Bronze Age from an epochal into a cultural basis has taken much longer, due to the impressive typological sequences which had been built up by Montelius and Sophus Müller, and the way in which these had been built up into a rigid framework of reference by such men as Kossinna and Hubert Schmidt. That these rigid typological sequences and the epochal inferences made from them was only a method of studying the material, rather than the discovery of historical facts, had been hinted at by Chantre in his suggested Uralian, Danubian and Mediterranean provinces of the Bronze Age. As detailed studies of Bronze Age material proceeded, the contemporaneity of different cultures became clear; Déchelette in France, Böhm, Reinecke, Schwantes and Sprockhoff in Germany, Fox in Britain, and Broholm and Forssander in Scandinavia demonstrated the coexistence of distinct cultures or groups of objects, and this was most clearly argued in Childe's *The Danube in Prehistory* (1929) and Åberg's great *Bronzezeitliche und früheisenzeitliche Chronologie* (1930–35).

The terms Hallstatt and La Tène had really always defined cultures and not epochs, but it was not until the twentieth century that it was clearly understood they were not merely periods of the Iron Age but cultures or civilisations. When C. F. C. Hawkes began studying the Iron Age in southern Britain he found that a division into subdivisions of the Hallstatt and La Tène "periods" was valueless, and was forced to introduce a fresh classification into Iron Age A, Iron Age B and Iron Age C—a classification which cut across the epochal idea and defined contemporary and overlapping cultures.[1]

These examples must suffice to show how detailed archaeological researches in a small area like southern France in the Palaeolithic, or Denmark in the Neolithic, or Britain in the Early Iron Age revealed a complex of cultural development which could not be dealt with only in a temporal sequence but by the recognition of an idea which was both temporal and geographical—the idea of a culture. The same lesson was taught by the application

[1] See Hawkes, "Hill Forts," *Antiquity*, 1931, 60 ff., and in Kendrick and Hawkes, *Archaeology in England and Wales, 1914–31*, chapter x.

of the geographical method with its detailed distribution maps of types, and by the extension of researches all over Europe and, gradually, all over the world. At first, attempts were made to find everywhere the same cultural sequence as had been worked out for western Europe, but gradually it became clear that, everywhere, the archaeologist was dealing with a sequence of cultures, not of cultural epochs, that each culture had a spatial as well as a temporal significance, and that the same sequence could not be expected even in areas very close together.

These purely archaeological lessons were driven home by the acceptance in archaeology of ideas derived from the new studies of human geography and anthropology. The anthropogeographers and anthropologists began to study the regional differentiations of material, moral and mental culture as they appeared among modern primitives and to explain these differences in terms of cultural diffusions. Ratzel's *Völkerkunde* was published in 1885–88, and his *Anthropo-Geographie* appeared during the period 1882–91; he clearly distinguished what he called "cultural complexes". Ratzel's pupil, Leo Frobenius, developed this idea into what he called the "geographical-statistical method" and worked out "culture-circles" in West Africa and in Melanesia in the last few years of the nineteenth century. The ideas of Ratzel and Frobenius were developed and extended in the first quarter of the twentieth century by German ethnologists such as Graebner, Schmidt, Foy, Lips and Ankermann into a complicated study of culture areas and culture strata. It is not our concern here to trace this development, which, through the more moderate working of the culture area idea in the hands of Boas and Wissler, may have a great deal to contribute to the detailed analysis of prehistoric archaeology; what was important in the early years of this century was that the general idea of cultures and cultural diffusion as set out by the German ethnologists was taken over by prehistoric archaeologists, and in the light of the Kulturkreis school they were able to interpret the spatially and temporally differentiated units which were appearing in the archaeological record. These constructs—so different from the geological epochs—they identified with the cultural complexes of Ratzel and Frobenius.

Finally the old epochal idea of prehistory was destroyed when prehistorians working in western and northern Europe absorbed the new approach to archaeological methodology which had developed in the Aegean and the Near East. When Schliemann had studied the archaeological remains he had discovered he did not nominate them with reference to some epoch of the Stone or Bronze Age; he just boldly called them Mycenaean. And in east Mediterranean archaeology the names Aegean, Mycenaean and Minoan, Helladic and Cycladic were being used not for periods, but for civilisations. What distinguished the "civilisations" of the Aegean and the Near East from the "epochs" of western and northern Europe prehistorians except the degree of complexity of their material remains? Were the epochs, now demonstrated anyway to be in many cases contemporary, really no more than types of civilisations? Should not prehistory then follow the examples of Schliemann and Sir Arthur Evans, abandon the three-age system, and refer instead to the Mousterian Civilisation, the Hallstatt Civilisation, and so forth? Some of these usages have remained and the immediately pre-Roman Celts are often described as possessing the La Tène Civilisation. But others felt chary of boldly using the word "civilisation" for the remains of people who were savage and barbarian, and would like to reserve the word civilisation for literate societies. We see this difficulty being met and resolved in Pumpelly's excavations at Anau, where he deliberately introduces the word culture for the levels of archaeological occupation recognised. "To avoid misunderstanding," wrote Pumpelly in 1908, ". . . it may be added that the word *cultures* is used as a synonym for *civilisation* and that the term culture-strata (Kulturschichte of the Germans) stands for the débris slowly accumulated during occupation of an inhabited site."[1]

These four things, in the first quarter of the nineteenth century, turned prehistory in Europe from a study of the epochs of man's development to the description of his cultures—his "barbaric" civilisations, to use an Irishism. It was a complete re-orientation of prehistoric material and marked the change from the study of man as an animal to the study of him as a human being. It was, in a word, the change from the geological to the historical and anthropological attitude to prehistoric man. Of course the old epochal idea of prehistory died hard. It was flourishing in the great textbooks of prehistory which were published in the early

[1] *Explorations in Turkestan: Expedition of 1904*, p. xxxv.

years of the twentieth century, such as Macalister's *Textbook of European Archaeology* (1921), H. F. Osborn's *Men of the Old Stone Age* (1918), MacCurdy's *Human Origins* (1924) and Burkitt's *Prehistory* (1921). Osborn, in his textbook, paid very especial attention to the sequence at Castillo, which he said "affords a unique and almost complete sequence of the industries of the entire Old Stone Age", and added, "these stages, at first regarded as single, have each been subdivided into three or more substages, as a result of the more refined appreciation of the subtle advances in Palaeolithic invention and technique". That was the key-note of the old epochal idea—that man's cultural development could be represented as a single sequence, and read in a cave section, just as the geological sequence could be read in a deep cutting through the sedimentary rocks. Reproduced opposite is the great master table printed by MacCurdy in his textbook. It must serve as a milestone in the development of prehistory. It is, in a way, the logical development of the tables of De Mortillet, one of which has been reproduced above (p. 237). But there is this great difference between the work of Gabriel de Mortillet and the tables of MacCurdy and Osborn: de Mortillet represented orthodox prehistory, and there were only a few who protested then at the epochal subdivisions. *Human Origins* and *Men of the Old Stone Age*, on the other hand, were already, in a way, out of date when they were published; with great erudition they were built up on a scaffolding which was already being destroyed by that very erudition they displayed. It is curious to reflect now that only eight years separates MacCurdy's *Human Origins* from *A Chronological Table of Prehistory*, produced by Childe and Burkitt in 1932, and ably demonstrating the realisation of the culture - civilisation approach to prehistoric archaeology. The change from the geological to the historical and anthropological approach to prehistory can be seen in the writings of one man, if we compare M. C. Burkitt's *Prehistory* (1921) with his *The Old Stone Age* published twelve years later, in 1933. And to put a finer point on the change in prehistory that was taking place we might think only of the year 1924–25, which saw the publication of both MacCurdy's *Human Origins* and Gordon Childe's *The Dawn of European Civilisation:* and if we want to think of beginnings, rather than achievement, we should think of the year 1913, which saw Reinach's *Répertoire de l'Art Quaternaire* and

Era	Age	Stage	Culture	Subdivision	Characteristics
RECENT	*Iron Age*		La Tène	III	100–Christian era
				II	300–100 B.C.
				I	500–300 B.C.
			Hallstatt	II	Antennae swords and poniards
				I	Long swords of both bronze and iron
	Bronze Age			IV	Winged and end-socket axes
				III	Axes with transverse ridges
				II	Plain-border axes
				I	Flat axes
	Stone Age	*Neolithic*	Carnacian		Stone cist Many-chambered dolmen Small dolmen
			Robenhausian		Polished flint implements
			Campignian		Pottery
			Maglemosean		
			Azilian-Tardenoisian		Painted pebbles, harpoons of staghorn
QUATERNARY (*Pleistocene*)		*Paleolithic*	Magdalenian	VI V IV	Evolution of harpoon of reindeer horn; Polychrome frescoes
				III	
				II	Evolution of the javelin
				I	
			Solutrean	Upper	Point with lateral notch at base
				Middle	Laurel-leaf point
				Lower	Font-Robert point
			Aurignacian	Upper Middle Lower	Art Graver (*burin*); Scratcher (*grattoir*)
					Transition
			Mousterian	Upper Lower	Evolution of the cleaver (*coup de poing*) and scraper (*racloir*)
			Acheulian	Upper Lower	
			Chellean	Upper Lower	
			Pre-Chellean		**Transition**
TERTIARY		*Eolithic*			Utilization of natural flint flakes; first attempts at artificial production

FIG. 5. G. C. MacCurdy's table, "The Chronology of Prehistory," printed in his *Human Origins: A Manual of Prehistory* (1924), vol. i, p. 27.

Schuchhardt's *Westeuropa als alter Kulturkreis.* Reinach was content to interpret prehistory in the strict epochs of de Mortillet; Schuchhardt had already seen that the periods had to be replaced by an interpretation of European prehistory in terms of the Kulturkreislehre.

There is sometimes a tendency to regard the idea of culture in prehistoric archaeology as the final discovery of archaeological methodology, yet it may prove to be merely a conceptual tool, as were the epochs. Indeed it may well be that the organisation of prehistory into epochs characterises the geological attitude to prehistory, the organisation of prehistory into cultures, the anthropological attitude to prehistory, and that, in our new historical attitude to prehistory, we shall be content with historical contexts and culture rather than epochs and cultures. Recently American scholars have criticised very sharply the easy way in which Old World prehistorians invent and multiply "cultures". Braidwood speaks of "the confusion of terms which exists in Old World prehistory" and says "it is high time for a house-cleaning in the terminology of Old World prehistory".[1] Braidwood and Taylor, more recently,[2] plead that the word culture should be restricted to its current usage in the social sciences, and that the archaeologist should call what are only assemblages of artefacts by other names. There is much justice in this criticism for, as Braidwood says, the "Chellean culture" is no more than "a single flint type tool and various 'atypical' flint flakes".[3] Americanist archaeologists dealing with pre-contact times have recently devised two different systems of prehistoric nomenclature; one is that of Gladwin, who distinguishes "roots", "stems", "branches" and "phases",[4] the other is the McKern taxonomic system, which deals with "patterns", "phases", "aspects", "foci" and "components".[5] These systems may not gain wide acceptance in Old World prehistory, but their very existence shows the need for a new vocabulary and a new taxonomy in prehistoric archaeology.

But this is no place for an analysis of the concept of culture in

[1] *American Journal of Semitic Languages and Literatures*, January, 1945.

[2] W. W. Taylor, *A Study of Archaeology*.

[3] *Op. cit.*

[4] W. W. and H. S. Gladwin, "A Method for the Designation of Cultures and their Variations," *Globe*, Arizona, 1934.

[5] J. B. Griffin, *The Fort Ancient Aspect* (Ann Arbor, 1943).

prehistoric archaeology. We are here concerned only in chronicling how the idea of cultures entered prehistory, and there is no doubt that it was Childe's *Dawn of European Civilisation* that did most in English to popularise this new approach to prehistory. Gordon Childe's *Dawn* was not merely a book of incomparable archaeological erudition but it provided a new starting-point for prehistoric archaeology. To it, and to the volumes of *The Corridors of Time*, produced by H. J. Fleure and H. J. E. Peake from 1927 onwards, the prehistorians of Europe in the middle of the twentieth century must ever look back, as they also look back to Sir John Myres's chapters in volume one of the *Cambridge Ancient History* (1923), as bridging the gap between the two prehistories.

The older European prehistory of the first quarter of the twentieth century was the outgrowth of the geological-epochal treatment of de Mortillet and the French school, and of the typological treatment of Montelius, Sophus Müller and the Scandinavian school. It was characterised by an uneasy marriage of geological and historical concepts, and this was natural in a subject like prehistoric archaeology, which had grown up from the twin roots of natural science and human history. We have already discussed the dominance of the epochal idea, and how this older concept of prehistory was prepared to modify this idea slightly on a regional basis. We have discussed, too, the unwillingness to face up to the mechanics of prehistoric culture change, an unwillingness which, when it was overcome by a belief in diffusion, went to violent extremes. One of these extremes was the school of Egyptocentric hyperdiffusionists started by Sir Grafton Elliot Smith and developed by his disciples, such as Perry. This Manchester school of hyperdiffusionists saw all culture, European and otherwise, as the result of the spread from Egypt of the Children of the Sun in their search for Givers of Life. The spread of this Archaic Egyptian culture or the Heliolithic Culture-Complex, as it was called, was argued by Elliot Smith from 1911 onwards, being set out most clearly in Elliot Smith's *The Migrations of Early Culture* (1915) and his *Human History* (1929) and in Perry's *The Children of the Sun* (1923).

Another extreme was the attempt to identify prehistoric movements and migrations with the spreads postulated by a comparative study of language or the occurrence of racial types.

The early writings of H. J. Fleure may be taken as typical of the attempt to equate physical groupings with archaeological facts, an attempt which springs from the work of Sergi, Denniker and Ripley. As good examples of the attempts to equate linguistic groupings with archaeological facts we may take the work of Sir John Rhŷs in Britain, or Randall McIver in Italy. The problem had changed since the days of Isaac Taylor and Max Müller; it was now no longer "who were the Aryans?"—although this question has retained a fine fascination for many protohistorians—the problem was now the detailed identification of Aryan languages with archaeological groups. Was Q-Celtic introduced by the Beaker folk at the end of the Bronze Age, and were the Brythons the Late Bronze Age invaders or the Hallstatt folk or the La Tène folk? And who introduced the Italic dialects into Italy—the Bronze Age *terramaricoli* as Pigorini, Colini and Peet held, or the Villanovans as MacIver and Von Duhn argued?

The new European prehistory which we see coming into being in the mid-twenties of the present century was, quite frankly, not geological in outlook. It used geology as a framework for the relative and absolute chronology of its cultural sequence but it conceived its sequence in terms of historical and anthropological concepts, in terms of civilisations and of cultures. It was, moreover, mainly diffusionist in outlook. Childe, in the *Dawn of European Civilisation* (1925) and in *The Danube in Prehistory* (1929), and Peake and Fleure in their *Corridors of Time* argued convincingly a moderate case for diffusionism which at once resolved the late nineteenth-century dispute between Orientalists and Occidentalists, and banished the doubts raised by the Manchester Egyptophiles. It was, too, characterised by a deliberate eschewal of linguistic and anthropological equations: no longer were archaeologists harassing themselves with the largely insoluble problems as to whether the Sicanians were the Neolithic people of Stentinello and Molfetta and the Siculans the collective tomb builders of Siculan I, or twisting their scholarship to answer insoluble questions about P- and Q-Celts which should never have been asked. And the spread of long heads and round heads into Britain became a matter of such minor importance to the archaeologist as would have shocked Rice Holmes and horrified Thurnam and Beddoes.

The new prehistory of the twenties shared nothing of the

geological epochal outlook of the older prehistory, but it had one great methodological device in common: both schemes of prehistory were built up on the framework of Thomsen's three ages as modified into Lower and Middle Palaeolithic, Upper Palaeolithic, Mesolithic, Neolithic, Bronze and Early Iron ages. Yet, although built around this framework, the new prehistory was demonstrating its uselessness.[1] In the first place, cultures which were formally Neolithic and those that were formally Bronze Age or Mesolithic appeared to coexist in small areas of Europe, and the transition lines between these three ages were blurred geographically and chronologically. Perhaps the most disturbing idea in the new prehistory was the thought that in northern and north-western Europe the Neolithic cultures might be, in fact, impoverished versions of Bronze Age cultures in the Mediterranean and Near East. This was argued cogently by Peake, Fleure and Forde in relation to the collective tombs of Iberia and is now a commonplace of current archaeological thought. It meant that the word Neolithic was used for several stages of culture; that it was in fact a relative term, and not an absolute stage in the development of all kinds of men. This lesson from European prehistory was also learnt when the prehistoric sequence outside Europe was squeezed into the development of the three-age framework.

There can be no doubt that the new prehistory realised the terms Palaeolithic, Mesolithic, Neolithic and so forth were ambiguous; to say the least of it they were used as denoting either chronological divisions or cultural stages. How was this ambiguity to be resolved? Some writers have suggested abandoning the three-age system. T. D. Kendrick, in his *The Axe Age* (1925), proposed the term "the Eochalcic Episode" for the periods of British prehistory usually known as Neolithic and Early Bronze ages, and both Childe in his *Dawn* and Hawkes in his *Prehistoric Foundations of Europe* (1940) emphasise the unity of the period from the introduction of agriculture to the fall of Knossos in European prehistory, while Peake would divide the corn-growing time of man's life in Europe into three great periods, the first of which lasted from the beginning of the Neolithic to the end of the Middle Bronze Age.[2] Menghin in his *Weltgeschichte der Steinzeit*

[1] For a discussion of this point see Childe, "Changing Methods and Aims in Prehistory," *Proc. Prehistoric Soc.*, 1935, 1 ff.; and Daniel, *The Three Ages* (1943).

[2] *Journal of the Royal Anthropological Institute*, 1940, 26.

(1931) proposed to group the Upper Palaeolithic and Mesolithic to form what he called the Miolithic, calling all that went before the Protolithic. And Jacques de Morgan had realised the break that existed between the Lower and Middle Palaeolithic on the one hand and the Upper Palaeolithic on the other by proposing

<table>
<tr><td>Early Iron Age
La Tène
Hallstatt</td><td rowspan="2">Full Prehistoric
Metal Age</td></tr>
<tr><td>Bronze Age
Late
Middle
Early</td></tr>
<tr><td>Chalcolithic</td><td rowspan="2">Eochalcic Episode
or Age</td></tr>
<tr><td>Neolithic</td></tr>
<tr><td>Mesolithic</td><td>Miolithic</td></tr>
<tr><td>Palaeolithic
Upper
Middle
Lower</td><td>Protolithic</td></tr>
</table>

FIG. 6. Diagram to illustrate the proposed reclassifications of Menghin and Kendrick. Reproduced from Daniel, *The Three Ages* (1943), 52.

to restrict the term Palaeolithic for all that went before the Upper Palaeolithic, and substituting Archaeolithic for what was Upper Palaeolithic.[1] In the accompanying table are set out diagrammatically the proposals of Menghin and Kendrick, compared with the framework of the older prehistory. They form as significant a grouping of human cultures as, or indeed a more significant grouping than, the left-hand column.

Other writers, while unwilling to abandon the three-age

[1] The term Archaeolithic is often used in France at the present day for the Upper Palaeolithic and Mesolithic industries.

system, realise its great limitations in the present state of European prehistory. Childe, in his Huxley Lecture for 1944, *Archaeological Ages as Technological Stages*, proposes that we abandon the use of the three-age derivative labels as chronological indications, and use them as technological stages only. But are they technological stages?

It does not seem likely that the three ages, reduced to the status of doubtful technological stages, will stay on in European prehistory. Over a hundred years ago they provided the only ray of light which enabled archaeology to develop out of mere antiquarianism. They were intellectual constructs which for a long time served as the greatest value in prehistory. Now their usefulness is probably over, and soon they will stand in the same relation to the mid-twentieth-century prehistoric scholarship as did the old labels "Ancient British" and "Gothic" to the "new" prehistory of Worsaae and Nilsson. To replace them we need not only the grouping into cultures which is the new face of prehistory, but also a new vocabulary and an objective chronology. It is the provision of an objective chronology into which, and against which, the facts of prehistoric development can be marshalled that has been, and still is, one of the great achievements of twentieth-century archaeological scholarship.

3. *Chronology*

Prehistoric archaeology employs two forms of chronology, the one relative, and the other absolute. By relative chronology is meant a temporal sequence based on the relation of artefacts and cultures to each other or to natural events. An absolute chronology, on the other hand, is a temporal sequence expressed in exact years. It is the aim of the archaeologist to establish the relation of cultures to each other, to natural events, and in exact years.

The three ages and their subdivision into the de Mortillet scheme was, of course, an attempt at relative chronology of a kind. Early in the development of Palaeolithic archaeology, archaeologists became interested in the problem of the relations of the subdivisions of the de Mortillet scheme to the phenomena of the Pleistocene Ice Age, namely, the glacial and pluvial periods, and the changes in sea-level. In many places the Magdalenian was shown to be post-glacial. The evidence from Wildkirchli, Drachenloch, and from Taubach, Ehringsdorf (Weimar), and from Cotencher (Neufchâtel) and Bouchieta (Ariège) showed that the Mousterian was in part earlier than, and in part contemporary with, the last glaciation. In 1889 Marcellin Boule found a Mousterian hand-axe (although he at the time claimed it to be Chellean) at Aurillac (Cantal) dating from the last interglacial, and declared that man in Europe was contemporary at least with the last interglacial if not with the penultimate glaciation. Boule based his findings on a very few sites then available, including that pioneer discovery of John Frere at Hoxne.

James Geikie, in his *The Great Ice Age and its relation to the Antiquity of Man* (1874, 2nd ed., 1894) and his *Prehistoric Europe* (1881), propounded a system of four large glaciations and a fifth smaller one for the Pleistocene, and argued that man had appeared for the first time in the second interglacial. Between 1910 and 1919 Penck and Bruckner produced a system of four Pleistocene glaciations, which they termed Günz, Mindel, Riss and Wurm, and argued that man first appeared in Europe during the Mindel-Riss period. A half-century of research and controversy on this problem by geologists and archaeologists now suggests that the Abbevillian and the Clactonian are to be dated to Günz-Mindel times rather than Mindel-Riss, while the various "pre-Chellean industries", as they used to be called, date to the Günz glaciation.

Meanwhile new terminologies have been suggested for the glaciations and interglacial periods; Soergel distinguishes nine glacial maxima in the Pleistocene, two corresponding to each of the first three of the Penck-Bruckner glaciations, and three to the Wurm glaciation. Zeuner very properly insists on the necessity of a terminology not derived from the local study of glacial phenomena but objective and applicable to the whole of Europe, or indeed the world, and proposes to refer to the four main glaciations as Early, Ante-Penultimate, Penultimate and Last, and the three interglacials as the Ante-Penultimate, the Penultimate and the Last Interglacials.[1] A better suggestion is the recognition of Lower, Middle and Upper Pleistocene periods, the Lower including from Günz 1 to Mindel 2, the Middle from the Great or Penultimate Interglacial to Riss 2, and the Upper Pleistocene from the Last Interglacial to the end of Wurm 3 times. Here is at last a reasonably objective framework into

[1] Zeuner, *Dating the Past* (1946), *passim.*

which the Palaeolithic succession of cultures can be fitted; the Abbevillian and pre-Chellean industries to the Lower Pleistocene, and the Acheulian and Early and Middle Levalloisian to the Middle Pleistocene.

In post-glacial times the place of the glacial and interglacial phenomena has been taken by raised beaches and especially by climatic phases. Blytt and Sernander distinguished by a macroscopic study of plant remains five divisions of post-glacial times, namely, pre-Boreal, Boreal, Atlantic, sub-Boreal and sub-Atlantic. These phases were confirmed by pollen-analytical methods, developed first by Lennart von Post. In a general way von Post found the Blytt-Sernander periods too complicated, and suggested three major divisions of post-glacial climate and vegetation history: first, the approach of a warm period, then the warm period with a flourishing of relatively heat-loving trees of various kinds, and thirdly the decrease of the warmth-loving trees and the appearance or return of the dominant forest constituents of the present day. Apart from these general periods, von Post has distinguished a series of eleven zones in the forest history of the island of Gotland, and similar zones have been distinguished by Nilsson in Scania, by Jessen in Denmark, and by Godwin in England. With these climatic and vegetation phases as a relative framework it has been possible to date the post-Pleistocene cultures relatively. Such work of correlation has been developed notably in northern Europe, but also by the work of Godwin, J. G. D. Clark and others in England in the last twenty years.

The transformation of these sequences of archaeological and natural events into an absolute chronology expressed in years has been achieved in two ways, one archaeological, the second geochronological. The archaeological method depends on correlations with historic chronologies, mainly, of course, the historic chronologies of Egypt and Sumer.

The extension of accurate dates in European and world prehistory, behind the first fixed historic dates in Europe and the Near East, depends, however, on geochronological techniques only. Of these the first is based on calculations of the rate of formation of deposits, either occupation deposits, or such natural deposits as river gravels. We have seen that, in the late nineteenth century, archaeologists attempted to give exact dates by dead reckoning from the thickness of deposits. Estimates of the Neolithic as 10,000 years ago were based on this technique, and Pumpelly's chronology for Anau I was based on similar calculations. Indeed, even at the present, all dates given for the predynastic cultures of Egypt and Sumeria are based on this dead reckoning. Many estimates were made of the duration of the Pleistocene Ice Age by the thickness of deposits; Penck himself estimated 600,000 years.

More exact geochronological figures have been obtained by the counting of tree-rings and clay-varves. Tree-ring analysis, or dendrochronology, was developed as a scientific technique by A. E. Douglass in 1901, though as early as 1811 De Witt Clinton had been using it to date earthworks near Canadaigua (New York State). The modern principles of this technique have been summarised by W. S. Glock in his *Principles and Methods of Tree-ring Analysis* (1937). By tree-ring analysis the early Basket Maker cultures in America have been dated to the early years of the Christian era. The main development and uses of this technique have been in North America, but some attempts have been made to extend this technique to Sweden and England, and the possibility of tele-connections between America and Europe exists. But of course tree-ring analysis, at its best, only takes one back for 3,000 years—not as far as synchronous cross-dating with the Egyptian and Sumerian chronologies.

Clay-varve analysis, on the other hand, goes back very much further. In fact, de Geer's famous paper of 1910 is entitled "A Geochronology of the last 12,000 years." The technique owes its origin to Baron Gerhard de Geer, who as long ago as 1878 had gauged its potentialities and who began his field work in 1905. The work of de Geer and his collaborators in Sweden was followed by that of Sauramo in Finland, Antevs in North America and Vierke in Pomerania. De Geer took his zero-point of 6839 B.C. as designating the end of the Late Glacial and the beginning of the post-Glacial. Others have preferred the limit between the Gotiglacial and Finiglacial, namely, 7912 B.C., which coincides with the breakdown of the glacial anti-cyclone and the beginning of climatic changes in northern Europe. There has been considerable confusion about de Geer's dates. The important thing for the prehistoric archaeologist is that these geochronologically derived dates do enable us to say that the Magdalenian was flourishing somewhere between 13,000 and 20,000 years ago. It is no longer a matter of guesswork to say when man first made works of art on bones and on the walls of caves in the south of France and the north of Spain.

Two other methods have been used for dating the Pleistocene. The first—the solar radiation method—is based on the cycle of perturbations of the earth's orbit. Milankovitch and Michkovitch, working on earlier calculations by Leverrier and Stockwell, produced a radiation curve which agrees well with the sequence of glacial phases and with Penck's estimate, and suggests that the Pleistocene/Pliocene boundary might be about 600,000 years B.C. The second—the radioactive method—while of more value in the geochronology of pre-Pleistocene times, also suggests a million years as the maximum time that must have elapsed since the beginning of the Pleistocene.

These geochronological techniques have been used mainly, hitherto, to date archaeological material between the end of the Ice Age and the beginning of the second millennium B.C., when an absolute chronology based on cross-dating with the Near East historic civilisations has been possible. Recently, in his *Stratigraphie comparée et Chronologie de l'Asie Occidentale* (1948), C. F.A. Schaeffer has proposed what is virtually a geochronological technique for the elucidation of the chronology of protohistoric and prehistoric civilisations of the Near East. Impressed by the arguments of de Montessus de Ballore in his *Les Tremblements de Terre* (Paris, 1906), and by the evidence of his own excavations at Ras Shamra, Schaeffer proposes to recognise two great earthquakes in protohistoric times, the first between 2200 and 2100 B.C. at the end of Troy III, and marking the break between the Early and Middle Bronze Age in Palestine, and the second, which he dates accurately to 1365 B.C. and equates with the end of Troy VI. He traces the occurrence of phenomena associated with these earthquakes in all the recorded stratigraphical sequences in the Near East, and, granted the validity of his method and his inferences,[1] seems to have discovered not only a way of accurately establishing the comparative stratigraphy of the Near East, but

[1] Professor H. Jeffreys tells me that the validity of Schaeffer's premises are doubtful, and that the problem is rather for the archaeologist to prove to the seismologist the contemporaneity of the observed phenomena, than for the archaeologist to assume their contemporaneity and date his sections from this assumption.

also a geochronological method for providing an accurate chronology to be extended into prehistoric Europe.

The purely archaeological method of obtaining an absolute chronology for prehistoric Europe depends on tying the culture sequence of prehistoric Europe with the historically dated sequences in Egypt and Sumer. But too much cannot be expected from this method. Even the historic chronologies are liable to considerable variation, as we may see from the two chronologies set out for early Egypt within one year of each other by Meyer and Petrie, the former dating the first dynasty at 3315 B.C. in 1904, and the latter dating it the following year at 5510 B.C., while a generally accepted date at the moment is 3100 B.C. for this event. In the last few years we have seen a re-dating of Mesopotamian chronology following the publication of Sidney Smith's *Alalakh and Chronology* (1940), which brings down the date of Hammurabi. The equation of the relative chronologies of Europe with the absolute chronologies of Egypt and Mesopotamia is achieved by cross-dating synchronous imports, a technique first developed, as we have seen, by Flinders Petrie, who dated the early Greek civilisation in terms of Egypt. Montelius followed up Flinders Petrie's technique and devised a chronology for prehistoric Europe, and his chronology, with minor modifications, served as the basis for the chronologies adopted by the new prehistory of the twenties. These, in a general way, saw the beginning of the Neolithic cultures of south-east Europe in the first half of the third millennium B.C. and in southern Britain and Scandinavia in the second half of the third millennium, and the beginning of the Bronze Age in the first half of the second millennium B.C. This was a considerable deflation of the old ideas which conceived of the European Neolithic as beginning eight to ten thousand years ago, and the Bronze Age early in the third millennium. A further drastic deflation was proposed by Nils Åberg in his *Bronzezeitliche und früheisenzeitliche Chronologie* (1930–35). The keys to European chronology are Crete and Troy, and these cannot even now be regarded as having chronological limits fixed beyond doubt. They in their turn depend on synchronisms with Egypt and Sumeria, and the whole process is such that, as Childe has shown brilliantly in his *The Orient and Europe*,[1] it is possible

[1] *The Advancement of Science*, 1938, and *American Journal of Archaeology*, 1939, 10 ff.

to establish European chronologies for an event like the beginning of the Aunjetitz culture varying by as much as nearly a thousand years. In view of this it is more than ever necessary to accumulate and analyse more and more evidence for cross-dating synchronisms and to subject all accepted dates to the most careful scrutiny. The "Beaker Horizon" of 1900–1800 B.C., which has for a long time appeared as a fixed date in prehistory, is now much in question, and Hencken and Åkerström, from an examination of the same Italian evidence which was first used by Montelius to establish his European chronology, have wanted to scale down the date of the beginning of the Late Bronze Age in Central Europe.[1] The truth is that a too refined dating of European prehistoric cultures may never be possible, and that disputes whether La Tène I began in 450 or 425 B.C. or whether the Windmill Hill culture in Britain should be dated 2300 or 2200 B.C. are disputes about academic fictions.

Childe, in his *Prehistoric Communities of the British Isles* (1940), realising the difficulty of using absolute dates in describing the Neolithic, Bronze and Early Iron ages in pre-Roman Britain, has proposed a system of Periods "defined by the cultural sequence deduced from stratigraphy". This is in a way a form of sequence-dating, only it deals with a sequence of cultures instead of a sequence of pottery types. It has, as he himself admits, obvious drawbacks, but it is a step on the way to an objective chronological system for later European prehistory. It gets away completely from the confusion which was besetting British prehistory in its analysis of the cultures from the first Windmill Hill settlers through to the Middle Bronze Age, a confusion which was becoming twice confounded by the arbitrary ascription of some cultures to the Neolithic and others to the Early Bronze Age. The present writer has elsewhere [2] expressed his opinion that the real solution of this problem of chronology lies in the establishment of approximately dated periods, not based on the cultural sequence, but on groups of centuries. Thus the period in western Europe from the first food-producing communities to the Urnfield invasions could be conveniently divided into four chronological periods, viz. Period I from 2500 to 2000 B.C., Period II from 2000

[1] For a recent discussion of Late Bronze Age and Early Iron Age chronology see Childe, *Proc. Preh. Soc.*, 1948, 177 ff., and Hawkes, *Ibid.*, 196.

[2] *The Three Ages*, passim.

to 1700 B.C., Period III from 1700 to 1400 B.C. and Period IV from 1400 to 1000 B.C. These periods correspond roughly to Childe's first four periods, but they are objective chronological periods. In relation to such a system of approximately dated periods, the problem of the prehistoric archaeologist is not whether the periods are correctly dated, for by definition they are so, nor whether any events inside these periods can be more narrowly dated—for this will probably prove impossible—but to fit the cultural sequence in its regional variations against this framework of periods, to decide, for example, whether Los Millares dates from Period I or II or III, and whether the so-called Windmill Hill pottery from Yorkshire and Scotland and Ireland dates from the same period in Period I as do the Causewayed Camps. Such a system of approximately dated periods needs agreement on an international basis before it can be widely used, but it seems to the writer a prerequisite of further advance in the study of the Neolithic, Bronze and Iron ages in prehistoric Europe.

CHAPTER EIGHT

THE DEVELOPMENT OF WORLD PREHISTORY

FROM the point of view of the Old World archaeologist prehistory had geographically two beginnings. One was in Europe—in the bogs of Denmark, the lake dwellings of Switzerland, the gravels of the Somme, the caves of Devon and the Dordogne—and the other was in the Near East—the Aegean, in the gradually revealed prehistoric civilisations of Anatolia, Greece, Egypt and Mesopotamia. These European and Near-Eastern beginnings, which so much influence still the balance of prehistory in textbooks and lectures, became transformed into a world prehistory by two main events, first the discovery of the ancient prehistoric civilisations of India, China and America, and secondly by the extension of Palaeolithic studies all over the Eurafrasian land-mass, particularly to South and East Africa, and parts of Asia. These two developments, with which we are concerned in this chapter, had far-reaching effects on the development of prehistoric archaeology, not only by their new content of fact, but because of the challenging light they throw on the problems of the nature of cultural change.

1. *India*

The ancient prehistoric civilisation of north-west India was the most recently discovered of the Chalcolithic civilisations, and its revelation by excavation and comparative study has taken place only in the last thirty years. In 1913 Barrett began his book on *The Antiquities of India* with the Rig-Veda hymns and remarked: "In India there is no twilight before the dark." In his article on "The Monuments of Ancient India" in volume one of *The Cambridge History of India*, published in 1922, Sir John Marshall wrote: "It is the misfortune of Indian history that its earliest and most obscure pages derive little light from contemporary antiquities" [1]; and his account of the pre-Vedic antiquities of

[1] Page 612.

India was little more than a passing reference to the palaeoliths of the Deccan, the megaliths of southern India, and various hoards of copper objects, including the Gungeria hoard, which Vincent Smith had studied.[1] Yet two years later Sir John was announcing, in *The Illustrated London News*, the excavations at Harappa and Mohenjodaro and comparing their discovery with Schliemann's discovery of Tiryns and Mycenae. Such was the dramatic suddenness with which the Chalcolithic Indus civilisation was revealed.

In many ways Sir John's comparison was most apt. The discoveries at Mohenjodaro and Harappa and the other sites in the Sind, the Punjab, and Baluchistan of what is now generally known as the Indus civilisation brought to light a flourishing Chalcolithic civilisation supporting large, well-planned cities many centuries before the Aryan invasion of India, an event which, since the time of Max Müller, it had been customary to date at about 1500 B.C. and to regard as the beginning of Indian prehistory. Oral traditions preserved in the Rig-Veda refer to the aborigines whom the Aryans found in north-west India as Dasas or Dasyus, and describe them as small, with black skins, "noseless", "hostile-speaking", living in town and forts, skilled in various arts, and practising a religion which they despised. Little credence obtained to these traditions among modern historians, but Bishop Caldwell argued from them that the pre-Aryan inhabitants of India had possessed temples, kings, cities, metal instruments and written books.

Harappa lies about three hundred miles north-west of Delhi, in the Montgomery district of the Punjab and near an old bed of the River Ravi. It is close to the railway line from Lahore to Multan, which is ballasted for about a hundred miles of its length by bricks from the ruined Chalcolithic city. In 1873 General Sir Alexander Cunningham, first Director of Archaeology in India, made several small excavations at Harappa and found pottery and a polished stone seal engraved with a bull and pictographic writing. Cunningham was at this time mainly interested in the travels of the Chinese monks Fa-Hien and Hieun-Tsang, but he was also interested in the seal, suggesting the pictographs were ancestral to the early Brahmi script of the fourth century B.C.,

[1] "The Copper Age and Prehistoric Bronze Implements of India," *Indian Antiquary*, 1905, 229 ff.; *Ibid.*, 1907, 53 ff.

a suggestion supported more recently by Professor Langdon. The seal was acquired by the British Museum and studied by J. H. Fleet and others, but no further work was done at Harappa until 1921, when Daya Ram Sahni dug three of the mounds, and established the prehistoric nature of the site. The excavations at Harappa were continued in 1923–25 by Sahni and in 1926–34 by M. S. Vats, whose complete publication of the site appeared in 1940.

About the same time as Sahni was excavating at Harappa, R. D. Banerji began digging at Mohenjodaro—"the place of the dead"—a similar site four hundred miles to the south, and in the province of Sind, about a hundred and forty miles north-east of Karachi. Banerji's excavations in 1921–22 cut through buildings of the historic Indian period and came to levels yielding seals like those from Harappa. His excavations were continued in 1923–24 by Vats, and in 1924–25 by K. N. Dikshit. In 1925–26 more extensive excavations were carried out under the direction of Sir John Marshall, assisted by Hargreaves, Dikshit and Mackay. In 1926 these were continued by Sahni and Mackay, and in 1927–31 by Mackay. The results of these ten years of excavations were published by Marshall and Mackay, the 1921–27 excavations in Marshall's three fine volumes, *Mohenjodaro and the Indus Civilisation*,[1] and the 1927–31 excavations in Mackay's two volumes, *Further Excavations at Mohenjodaro*.[2]

The excavations at Mohenjodaro and Harappa revealed an ancient urban civilisation—the Harappa culture, as it is called—with densely peopled cities, carefully planned, with buildings of burnt bricks, elaborately laid out with wells, drains, bathrooms and lavatories, a civilisation based on agriculture and trade. The crops grown were wheat, barley, rice, dates and cotton, and the domesticated animals included humped and unhumped cattle, buffalo, sheep, pig, dog, elephant and camel. The Harappa folk had wheeled vehicles, a system of weights calculated on the binary and decimal systems, and a pictographic form of writing not yet deciphered. They had weapons of copper, bronze and stone and ornaments of gold, silver, electrum, copper, bronze, faience, terracotta, ivory and cornelian. Most of their pottery was plain, but they also made pottery painted with black designs on a bright red slip. They were skilful metal-workers and stone-carvers,

[1] London, 1931.

[2] Delhi, 1938.

their intaglio work on small stone seals being especially remarkable. There is no public art in their cities, their art being represented by the pottery designs, the engraved seals, countless clay and terracotta figurines, and some sculpture in the round. Piggott complains of the "dead level of bourgeois mediocrity in almost every branch of the visual arts and crafts" [1], but there are four works of art from the Harappa cities—the red sandstone torso and the grey figure from Harappa, and the bronze dancing girl and the head of a man in a trefoil-decorated robe from Mohenjodaro—which are of outstanding merit. Marshall describes how, when he first saw the Harappa figurines, he found it difficult to believe that they were prehistoric: "they seemed to upset all established ideas about early art", he wrote [2]; and Carleton declared roundly that the nude torso from Harappa was "the finest ancient work of art ever found in the Middle East until the Assyrian bas-reliefs 2000 years later" [3], and compares it with the Greek sculpture under Pheidias and Praxiteles.

While the excavations of the cities had been proceeding, Majumdar in Sind, and Hargreaves and Stein in Baluchistan, had been finding other sites of the Indus civilisation. Majumdar's field surveys and excavations discovered in 1927–31 many new sites in Sind, such as Chanhu-daro, Amri, Ali Murad, Lohri, Pandi Wahi, Lohumjo-daro, Jhukar and Jhangar.[4] Ali Murad was a fortified site in the hills, Chanhu-daro a small town, the other sites were villages. At Amri, Lohri and Pandi Wahi, Majumdar found settlements beneath the Harappa culture levels of a culture characterised by buff pottery decorated with black painted ornament and a frequent use of red in zones or lines, and with no objects of metal except copper beads, to which the name of the type site of Amri has been given. At Jhukar, not far from Mohenjodaro, Majumdar found, above levels of the Harappa culture, a culture characterised by a buff ware with black and red painted decoration, stone and clay stamp seals, to which the name Jhukar culture has been given. The small town of Chanhu-daro was excavated in 1935 by a field expedition of the School of Indic and Iranian Studies of the U.S.A. and the Boston Museum of Fine

[1] *Some Ancient Cities of India*, 16. Bombay, 1945.
[2] *Mohenjodaro and the Indus Civilisation*, 45. 1931.
[3] *Buried Empires*, 153. 1939.
[4] N. G. Majumdar, "Explorations in Sind," *Memoirs of the Archaeological Survey of India*, No. 48. Delhi, 1934.

Arts under Mackay, and here a succession of three cultures was observed, the oldest, Chanhu-daro I, belonging to the Harappa culture, the second, Chanhu-daro II, belonging to the Jhukar culture, and the most recent, Chanhu-daro III, belonging to a culture noted by Majumdar at Jhangar, and called by the name of that site, characterised by a black or grey polished pottery well decorated with incised designs of triangles, chevrons and zigzags.[1]

In 1925–26 Hargreaves dug a large cemetery of inhumed fractional burials in the top levels of a tell at Nal, in the Kalat state in Baluchistan, which yielded a buff pottery with black painted ornament as well as additional painted ornament in red, yellow and blue, to which the name of the Nal culture has been given.[2]

While the archaeological reconnaissances and excavations of Stein, Majumdar and Hargreaves extended our knowledge of the Chalcolithic Indus civilisation into southern Sind and Baluchistan, other discoveries showed the extension of this civilisation south towards the Gulf of Cambay and north-west towards the Siwalik Hills. Vats found Indus sites in the Limbdi state of Kathiawar at Rangpur, and at Kotla Nihang, Rupar, near Ambala. The area over which known remains of the Indus civilisation have been found is now very large: from south Baluchistan to the north-east Punjab, and from north Baluchistan to Kathiawar, an area as large as the British Isles and immensely larger than the areas occupied by the Chalcolithic civilisations of Egypt and Sumeria. It is possible that the full extent of the Indus civilisation has still not been discovered: there may be Indus sites on the coast of the Deccan in Bombay Presidency, and Sir John Marshall was convinced that the civilisation had penetrated into the Ganges Basin. The Indus remains, however, the centre of the civilisation and the one area in which the urban Harappa culture flourished. It seems likely that, when the Indian Chalcolithic civilisation was flourishing, Sind was not the desert that it now is. The evidence of animal bones from the Indus sites suggests this, and there was a second

[1] The Chanhu-daro excavations are published by Mackay in his *Chanhu-daro Excavations*, 1935–36 (American Oriental Series, vol. 20). New Haven, 1943. I have used the renaming of occupation levels proposed by Piggott (*Ancient India*, 13. 1946).

[2] H. Hargreaves, "Excavations in Baluchistan, 1925," *Memoirs of the Archaeological Survey of India*, No. 35. Delhi, 1929.

river—the Mihran or Hakra or Wahindah—flowing through Sind east of the Indus even as late as the time of the Arab geographers.

The mounds or tells at Mohenjodaro and Harappa stood sixty feet above the surrounding plains. Owing to the rise in the level of the Indus since prehistoric times it was impossible to excavate the lowest levels at either site, but an extraordinary absence of any change in material culture is visible throughout the levels excavated. At Mohenjodaro excavations were made through forty feet—two-thirds—of the mound, and although nine or ten building periods were distinguished, and it is difficult to disagree with the conclusions of the excavators that they probably represent a continuous occupation of about five hundred years, no significant changes were found throughout, even in features like figurines, pottery and writing, which one would expect to show considerable change over such a period. It is this which leads Piggott to speak of the "uniformity which becomes an inescapable dull sameness" of the Harappa cities. At Harappa itself the same uniformity was noted, but the so-called "H" Cemetery had been dug into a rubbish tip on the edge of the town and was later than the main occupation of the city: it yielded a distinctive black on red ware, sherds of which were also found scattered in the top levels of the town.

The war of 1939–45 produced tremendous advances in Indian archaeology. This was mainly due to two causes, first, the appointment of Dr R. E. Mortimer Wheeler as Director-General of Antiquities in India in 1942, and secondly the work which Professor Stuart Piggott was able to achieve in India during the leisure hours of his military duties there. Wheeler brought to India the scientific methods of archaeological excavation which he had developed in England in the twenties and thirties from the earlier techniques of Petrie, Pitt Rivers, Curtius and Dörpfeld, and the administrative genius which he had displayed as Director of the National Museum of Wales, and of the London Museum. He revitalised Indian archaeology and trained archaeologists, as well as himself conducting excavations and surveys of the greatest importance. His first task was the re-study of the Indus cities. Since Marshall's first publication of Mohenjodaro it had been customary to regard the two Indus cities as unique in the Ancient East, a communal organisation dominated by a wealthy merchant class, and having no priest-king or citadel area as had the Sumerian cities. Wheeler and Piggott pointed out in 1945 that the Stupa mound at Mohenjodaro, with its ritual bath and public buildings, was very like a citadel, and that the AB mound at Harappa contained traces of brick bastions. Wheeler's excavations at Harappa in 1946 brought the citadel there to light and exploded the idea of the special character of the Indus cities.[1] In the second place, Wheeler attempted to bridge, if not to close entirely, the gap in Indian prehistory between the end of the Indus Chalcolithic civilisation and the beginnings of Indian history. His study of the upper levels of Harappa and his excavations at Taxila were steps in this direction, although the gap has not yet been closed, and it is not possible with any certainty as yet to point to the material remains of those Aryan speakers in India. In the third place, by his discovery of an Indo-Roman trading station on the east coast of India at Arikamedu,[2] Wheeler was not only to reveal the first settlement of its kind in India, but to produce dating points for some of the prehistoric ceramics of India, carrying his work across the Deccan to date the Indian megalithic structures to the centuries immediately before the Christian era.

Piggott, starting from an earlier analysis of Childe's, studied the Indian Chalcolithic material in its widest contexts, and with special reference to McCown's analysis of Iranian material. Piggott has made a special analysis of the finds from Baluchistan and distinguishes, in addition to the Nal culture, four other cultures and wares [3]: (i) the Zhob culture from north Baluchistan sites such as Sur Jangal, Rana-ghundai, Mogul-ghundai and Periano-ghundai, characterised by red slipped pottery with painted designs in black and sometimes red, no use of metal, cremation burial, clay figurines of women and cattle, and phallic representations; (ii) Quetta ware, a buff pottery decorated with black paint, found localised in the Quetta area; (iii) the Kulli culture in south Baluchistan characterised by buff pottery decorated with black painted ornament (occasional red), clay figurines of women and cattle, copper pins, and found at sites such as Kulli and Mehi, and (iv) the Shahi-tump culture, known from a cemetery in south Baluchistan, and characterised by buff or grey wares with black painted ornament, copper stamp seals, and

[1] *Ancient India*, 1947, 58 ff.
[2] *Ibid.*, 1946, 17 ff.
[3] S. Piggott, "The Chronology of Prehistoric North-west India," *Ancient India*, 1946, 8 ff.

inhumation burials. Despite these archaeological distinctions, the culture of the Baluchistan sites has a general uniformity—it is a culture of unfortified village settlements set in the valleys among the Baluchistan hills. These early Baluchistan villagers lived in little groups of stone or mud-brick houses, cultivated grain, had domesticated cattle, hunted ibex and wild goat, made painted pottery and, for the most part, worked copper for some of their implements. It is no wonder that these small self-sufficing communities probably developed regional styles of pottery-making reflected in Piggott's classification.

Piggott argues that the Zhob and Quetta cultures are contemporary with the Amri or pre-Harappa phase in the Indus Valley, that Kulli is contemporary in part with the Harappa culture, Nal part contemporary and part later, and that Shahi-tump is post-Harappa in date. The date first suggested by Marshall for the Harappa culture was between 1000 and 400 B.C., but after the various Indo-Sumerian connections had been commented on and studied by Sayce, Gadd and Sidney Smith he put forward the dates of 3250 to 2750 B.C. for the *floruit* of the culture, which Mackay proposed to alter to 2500 for the upper levels of Mohenjodaro and Harappa. The more recent analysis of Wheeler and Piggott would suggest that the Indus civilisation is to be dated somewhere in the millennium 2500 to 1500 B.C. and that from the thickness of the deposits it seems likely that the Indus cities were occupied for at least three-quarters if not the whole of this time.

2. *China*

Until 1920, although the antiquity of Chinese civilisation was appreciated, it was thought that China had not been occupied by man in the remote human past. In his *Prehistoric Man*, Jacques de Morgan declared: "Chinese civilisation dates from the seventh or eighth centuries B.C.; we are completely ignorant of its prehistory." While it still remains true to say that Chinese civilisation, defined as the culture of people using the Chinese written language, is a recent event compared with the rise of the literate Egyptian and Sumerian civilisations, we can now date its beginnings as far back as the fourteenth century B.C., and can describe a succession of prehistoric cultures in China anterior to the earliest Chinese writing and going right back to the Lower

Pleistocene. The lateness of the discovery of Chinese prehistory as compared with the prehistory of south-west Asia is due to many causes. Creel lists "a general and deep-rooted antipathy to archaeological excavation", the belief that "cutting into the earth is believed to disturb the magical influences of the region", the widespread scatter of historic Chinese graves and the desire not to disturb the susceptibilities of ancestral spirits, and the presence of bandits and terrorists who regard archaeologists as rivals or wealthy victims.[1] It has been estimated that the excavators at Anyang spent sixty per cent. of their time preventing looting and ensuring that excavation could take place, and only forty per cent. in actual archaeological work. The Anyang excavations had eventually to be carried out under an armed guard, and were then only made possible at all by the personal intervention of General Chiang Kai-shek.

The discovery of the Palaeolithic and Neolithic cultures of China were due, in the first instance, to the energy, interest and initiative of J. Gunnar Andersson, a Swedish geologist, who, in 1914, went to China as adviser to the Government on coalfields and oil resources. He has traced his own career in China from mining expert via collector of fossils to archaeologist in his *Children of the Yellow Earth: Studies in Prehistoric China* (1934). In 1921 he discovered a Neolithic dwelling site at Yang Shao Tsun, in Honan. It was characterised archaeologically by black painted designs on a red polished surface. Later, other sites of the same characteristic pottery were discovered in the Yellow River area of Honan, Shensi and Shansi, and a preliminary account of them was given by Andersson in his *An Early Chinese Culture*, published in Peking in 1923,[2] and in two articles in *Ymer*.[3] T. J. Arne published a special study on the *Painted Stone Age Pottery from the Province of Honan* in 1925.[4] These works defined what has since been known as the Yangshao culture. Andersson made further discoveries of this culture in Kansu and further westwards as far as Lake Kokonor. The Yangshao villagers had domesticated animals and cultivated grain with shoe-last hoes; Edman and Söderburg were able to show that one sherd of their pottery had on

[1] *The Birth of China*, 1936, 27.
[2] *Bulletin of the Geological Survey of China*, 5.
[3] *Arkeologiska studier i Kina*, 1923, and *Arkeologiska Fynd i provinsen Kansu*, 1924.
[4] *Palaeontologia Sinica*, D, 1, 2.

it the imprints of rice husks. Andersson drew parallels between the Yangshao pottery and that found by Pumpelly at Anau, and at various sites in south-east Europe, and these parallels were examined carefully by Arne. It now seems probable, as Andersson and Arne argued, that the Yangshao culture is certainly in part apparented to the painted pottery Neolithic/Chalcolithic cultures of south-west Asia, which spread to eastern Asia via Turkestan, and through the Dzungarian gate between the Altai and Tien Shan mountains or across the Tarim Basin to the north of the Kun Lun mountains.[1] In 1923 Andersson estimated the date of the Yangshao culture as 3000 to 1500 B.C. Menghin, however, would not date any of the Yangshao sites before 2000 B.C. and Spinden would date the *floruit* of this culture in China to between 2200 and 1800 B.C.

Andersson at first regarded his Yangshao discoveries as revealing the first Neolithic culture of China. Painted pottery was not, however, the only ceramic in the Yangshao Neolithic villages and tombs. There were also unpainted wares, and at some comparable sites only unpainted wares were found. Andersson himself excavated some unpainted pottery Neolithic sites, such as Ch'i Chia P'ing in Kansu, but he regarded this and similar sites as contemporary variants of the Yangshao culture, which to him was a totally intrusive complex in China. Creel and others would now regard the Yangshao culture as a fusion of Western influences with an earlier Chinese Neolithic, and Carl Whiting Bishop distinguishes in the pre-Yangshao Chinese Neolithic three cultures: a north-western, characterised by sites such as Ch'i Chia P'ing, often referred to as the Pekin culture, a north-western characterised by sites such as Pu Chao Chai, and a southern culture characterised by pile dwellings. The general culture pattern of these three Chinese Neolithic cultures Bishop lists as sedentary planters, practising a *milpa* type of cultivation with the aid of stone-bladed hoes, cultivating millet as the only cereal, with dog, pig and fowl as their domesticated animals, using coarse hand-made pottery, living in winter in beehive-shaped earth houses, and in summer in houses some of which were built on stilts.

[1] Dr D. L. Yüan, of the Sino-Swedish Central Asiatic Expedition, found painted pottery related to the Chinese wares and in a Neolithic association from the vicinity of Urumchi and Hami in Chinese Turkestan (Bishop, *Antiquity*, 1933, 399).

Yet another Neolithic culture in China was discovered in 1930–31, through excavations by the National Research Institute, at Ch'eng Tzu Yai, Lungshan, east of Tsinan, in the province of Shantung. This culture, now generally known as the Lungshan culture, is characterised by thin, highly polished, black pottery made on a potter's wheel, the use of horse and cattle, scapulomancy, and by cities protected by elaborate rectangular walls of beaten earth. The Lungshan culture shares with the Yangshao culture some types of unpainted pottery and some decorative *motifs*, but also has affinities with the early Neolithic wares. Creel has described the Lungshan culture as "a variety of Neolithic culture developed in and chiefly peculiar to north-eastern China" [1]—*i.e.* in Honan, Shantung and southern Hopei: but more recently sites of Lungshan type have been found near Hangchow, in the province of Chekiang and at Chin San Lake—four hundred and fifty miles to the south of the Shantung sites.[2]

During the last few decades of the nineteenth century, farmers tilling their fields near the tiny village of Hsiao T un, near Anyang city in the north tip of Honan province, found curious bits of bone, some of which were decorated with characters. It was not until the present century that these were studied in detail by Lo Chen-yu, Sun I-jang, Menzies and R. S. Britton and correctly diagnosed as oracle bones. In 1928 the National Research Institute of History and Philology of the Academia Sinica, together with the Freer Gallery of Art of the Smithsonian Institute, began excavating at Anyang under the direction of Dr Li Chi and Mr Liang Ssu-yung. Four volumes of their reports have been published in their *Preliminary Reports on Excavations at Anyang* (1929–33), and their results have been summarised in more accessible form in Creel's *The Birth of China* (1936) and his *Studies in Early Chinese Culture* (1938). The detailed work of studying the material from Anyang still proceeds; over 200,000 inscribed pieces of these oracle bones are known to exist. The excavations revealed the old city of Anyang as the capital of the Shang dynasty, the centre of an ancient urban culture making fine bronze weapons and vessels, and exquisite carvings in bone, stone and ivory. In fact, as Andersson has pointed out, here, at Anyang, in the middle of the second millennium B.C., are all the elements of the historic Chinese

[1] *Studies in Early Chinese Culture* (1938), 194.
[2] On these new sites see S. S. Beath, *Asia*, 1941.

urban culture—statesmanship, religion, a literary language, a calendar and an art comprising all the motives we call archaic Chinese.

The interrelation of the early Chinese cultures discovered in the twenties was established by Liang Ssu-yung's excavations at Hou Kang in 1931. Here he distinguished three separate occupations: Hou Kang I, a Neolithic unpainted pottery culture; Hou Kang II, a Lungshan black pottery level, and Hou Kang III, a Shang/Anyang level. Students of these newly discovered cultures in China have been at pains to equate these archaeological stages with the legendary Chinese histories, particularly with the Hsia dynasty, the Shang dynasty, and the Chou dynasties, whose traditional dates are 2205 B.C., 1765 B.C. and 1122 B.C. respectively. There seems little doubt that the people of the Anyang Bronze Age city were the Shangs. The Hsias are generally located in the same Yellow River Valley region that has always been considered the ancestral home of the Chinese civilisation; Hsu Chung-shu argues that the Yangshao culture of N. W. Honan is that of the Hsia people.

A second problem in the interpretation of this newly discovered Chinese sequence of Neolithic and Bronze Age cultures concerns the extent to which this sequence is indigenous or dependent upon contacts with the West—with the culture sequence of south-west Asia. Andersson saw the Chinese Neolithic of the Yangshao culture as a direct translation to eastern Asia of one of the painted pottery cultures of south-west Asia, and others have seen the Anyang city as a direct transplanation of some urban community in south-west Asia. But we now see that Yangshao is a fusion of Western and native Chinese Neolithic cultures, and the Anyang Shang urban culture of China, while it owes much to the West, also has distinctive Eastern elements (*e.g.* the handleless crescent-shaped and rectangular knife-blades, divination bones, tripods). The problems of east Asian prehistory can only be solved when much greater information is available regarding the Chinese cultures, and when they are studied in relation to the Neolithic and Bronze Age cultures of east Asia in general. The likenesses between the Yangshao painted pottery and the Chalcolithic painted potteries of south-west Asia have prompted Western prehistorians to study in isolation one or two points in Chinese prehistory and to give an apparent clarity to a story as certainly complicated as the prehistory of Europe or the Near East. Both north and north-east of China and in south-east Asia the story of cultural development awaits detailed study. Mr and Mrs Torii have discovered painted pottery and associated stone types in east Mongolia and in Japan, where more than four thousand "Neolithic" dwelling places are said to exist! N. G. Munro in his *Prehistoric Japan* (Yokohama, 1908) lists painted sherds from Japan not unlike some of the Yangshao fabrics. The whole prehistory of Japan needs detailed study in its relation to China and India, especially the remarkable megalithic tombs, which seem to flourish there in contexts which in Europe would be described as Neolithic, Bronze Age and Iron Age.

3. *America*

The story of the rediscovery of the ancient American civilisations begins about 1840 with the work of John Lloyd Stephens.[1] Stephens was a traveller and archaeologist who had spent some time in Europe and had been fascinated by vague accounts he had read of the buried and abandoned cities of Central America. Stephens got himself appointed Special Confidential Agent of the United States in Central America, and accompanied by his friend, the English artist and antiquary, Frederick Catherwood, spent two visits studying the Mayan cities. The first visit was 1839–40 and the results were published in his *Incidents of Travel in Central America, Chiapas, and Yucatan* in 1841; the second expedition was 1841–42 and the results were published in *Incidents of Travel in Yucatan* in 1843. Both books were illustrated by Catherwood, who, after Stephens's death, produced a more popular version of the two volumes of *Incidents*. These fascinating and beautifully illustrated books, the record of great achievements in the face of enormous difficulties, interested people for the first time in the archaeological aspects of American prehistory. Speculations were made as to the date of these abandoned cities; were they monuments of the historic period like the abandoned cities of Siam and Indo-China, or were they the remains of some forgotten civilisation like the Egyptians?

These speculations about the Mayas—the Egyptians or Greeks

[1] On Stephens, see V. W. Van Hagen's *Maya Explorer: John Lloyd Stephens and the Lost Cities of Central America and Yucatan* (1947).

of the New World, as they were called—were not for a while accompanied by any fresh study of their monuments. Desiré Charnay was entrusted by the French Minister of Public Instruction with the study of the ancient American civilisations. He travelled and explored in Central America between 1857 and 1882. The result of his work, first published in French, was translated into English under the title of *The Ancient Cities of the New World* in 1887. Charnay emphasised the lateness of the ancient American civilisations in relation to the old civilisations of Egypt and the Aegean, but thought they were still interesting even if not, as some had hoped, the oldest civilisation in the world: "Why should the people who raised the American monuments be less deserving of our regard", he asked, "because they built them ten centuries sooner or ten centuries later?"

The real foundations of Central American archaeology were laid by an Englishman, Sir Alfred P. Maudslay, who worked systematically among the Maya remains for fifteen years, from 1881 to 1894. Maudslay describes this first journey through the Central American forests in search of the ruins of ancient cities as "merely a journey of curiosity", and wrote: "I had no intention whatever of making a study of American archaeology. However, the interest awakened by the sight of the truly wonderful monuments which it was my good fortune to behold induced me to undertake other and better equipped expeditions." This was fortunate for prehistoric archaeology: the results of Maudslay's work were published in *Biologia Centrali-Americana* (London, 1889–1902), in four volumes of archaeological text describing the cities of Copan, Quiriqua, Chichen Itza and Palenque, a volume of plates, and a long appendix by J. T. Goodman on the archaic Maya inscriptions. Maudslay's volumes constituted the first scientific account of Central American archaeology.

Maudslay attributed the neglect since 1840 of Central American archaeology as due to the difficulties of travel and the disturbed state of the country, but he prophesied that such neglect was never likely to occur again for, "although many of the ruins are as deeply buried in the forest as they were in Stephens's time, steamboats and railways have now brought the points of departure for exploring expeditions within at most a fortnight's journey from New York, and the universities and learned societies of the United States are becoming fully alive to the rich fields of research within easy reach." His prophecy was amply justified, and from Maudslay's time onwards research and excavation on the Central American ancient civilisations has been intensified. Notable among the universities and learned societies closely associated with this work have been the Peabody Museum of Archaeology and Ethnology, of Harvard University, which, between 1888 and 1915, sent many expeditions to Central America, and the Carnegie Institute of Washington, which has carried out great work in Central America since the end of the 1914–18 War. British excavations in British Honduras, like the British Museum campaigns at Lubaantun in 1927, have supplemented the great American and Mexican work in Middle America.

The extent of this work and our modern knowledge of the Middle American civilisations may be seen in such summaries as Spinden's *Ancient Civilisations of Mexico and Central America* (1922), Morley's *The Ancient Maya* (1946), Means's *Ancient Civilisations of the Andes* (1931), T. A Joyce's *South American Archaeology* (1912) and J. H. Steward's *Handbook of the South American Indians* (1946).

Parallel with the development of the archaeology of the Middle American civilisations has proceeded the study of the archaeology of North America. Squier and Davis published their *Ancient Monuments of the Mississippi Valley* in 1848, Squier's *Aboriginal Monuments of the State of New York* appeared in 1849, Lapham's *Antiquities of Wisconsin* in 1853 and Samuel Haven's *Archaeology of the United States, or Sketches, Historical and Biographical, of the Progress of Information and Opinion respecting Vestiges of Antiquity in the United States*, in 1855. Lord Avebury was able to include a study of these and other memoirs in his *Prehistoric Times* when it was first published in 1865. Indeed he devoted a whole chapter to "North American Archaeology", and it looked to some in the sixties and seventies as though America might prove as fruitful a field for prehistorical research as Europe and the Near East. The last thirty years of the nineteenth century saw a great increase in the interest of north American archaeology, among which Charles Jones's *Antiquities of the Southern Indians* (1873), Abbott's *Stone Age in New Jersey* (1877) and Bandelier's work on the archaeology of Mexico and the south-western United States should be mentioned. This work has been intensified in this century under the auspices of American universities and institutes and museums, and the complexity and detail of the archaeological picture of North America at the present day may be seen by consulting such an admirable summary as that of Martin, Quimby and Collier in their *Indians before Columbus* (Chicago, 1947). Here, well over a hundred cultures are described, going back to the Original Eskimo Culture and the first Basket Maker Culture at the beginning of the Christian era.

This great story of the development of north American archaeology differs in many ways from the problems of Old World archaeology. In the first place, many of these prehistoric American cultures are interpreted far more completely than are European prehistoric cultures, because many of the present-day Indians are living more or less as did their prehistoric ancestors, substantially unaltered by Spanish and American culture; in North America, to use Lummis's phrase, we can "catch our archaeology alive". Then, because of this, it is impossible to study north American archaeology except in the closest association with north American ethnology, particularly in the light of works such as Wissler's *The American Indian* (1922). The ideas of culture-traits and culture-areas which were first set out clearly by Wissler in his *Man and Culture* (1923) may, indeed, in the end, have produced a conceptual tool of greater use to the prehistoric archaeology of the Old World than the old ideas of epoch derived from the geologists, or of culture and civilisation derived from the historians and the late nineteenth-century anthropologists. North American archaeology is still forging this tool into the fashion it will be best suited for Old World archaeology. It was clear that the north American cultures could not be classified in terms of the Old World framework of Palaeolithic, Mesolithic and Neolithic, and they have been given a nomenclature based on types or areas, and placed in a chronological sequence established absolutely by dendrochronology, or the Maya records. Braidwood has criticised the loose use of terms like industry, culture and civilisation with reference to American archaeology, while students of the Mississippi Valley cultures, notably McKern, have been devising an entirely new terminology in which a find becomes a *focus*, grouped together to form an *aspect*—what Old World archaeologists would call an industry—of a *phase* of a *pattern*. The pattern, by itself or together with other patterns, characterises an entire area. Cole and Duel, in their *Rediscovering Illinois* (Chicago, 1937), distinguish, for example, in the Mississippi drainage area, two patterns which they named Woodland and Mississippi.

The detailed study of the middle American civilisations and of the cultures of north American archaeology posed from the beginning two problems regarding the antiquity and origins of these cultures. It is difficult to take the origin of the Basket Maker or Maya cultures back at most before 1000 B.C. Was this the earliest appearance of man in America? In 1839 Koch, in his *Mastodon Remains in the State of Missouri*, claimed the association of stone points with mastodon bones. In 1846 a human pelvic bone was found at Natchez, Mississippi, in association with extinct animals, and in the same state of mineralisation. In 1872 Abbott claimed to have found Palaeolithic implements from glacial deposits near Trenton, New Jersey, which Spier described as the Trenton Argillite culture. From then on, claims and counter-claims of the finds of early man and his culture have been made from North America, of which the most notorious have been *Hesperopithecus* H. Cookii—the Nebraska pig-tooth, Minnesota man—and *Homo Novus Mundus*.

The whole problem was put on a new and scientific basis in the late twenties by the discoveries at Folsom, in the Guadalupe mountains of New Mexico. In the quarter-century between the first Folsom discoveries and the present day, really authenticated remains of early American cultures have been found from many localities; suffice it to mention here, in addition to the finds of the Folsom culture, the Sandia culture of New Mexico, the Gypsum Cave culture of Nevada, the Cochise culture of Arizona, the Lake Mohave culture of California, the industry in the lowest layer of the Ventana Cave of Arizona, and the Lake George industry of Ontario. The Folsom finds are the best known, and it was they which produced a scientific archaeological basis for the discussion of the origin of man in America, hitherto conducted on the basis of the possible authenticity of disputed human remains, or the preconceived notions of cultural diffusion from the Old World. It was in 1925 that the residents of Raton, in New Mexico, reported to J. D. Figgins, then director of the Colorado Museum of Natural History at Denver, the finding of bones of extinct animals with flint tools at Folsom. Expeditions of the Colorado Museum, and of the American Museum of Natural History under Dr Barnum Brown, in the next few years, established the authenticity of the Folsom finds. A second area in New Mexico with finds of the Folsom culture was reported in 1932, when Dr E. B. Howard studied a group of sites between Clovis and Portales, some hundred and sixty miles south-east of Folsom, and near the Texas/New Mexico boundary. From 1932 onwards expeditions connected with the Academy of Sciences of Philadelphia, the University of Pennsylvania Museum and the Carnegie Institution of Washington worked on these new sites in the Clovis-Portales area, under the several auspices of Dr Howard, Dr J. C. Merriam and Dr Chester Stocks. The third important site of the Folsom culture—that at Lindenmeier—is twenty-eight miles north of Fort Collins in Colorado. It was discovered in 1924 by Judge Coffin and his son, and in 1935 and later excavated by the Colorado Museum of Natural History.

The Folsom and associated finds have brought in a new era in American archaeology. We now see the archaeological counterparts of the first American cultures postulated by the anthropologists, even if we have as yet no skeletal remains of these first Americans. Prehistoric archaeology now lends its support to the view that the first settlers of America came from north-east Asia in post-glacial times bearing a culture that may be formally classified as Mesolithic or Epi-Palaeolithic. As yet, however, it is not possible to give even approximate dates for these cultures—they have been dated between 20,000 and 2000 B.C.—nor to work out in detail the succession of cultures in America between the Folsom-Sandia-Cochise stages and the Basket Makers on the one hand, and the archaic Middle American and Chavin civilisations on the other. In a way, the Folsom discoveries are to New World prehistory what the acceptance of the finds of Boucher de Perthes and Pengelly were to Old World prehistory. They provide an agreed basis on which to build.

But the Folsom finds, while they lend support to the anthropologists' postulate as to the Asiatic origin of the first Americans, do not, and indeed could not, answer definitely the second problem of American prehistoric archaeology—that of the origin of the great Central American civilisations. Three quite different views are still held about this problem of the origins of the Maya and Peruvian civilisations, which are in so many ways like the Old World civilisations, and in so many ways quite different. Ever since the New World civilisations had been apprehended by the scholars of the Old World, theories have been woven to account for their origins in terms of the Old World civilisation. They were said to be due to Egyptians, or Phoenicians, or Greeks, or the ten lost tribes of Israel, or Madoc and the Welsh, or St Brandon and the Irish. The Chinese and Polynesians were claimed as the parents of Middle American civilisation as well as the mythical inhabitants of the supposed lost continents of Atlantis and Mu. As early as 1823 John Ranking wrote his *Historical Researches on the Conquest of Peru, Mexico, Bogota, Natchez and Talomeco in the Thirteenth Century by Mongols, accompanied with Elephants.* The diffusionists have stuck to Ranking's elephants, and in his clearest statement of the origin of Central American civilisation from Egypt, via Polynesia, Sir Grafton Elliot Smith calls his book *Elephants and Ethnologists.* Professor Leo Wiener provided an alternative to the Perry-Elliot Smith Egyptian origin of American civilisation by deriving the old American cultures from Gambia and Sierra Leone. As a complete contrast to these hyper-diffusionists come those who would derive Old World civilisations from the Americas. Ameghino claimed that man and civilisation had originated in South America, basing his views on his own investigations from 1870 onwards in the Argentine, and on the work of the Danish palaeontologist Lund, who had worked in the province of Minas Geraes in south-west Brazil between 1835 and 1844, excavating no less than eight hundred caves—in six of which, near Lagoa Santa, he found about thirty skulls. Ameghino's extreme views have been revived recently by the late G. N. Lewis, Professor of Chemistry in the University of California.[1]

The third school of thought regards the Central American civilisations as having originated independently in the Americas, from the primitive food-gatherers of the Folsom-Yuma stage or comparable cultures. This is the orthodox view of American anthropologists and archaeologists, and it is certainly the one which the archaeological evidence, imperfect though it still is, would seem to support. Charnay was inclined to belittle the interest in American origins: in his study of the ancient American cities he declared "the question of first origins" to be "unnecessary for our purpose" and "an idle pursuit". It certainly becomes an idle and dangerous pursuit when it leads to the speculations of Poznansky, and to works like Elliot Smith's *Elephants and*

[1] "The Beginning of Civilisation in America," *American Anthropologist*, 1947, 1.

Ethnologists, and Bellamy's *Built before the Flood*. But, properly conducted, it is one of the most fruitful enquiries, and likely to be of great profit to Old World prehistorians. For the more we study the question "What is the origin of the Middle American civilisations?" the more we begin to wonder what the phrase "the rise of a civilisation" means. Is civilisation, as used by prehistorians and protohistorians, no more than a label for a complicated culture pattern which included writing and city life? Granted an increasing complexity in culture and an assured food supply, may not civilisations have arisen independently in the Old World? The New World evidence needs digesting by Old World prehistorians, and in the light of it a re-examination of Old World protohistory may show that developments of the Old World protohistoric civilisations were parallel and not the result of diffusion from one centre. This is particularly so in regard to China and India. We know very little from archaeology about the mechanics of culture diffusion; the study of American archaeology may help us to clearer thinking in these matters. We often talk of the development of agriculture as a stage in prehistoric development; it is a hall-mark of the Neolithic of the textbooks, the Food-producing Revolution of Peake and Elliot Smith, and the Neolithic Revolution of Childe. Do not these phrases merely mean the discovery of wheat cultivation in south-west Asia? A study of American archaeology and anthropology suggests that manioc was developed in the lowlands of South America and maize in the Central American highland. Are these evidences of two more Neolithic revolutions? And what of rice cultivation, which seems to have originated in South China, Indonesia and Bengal? It certainly looks as if "agriculture" may well have been invented four times, or, rather, that it is an omnibus word for four separate developments in man's economic life. American archaeology teaches us at the present day very clearly that words like agriculture and civilisation may well be no more than the conceptual tools by which the prehistorian has so far advanced his subject, and that what really has happened in human history is not necessarily just what has happened in the Near East and Europe.

4. *The Development of Palaeolithic Studies*

Writing in 1922, in his *El Hombre Fossil*, Obermaier said that in parts of the world other than Europe "the ancient past of

Humanity is as yet unexplained and shrouded in impenetrable obscurity". He was thinking of the Palaeolithic, and, although it is true that there has been an enormous extension of our knowledge of the Palaeolithic in the quarter-century since Obermaier wrote, yet it must not be thought that the world-wide nature of the Old Stone Age was unknown before these intensive researches. As early as 1868 Bruce Foote had found palaeoliths in the Narbada valley in the Madras presidency, and even earlier, in 1855, Colonel Bowker had collected and presented stone implements to the museum at Capetown. At the Edinburgh meeting of the British Association in 1871 the Abbé Richard exhibited palaeoliths found near Lake Tiberias. All these were, of course, isolated discoveries, but their cumulative effect was such that by 1873 de Mortillet could claim that the Stone Age was a universal stage of early history "preceding all civilisations", even the most ancient, found all over the world, and he lists Italy, Greece, Palestine, Assyria, China, India and Egypt as having yielded evidence of the Palaeolithic.

But for all this, Obermaier is right in saying that even in the early twenties of this century it was still only the European Palaeolithic that was understood in detail, and the transformation of Palaeolithic studies from a European or even western European basis to a world basis is the result of discoveries and comparative studies made in the twenties and thirties of this century in Africa, Hither Asia, Russia, India, China and south-east Asia. This is no place to chronicle these discoveries in detail but some of the most important work must be mentioned.

The French had, from an early time, been interested in the Paleolithic of North Africa, and the work of Breuil and Vaufrey there has been extended and supplemented by the work of Sandford and Arkell in the Nile Valley,[1] the work of Caton-Thompson in the Kharga Oasis,[2] and the most recent work of the Cambridge expeditions in Cyrenaica under McBurney,[3] and the American expeditions to Tangier.[4] The presence of Palaeoliths in East Africa was first recognised in 1893 by Professor J. W. Gregory.

[1] Sandford and Arkell, *Palaeolithic Man and the Nile Faiyum Divide* (1929): ibid., *Palaeolithic Man and the Nile Valley in Nubia and Upper Egypt* (1923); Sandford, *Paleolithic Man and the Nile Valley in Upper and Middle Egypt* (1934).

[2] Caton-Thompson and E. W. Gardner, *The Desert Faiyum* (1934). Caton-Thompson, "The Kharga Oasis," *Antiquity*, 1931, 221.

[3] *Proc. Preh. Soc.*, 1948, 33.

[4] Henckel, *Proc. Am. Philosophical Society*, October 1948.

After the 1914–18 War, E. J. Wayland, Director of the Geological Survey of Uganda, began work there; from 1926 onwards L. S. B. Leakey began studying the Stone Age cultures of South Africa. Between them Wayland and Leakey have demonstrated an impressive sequence of prehistoric cultures, leading from simple pebble-tool industries like the Kafuan of Uganda and the Oldowan of Kenya through to Mesolithic and Neolithic cultures.[1] In South Africa recent workers like van Riet Lowe, Goodwin and Breuil have worked out a similarly impressive sequence of prehistoric cultures, summarised by Burkitt in his *South Africa's Past in Stone and Paint* (1928) and by Goodwin and van Riet Lowe in their *The Stone Age Cultures of South Africa* (1928),[2] and by the Abbé Breuil.[3] In central and western Africa the advance of our knowledge of Palaeolithic studies must always be associated with the work of the Rev. Neville Jones in southern Rhodesia.[4]

Between 1897 and 1900 Zumoffen had identified a Chelleo-Acheulian industry in Palestine, and later Neuville found a flint industry of middle Palaeolithic date. In 1925 Turville-Petre found the famous Galilee skull associated with an Acheulian-Mousterian industry.[5] The real advance of our knowledge of the Palaeolithic in Palestine dates from the excavations by the Institut de Paléontologie Humaine under Neuville and Stékelis, and the American School of Prehistoric Research and the British School of Archaeology in Jerusalem under (Professor) D. A. E. Garrod, at sites such as Skhul, el-Wad and et-Tabun in the Wady el-Mughara on Mount Carmel. Here was found a sequence from the Tayacian of the Middle Pleistocene through the Levalloiso-Mousterian of Middle Paleolithic times to the blade industries of the Upper Palaeolithic, and on to a new Mesolithic industry which was named the Natufian.[6]

[1] E. J. Wayland, "Rifts, Rivers, Rains and Early Man in Uganda," *Journal of the Royal Anthropological Institute*, 1934. L. S. B. Leakey, *The Stone Age Cultures of Kenya Colony* (1931). T. P. O'Brien, *The Prehistory of Uganda Protectorate* (1939).

[2] For a general summary of the Stone Age cultures of Africa see L. S. B. Leakey, *Stone Age Africa* (1936).

[3] *Cahiers d'Art*, 1931.

[4] Neville Jones, *The Stone Age in Rhodesia* (1926). A. L. Armstrong, "Excavation in the Bamtak Cave," *Jour. Roy. Ant. Inst.*, 1931. J. Desmond Clark, *Stone Age Sites in Northern Rhodesia* and the *Probabilities of Further Research* (1939).

[5] F. Turville-Petre, *Researches in Prehistoric Galilee, 1925–26, and Report on the Galilee Skull*, London, 1927.

[6] *Bulletin of the American School of Prehistoric Research*, 1931–36; D. A. E. Garrod, *Antiquity*, 1934, 133, and *The Stone Age of Mount Carmel: Excavations at the Wady el-Mughara*. Oxford, 1937.

Study of the Palaeolithic of India had begun soon after the discoveries of Boucher de Perthes and Pengelly in Europe had won acceptance for the antiquity of man and the authenticity of stone tools. Bruce Foote of the Indian Geological Survey immediately began to look for what he called similar traces of "early human art". In 1863 he discovered a palaeolith near Madras, and then for forty-three years collected stone tools from the whole of south India, his great collection ultimately finding its way to the Madras Museum, and being published by himself in 1914 in two volumes called *The Foote Collection of Indian Prehistoric and Protohistoric Antiquities* (Madras, 1914). In 1930 M. C. Burkitt studied the collection of palaeoliths made from the Kistna Basin in south India by L. A. Cammiade, discovered a chronological sequence of types comparable with that recognised in Africa, and analysed the tools into the accepted framework of Palaeolithic epochal nomenclature.[1] In 1935 de Terra led the Yale-Cambridge North Indian Expedition, consisting of himself, Teilhard de Chardin and T. T. Paterson, to resolve problems of the Indian Stone Age in Kashmir and the Punjab. Here de Terra found an industry with pebble choppers, and flake and cores of Clacto-Levalloisean types, but evolved on its own lines, to which he gave the name Soan. De Terra also distinguished a pre-Soan industry, a flake industry recalling the Clactonian.

There would then appear to have been in India in Mid and Upper Pleistocene times what Krishnaswami describes as "two different manufacturing traditions working together and of equal antiquity",[2] the first the Soan chopper-chopping pebble tradition and the second the Abbevillio-Acheulian hand-axe tradition. A true Upper Palaeolithic comparable with the Solutrean and Magdalenian does not exist in India, though some blade industries have been distinguished, and there are widespread microlithic industries, which have been compared with the Capsian of Syria and Africa, and which merge into the "Neolithic" industries of India.

Two years after his first expedition, de Terra led an expedition under the auspices of Harvard University to Burma. He was accompanied by Teilhard de Chardin and Movius. They discovered an industry of chopping tools and coarse scrapers as

[1] Burkitt and Cammiade, *Antiquity*, IV, p. 327 ff. Burkitt, Cammiade, and Richards, *Geological Magazine*, LXIX.

[2] *Ancient India*, 1947, 40

well as chopping tools of petrified wood, and to this industry Movius gave the name Anyathian. The Anyathian was thought to be generally contemporary with the Soan of India. Tools comparable with the Anyathian of Burma have been found in Malaya, at Patijan in Java, and at Choukoutien in China,[1] as well as during the last war by van Heekeren at Ban-Koa in the Mekong valley in Siam.[2]

Meanwhile Chinese prehistory has had added to it a variety of Palaeolithic cultures as well as the Neolithic and Bronze Age oultures. The story of the discovery of Peking Man has often been told. Andersson excavated at Choukoutien, just under forty miles south-west of Peking, early Pleistocene cave deposits in 1921 and the following years, and in 1926 discovered two human teeth. The following year Birger Bohlin continued the excavations in the Choukoutien cave and discovered another tooth, which Davidson Black attributed to a hitherto unknown variety of early man, which he christened *Sinanthropus Pekinensis*. Following these discoveries the Choukoutien site was systematically excavated under the direction of Dr Wong Wen Hao and with the assistance of Father Teilhard de Chardin. By 1939 thirty-eight specimens of the new species had been found, as well as artifacts. Apart from a single chert implement from Locality 13, described as a core tool and compared with Abbevillian hand-axes, the industry associated with the Choukoutien *Sinanthropi* is a flake industry, including scrapers, points, chisels, choppers and gravers, as well as worked utilised bones. This classical *Sinanthropus* industry is found at Choukoutien, Locality 1, together with evidences of fire and apparently of organised cannibalism. Both Localities 1 and 13 are dated to the Lower Pleistocene. Elsewhere at Choukoutien, at Locality 15, another industry was discovered in what were perhaps Lower Middle Pleistocene contexts; this industry has been classified as perhaps a later development of the classical industry of Locality 1.

The gap between the Lower Palaeolithic industries of Choukoutien Localities 1, 13 and 15 and the early pre-Yangshao Neolithic cultures has been filled in part by discoveries in the Mongolian Gobi desert, the Ordos desert and by further

[1] On the Anyathian and the Burma excavations see Movius, *Early Man and Pleistocene Stratigraphy in Southern and Eastern Asia*, 1944.

[2] H. R. van Heekeren, "Prehistoric Discoveries in Siam, 1943–44," *Proceedings of the Prehistoric Society*, 1948, 24 ff.

discoveries at Choukoutien. In 1923 and 1924 Father Teilhard de Chardin and Father Licent discovered in the Ordos desert region, at sites such as Choei-tung-kiau and Sjara-osso-gol, a Middle Palaeolithic industry dated to the Late Middle Pleistocene, while between 1930 and 1939 the Upper Cave industry at Choukoutien was discovered and described. It is an industry poor in stone tools but rich in bone artifacts, such as needles and pendants, perforated shells, painted red stone beads, and associated with the remains of seven human beings which had haematite powder scattered over and around their bones.[1]

The gap in our knowledge of the world Palaeolithic between eastern Europe and China has been filled in part by the work of Russian prehistorians such as Gerasimov, Efimenko, Zamyatkin and Bontch-Osmolovski, who, while not finding any Lower Palaeolithic industries, have discovered rich Upper Palaeolithic industries at sites in European Russia like Kostienki and Gargarino, and in Siberia like the famous site of Mal'ta dug by Petri near Irkutsk.[2]

This bare chronicle of some of the important Palaeolithic discoveries of the last thirty years must suffice to indicate the way in which, between 1920 and 1950, world Palaeolithic studies have been born. Their interest to us is not only in the wide extent of Palaeolithic cultures; they have also changed our ideas of the content of Palaeolithic culture as a whole. Our knowledge of prehistoric art has been extended by the discovery of statuettes comparable with those from Willendorf, Vistonice and Grimaldi at the south Russian sites of Kostienki and Gargarino, and from Mal'ta in Siberia: and by the study of the cave paintings and wall engravings of South Africa and southern Rhodesia. The picture of Palaeolithic dwellings given by researches in the nineteenth century in western Europe was one based entirely on rock shelters and "open sites", although no clear evidence was available as to what these open sites might be. The Russians have now

[1] On the Chinese Palaeolithic see Teilhard de Chardin, "The Pleistocene of China: Stratigraphy and Correlations" in MacCurdy, *Early Man*, 211; and Pei Wen-Chung, *Palaeolithic Industries in China*, ibid., 221; and Boule, Breuil, Licent et de Chardin, *Le Paléolitique de la Chine*, 1928.

[2] For an account of Russian prehistoric discoveries see Childe, *Proceedings of the Prehistoric Society*, 1935, 151; Tallgren, *Europa Septentrionalis Antiqua*, X, 129; Golomshtok, *American Anthropologist*, 1933, 301, and *Trans. American Philosophical Society*, 1938; Field and Prostov, *American Anthropologist*, 1936 and 1937; Zolotarev, *American Anthropologist*, 1938.

excavated, at Kostienki and Gagarino, Palaeolithic house sites; these were hollowed in the earth, with hearths, store-pits, and post-holes for roof supports. And in 1946 Leakey found at Mount Olorgasailie, near Nairobi, an Acheulian living site with quantities of hand-axes and bolas.

This great accession of information about the Palaeolithic all over the world has brought with it great problems of nomenclature and comparative archaeology, and there is still no general agreement on the correlations of these cultural sequences with each other, or with the geological phenomena of the Pleistocene.[1] The problems of nomenclature have been as difficult as those of correlation; Leakey has been criticised for labelling industries in East Africa with the regional labels of old western European prehistory; in South Africa names of industries were deliberately chosen, like Stellenbosh and Fauresmith, from local sites. The problem is a complicated one and is of course closely involved with the taxonomic basis of nomenclature; to what archaeological isolates are we giving the names industry, cultures, tradition, civilisation?[2]

We have seen in the previous chapter how, gradually, Obermaier and Breuil arrived at the notion of two great contemporary civilisations in the Lower Palaeolithic. As the knowledge of world prehistory developed it seemed that these two civilisations embraced the world, and that in early Palaeolithic times the inhabited world could be divided into these two great provinces of flake and core tool-makers; the flake province was seen to include China and south-east Asia, as well as eastern Europe, while the core province comprised western Europe, Africa and India. These provinces were fully described and set out by Menghin in his *Weltgeschichte der Steinzeit* (1931). Here Menghin also argues for a third great province of Lower Palaeolithic cultures —a bone civilisation, and that the three great Lower Palaeolithic civilisations arose directly from an earlier wooden stage, or Palaeoxylic period. Menghin's work is important not only for his attempt to define these early provinces, and because it is the first great survey of the world Palaeolithic, but because he also

[1] The most ambitious correlation is that attempted by T. T. Paterson in *Nature*, 1940, 12 and 49. For another world correlation see Zeuner, *Dating the Past*.

[2] For a useful *exposé* of this problem see T. T. Paterson, "Core, Culture and Complex in the Old Stone Age," *Proceedings of the Prehistoric Society*, 1945, 1.

attempts a complete reclassification of the Stone Age. As he studied the problem of Stone Age cultures on a world basis he saw that it would be hopeless to retain for their description what Grahame Clark has aptly described as "the time-honoured hash of French place-names provincial in both space and time".[1] Menghin therefore proposed to abandon the words Palaeolithic and Neolithic, invented by Lubbock, and to produce three new divisions of the Stone Age: the Protolithic, the Miolithic and the Neolithic. By Protolithic he meant all industries earlier than the Upper Palaeolithic; the Miolithic included the Upper Palaeolithic and Mesolithic, while his newly defined Neolithic comprised Neolithic and Eneolithic cultures.[2] This new scheme of Menghin's has not been adopted, and indeed at the present moment the idea of the two great civilisations of core tools and flake tools is undergoing very considerable modification. Perhaps, like the epochs of the West European Palaeolithic, it will be shown to be a useful conceptual tool, rather than the final classification of Stone Age man.[3]

Miss Caton-Thompson has insisted that in all this analysis of cultures and civilisations we must be sure that we are dealing with realities and not merely "techno-typological devices", and Harper Kelley has very rightly said that "all biface cultures have their flake tools as well".[4] Movius, de Terra, Paterson, and more recently van Heekeren, would distinguish a third civilisation, neither core nor flake, but associated with the chopper-chopping tool or pebble-tool, and group together the Soan of N.W. India, the Anyathian of Burma and Indo-China, the Choukoutienian of China, the Tampanian of Malaya, the Patjitanian of Java and the Fingnoian of Siam into the third Palaeolithic "civilisation".[5] It may well be that we are still at too early a stage of our knowledge of the world Palaeolithic to devise these large civilisations. As Professor Garrod has remarked, the stultification of Palaeolithic studies for many years was due to "the canonisation of a scheme

[1] *Antiquity*, 1931, 518.

[2] Menghin also devised a system of what he called "phaseological chronology," by which a Protolithic culture survived into Miolithic times was called epi-protolithic, and a Protolithic culture survived into Neolithic times was called opsi-protolithic.

[3] On this see Caton-Thompson: *The Aterian Industry, its Place and Significance in the Palaeolithic World.* Huxley Memorial Lecture, 1946.

[4] *Proceedings of the Prehistoric Society*, 1937, 15.

[5] Van Heekeren has christened his Mekong finds as Fingnoian, after Mei Fingnoi, the name of the river (*Proc. Preh. Soc.*, 1948, 28).

which could only be applied locally"[1]; we do not want to stultify further research in the Lower Palaeolithic by canonising too soon these two to four civilisations that have been so far distinguished.

The extension of prehistoric studies which we have very briefly chronicled in this section has not, of course, stopped with the end of the Palaeolithic, and a welter of subsequent industries formerly described as Mesolithic and Neolithic have been distinguished in various parts of the world, from the Angara-Yenesei Neolithic of Siberia to the Hoabhinian culture of south-east Asia, Australia and Japan, first distinguished in Siam by Sarasin,[2] and the much-disputed Tumbian of Central Africa.[3] The Neolithic cultures of the Near East and Europe are usually one of two things, either the early peasant village communities which had not yet acquired a knowledge of metallurgy, or impoverished village communities derived from metal-using centres. As yet the relations of these various Neolithic communities in Africa, south-east Asia and Siberia to the Neolithic-Chalcolithic peasant village communities of the Near East is very obscure; it is one of the most important fields for future research in world prehistory.

[1] *Proc. Preh. Soc.*, 1938, 1.

[2] *L'Anthropologie*, 1933, 1 ff.

[3] For an excellent account of the Tumbian problem see C. T. Shaw, *Proceedings of the Prehistoric Society*, 1944, 51–60, and R. Vaufrey "Le Néolithique Para-Toumbien," *La Revue Scientifique*, 1947.

CHAPTER NINE

THE DEVELOPMENT OF TECHNIQUES & METHODS: 1900–50

THE average reader asked to say what was the most single significant development of prehistoric archaeology in the present century would say, unhesitatingly, the development of archaeology into a scientific study, and by this would mean the development of scientific techniques and methods. It is probable that every generation of thoughtful archaeologists with a conscious and deliberate technique of discovery, excavation, analysis and interpretation will make notable advances on a previous generation and will, to a certain extent, regard themselves as scientific and their predecessors as unscientific. Already we can detect this process in considering the generations that separate Loftus and Layard from Rassam, Rassam from Koldewey and Andrae, and the work of the Deutsch Orient Gesellschaft from the work of the British, American and French expeditions in Mesopotamia between the two world wars. Yet, even when we have made allowance for the inevitable development of technique that must accompany the growth of a young and energetic branch of learning, it is true that the first half of the twentieth century has seen an enormous advance in methods and technique and that, from the viewpoint of future generations, it may well be that this advance of scientific technique will be regarded as of equal importance in the history of archaeology with the great discoveries made in that half-century.

What exactly has been involved in this development of new techniques, methods and attitudes? In the first place, twentieth-century archaeology has become conscious of the need for planning and method in all aspects of archaeological work—in discovery, in excavation, in the recording, preservation and disposal of remains, and in research. A conscience regarding the disposal of antiquities dates back, as we have seen, to Mariette and to the action of the Germans at Olympia: the Iraq Antiquities Service and legislation created by Gertrude Bell before the 1914–18 War may be taken as an exemplar of the national organisations and legislations that have come into existence in most countries since that time, of which the Irish and Danish organisations provide the most striking modern developments. The deliberate elaboration of excavation technique may be said to start with the Germans at Olympia, with Petrie in Egypt, and with Pitt Rivers in England. This consciousness of technique in excavation is shown by the publication of Petrie's *Methods and Aims in Archaeology* (1904), the *Manuel de Recherches préhistoriques* published in 1906 by the Société Préhistorique de France, and Droop's *Archaeological Excavation* (1915). The advice of Montelius that it is better not to carry out any excavations than to work in such a way that facts are irreparably lost gradually became a *sine qua non* of archaeological work. We may at the present day gauge the extent of the conscious direction towards a technique of excavation in Atkinson's *Field Archaeology* (1946), Du Mesnil du Buisson's *La Technique des Fouilles archéologiques: Principes généraux* (1934), and the *Manual on the Technique of Archaeological Excavations* published by the International Museums Office of the International Institute of Intellectual Co-operation after its International Conference on Excavations held in Cairo in 1937.

Secondly, the new scientific method in archaeology involves not only a conscious study of technique, but a study of the totality of phenomena. The archaeologist is no longer concerned with a few sites, or a few works of art, or a few interesting things dug out of an ancient site. He is now concerned with all the evidence that can be obtained from an excavation down to the domestic pottery and the bones and seeds preserved in refuse heaps. The archaeologist has long ago ceased to be a connoisseur; indeed so much so that it may sometimes be complained justifiably of the prehistoric archaeologist that he has entirely set aside aesthetic judgements. The detailed excavation report, with its emphasis on the study of all material remains found, and the distribution map, itself the visual presentation of all the sites of a particular artefact or culture, are witness to this emphasis on the study of the totality of archaeological evidence.

Thirdly, archaeology has become increasingly dependent on information from specialists in the natural sciences regarding the material and associated finds of the prehistoric human past. We have seen that in the late nineteenth century archaeology was busy establishing itself as the paramount source of information regarding the prehistoric past, and denying the usefulness of alleged prehistoric facts obtained from a study of physical anthropology, linguistic palaeontology, folk-lore, survivals, and oral literature. Having established itself as the paramount source, archaeology now finds that it is able to provide only part of the story needed by the prehistorian, and turns, for example, to the geologist for analyses of rocks, the metallurgist for analyses of prehistoric bronzes, the botanist, the pollen analyst and zoologist for information about the flora and fauna of prehistoric times, the geochronologist for absolute time scales, the pedologist for information regarding the ecological conditions of human settlement. Indeed so widespread is this dependence that the Council for British Archaeology published recently a small pamphlet of *Notes for the Guidance of Archaeologists in regard to Expert Evidence*, while works like Lucas's *Ancient Egyptian Materials* (1916) and J. R. Partington's *Origins and Development of Applied Chemistry* (1935) show the wealth of data to be obtained by the scientific analysis of material and associated finds.

Let us briefly consider these three trends in relation to the advance in techniques of excavation, discovery and interpretation.

1. *Techniques of Excavation*

We have already traced the beginnings of scientific excavation, assisted by architects and photography, in the work of Curtius at Olympia, Petrie in Egypt and Pitt Rivers in England. These great excavators built up a body of excavational technique which formed the basis of twentieth-century excavational methods. The excavations at Anau occupy an important place in the development of archaeological technique. Anau was excavated in 1904 under the general direction of Pumpelly. The actual digging, preservation and recording were undertaken by Hubert Schmidt, of the Museum für Völkerkunde in Berlin: Schmidt had been trained by Dörpfeld at Troy. He set about the Anau excavations by sinking large pits, which were deepened two feet a day, and by marking the position of everything found. We read in the Anau report such phrases as "Much of the earth was sifted to save small objects", and "The importance of considering even apparently insignificant objects as documents containing a story, and of recording their vertical and horizontal position in the column of culture strata became evident at every stage of the analysis of results". The human skulls from Anau were studied by Sergi, the long bones by Mollison, animal bones by Duerst of Zürich, the remains of cultivated grains by Schellenberg, while F. A. Gooch made chemical analyses of the metal implements. Schellenberg was able to identify wheat and two-rowed barley from casts and from siliceous skeletons of the chaff of these cereals. Duerst, who was sent half a ton of animal bones (and complained that their analysis occupied his whole time for three years!), alleged that, from his studies alone, he was able to show the translation of *Bos nomadicus*, pig and sheep from a wild to a tame state, a conclusion, if confirmed, of the greatest importance to the prehistorian.

The techniques of excavation developed in classical lands were brought to Mesopotamia by Koldewey. We have already spoken of the work of Koldewey at Babylon and Andrae at Ashur. The work at Ashur has been described by Seton Lloyd as "a brilliant feat of excavating and the prototype of all stratigraphical investigations in later times".[1] Egypt was, in a way, a paradise for excavators, but did not perhaps lead to such advances in technique as did Mesopotamia. In Egypt every monument was built of stone or cut in the solid rock, and the arid climate permitted preservation in a remarkable manner of objects of wood, cloth and other perishable materials which would have been destroyed elsewhere. Egypt, moreover, had so many sites occupied only once. It was, therefore, in Mesopotamia that the classical techniques were reshaped and that new techniques of stratigraphical examination, and of the excavation of perished and semi-perished materials, were developed. The architecture of Mesopotamia is executed in sun-dried bricks; the techniques of tracing these were quite unknown to earlier excavators. Koldewey and Andrae first successfully traced the walls of sun-dried brick, and this work reached its highest technical achievements in the work of Delougaz, at Khafajah, where every single brick was articulated, the chips being blown away by compressed air. The excavations at Ur were a noteworthy model of the whole modern technique of archaeology, from extraction and preservation to interpretation and publication. Among the most remarkable technical achievements at Ur was the recovery of destroyed objects

[1] *Foundations in the Dust*, 202.

like Shub-ad's harp by the study of the "ghosts" of the strings, an achievement comparable with Professor Garrod's reconstruction of a wooden spear from the hole it had left in the pelvis of a Palaeolithic hunter in Palestine, and Badè's use at Tell en-Nasbeh of the fingerprints of Bronze Age potters for tracing the contemporaneity of strata.

But it would be a mistake to suppose that the development of archaeological excavational technique in the first half of the twentieth century was due only to work in the Near East. Work in Europe, too, has contributed a great deal to the development of technique. Special mention should be made of the Danish examination of tree coffins, excavations in Germany like those of Buttler at Köln-Lindenthal, British excavations such as those of Wheeler, Hawkes, Grimes and Fox, and the work of van Giffen in Holland. Buttler at Köln-Lindenthal and other sites used a technique which Crawford has called that of the horizontal section, and Mahr that of the study of monumental palimpsests. The sites above ground had been entirely destroyed and excavation consisted of the careful recovery of post-holes and pits—even outlines of skeletons were found. The same techniques of post-hole and ghost studies were developed by van Giffen in the Dutch provinces of Groningen and Drenthe.[1]

It would also be a mistake to suppose that the first half of the twentieth century saw nothing but the development and practice of a slowly perfecting technique of excavation. Far from it; the record shows that the principles of modern excavation were only very slowly learned. We have stressed the importance of Koldewey's work at Babylon in that he excavated a whole site and paid attention not only to palaces and sculptures but to the domestic and commercial quarters of the city. But, as Childe has pointed out, Koldewey himself was "culpably neglectful of pottery, implements and even graves, to say nothing of human skeletons"[2]: and, as late as 1907, A. H. Sayce was in a position to deplore the absence of a ceramic record for Babylonia and Assyria.[3] The modern excavations in India, which brought to light the great Indus civilisation, were technically inspired by Sir John Marshall and Ernest Mackay. Mackay brought to the problem his training

[1] See *Die Bauart der Einzelgräber* (1930) and "La Technique des Fouilles aux Pays-Bas," *Mouseion*, vol. 43, 44.

[2] *Occasional Papers, Institute of Archaeology, University of London*, No. 5, p. 21.

[3] *The Archaeology of the Cuneiform Inscriptions.*

in Egypt and Mesopotamia, and one of the main reasons why Sir John Marshall was made Director-General of Archaeology in India, as he himself admits,[1] was that he might introduce into India the scientific methods of digging he had learned in Greece. Yet, as Piggott and Wheeler have pointed out,[2] the real significance of stratigraphy on archaeological sites as demonstrated by Dörpfeld, Schmidt, Petrie and Pitt-Rivers does not seem to have been understood, and the so-called stratification of the Indus Valley civilisation depended not on the recognition of occupation levels but on levelling every object found and tying it at long range with the sea-level at Karachi, a system which Wheeler has, with commendable restraint, described as "incredible".

The development of complex and detailed excavation techniques has meant the growth in size and complexity of excavation staffs. The staff of the Carnegie Institution of Washington Excavations at Chichen Itza, in Yucatan, for example, consisted of the director (S. G. Morley), a chief assistant, an assistant in charge of each unit of the excavation, a supervisor for the restoration of buildings, an epigrapher, an architect, a surveyor, artists to copy the frescoes and murals, a photographer and an engineer, not to speak of a trained housekeeper-nurse.[3] Excavational organisation has indeed progressed a long way from the days of Belzoni and Rassam. And together with the complexity of excavation has gone the complexity of excavational reporting. We have only to glance at the size and comprehensiveness of Wheeler's *Maiden Castle*, the Hawkes and Hull report on *Colchester*, Sir John Marshall's *Mohenjodaro*, the *Ur* reports, or the reports of the Oriental Institute of Chicago on Alishar Hüyük, to see how complicated and forbidding the primary sources of archaeology have become through a half-century of scientific digging.

2. *Techniques of Discovery*

Apart from excavation, archaeological discovery depends largely on chance and on field survey. Many of the important archaeological discoveries in the nineteenth century were due to chance, and in the first half of the present century chance remained, as it must always do, a most vitally significant factor in

[1] *Revealing India's Past* (ed. J. Cumming), 1939, 23.
[2] *Ancient India*, No. 3 (1947), 143–150.
[3] *Manual of the Technique of Archaeological Excavations*, 53.

discovery. Mari was discovered following the chance finding by villagers of a Sumerian statuette, the excavations at Ras Shamra-Ugarit followed on the discovery by a peasant, when ploughing, of a corbelled tomb, the fine La Tène hoard of Llyn Cerrig Bach was brought to light by accident during the construction of an aerodrome, while the painted caves of Lascaux were found because some French boys lost their dog down a hole in the ground. But, increasingly in the last fifty years, discoveries have been made as a result of deliberate field archaeology, often based on clues in maps, charters, or early written accounts.

Field archaeology—the study of the prehistoric sites in the field as distinct from their excavation—is as old as British antiquarianism itself, and has its roots in the work of Leland, Lhwyd, Camden and Aubrey. General Roy's *The Military Antiquities of the Romans in Britain* (1793) was a fine work of field archaeology. Roy bequeathed to the Ordnance Survey the tradition that its maps should bear indications of antiquities, or the non-functional as well as the functional aspects of the cultural landscape, a tradition very much lacking in many other national surveys, such as the French. Colt Hoare and Cunnington were great field archaeologists as well as excavators, and so were Greenwell and Pitt-Rivers. Randall[1] has stressed the contribution of the Oxford historians of the seventies such as Freeman, Stubbs and Green to field archaeology, and especially the importance of Edwin Guest, Master of Caius, who, though not an excavator, spent a great deal of his time exploring the countryside, often "with half the village in company".

Springing both from the antiquarians and the historians, there came into existence the fine tradition of English field archaeology which is one of our greatest contributions to the development of prehistory. The greatest development of this tradition was, however, after 1900, and was associated first with men like Williams-Freeman, Harold Peake and W. G. Collingwood, next with Crawford and Fox, and in the last quarter-century with Phillips, Grimes and Grinsell, to mention only a few names. Among the special achievements of field archaeology in Britain must be mentioned the archaeological maps of the Ordnance Survey, Fox's work on the East Anglian and Welsh dykes, Grimes's survey of Welsh megaliths, the survey of a team of north Irish

[1] *History in the Open Air* (1936), 9–11.

workers under Estyn Evans of the antiquities of Ulster, Hansford Worth's field surveys of Dartmoor antiquities, and Grinsell's field surveys of the barrows of many of the counties of southern England—all good examples of the necessity of the study of the totality of phenomena in field archaeology. We should mention here, too, the archaeological travels of Sir Aurel Stein in India, Iran and Central Asia, which are among the most remarkable pieces of field archaeology that have ever been undertaken.

New techniques had been added to those already employed in nineteenth-century field work—techniques such as bosing, phosphate determination, resistivity survey and echo-sounding. Special techniques have been devised for carrying out field work beneath the sea. The recovery of ships such as that off Mahdia (Tunis) and those from Lake Nemi in Italy are well known. Less well known is the submarine field work of Père Poidebard in Syria, where, with the use of submersible cameras, divers, and the *lunette de calfat*—the "caulker's bucket glass"—he made a survey of the ancient port and roadstead of Tyre. But, unquestionably, the greatest single technical advance in recent archaeological discovery has been the archaeological use of air photography.

Photography from the air was first suggested as a joke in a French lithographed caricature published in the middle of the nineteenth century. The joke became fact when, in 1858, the Parisian photographer Gaspard Felix Tournachon, who went by the name of Nadar, took air photographs of Paris from a balloon. Honoré Daumier drew a caricature of this exploit, declaring that Nadar had elevated photography to be the "highest" of the arts. In 1860–61, King and Black took air photographs of Boston, America, from a captive balloon, and in 1863 Negretti took air photographs of a London suburb. Nadar was urged to use air photography for military purposes during the Franco-Italian war of 1859, but declined. The first military use of air photography occurred during the American Civil War.

The pioneer of air photography in the British Army was Major Elsdale, who served in the Army's Balloon Establishment and, between 1880 and 1888, carried out photographic experiments from free balloons, as well as inventing a method of using small passengerless balloons. These latter balloons were just large enough to carry a camera which automatically exposed a number of plates, after which the balloon descended with the photographs it had taken. Sir Charles Close (then a lieutenant in India) suggested in 1891 that apparatus similar to that used by Major Elsdale should be used for photographing archaeological sites near Agra, such as Fatehpur Sikri. The scheme was approved by the Surveyor-General of India, but eventually came to no more than a few air photographs of Calcutta. Close's purpose had been to get a bird's-eye overall view of the cultural landscape around Agra and to construct a map from these photographs. This purpose was not achieved until the end of the 1939–45 War.

The first archaeological air photographs were taken in 1906 by Lieutenant P. H. Sharpe, R.E.—nearly half a century after Nadar had demonstrated the practicability of such photography. Sharpe took an oblique and a vertical photograph of Stonehenge from a military balloon. These were displayed at the Society of Antiquaries in December 1906 by Colonel J. E. Capper, and were published next year in *Archaeologia* (vol. 60, 1907, plates 69 and 70). These two photographs are interesting as curiosities: they were the earliest examples of air archaeology, and revealed very clearly the value of air photographs in depicting ancient remains as a whole and from a fresh perspective unobtainable on the ground. They also showed up, as dark marks, features like the avenue, which were no longer visible on the ground as surface features; in fact they provided at once a demonstration that air photography could reveal not only the functional and non-functional cultural landscape visible to a ground observer, but traces of the non-functional cultural landscape now hidden from the gaze of earthbound scholars. This was, of course, the great contribution of air archaeology to the development of prehistoric archaeology, namely, that it was a prime source for the discovery of new sites. But it was not realised in 1906 that the air camera had added a fourth to the three other sources of archaeological discovery hitherto available — chance, field work and excavation. This realisation had to wait until the 1914–18 War.

In the years immediately preceding the 1914–18 War, H. S. Wellcome used large box-kites with special automatically controlled cameras for photographing his excavations in the Sudan, but it took the war itself to make air photography an efficient instrument for collecting information and to reveal fully its archaeological purposes. In the first place, it trained archaeologists and geographers, among others, in the new techniques of photography and photographic interpretation, and secondly, it provided, incidentally to military requirements, photographs of archaeological sites, many hitherto unknown. The archaeological value of air photography was recognised by German, English and French scholars working on military photographic duties. M. Léon Rey used air photographs for archaeological purposes in Macedonia in 1915. Dr Theodor Wiegand traced the eastern end of the Roman *limes* in the Dobrudja from air photographs, and was later sent out specially with the German forces in south Palestine and Sinai to photograph archaeological sites and describe his results, which he did in a monograph published in 1920 in Berlin. At the same time, and later, the Royal Flying Corps and the French Air Force were taking air photographs of archaeological interest in the Near East, and the value of these was appreciated by Poidebard, Hamshaw Thomas and Beazeley. Father Antoine Poidebard, a Frenchman, studied air photographs in the Near East during the war and in 1918 flew across Persia with General Dunsterville's force.

Colonel Beazeley was a sapper with the British forces in Mesopotamia, and on his routine military flights he noted the strange patterns of canals and the *karezes*, or underground water channels, and was able to pick out the plans of ancient cities. Describing his discovery of the ancient city of Eski Baghdad, north of Samarra, he wrote "much of the detail was not recognisable on the ground, but was well shown up in the photographs, as the slight difference in the colour of the soil came out with marked effect on the sensitive film". Beazeley also describes his discovery of detached forts: "When riding as a passenger in an aeroplane, *en route* for survey over enemy territory, I could clearly see on the desert the outline of a series of detached forts . . . whereas when walking over them on the ground no trace was visible." He also records "the outline of an ancient irrigation system", but adds "unfortunately I was shot down and captured before being able to make a detailed survey of the system during a lull in the military operations". Nevertheless, before his capture, Beazeley had laid the basis of the archaeological interpretation of air photographs which he was able to set out in his paper on *Surveys in Mesopotamia during the War*, which he read to the Royal Geographical Society (*Geographical Journal*, 1920).

Less of archaeological interest was seen on air photographs of the Western Front than on those of the Near East, for various reasons, notably the greater height at which photographs were taken on the Western Front, and the barren or overgrown nature of the cultural landscape in north France and Belgium. But at least one observer on the Western Front, O. G. S. Crawford, realised the value of archaeological air photography. Before the war Crawford had often discussed with Williams-Freeman the possibilities and advantages of the overhead view in archaeology: during the war he had considerable experience as observer and photographic interpreter; after the war, and especially after he had been appointed Archaeological Officer to the Ordnance Survey, he was able to lay the real foundations of the scientific study of archaeological air photography.

To many, the development of air archaeology is synonymous with the name Crawford, and most who write the history of this new archaeological technique very properly pay high tribute to his work. Crawford himself has insisted that the credit for the first actual application of aeroplane photography to archaeology should go to Beazeley. Actually, before photography from aeroplanes or balloons, some archaeologists had realised the value of the detached overhead view with its new perspective. In a discussion in the Royal Geographical Society in 1923, following the reading of a paper by Crawford, two very interesting comments were made. Sir Charles Close instanced how, from the top of the rock of Gibraltar, it was possible to see, on the ground to the north, remains of old Spanish lines which were invisible on the level; and Dr Williams-Freeman said he had often noticed, on the ground, features shown up by shadow, soil differences and snow which he would otherwise have missed, and had noticed, moreover, how these features showed up more clearly when viewed from the top of a hill. "I remember thinking", said Williams-Freeman, "that one ought to be a bird in order to be a field archaeologist." The air camera and the aeroplane enabled the field archaeologist to carry out this obligation. Many realised this during the stress of military operations in the 1914–18 War, but none perhaps as clearly as Crawford.

In the years following the war the Royal Air Force began taking photographs of England. These were bound, sooner or later, in a country whose cultural landscape is a crowded palimpsest, to include archaeological sites. It was found that these were of three kinds: first, sites such as barrows and hill forts already known from ground survey but now revealed for the first time from a new overhead viewpoint and in their correct topographical relationship; second, sites which were recognisable on the ground merely as a jumble of curious ditches and banks but which now, in air view, could be properly seen in totality and in their appropriate interrelationships, and which could be sorted out into the remains of prehistoric fields and farms; and third, sites which were unrecognisable as archaeological sites from ground survey alone. It was this third type of photograph, showing the vanished or non-apparent cultural landscape, that most excited archaeologists. In 1922 Air Commodore Clark Hall showed Williams-Freeman and Crawford air photographs of parts of Hampshire showing curious marks not readily apparent to the ground archaeologist, but which now stood out as a prehistoric pattern of what Crawford called Celtic fields. The two archaeologists at once realised the potentiality of air photography in the discovery of half-destroyed and levelled sites surviving as soil, shadow and crop marks. Public interest was aroused by the publication in the London *Observer* in 1923 of air photographs of Celtic fields and the Stonehenge Avenue, and has been consistently maintained in this, one of the strangest and most spectacular techniques of the archaeologist.

The development of archaeological air photography between the two wars was due in the main to the initiative and energy of three people—Crawford, Allen and Père Poidebard. In 1924 Crawford and Keiller hired an aircraft and took three hundred photographs of archaeological sites in two months—in a wet season. These sorties formed the basis of *Wessex from the Air*, published in 1928, a magnificent work which can be called the foundation stone of air archaeology. Crawford had set out the principles of air archaeology in a lecture to the Royal Geographical Society, reprinted under the title *Air Survey and Archaeology* in the *Geographical Journal* for 1923, and later republished as a Professional Paper of the Ordnance Survey (first edition, 1924, second edition, 1928). A second Professional Paper, *Air Photography for Archaeologists*, was published in 1929. In the pages of *Antiquity*, and elsewhere, Crawford drew attention to new discoveries made by air photography, notably those of Woodhenge, the Arminghall Woodhenge and Little Woodbury.

Major Allen's interest in air archaeology was stimulated by reading *Wessex from the Air*. Subsequently, in a few seasons' flying, he took many thousands of photographs, piloting his own aircraft and operating his own hand-made camera. Crawford, and many of the other war-time photographic interpreters, had emphasised the value of vertical air photographs. Allen was the first to stress the great value of oblique air photographs to archaeology, and his magnificent oblique views of Maiden Castle, Celtic fields and other sites have done a great deal to make air photography intelligible to those who remained puzzled by the unfamiliar appearances of the cultural landscape and the fundament in vertical view.

Poidebard's work has been concentrated in the Near East, where his interest in air photographs had been aroused during the 1914–18 War. As a result of work in the twenties he published in 1934 *La Trace de Rome dans le Désert de Syrie: le Limes de Trajan à la Conquête arabe; recherches aériennes 1925–32*. In 1939 he published *Un Grand Port disparu, Tyr; recherches aériennes et sous-marines 1934–36*, and in 1945 (with R. Mouterde) *Le Limes de Chalcis*. All these three works are of remarkable distinction and interest. His work in Tyre combines ground and air archaeology in a most exemplary and profitable way, together with special submarine researches which he carried out, first by aerial photography, and, where their value was limited by depth and movement of water and reflection from its surface, by reconnaissance divers and the use of the *lunette de calfat*.

The 1939–45 War saw a tremendous increase in air photography, due to the improvements in the performance of air cameras and aircraft, to the very great numbers of aircraft and cameras then available, and to the increased importance of photographic intelligence, especially when more normal sources of intelligence were cut off after the fall of France and Singapore. As a result, this war provided hundreds of thousands of air photographs of areas from Norway to China, and these, though not deliberately taken for archaeological purposes, contained a vast mass of unrecorded archaeological data. Many archaeologists found themselves employed, very appropriately, as photographic intelligence officers during the war and were able to make use of the new data at once. Most notable in this respect is

J. S. P. Bradford's work on air photographs of Italy, some of which has been published in *Antiquity*.[1]

The war not only increased the range of air photography and produced air photographs of areas hitherto unphotographed, but it increased the intensity of photographic cover. Indeed there had hardly been much attempt at total photographic cover of areas before the 1939 War. Until 1939, and with the exception of military training mosaics, aerial photo-reconnaissance had been mainly a matter of pinpoint photography, *i.e.* the photography of selected sites. During the war it became a matter of total cover, and the archaeologist of western Europe has now available to him complete air maps of the cultural and natural landscape of the areas he is studying. Archaeological air photography is no longer a technique which we should understand as it *may* lead to interesting discoveries: it is now an essential part of archaeological technique which we must understand if we are to make use of the discoveries already made that are locked up in the photographic archives of the national air forces, and which are being added to daily.

The work of military photographic interpretation during the war taught those prehistorians who were so employed the value of the stereoscopic examination of air photographs. Before 1939 archaeological air photography was conceived of rather in terms of large-scale low-flown single verticals. Now we see that smaller-scale overlapping cover susceptible of stereoscopic examination can give as good results at least in the discovery of surface and shadow sites, and that, in any case, the three-dimensional photograph is immensely useful in the appreciation of all relief features, and in seeing them against the background of the country.

We may perhaps, then, distinguish three phases in the development of archaeological air photography: the first, before 1914, when air photography was conceived of as a valuable aid to the record of known monuments like Fatehpur Sikri and Stonehenge; the second, from 1914 to 1939, associated with the pioneer work of Beazeley, Crawford, Allen and Poidebard, which was concerned with the discovery by pinpoint vertical and oblique photography of hitherto unknown sites revealed by soil, shadow and crop marks;

[1] "Etruria from the Air," *Antiquity*, 1947, 74; "A Technique for the Study of Centuriation," *Antiquity*, 1947, 197; and (with P. R. Williams Hunt) "Siticulosa Apulia," *Antiquity*, 1946, 191.

and the third, from 1939, concerned with the stereoscopic examination of total vertical cover of extremely large areas. Throughout phases two and three air photography has been a prime source of archaeological discovery and record, and has more than justified Crawford's claim in 1923 that the invention of the air camera was "as valuable to archaeology as that of the telescope has proved to astronomy" and inaugurated "a new epoch in the history of British archaeology". Air photography continues on a large scale at the present day, and the National Survey of the British Isles on a scale of 1/10,000 being undertaken by the Royal Air Force is providing a wealth of archaeological material. Even so, being made primarily for non-archaeological purposes, with no special attention to the conditions of light and cropping best suited for archaeological air photography as summarised in D. N. Riley's paper on *The Technique of Air Archaeology* [1], this National Survey does not record all the sites potentially visible to the air camera. This has been shown very clearly in the last ten years by the work of J. K. St Joseph and others who have discovered new sites by independent photography from charter aircraft. St Joseph, carrying on the work of Crawford and Allen, has made many spectacular discoveries, especially of sites from Romano-British times. Nor must it be thought that intensive official photography during and after the war has covered more than a small portion of the cultural landscape of the Old World. E. F. Schmidt's *Flights over Ancient Cities in Persia* (1940) shows what can be done in the way of archaeological discovery and record in an area where no National Air Survey has hitherto been attempted.

Air photography has, then, become a major instrument of archaeological discovery and record, and no archaeologist can consider himself completely trained who is not as expert in the interpretation and reading of air photographs as he is in map interpretation and reading. Air photography has not yet become a major instrument in archaeological exposition. It remains to use air photographs much more in excavation reports and in general works. Aerial mosaics are a clearer and more impartial way of depicting the cultural landscape than a map, with its extensive conventionalisations, and stereoscopic photographs are an essential for a full understanding of an archaeological site and its topography. One of the great difficulties of using air

[1] *Archaeological Journal*, 1946.

photographs for exposition is this necessity for providing facilities for stereoscopic examination. As early as 1857 a work entitled the *Geologische Bilder* was published with stereoscopic photographs, and one of Duboscq's stereoscope lorgnons was sold with each book. The use of anaglyphs and vectographs for illustration gets over this difficulty in part, since anaglyphoscopes and polaroid viewing spectacles can be more easily enclosed in books than can lens stereoscopes, while of course devices like Deep Pictures need no viewing device to give a three-dimensional photograph. The ideal is probably to illustrate archaeological reports and books with stereograms constructed for an average interocular distance and to assume, as the *Illustrated London News* did occasionally during the 1939 War, that every home possesses a lens stereoscope. Only then will the full uses of air photographs to the archaeologist be realised.

3. *Techniques of Interpretation*

Two notable advances in the techniques of archaeological interpretation have been made in the last fifty years. The first is the analysis of materials, and the second the development of distributional and ecological studies. We have already mentioned briefly the first in discussing the increasing dependence of the archaeologist on the natural scientist for detailed reports on soils, pollens, metals, stones, flora and fauna. A hundred years ago, when Rutimeyer and Heer reported at length on the flora and fauna from the Swiss lake dwellings, archaeologists were astonished at the amount of information that could be obtained by specialist analysis. Now it has become a matter of course, and we need only mention here Dr H. H. Thomas's work on the foreign stones of Stonehenge, Watson's work on the fauna of Skara Brae, the work of the Danes on prehistoric grains, to show what far-reaching effects the analysis of material has in archaeological interpretation.

The geographical method in prehistoric archaeology has had equally far-reaching effects. There was a tendency during the nineteenth century to regard antiquities merely as antiquities—the material relics of the past, whether at the beginning of the century they were mainly works of art or towards the end of the century, under the beneficent influences of Flinders Petrie and Pitt Rivers, the common objects of everyday life. There had been little attempt to study the find-spots of antiquities in their geographical and ecological relationships, or to map the overall distribution pattern of a type of antiquity or of all the antiquities of a period.

Admittedly Worsaae had stressed the importance of knowing where antiquities had come from. He had emphasised that prehistoric archaeology could not proceed only by excavation and by the study of museum collections. The objects in the museum collections must be related to their find-spots and he conceived of these find-spots in time as well as geographically. Worsaae appreciated the succession of vegetation types revealed by the Danish bogs, and considered that all antiquities should be studied in relation to the prehistoric vegetation. But, as in so many other things, the Danish and Swedish archaeologists of the early nineteenth century were well in advance of their time.

As we now see it, the geographical approach to archaeological interpretation involves two things: first, the study of antiquities or groups of antiquities as distribution patterns, and second, the study of these patterns and the occurrence of antiquities against the background of the prehistoric landscape. We have mentioned the part played by the Oxford historians and by Guest in the development of field archaeology; this interest naturally provided a stimulus as well for the geographical interpretation of the archaeological facts. Guest's *Origines Celticae* (*a fragment*), *and other contributions to the History of Britain*, was published in 1883. Guest taught that the settlements and invasions of Britain were largely determined by the natural landscape of the country, and that the story of British history must be seen at all times against the background of British geography. It was Guest's influence that lay behind Freeman's *Historical Geography of Europe* (1881) and the maps in Green's *The Making of England*.

One of the first distribution maps to be published was that of inscribed British coins, published by J. Y. Akerman in 1849. Some distribution maps were exhibited at the Paris Exposition of 1857. They were made by Ogérien, and were of antiquities in the Jura. These maps were severely criticised by Gabriel de Mortillet, largely because of their curious categories—one was "cavernes habitées par les animaux diluviens et par l'homme après le cataclysme", and another "fossiles de l'époque gallo-romaine". But, despite their inadequacy, the efforts of Ogérien *were* distribution maps, and their exhibition at the Paris Exposition is a landmark. In 1876 de Mortillet himself was exhibiting to the Société d'Anthropologie de Paris a "Carte Préhistorique de la Loire-Inférieure" which comprised, *inter alia*, 89 polished axes, 59 menhirs, and 36 dolmens,[1] and the International Congress at Stockholm in 1874 adopted an international series of symbols for distribution maps.

Megalithic monuments were among the first field antiquities to be plotted on distribution maps. Pitt Rivers had, in 1869, produced a distribution map of megalithic monuments, and Fergusson included one in his *Rude Stone Monuments* (1872). These were world-wide distribution patterns. In 1864 Alexandre Bertrand published a distribution map of megalithic monuments in France [2]; a fresh map appeared in the *Dictionnaire archéologique de la Gaule*, and in 1901 Adrien de Mortillet published a new map based on the *Inventaire des Monuments mégalithiques de la France*.[3] In the last decade of the nineteenth century Sir John Evans published a new map of inscribed British coins, and Heierli and Oechsli issued maps of the Swiss cantons showing antiquities of the Stone, Bronze and Iron ages in different colours. The regional surveys of the Society of Antiquaries and the chapters on Early Man published in the volumes of the *Victoria County Histories* were also now including distribution maps of antiquities.

In 1904 Abercromby published in the *Proceedings of the Society of Antiquaries of Scotland* a distribution map of the Bronze Age ceramic type, which he had distinguished as "the drinking cup or Beaker class of fictilia in Britain" [4], and his *Study of Bronze Age Pottery* published in 1912 contained further distribution maps. Between 1904–7 Lissauer published in the *Zeitschrift für Ethnologie* distribution maps of Bronze Age types such as implements and pins. His maps, which were a great advance on nineteenth-century distribution maps, were on the scale of 1/2½ million, and had clear symbols overprinted in red and blue.

Meanwhile, in 1898, the geologist Robert Gradmann, in his *Das Pflanzenleben der Schwäbischen Alb*, and in subsequent articles in the *Geographische Zeitung*, set out the theory that prehistoric settlement was virtually confined to open country

[1] *Revue d'Anthropologie*, V, 1876, 112–113.

[2] *Revue archéologique*, 1864, II, 144.

[3] "Distribution géographique des Dolmens et des Menhirs en France," *Revue mensuelle de l'École d'Anthropologie de Paris*, 1901, 32.

[4] Vol. 37, 323–410.

of a steppe-like character, among which the loess was of course included. Gradmann insisted that early man was incapable of clearing forest and therefore shunned it, cultivating areas which were naturally devoid of trees or which were at most lightly forested. He claimed that these "open" areas had borne nothing denser than a steppe and heath flora. His *Steppenheidetheorie* gained many adherents. In 1906 Schliz studied in detail the relation of the loess deposits of Central Europe to the Neolithic population. Ernst Wahle carried on the principles and teachings of Gradmann and Schliz, arguing that this method should be tested in small areas. In 1923 Max Hellmich's *Die Besiedlung Schlesiens in vor und frühgeschichtlicher Zeit* provided a regional survey applying Gradmann's principles.

Crawford, himself a geographer trained in the Oxford school of Mackinder, Herbertson and Myres, and a field archaeologist encouraged and inspired by Williams-Freeman and Peake, became interested in combining the distributional approach of Abercromby and Lissauer with the geographical analysis of distribution suggested by Gradmann and Schliz. In his paper on "The Distribution of Early Bronze Age Settlements in Britain", read to the Royal Geographical Society in 1912, and published in the *Geographical Journal* for that year, he first plots the distribution of flat bronze axes, beakers and gold lunulae, and then studies this distribution pattern in relation to the geography of Britain. His purpose was, as he said in the opening words of his paper, "to isolate a single culture period and to examine it from a geographical point of view". Crawford fully realised that, if the geographical approach was to be properly applied, two things were essential—first the plotting and the graphical representation of complete distribution patterns of the antiquity or group of antiquities being studied and, secondly, the reconstruction of the prehistoric geography of the time. He appreciated, as had Gradmann and his school, that prehistoric cultural landscapes must be studied against the background of prehistoric, not modern, natural landscapes. The most important element in prehistoric geography was likely to be vegetation cover. Crawford had often discussed the desirability of restoring primitive vegetation upon the basis of soil distribution with Williams-Freeman, whom he refers to as the pioneer of vegetation restoration,[1] and whose *Field Archaeology*

[1] *Antiquity*, 1934, 9.

as illustrated by Hampshire, with its map, appeared in 1915. Subsequently, as Archaeology Officer of the Ordnance Survey, Crawford continued and developed his geographical approach to prehistory, and primitive vegetation was restored by him on the Survey's maps of *Roman Britain* and *Neolithic Wessex*.

In the same year as Crawford's paper was published in the *Geographical Journal*, and Abercromby's maps appeared in his *Study of Bronze Age Pottery*, Leeds published in *Archaeologia* a paper on "The Distribution of the Anglo-Saxon Brooch in relation to the battle of Bedford," which was accompanied by a distribution map.[1] The following year saw the publication of Coffey's *Bronze Age in Ireland* and Déchelette's *Manuel*, vol. ii, part 2 (the Hallstatt volume), both of which had distribution-maps. Since this time the distribution map has become an essential of the study or exposition of any problem in prehistoric archaeology, and the graphic representation of areal distribution a canon of prehistoric methodology.

Meanwhile the study of these distribution patterns against the prehistoric landscape pattern was continued in England parallel with, though independent of, similar researches in Germany. In 1916 Fleure and Whitehouse published a paper on "The Early Valleyward Movement of Population in Southern Britain." [2] In *Man and his Past* (1921) Crawford summarised the possibilities and techniques of the geographical approach to prehistory and early history. Two years later Fox published *The Archaeology of the Cambridge Region* (1923).

The subtitle of Fox's work is important: it was "a topographical study of the Bronze, Early Iron, Roman and Anglo-Saxon Ages, with an Introductory Note on the Neolithic Age". Fox, in his approach, was indebted to the work of Fleure, Williams-Freeman, Crawford and Peake, and encouraged in its application by H. M. Chadwick and Crawford. He applied the general notions of Crawford to a small region—a region extending twenty to twenty-five miles around Cambridge. Here he studied prehistoric distributions against the background of the natural vegetation. He used as a base map a map with the prehistoric vegetation restored, and overprinted the prehistoric patterns against the modern topography and the restored prehistoric vegetation. The results of this study have become an archaeo-

[1] LXIII, 159.

[2] *Archaeologia Cambrensis*, 1916, 101 ff.

logical classic. Fox was able to show in detail that the prehistoric distribution patterns are not related to the present vegetation pattern but to a prehistoric vegetation cover. He showed that in the Bronze Age, and to a certain extent in the Neolithic, settlement was mainly on the lighter pervious soils, such as sand, gravel and chalk, and that later, in the Iron Age, and especially in the Anglo-Saxon period, settlement shifted to the less pervious, heavier loam clays. He was thus able to distinguish between the primary and secondary areas of settlement in the Cambridge region, and to show that the phenomena observed in Wales by Fleure and Whitehouse—the shift to the valleys—was only one instance of what he regarded as the general trend of early British history—the shift from primary to secondary areas of settlement.

Many advances in prehistory have taken place in the quarter-century since 1923, and the details of Fox's thesis have had to be modified, as he recognises in his *Reflections on the Archaeology of the Cambridge Region.*[1] We now see that it is not possible to use one single base map for the period 2500 B.C. to 1000 A.D.: the fundament was changing during this period just as the pattern of human settlement was changing. It now appears, as the ecological botanists were saying as early as in 1911, that the primary areas of settlement in Neolithic and Early Bronze Age times must not be thought of as "open" country but as lightly forested country, and that the open chalk-down lands are a "biotically determined sub-climax association". Few archaeologists would now agree with Gradmann that early man could not clear forest: Crawford's study of megalithic settlement in the Cotswolds and Grimes's study of megalithic settlement in Wales show that Neolithic and Early Bronze Age man sometimes settled by preference in heavily wooded areas. The change from the primary areas of settlement to the secondary areas may now be seen as a reflection of improved technology—the exploitation of the less pervious soils depends on the possession of iron tools and a heavy plough.

Following on his studies of the Cambridge region Fox applied his theories to East Anglia as a whole, and then to the British Isles, in his *Personality of Britain* (1932). In this justly famous work Fox combined the ecological-distributional approach of Crawford and Gradmann, with the positional geographical notions which

[1] *Cambridge Historical Journal*, 1948.

Mackinder had set out in his *Britain and the British Seas*, and the "personality" idea of the French human geographers like Vidal de la Blache, to produce a startlingly new approach to the facts of prehistory. Even to those who felt Fox's general theories savoured too much of geographical determinism, there was no denying the fresh impetus to geographical and prehistoric studies given by this work. Professor E. G. R. Taylor has described the publication of *The Personality of Britain* in its effect on geographers as "a minor earthquake corresponding to number 6 of the Rossi-Forel scale 'General awakening of those asleep. General ringing of bells . . . some startled persons leave their dwellings'".[1] And it was not only the geographers who were startled by this new geographical approach to prehistory.

[1] *Antiquity*, 1944, 103.

CHAPTER TEN

RETROSPECT AND PROSPECT

WE have now seen how, in the hundred years or so from 1840 to the war of 1939–45, archaeology, and especially prehistoric archaeology—in which specialist sense we have mainly used the word archaeology in this book—has become a recognised and distinctive branch of learning with a body of techniques, a great accumulation of facts, and a new set of interpretations of man's earliest history. The beginnings of archaeology lay in the antiquarianism of the eighteenth century, revived by the Romantic Movement, the second discovery of Greece and the growing interest in natural history. Geology provided a theory—the doctrine of uniformitarianism—which made sense of the record of the rocks and enabled the proof of the great antiquity of man to be given; the development of interest in the antiquities of Egypt and Mesopotamia showed what archaeological techniques could do in restoring man's lost past; and the northern antiquaries achieved a revolution in the study of antiquities alone by showing how the past of man could be induced from artifacts, and deduced from stratigraphy. The birth of archaeology must go back to that period before 1840 when Thomsen was arranging the National Museum at Copenhagen, Lyell was publishing his *Principles of Geology*, Champollion and Young were deciphering Egyptian, and Rawlinson was copying the Behistun inscription. Its coming of age dates from the sixties of the nineteenth century—the decade from 1859, when the *Origin of Species* was published and the authenticity of the stone axes from the Somme and south Devon publicly acclaimed, to 1867, when, at the Paris Exposition, de Mortillet arranged the prehistoric collections, and the Empress Eugénie was prevented from looting the Egyptian jewels by Auguste Mariette. From this time onwards, the story of the development of archaeology has been one of developing technique, the penetration of archaeological research into all parts of the world, and the gradual accumulation of an immense mass of factual information about prehistoric man.

The development of prehistoric archaeology has been paralleled by that of anthropology. Anthropology came into being later, at a time when archaeology was coming of age, and anthropology owes much in its origin to the stimulus given by the northern antiquaries and by Boucher de Perthes. From the sixties onwards anthropology and archaeology have grown up together; they have cross-fertilised each other with ideas, and of course they have much in common—both deal with new aspects of the humanities—the study of the uncivilised civilisations. They study preliterate and non-literate man—archaeology in the past and anthropology at the present day. But of course, while joined together in their common study of the primitives, each has the strongest bonds with other branches of learning—anthropology with psychology and sociology, and archaeology with the study of the literate civilisations which to many, and certainly to Professor A. J. Toynbee, means history. It is this inevitable dual allegiance, which he calls "the cultural anthropology—history ambivalence", that makes Taylor describe the archaeologist of to-day as "a Jekyll and Hyde, claiming to 'do' history but 'be' an anthropologist".[1] Yet it is this apparent feat of schizophrenia that the prehistoric archaeologist must achieve.

It is neither helpful nor in accordance with widespread modern usage to call either archaeology or anthropology "sciences", except in so far as they may claim, with so many of the humanities, to be miscalled the social sciences. Nor is it justifiable, as Childe has done, to regard archaeology and anthropology as twin branches of a single science.[2] While anthropology, in some of its branches, looks towards sciences like human biology, archaeology can only be called a science by a very special use of that term. Many of the nineteenth-century archaeologists claimed they were scientists, and Michaelis has declared that archaeology "may be classed among the conquering sciences of the nineteenth century".[3] But these fine precedents should not confuse us; nor should we confuse the issue because prehistory is rooted in geology. It is true, as Childe has argued, that "aided by archaeology, history with its prelude prehistory becomes a continuation of natural

[1] *A Study of Archaeology*, 6.
[2] *South-Western Journal of Anthropology*, ii, 3 (1946), 243 ff.
[3] *A Century of Archaeological Discoveries*, 1.

history",[1] but temporal continuity is in itself no argument: it no more makes prehistory and history into natural science, than it makes natural science into history. Nor should we confuse the issue because the archaeologist uses scientific techniques and engages in the microscopic examination of specimens and monuments, and because we build so much on the prime scientific doctrine of uniformitarianism. Archaeology is a technique by which facts are obtained for the construction of history and prehistory; and prehistory, like history, is humanity—a way of looking at man and his works, not at nature.

But, claimed as humanity or science, prehistory has at last come into its own; it is a recognised branch of learning and has a wide popular following. There are now Professorships of Archaeology in Oxford, Cambridge, London, Edinburgh and Dublin, as well as non-professorial departments to teach prehistoric archaeology in the Universities of Liverpool and Birmingham and the University Colleges of the South-West and South Wales. In 1948 the University of Cambridge, which for the previous thirty years had had an Honours School of Archaeology and Anthropology, introduced a new two-part Tripos in this School. Popular interest has outstripped the academic recognition of the place of archaeology in the scheme of knowledge. Popular interest began with the widespread sales of Layard's *Nineveh*, continued with the work of Schliemann, Petrie and Budge, and was established once for all by the excavations of the tomb of Tutankhamen and the Royal Graves at Ur, in the twenties of this century. Nor should we underestimate the part played in the dissemination of archaeological interest and the creation of a public for archaeology by the intelligent management of the *Illustrated London News*,[2] and by

[1] *What Happened in History*, 7.

[2] From its inception the *Illustrated London News* dealt sporadically with all sensational archaeological discoveries. From 1900, when Bruce Ingram took over the editorship, it adopted a more considered policy of covering the field of archaeological exploration. Mr Ingram writes: "As a boy at school, I was taken to Egypt by my father for an extended tour of most of the exploration sites, an experience which made a lasting impression on me. When the control of the paper fell to me in 1900, I made up my mind that there were a great many people who would have been equally interested if they were to be given an opportunity of seeing what was being done all over the world to throw light upon the civilisation of the past. The difficulty was to combine technical accuracy with an exposition simple enough for the comprehension of the layman, and by that means to stimulate his desire for further publication of a similar character" (Letter to the author, February 16, 1949). A survey of the *Illustrated London News* in the last half-century will show how brilliantly Ingram achieved his aims.

the archaeological correspondents of *The Times* and the *Daily Telegraph*. This general public interest is attested by the wide sales of popular archaeological books from the Pelican editions of Childe and the Hawkeses to more expensive works like Clark's *Prehistoric England*, the appearance of talks on prehistoric archaeology as regular and popular broadcast features, and the existence of flourishing journals like *Antiquity* and the *Archaeological News Letter* in England, and the magazine *Archaeology* in America. The quarterly review *Antiquity*, started in 1927 and still edited by its founder, O. G. S. Crawford, is more than a mine of information on all archaeological subjects, and a brilliant commentary on the development of archaeology in the last quarter-century. It is an index of the really widespread popular interest in archaeology. *Antiquity* has succeeded where its earlier predecessors like *The Antiquary* and *The Reliquary and Illustrated Archaeologist* and many others failed. This is, without doubt, in part due to the brilliance and vision of Crawford's editorship, but also in part due to the new general interest in prehistory—an interest which *Antiquity* has helped to create as well as benefited by.

It has been suggested that prehistoric archaeology has even yet not found its place in the scheme of organised knowledge, and that it should be taught in schools and become a subject for entrance scholarships to the University.[1] It depends on what view is taken as to the educative value of archaeology. Petrie claimed that archaeology "gives a more truly liberal education than any other subject, as at present taught", and in a remarkable recent statement Clark has declared that "to the peoples of the world generally . . . Palaeolithic Man has more meaning than the Greeks".[2] This passionate over-advocacy of the place of archaeology in education may easily distort the place which prehistory should properly have. There is no room for more subjects in the already overloaded curricula of primary and secondary education; but there is an imperative need that our teachers of geography and history, those basic subjects of any balanced education, should be informed by the lessons of prehistoric archaeology. Only thus can the perspective of history be extended in the minds of the young to include the prehistoric past, and an

[1] On this, see D. P. Dobson, *The Teaching of Prehistory in Schools*, 1928; Aileen Fox, "The Place of Archaeology in British Education," *Antiquity*, 1944, 153 ff.; J. G. D. Clark, "Education and the Study of Man," *Antiquity*, 1943, 113.

[2] *Antiquity*, 1943, 118.

intelligent interest taken and encouraged in the material remains of the ancient human past, whether they be artifacts like polished stone axes, or features of the cultural landscape like barrows and hill-forts. The teaching of prehistory must be largely visual and it is good to know that some instructional films in prehistory are now becoming available. Zotz was trying to bring German prehistory before the public in films before the 1939–45 War, and, since the war, the Crown Film Unit, with the technical advice of Jacquetta Hawkes, has made for the Ministry of Information the film "The Beginning of History," a very fine attempt at visual education in British prehistory. It is by such methods as those, by school broadcasts, and suitably written school history books, that the youth of the nation will become archaeologically-minded, And here our national and provincial museums have a great part to play in education; the National Museum of Wales has already developed an ambitious scheme of liaison between schools and the Museum.

The growth of archaeology has inevitably meant the growth of archaeological organisations. In Great Britain archaeology is officially organised under three bodies: the Office of Works, the Royal Commissions on Ancient and Historic Monuments, and the Ordnance Survey, which under its archaeological officer maintains an archaeological survey (topographical). The union of these three bodies into a national directorate-general of antiquities—perhaps under a restored King's Antiquary—is only at present a dream. Similar departments of antiquities exist in many foreign countries.[1]

The international organisation of prehistoric archaeology is well over eighty years old. The first international congress "pour les études préhistoriques" met at Neuchâtel in 1866. The next year, when it met in Paris, its name was changed to the "Congrès international d'Anthropologie et d'Archéologie préhistoriques". The following year the new Congress met in Norwich and London. Thereafter it did not meet annually and the fourteenth and last session was held in Geneva in 1912.[2] A revival of interest in international congresses came with the great interest in prehistory in the late twenties. A new congress, the International Congress

[1] On this subject see J. G. D. Clark, "Archaeology and the State," *Antiquity*, 1934, 414 ff.; C. L. Woolley, "Antiquities Law, Iraq," *Antiquity*, 1935, 84.

[2] The intervening meetings were held as follows: Copenhagen, 1869, Bologna, 1871, Brussels, 1872, Stockholm, 1874, Budapest, 1876, Lisbon, 1880, Paris, 1889, Moscow, 1892, Paris, 1900, Monaco, 1906, and Geneva, 1912.

of Prehistoric and Protohistoric Sciences, met first in London in 1932, then in Oslo in 1936; its third meeting, scheduled for Budapest in 1940, was postponed until 1950.

We should then ask, what has prehistoric archaeology produced in its hundred years of development which justifies these organisations and sustains the widespread interest in prehistory? The vast quantity of merely archaeological facts is apparent to anyone who opens an archaeological textbook or the report of an excavation. But what historical facts of importance to all interested in the humanities have emerged from prehistoric archaeology? Nelson has declared that the broad outstanding achievements of prehistoric archaeology to date are, the growth and organisation of the science itself, the accumulated body of facts from all parts of the world about early man, and "the growing body of interpretations and its obvious influence on modern thought."[1] Let us consider briefly some of these "interpretations".

In the first place, prehistoric archaeology has given an enormous perspective to man's story and revealed the relative lateness of what we call civilisation. Gone is the Ussher chronology of the diluvialist and fundamentalist days; no longer are we content with a history of six thousand years only. The first artifacts are now dated geochronologically to perhaps a million years ago, while the first villages are dated to the eighth millennium ago, and the first cities of Egypt and the Fertile Crescent to five millennia ago. To one schooled in the history of western Europe in the last two thousand years, dates like the sixth millennium B.C. seem still incredibly old; but against the perspective of a million years of human effort they are indeed recent. Man the food producer, man the village and city dweller, man the literate civilised animal is a very recent phenomenon. This perspective still needs to be stressed, although C. F. C. Hawkes thinks it banal from over-repetition,[2] and Ronald Knox has attacked the whole argument of the perspective of prehistory as the argument *obscurum per obscurius.*[3] The average historian still needs these facts stressed to him; civilisation occupies at most only one per cent. of man's time on the earth as a tool-making animal. This new perspective will bring about a great revolution in thought, when it is realised,

[1] Nelson, in Boas (Ed.), *General Anthropology*, 1938, 230.
[2] *Archaeology and the History of Europe.*
[3] *The Belief of Catholics*, 249 (Oxford, 1948), 11.

as Lowie has said, that written history is only "the final scene of a lengthy drama",[1] and that it is no longer possible to study history, as Toynbee does in his *Study of History*, by concentrating on the varied manifestations of the literate civilisations. Perhaps Childe goes too far in the other direction in boldly calling a book which deals mainly with prehistory and protohistory *What Happened in History*, but his is a most welcome reaction to those historians who have been trying, as Charles Letourneau said nearly half a century ago, "to reconstruct a book from its last chapter".[2]

Archaeology can, then, demonstrate the lateness of those complicated societies we call civilisations, with their cities, technologies and religions. It shows, too, the falsity of what Childe has termed "the illusion entertained by Spengler and Toynbee of a multiplicity of 'civilisations' any of which can be isolated from forerunners and contemporaries and still continue to behave as a living organism".[3] But can prehistoric archaeology go further? Can it demonstrate how the peasant village economies came into being, and how the urban civilisations arose? Can it isolate and document the Neolithic and Urban revolutions? The answer to this question, after a hundred years of archaeological research, is that prehistory is well on the way to doing this, although at present it cannot do so with certainty.

We have seen how Egypt replaced Central Asia as the cradle of civilisation, and how Mesopotamia has temporarily dethroned Egypt, with the Fertile Crescent—and particularly Palestine—and Iran appearing as possible claimants. Are these changes merely reflections of the changing state of archaeological knowledge, or do they represent a changed body of facts? In part they are an index of our increased knowledge of Near-Eastern archaeology, but it is true that at Mersin, Jericho, Nineveh, Hassunah and Sialk, peasant village communities older than any hitherto found have been excavated and described. But there are other areas to be studied. Vavilov, from the evidence of cultivated plants, drew attention to Abyssinia as a possible home of early civilisation, and Miss Caton-Thompson has recently redrawn attention to the possibility of a Central African origin for the Neolithic civilisation.[4] Although excavation has been intense in the Near East in

[1] *History of Ethnological Theory*, 9.
[2] *Le Condition de la Femme dans les diverses Races et Civilisations*, 1903, 3.
[3] *Antiquity*, 1941, 3.
[4] Huxley Lecture for 1948, *The Aterian.*

the present century, the number of unexcavated tells far exceeds those that have been excavated. What historical facts may lie buried, we wonder, in the great number of tells found by Von der Osten in the Kirul Ismak Basin of Anatolia, by Gjerstad and Garstang in the Cilician Plain, by Ellsworth Huntington in Askhabad, E. F. Schmidt in Iran, and Suydam Cutting in the Tien Shan Mountains? Huntington visited twenty-eight tells in eight days in the neighbourhood of Merv,[1] and Arne drew a map showing two hundred mounds in a small area along the Gurgan river on the Iranian side of the Transcaspian steppes.[2] "The entire land is sown with thousands of them," wrote Herzfeld, "but the most important ones are to be sought near the Oxus and Iaxartes, the Amu- and Syr-Darya. One day this alluvial land will reveal itself as the home of civilisation rivalling in age, if not in importance, the most ancient civilisations of the Indus valley in the East and the Tigris-Euphrates in the West." [3] Where, then, is the home of the Near-Eastern civilisation? The answer has still to be provided by archaeology.

Until we have worked out in detail the sequence of cultures in the Near East from the food-gathering Mesolithic economies to the food-producing Neolithic economies, we shall be unable to answer the age-old problem of the succession of economies. Did man proceed independently from a food-gathering stage to agricultural and stock-raising economies, or is pastoralism a specialised variant of the mixed-farming peasant villages of the Neolithic revolution? The problem of economies brings us up against one of the great limitations of prehistory. A first limitation, that of the incompleteness of the archaeological record due to the incidence of excavations, we have already noticed in discussing the origins of civilisation. The second, which we touch when we discuss the evolution of economies, is the great problem of the existence of cultures and civilisations without material remains. It is the nightmare of the serious prehistorian. Menghin postulated a bone civilisation in the Palaeolithic of which few remains survive. To what extent were there nomadic peoples in the Near East and Central Asia in the period 6000 B.C. to the beginning of the present era who might have had few or no

[1] A reconnaissance of the Kurgans of the Merv Oasis.

[2] T. J. Arne, "La Steppe Turkomane et ses Antiquités," *Geografiska Annaler*, 1935.

[3] *Iran in the Ancient East*, 95.

elements of material culture that would survive in the archaeological record yet who had a vital part to play in the development and transmission of culture? Does the prehistorian, by studying only the artifacts of early man, tend to streamline history into the technological development of those early cultures whose artefacts have survived? And here we touch on the third great limitation of prehistoric archaeology. Is prehistory doomed to record only certain aspects of the material development of early man? What of man's early intellectual development? Must the story of the intellectual adventure of early man always begin only with writing, *i.e.* with the dynastic periods of Sumer and Egypt? At the present moment it seems that it must, and to that extent the distinction between prehistory and history is a more real one than most prehistorians would care to admit.

But if we are hampered still by the process of discovery, and the limited nature of the surviving relics of early man, archaeology remains the only source for the record of prehistoric man. It is only from prehistory that we derive any exact information about the relative chronology of man's development and the nature of culture change in the days before writing. Archaeology, no less than anthropology, has for much of its hundred years of development been a battleground between diffusionists and evolutionists. We have seen how the northern antiquaries of the first half of the nineteenth century, and their mid-century successors in England and Switzerland, like Lubbock and Morlot, thought equally in terms of diffusion and independent evolution without defining the relative parts played by the two processes. De Mortillet and his disciples, while they admitted "invasions", were mainly wedded to developing sequences. Elliot Smith and Perry by their violent advocacy of an Egyptocentric hyperdiffusion, while not converting many to their cure-all prehistory which explained everything from British dolmens to Maya pyramids by the search of the Children of the Sun for the Givers of Life, at least made prehistorians think clearly about the mechanics of culture change. The result was the modified diffusionism of Childe's *Danube in Prehistory* and *The Dawn of European Civilisation*, and the clear-cut interpretation of prehistory as a series of invasions which we get in books like Obermaier's *Fossil Man in Spain*. At the present day prehistory is becoming too much a matter of invasions and folk movements; more examination is needed of the mechanics of cultural diffusion and change, and this is where the study of anthropology and of early historic times can be of the greatest value to prehistorians. It may well be that in many cases we shall never be able to do more than indicate contacts and areas of possible origin for foreign types that occur for the first time in an archaeological sequence, that we shall be unable to speak of invasions and folk movements, and may have to take refuge again behind the much-maligned word "influence". Even so, there is certainly one thing the prehistorian can tell the later historian, and that is the foreign influences or the outside ethnic elements that make up the prehistoric background of any country's history, although he may not be able to translate these influences into terms of human beings, or estimate the relative strength and importance of the ethnic elements.

There is one great change which is coming over prehistoric archaeology at the present: we are moving from a study of cultures to a study of culture. We have seen in this book how the first analysis of archaeological material was geological: the analysis that produced the epochs and periods of de Mortillet. A second analysis was formal and classificatory: the approach that produced the periods of Montelius and his followers. The third analysis distinguished significant associations of types distributed in time and space, and these it defined as *the* culture of a society. We have argued that this third analysis owed much to the *Kulturhistorische Schule* of Graebner, Ankermann and Schmidt, and to the recognition of prehistoric civilisations in the Aegean and the Near East. In a natural revolt from the geological and taxonomic approaches of the late nineteenth century the study of cultures has become the new approach of the prehistorian in the last quarter-century. Indeed Childe and Clark have defined this as the main task of the prehistoric archaeologist. Clark writes: "The science of archaeology might well be defined as the study of the past distribution of culture traits in time and space, and of the factors governing their distribution" [1], and Childe says that prehistory is "largely devoted to isolating . . . cultural groups or peoples, tracing their differentiations, wanderings and activities".[2]

There are two objections to these definitions of archaeology. The first relates to the nature of a culture. Does the archaeologist really distinguish cultural differences, or does he merely list varying

[1] *Antiquity*, 1933, 232. [2] *Ibid.*, 1933, 417.

patterns in what Taylor would call the "material objectifications of culture"? To put a point on a theoretical discussion, it is customary in the description of pre-Roman Britain to distinguish in the first half of the second millennium various "cultures", such as the Windmill Hill culture, the Peterborough culture, the Skara Brae culture, the Beaker culture, the Western or Megalithic culture, and so forth.[1] Are these in fact cultures, or is the archaeologist merely misusing the notion of culture to apply to regional variations of material objects? Braidwood has registered an eloquent protest against this archaeological misusage,[2] and Tallgren has pointed out that often the cultures of the archaeologist "are not functions of a people; they may be the result of social classes and commerce".[3]

Prehistory, or prehistoriography, has arrived in its conceptual development at the stage which historiography reached in the late nineteenth century. Seeley said to his students: "Break the drowsy spell of narrative; ask yourselves questions, set yourselves problems"; and Lord Acton in his inaugural lecture in 1895 declared: "Study problems in preference to periods." It is now time for prehistory to break the drowsy spell of listing cultures, and to study problems in preference to periods. Prehistory cannot develop into one of the important humanities until it has a sense of problem; without this sense of problem it must remain a technique and the accumulation of facts. The distinction and description of cultures is not the problem of prehistory; the cultures of the modern archaeologist, like the periods and epochs of his predecessors, are merely conceptual tools. His problem is the description and analysis of prehistoric culture, and the writing of prehistoric contexts. This cannot be put more clearly than has been done recently by Taylor in his *Study of Archaeology*. Taylor, after an exhaustive analysis of the nature of history, archaeology and anthropology, and the concept of culture in archaeology, declares that while anthropology is concerned with the nature of culture and cultural dynamics, history is the construction of cultural contexts with due regard for time, not merely the arrangement of events and cultural phenomena in temporarily sequential

[1] The present writer has been guilty of distinguishing several megalithic cultures when all he was studying were regional variations in tomb plan, and grave goods.

[2] *American Journal of Semitic Languages and Literatures*, January 1945.

[3] *Antiquity*, 1937, 152.

order. Prehistory—and it is the writing of prehistory which is the goal of the archaeologist—is, then, not merely the arrangement of artifacts and other cultural phenomena in temporarily sequential order but the construction of prehistoric cultural contexts. As Brønsted wrote in the preface to his *Danmarks Oldtid*: "the goal of archaeology is the history of culture".

There are two obvious problems which beset the archaeologist who is trying to reconstruct the early history of culture. The first is the development of economy, and the second the development of art. Lubbock was interested in the development of economy in prehistoric times, and it should be remembered that even Gabriel de Mortillet, archpriest, as we think of him, of the taxonomic epochal approach to prehistory, wrote an essay on the origin of fishing. Attempts have been made to survey the whole economic development of prehistoric man, such as those of Renard in his *Life and Work in Prehistoric Times* (1929) and of Georges Heyman in his *Préhistoire Economique Générale* (1944). Bandi in his *Die Schweiz zur Renntierzeit* (1947) has attempted the description of the economic life of the Magdalenian reindeer hunters of Switzerland, and in Clark's *Prehistoric England* (1940) and Childe's *Scotland before the Scots* (1946) brilliant attempts have been made at the reconstruction of the economies of pre-Roman Britain. But unquestionably the most serious and important approaches to the economic history of prehistoric Europe have been made by Clark in an extremely important series of papers published between 1940 and the present day.[1] Here is a clear sense of problem—the economic development of prehistoric life: and painstaking researches leading towards the solution of that problem.

Less attention has been paid to another obvious problem that faces the prehistoric archaeologist — the development of prehistoric art. Palaeolithic art has attracted a great deal of attention, due partly to its antiquity, and to its very remarkable character. Apart from extensive treatment in all the standard works on the Palaeolithic there have been special memoirs like Baldwin Brown's *The Art of the Cave Dweller* (1928), Luquet's *Art and Religion of Fossil Man* (1930) and Parkyn's *Introduction to the Study of Prehistoric Art* (1915), which carry on the interest

[1] See, for example, *Antiquity*, 1942, 208; 1944, 1; 1945, 57; 1947, 122; 1948, 116; *Economic History Review*, 1947, 45; *Antiquaries Journal*, 1948, 45.

created by Piette's *L'Art pendant l'Age du Renne* (1907) and Reinach's *Répertoire de l'Art quaternaire*, and serve as introductions to the magnificent volumes published by the Institut de Paléontologie Humaine on individual caves. At the other end of the prehistoric time-scale the art of the La Tène Celts has received very special attention in memoirs such as Romilly Allen's *Celtic Art in Pagan and Christian Times* (1904) and recently in E. T. Leeds's *Celtic Ornament* (1933) and the magnificent publication of Jacobsthal's *Early Celtic Art* (1944). But apart from Upper Palaeolithic and La Tène art, the art of prehistoric man has received very cursory treatment. Of course full publication in expensive series of corpora is the prerequisite of the study of early art. The *Corpus des Signes gravés des Monuments Mégalithiques du Morbihan*, produced by Le Rouzic and the St Just Pecquarts in 1927, is an example of the way in which works should be attempted. It is indeed a matter for great regret that no adequate publication as yet exists of the art of pre-Roman Britain; the first prehistoric volume of the *Ars Hispaniae* (1947) is an indication of how such an adequate publication can be achieved.

The study of prehistoric art is not only one of the most obvious ways in which prehistoric studies can be made to interest the general reader—and some effort is required for the historically minded person to be made to think in terms of an anonymous prehistoric past—it is also one of the few ways in which the prehistorian can get towards the non-material values of the peoples he studies, and perhaps catch a glimpse, however fleeting, of the intellectual adventure of prehistoric man. That this glimpse can never be more than fleeting is unfortunately true; to write of the moral, material and religious culture of prehistoric man is at best, as Hogarth described it, "no more than subjective guessing at the causes of surviving products of human activities".[1]

But this subjective guessing has a great fascination for prehistorians. Much has been written about the purpose behind Upper Palaeolithic art; and much has been and is being written regarding the motives behind the development of prehistoric culture in general. Many of the late nineteenth-century prehistorians explained the changes in prehistoric culture as due to different races: such was Sir John Rhŷs's threefold explanation of Welsh prehistory in terms of Iberians, Goidels and Brythons.

[1] D. G. Hogarth, *The Twilight of History* (1946).

Elliot Smith and Perry's Children of the Sun diffusing a Heliothic Culture is not far removed from the Master Race interpretation of prehistory; and Lord Raglan in his *How Came Civilisation* (1939) has transferred the Master Race from Egypt to Sumeria. In England, Fleure and Fox, and in America, Ellsworth Huntington and Griffith Taylor, have stressed the geographical factors in the distribution of prehistoric settlements and the movements of peoples. In particular Fox's *Personality of Britain*, first published in 1932, has had an enormous effect on the orientation of prehistoric thought towards a geographical determinism, his statements on prehistoric man's possible utilisation of his geographical possibilities having been canonised by Collingwood, Hawkes and others into "Fox's Laws". Arnold Toynbee, on the other hand, in the sections of his *Study of History*[1] dealing with the genesis of civilisations, has advocated a thesis which, while claimed to be a negation of the geographical factor in prehistory, is in reality a subtle variation of the theory of the geographical causation of human activity: Toynbee sees the environment as a challenge to early man; to Fleure and Fox the environment is an all-powerful control. Others, from Camille Jullian to Hawkes, in his *Prehistoric Foundations of Europe*, see in the prehistoric record already formed much of the national and international characteristics of the present day. Finally, the Russian prehistorians, and in this country Childe, see the rise and fall of prehistoric cultures in terms of Marxian dialectical materialism.

This is not the place to discuss the development and usefulness of these interpretations of the motivations of prehistoric culture. They are, from the very nature of the evidence, subjective guesses. One of them may be right; in the absence of writing shall we ever be able to say which? What must be guarded against is the prehistorian who declares to the historian that this or that particular interpretation of history is the correct one, because it has been proved right in prehistory. We cannot, alas, prove what were the main motivating forces in prehistory, but it is unreasonable to suppose that they were other than those which motivate primitive peoples at the present day. Goldenweiser has

[1] The first three volumes of *A Study of History* were published in 1933: the next three in 1939. D. C. Somervell's abridgment of volumes i–vi appeared in 1946.

put the matter very well when he says: "It is evident that human history during the last several thousand years is altogether too richly varied for us to believe that the only slightly less rich story of man before he began leaving written documents for professional historians will prove essentially more expressible by such formulas." [1] These formulas are in the end the same *simpliste* errors which have beset anthropology and human geography for a long time.[2] But while they are valid bases of discussion in branches of learning where all the facts are available, they are of only very doubtful validity in prehistory, when all the facts are not available, and will probably never be available. We may be able one day to say what happened in history, but surely never what exactly happened in prehistory, because there is not, and never can be, a history of prehistoric thought. The history of ideas begins with writing.

We cannot unfortunately develop this point here, nor, again, can we here study another interesting aspect of the utilisation of prehistory, namely the perversion of the facts of prehistory for national and political ends, as was done by Italians and Germans during and before the 1939–45 War, and as is now being done by Russian prehistorians.[3] Here is a very real danger and a grave warning; apparently the history which is most controversial, and whose sources are most difficult to understand, is the easiest to pervert.

The way in which prehistory has been perverted deliberately by politicians, and interpreted from special angles by prehistorians themselves, makes it more than ever necessary that at all times the facts of prehistory, such as they are, should be summarised and available to historians and other students of the humanities, who cannot be expected to read excavation reports and to whom, for example, the comparative stratigraphies of McCown and Schaeffer are so much professional mumbo-jumbo. Breasted's *Ancient Times* (1916) was a beginning in the difficult task of synthesising the results of prehistoric archaeology for the historian; Elliot Smith's *Human History* (1930) was vitiated by his prepossession with the Egyptians; despite their frankly Marxist bias, Childe's three little books—*Man Makes Himself* (1936), *Progress*

[1] Goldenweiser, *Anthropology*, 631.

[2] On this, see Lowie, *History of Ethnological Theory*, passim.

[3] For an account of this see J. G. D. Clark, *Archaeology and Society*, chapter vii.

and Archaeology (1944) and *What Happened in History* (1942)—are admirable modern syntheses of prehistory designed for the non-archaeologist. And it should be noted here that Wells, in his *Outline of History* (1920), achieved a good integration of archaeology and history, as do his more scholarly successors, such as Ralph Turner in his *The Great Cultural Traditions* (1941).

We have no word in the English language like the German *Urgeschichte*, which means prehistory, protohistory and early history, and it is because of this, among other things, that it is still possible for historians to be trained and flourish without any sound knowledge of prehistory. This is why summaries of prehistoric archaeology must always be a main charge on the activities of archaeologists. It is useless to complain that the *Oxford History of England* starts only with the Roman conquest, and that A. L. Rowse's series *Teach Yourself History* confines itself only to the last one per cent. of man's time on this earth, unless archaeology is prepared to provide the constant vulgarisation of its results necessary to remove this old-fashioned idea of history. Eileen Power once said: "It is the greatest error to suppose that history must be something written down" [1]; it must now be one of the main tasks of prehistoric archaeologists to see that this error is not perpetuated, because hitherto it is only the history written down which is made generally intelligible.

But there remain greater things to do than merely to ensure that the history of man as taught and appreciated is the whole history of man. Archaeological scholarship itself has a great way to go, and it is wrong, even after a hundred years of work, to suppose that archaeology is anywhere except at a very early stage in its development. The new weapon of research of total air photography is only beginning to reveal the incredibly rich nature of the hidden sites. The techniques of excavation are still developing, and it may well be that in another quarter-century or so we shall look back at the present as only the beginnings of scientific digging. On the other hand, in one way the development of archaeological excavation has already reached a high point in its development. The cost of excavations has now become so great that far fewer excavations are likely to be undertaken. When Théophile Homolle began work at Delos in 1877 he had only 1.300 francs (about £52) at his disposal to finance his excavations;

[1] *Mediaeval People*, 149.

his work cost much more, and soon the Duc de Loubat was paying £2,000 a year towards the cost of the work. The cost of four seasons' work at Maiden Castle was estimated by Dr Wheeler as over £5,000, and this was before the 1939–45 War. The rising costs of excavation must mean that only carefully selected sites can be excavated, which in itself is a good thing.

The reduction in excavation may also mean that more energies are available for the collation and analysis of the material already excavated. Indeed Herzfeld has declared that "the task of systematic research and elaboration is more cogent than the continuation of excavation"; and develops this point in a passage of such importance that it must be quoted here *in extenso*: "The great public interest in archaeological exploration brings financial support to excavations more readily than to studies and publications, and contributes to the fact that students with insufficient archaeological training develop, for the romance of it, into 'excavators'. Excavating is but one method of archaeological research; it is what experiment is to natural science. It produces evidence for problems that change with and depend upon the momentary stage of our knowledge. Excavating is an art, but no autonomous branch of archaeology. Without intimate knowledge of the exact position of the problems, the excavator cannot solve them, nor even observe correctly, in spite of all good will. If research does not keep pace with excavating, the explorer is like an experimenter away from the scientist; he collects at random and misses the things that matter. For not everything is of equal importance and the scale for importance is the ever-changing state of our knowledge."

Taylor has said much the same thing in his recently published *Study of Archaeology*, arguing that excavation by itself is not enough, and that the aim of the archaeologist must not be accurate digging and publication, not even accurate comparative stratigraphy and the isolation of artefact patterns which he miscalls cultures, but the writing of history. He urges what he calls the conjunctive approach to archaeology, which is much what we have been arguing for here: the total study of the culture of a period of prehistoric time. It is true, as Crawford has recently claimed, that "we are all dirt archaeologists"; but it is not enough to be a dirt archaeologist. Unless archaeologists write history they are in danger of justifying Hooton's jibe at them, that they are "senile playboys of science, rooting in the rubbish heaps of antiquity . . . unregardful of the necessities of the present". The scale of importance of the archaeologist's work at the present day is not the number and size and frequency of his excavations, but the extent to which he has contributed to the writing or rewriting of the early history of man. Without a sense of history, and of historical problem, archaeology can revert again to mere collection; and there is always the danger of a new antiquarianism.

There is, of course, always at the base of the archaeologist's mind the collector's joy. It would be wrong if this were allowed to develop because, allegedly, all the major historical lessons from prehistoric archaeology had been learnt, and there was no more to do than add details. The inscription on the medal struck in honour of Oscar Montelius said: "Fifty years of research have mastered millennia of human culture": but this is not true; the mastery is a long way off. Marett, in discussing the generation of Lyell, Lubbock, Tylor and Sir John Evans, said sadly: "theirs was the age of prophets, whereas ours are rather the days of mass production, when factory hands are more in demand than masters of glamour who can read the signs in the sky". It is a great mistake, and one which must be guarded against in writing the history of archaeology, to suppose that archaeology was a great development of the nineteenth century, and that we have no more to do now than specialise microtomically and to summarise. The next hundred years of archaeology will yield as many prophets and masters of glamour as the first hundred years of archaeology. The state of our knowledge is ever-changing, and the present is only a moment in the development of archaeology. It is a brief picture of this ever-changing state of archaeological knowledge during the last hundred years or so that has been attempted here.

CHAPTER ELEVEN

ARCHAEOLOGY 1945–1970

The previous ten chapters, written in 1945–48, surveyed the development of archaeology from its beginnings as a serious discipline in the early nineteenth century until the outbreak of the Second World War in 1939—the year in which the Sutton Hoo ship-burial was discovered near Ipswich in Suffolk. The 1939–45 war locked up the energies of most archaeologists in military or semi-military pursuits and held up further discovery by excavation for some while. Yet major discoveries were made during the Second World War, some entirely by chance, such as the discovery of the cave of Lascaux in Dordogne, with its remarkable paintings and engravings of Upper Palaeolithic date, on 12 September 1940; and some by the fortunes of war and the necessity of continuing non-military work during a war—it was the extension of the runways of London airport at Heathrow that enabled W. F. Grimes to discover a Celtic temple.

Some archaeologists were able to turn their enforced military activities to scholarly advantage. In the intervals of his work in military intelligence in India, Stuart Piggott was able to make a survey of the prehistoric archaeology of that great sub-continent, and to summarise his findings in his *Prehistoric India* (1950), and J. S. P. Bradford to use the opportunities of aerial reconnaissance in Italy to do research in the main tradition of Crawford, Poidebard and Allen. Bradford, alas, no longer a functioning archaeologist, has summarised his work in his *Ancient Landscapes* (1960).

With the return in 1945–46 of the archaeologists to their peacetime jobs, and the renewal of opportunities for reconnaissance, excavation and research, all activities started up again with renewed vigour. Certainly, since the Second World War, archaeology has never looked back, professionally, although of course its profession is to look back. A quarter of a century after the end of the war archaeology has never been more booming. In universities, and in the world in general, it is now an important, recognised and respected discipline and its role in the study of man understood or at least appreciated. In 1932 there were less than ten archaeologists with posts in British Universities: now, including extramural departments, it is about two hundred. No major newspaper and no major television agency can now afford to neglect archaeology. In Britain the success of *Animal, Vegetable, Mineral?*, *Buried Treasure*, and the *Chronicle* series on the BBC, and series like *Who were the British?* and *The Lost Centuries* on Anglia TV, and in America the amazing success of Froelich Rainey's *What in the World?* (which ran for twenty-five years) show how archaeology has conquered the media. Piggorini opens his *The Meaning of Archaeology* (1967), with the words "Archéologie est aujourdhui à la mode", and this is very true.

A hundred years ago Tylor wrote in his *Primitive Culture* (1871): "The history and prehistory of man take their proper places in the general scheme of knowledge", and this sentence was quoted at the end of Chapter 3. Tylor was optimistic: it was not so in 1871. But it is so now: archaeology is now taking this proper place in the study of man. Our concern in this chapter is with what happened in the development of archaeology since 1945 to make it not only academically acceptable and necessary, but also interesting and relevant to the ordinary person—for what is now clear a century after Tylor's apothegm is that an understanding and appreciation of archaeology is mandatory for anyone interested in human history.

The period under review has seen major discoveries in all parts of the world but, from the most general point of view, the four main changes in archaeology have been these: first, prehistoric archaeology has become world-wide, secondly, American archaeology has come into its own, thirdly, scientific techniques have come to the aid of the archaeologist in a most remarkable way, and fourth, the archaeology of post-prehistoric, protohistoric and historic times has developed and established itself to the great benefit of historians and archaeologists.

Without any doubt the most important scientific technique developed for archaeology in the last twenty-five years is that of radiocarbon dating (discussed more fully later on), and it is on exaggeration to say that this technique has revolutionised prehistoric and protohistoric archaeology. It has recently become the custom to quote dates obtained by C14 dating in two ways: to use lower case letters b.p., a.d. and b.c., when they are actual C14 dates, and only to use upper case letters namely B.P., A.D. and B.C., when the dates have been calibrated to represent calendar years. For a clear account of these problems see Colin Renfrew, *Before Civilisation: the Radiocarbon Revolution and Prehistoric Europe* (1973), chapter 4.

1. *World Prehistory*

For a survey of the way in which prehistory has become world prehistory reference should be made to Grahame Clark's *World Prehistory: A New Outline* (Cambridge, 1969) and *Archaeology: Horizons New and Old* being papers read in November 1965 at the Autumn General Meeting of the American Philosophical Society (Philadelphia, 1966, *Proc. Am. Phil. Soc.*, 110, 91–152) and for Palaeolithic discoveries on a world-wide basis, J. Coles and E. Higgs, *Early Man* (London, 1968). Until very recently the date of the Pleistocene was given as one million years, but Bed 1 at Olduvai has yielded a date of 1.7 to 2.2 million years, and the full length of the Pleistocene may well be 3 to 4 million years. The discoveries of the Australopithecines have been discussed by Broom in *Finding the Missing Link* (London, 1950) and by Dart and Craig in their *Adventures with the Missing Link* (London, 1959). Archaeological research in the Olduvai Gorge in East Africa, one of the most important prehistoric sites in the world, began in 1931. Twenty years later L. S. B. Leakey (who died in 1972) published his *Olduvai Gorge* which summarised work up to 1947. In 1972 Richard Leakey announced the finding of many Australopithecines in East Rudolf and of the skull of a member of the genus *Homo* earlier than 2.6 million years ago. In Africa the early stages of man's physical and cultural evolution seem now well attested and Charles Darwin's dictum that Africa was probably the cradle of mankind a very shrewd guess.

The war brought excavation to an end in Egypt, as elsewhere, and since the war the unsettled nature of Egyptian politics, the declaration of the republic in 1952, the withdrawal of the British in 1956, the Israeli invasion and the Anglo-French intervention in the same year, the six-days Arab-Israeli war of 1967, the conflict of 1973 made archaeology difficult and the participation of foreign archaeologists quite naturally, and at least for a while, unacceptable. The British and French schools in Cairo were closed down in 1956, but the Antiquities Department of the Egyptian Government has itself achieved a great deal in the way of excavation and conservation. In the winter of 1953–54 the Egyptian Antiquities Department, while clearing away small sandhills near the south side of the great Pyramid of Cheops found a grave containing a perfectly preserved wooden boat. The boat had been taken to bits but every piece was there including the esparto grass covering of the bridge. The hull, over forty yards long, was made of cedarwood from the Lebanon—the scent of the wood was still discernible. The ship has been dated to 2700 B.C. It is curious that this discovery was made so recently in an area of Egypt so well studied for so long.

In 1953 Zakariah Goneim discovered the foundations of a Third Dynasty step Pyramid at Saqqara, near the famous step Pyramid of Zoser. The next year the excavators reached a burial chamber containing a great sarcophagus which appeared to be intact. In his *The Lost Pyramid* (London, 1965) Gonheim wrote: "One by one my workmen clambered through the hole in the blockage and scrambled down into the chamber. They were mad with excitement and, catching their enthusiasm, I gave way completely to my pent-up feelings, kept in check for so long. We danced round the sarcophagus and wept. We embraced each other. It was a very strange moment in that chamber, 130 feet beneath the surface of the desert. Many of these workmen had been employed by great archaeologists such as Reisner and Junker and Petrie; and they told me that never in their whole lives had they seen such a thing." In June 1954 the sarcophagus was opened: it was empty—the Pyramid was a dummy or a cenotaph.

The project for the Aswan High Dam had been one of President Nasser's dreams for many years and in 1955 the construction of the Dam was announced with a completion date of 1968. A Documentation and Study Centre for the History of the Art and Civilisation of Ancient Egypt was founded in Cairo. The High Dam, four and a half miles upstream of the Old Aswan Dam, was to have, and now has, a storage reservoir behind (Lake Nasser) which would submerge a large region now divided between Egypt and the Sudan, and known from antiquity as Nubia. The widening Nile north of the Dam would threaten many riparian sites. In 1959 Egypt and the Sudan appealed to UNESCO and the following year a campaign to salvage the archaeological heritage of Nubia was mounted under the sponsorship of UNESCO. Within a year Nubia became an archaeological camp: more than twenty-two different nations took part in this remarkable co-operative archaeological campaign.

Without doubt the most exciting and dramatic aspect of the emergency Nubia campaign was the bodily removal of twenty-two temples from the area between Abu Simbel and Aswan to higher, safer sites. The Graeco-Roman temple of Kalabsha was moved by the West Germans: it was cut into 1,600 blocks, many of them weighing 20 tons, floated down the Nile on barges and re-erected at Aswan. The greatest achievement of this campaign was the removal of the famous temples at Abu Simbel: fifty-one nations subscribed to the cost of this operation which eventually cost 34 million dollars—twice the original estimate. The United States of America bore the main burden of this cost.

The 22-nation campaign through UNESCO for the work in Nubia is a very great event in the history of archaeology. The then Director-General of UNESCO, M. René Maheu said: "This is the first time that an international common effort has assumed such scope in matters of culture and that governments have committed their states to an understanding of this kind. It is also the first time that such an effort has been based on the idea that certain religious, historical, and artistic monuments . . . belong to the whole human race and form part of its common heritage." Now UNESCO is mounting a similar campaign to save Carthage, threatened by complete destruction.

The last thirty years have revolutionised our knowledge of the development of early cultures in what Gordon Childe called the Most Ancient Near East. The Natufian culture in Jordan and Israel was defined by Dorothy Garrod in 1928. Diana Kirkbride's excavations at Beidha revealed Natufian encampments overlain by settlements of people growing wild barley, emmer, pea and pistachio and owning domesticated goats. Since 1950 the transition from hunting to farming has been established in rock shelters and open settlements. In the cave of Zami Cheni Shanidar in Iraq, Ralph Solecki found in the bottom of his Layer B dating from 10,000 B.C. a stone industry associated with the remains of wild goats, and in the upper part of this layer (dating to the early half of the ninth millennium B.C.) the same lithic industry but now, in addition, with slotted blades for reaping, knives, querns, baskets and the bones of domestic sheep (see *Science*, 1963, 179 and *Shanidar: the Humanity of Neanderthal Man* by R. S. Solecki, London, 1972).

R. J. Braidwood was one of the great pioneers in the exploration of sites in the Near East that could document and explain the transition from non-food producing societies to those that were food-producing. In 1948 he led expeditions into the hills of Kurdistan in Iraq and Iran and from 1948 to 1955 dug at Jarmo, a site in the foothills of northern Iraq, east of Kirkuk. The results of these excavations were published in Braidwood and Bruce Howe, *Prehistoric Investigations in Iraqi Kurdistan* (Chicago, 1960). The old Tell at Jericho—Tell-es-Sultan—first dug by the Germans in 1907–09 and then by Garstang between 1930 and 1936 was re-excavated by Kathleen Kenyon from 1952 onwards. In eight seasons she revealed the great importance of this remarkable site. Among the most exciting modern excavations in Turkey have been those of Beycesultan, Çatal Hüyük, and Haçilar. Çatal Hüyük is on the edge of the Konya plateau in south-central Turkey and was dug by James Mellaart in the fifties and sixties. He discovered twelve building levels dating from 6500 to 5720 B.C. This was an early town of rectangular mud-brick houses entered through openings in the roof. The inhabitants practised a fully developed agriculture with emmer, einkhorn, bread wheat, barley, peas and vetches: they had domesticated sheep and cattle. There were many shrines with outlines of animals in low-relief, many wall frescoes, painted modelled bulls' heads with horn cores incorporated and a number of carved stone figures of the Mother Goddess or her consort (see J. Mellaart, *Çatal Hüyük*, London, 1971).

Braidwood's pioneer work in the oak-pistachio woodland belt on the hilly flanks of the Fertile Crescent was continued by Hole and Flannery in the excavation of Tepe Ali Kosh and other sites in the Deh Luran plain of Khuzistan in Iran from 1963 onwards (see Frank Hole, Kent V. Flannery and James A. Neely, *Prehistory and Human Ecology of the Deh Luran Plain: an Early Village Sequence from Khuzistan, Iran* (Ann Arbor, 1969). The three phases at Ali Kosh show the transition from food-gathering to food-production, and this is precisely what the excavators were hoping to reveal: their most successful, interesting and well-published excavation was a problem-oriented job. They were looking for a test case of the origins of agriculture in the Near East: as they write themselves, "while most Near Eastern archaeologists have dug for buildings and incidentally recovered a few seeds in the process, we dug for seeds and incidentally recovered fragments of buildings in the process". Theirs was also a study of the micro-environment and it is by such studies that we shall get to grips with the reality of the process in the past which involved change from food-gathering and hunting to subsistence agriculture. These problems can no longer be studied in terms of large geographical areas as vegetational zones. As Robert Adams has said, "gross descriptive categories like 'semi-arid steppeland' may be as inadequate for a deeper historical understanding as they are for the contemporary planner". Adams's own book *Land Beyond Baghdad* (Chicago, 1965) is itself a fascinating and important survey, based on air photographs and ground survey, in which prehistoric settlement patterns are related to hydrological, social, historical and geographical patterns.

We can mention only some of the other important excavations in recent years in the Near East such as Eridu, Tell al Dhibai, Tel es-Sarwan, Nippur, Nimrud, Warka, Larsa and Tell al-Rimrah. From 1951–52 onwards Sir Max Mallowan mounted a series of highly important excavations at Nimrud which revealed among other things remarkable Assyrian ivories. His book *Nimrud and its Remains* (London, 1970) well deserves a place on the shelf of classic Near Eastern archaeological monographs alongside Layard, Rawlinson, and Woolley. Professor Claude Schaeffer has continued his excavations at Ras Shamra which he started in 1929 and their publication appears in a steady stream of books in the series *Ugaritica*. Parrot, later Director of the Louvre, excavated a second-millennium palace at Mari, and Dunaud went on digging at Byblos.

The state of Israel has devoted itself to archaeological research in a big and efficient way, and among their most notable enterprises was the excavation from 1963 onwards by Yigael Yadin of the great rock fortress of Masada, overlooking the Dead Sea and built by Herod the Great. The Dead Sea will, however, be best remembered in the history of mid-twentieth-century archaeology because of the chance discovery in 1947, by a Bedouin shepherd at Qumran near the then Jordanian frontier, of scrolls, most of them books of the old Testament over a thousand years older than any previous copies. Their original preservation was due to the Essenes, an old Jewish sect which sought to maintain its austerity by settling in the desolate and inhospitable regions near the Dead Sea. The publication of these scrolls has caused a revolution in Biblical studies and controversies about the nature, date and significance of the scrolls still rage.

From 1953 onwards a Danish archaeological expedition under P. V. Glob and Geoffrey Bibby has worked on the island of Bahrein in the Persian Gulf and at other sites near the Arabian Sea such as Qatar, Abu Dhabi and Failaka. The reports of seventeen years' work are now beginning to be published: Bibby has written an account for the general public in his *Looking for Dilmun* (London and New York, 1969). Sumerian texts going back to 2520 B.C. refer to three areas with which prehistoric Mesopotamia traded, namely Dilmun, Mahhan, and Melluḥha. Scholarly opinion now suggests that Dilmun extended along the Arab coast of the Gulf from Kuwait to Bahrein (its most important centre): that Mahhan consists of Makran and the Oman peninsula, and that Melluhha referred to the Harappa civilisation of the Indus Valley. The identification of Dilmun seems to be confirmed by the Danish excavations which have given "a new dimension . . . to the archaeology of the Middle East, but also to the history of the modern Arab states on the Persian Gulf" (Tosi, *Antiquity*, 1971, 22). In Iran Ghirshman has dug at Susa and Tchoga Zambil and Carl Lamberg-Karlowsky has directed the Harvard University expedition which excavated Tepe Yahya. Italian, Russian and American excavations in Iran have shown that the process of synoecism was already well advanced by the third millennium, and for a summary of parallel developments in south central Russia see V. M. Masson and V. I. Sarianidi, *Central Asia: Turkmenia before the Achaemenids* (London, 1972).

A new inspiration was given to Indian archaeology in the last years of the Second World War and the years following by Sir Mortimer Wheeler. After partition, work on Harappan sites continued apace. J. M. Casal dug at Amri in 1959, F. A. Khan at Kot Diji in 1955, and B. B. Lal and B. K. Thapar at Kalibangan. The geographical extent of the Harappan civilisation was revealed by excavations at Rupar and Alamgirpur, north-east of Delhi. Perhaps the most interesting new site was that of Lothal dug in the late 1950s and early 1960s by Shri S. R. Rao. The site is in

Gujerat: excavation revealed a town divided into six rectangular blocks with the remains of a dock measuring 710 by 120 feet with an inlet channel 23 feet wide and a 80-feet-long platform for loading and unloading merchandise. The site dated from early to mature Harappa: a contemporary Persian Gulf seal was found there. For summaries of these and other discoveries in Indian archaeology see R. E. M. Wheeler, *Ancient India and Pakistan* (London, 1959), and *The Indus Civilisation* (Cambridge, 1968), H. D. Sankalia, *Prehistory and Protohistory in India and Pakistan* (Delhi, 1969), and Bridget and Raymond Allchin, *The Birth of Indian Civilisation* (Harmondsworth, 1968).

Among the most exciting discoveries in Russian Palaeolithic archaeology are burials. At Teshik-Tash in Uzbekistan a Neanderthal child's grave had a ring of ibex horns carefully placed on it. At the Sungir site near Vladimir the garments of the deceased were richly decorated with ivory beads, and it was possible to reconstruct their form as a pullover shirt with round neck and a pair of trousers with boots, and a possible head covering. Unquestionably, the most startling Russian discoveries have been those of the fifth-century B.C. Scythian tombs of the Altai region of Siberia. The first of the sixty or so mounds at Pazyryk in the Altai were examined in 1929 by M. P. Gryaznov and S. I. Rudenko: five barrows were then dug revealing that the dead had been buried in wooden chambers in shafts below the mounds. It was not until 1949 that Rudenko carried out more extensive excavations and seven more of the larger mounds were dug. The timber roofing had been removed by looters, rain water had seeped on to the corpses and frozen, resulting in the preservation of clothing, leather, wood and felt. The unusual preservation of materials and bodies from the ancient and prehistoric past of man is one of the great fascinations of the archaeological record. Few examples are more fascinating than the Pazyryk mounds which produced, to mention a few remarkable survivals, a wool-pile carpet, a tattooed man, embroidered Chinese silk and woven Persian stuffs. Rudenko's account of these discoveries was first published in Russian in 1953: and in 1970 a revised English translation appeared under the title of *Frozen Tombs of Siberia: the Pazyryk Burials of Iron Age horsemen*. For a brief account of these spectacular finds see M. I. Artamonov in *Scientific American*, 1965, 242, 100–109.

Chinese archaeology has made enormous advances in the last

thirty years, although during the years following the Cultural Revolution contact between Chinese archaeologists and their colleagues in the rest of the world has been very difficult. Now however relations have been resumed and we are beginning to see some of the discoveries made in the last few years. They have been illustrated in *Historical Relics Unearthed in New China* (Foreign Languages Press, Peking, 1972) and range from the skull of *Sinanthropus lantienensis* discovered at Lantien, Shensi, and pieces of the skull of a new *Sinanthropus pekinensis* found in 1959 and 1966, to the discovery of the tombs of Liu Sheng and his wife Tou Wan in 1968. These tombs of the Western Han dynasty, dating from 100 B.C., were found in 1968 at Mancheng in Hopei Province: Liu Sheng's clothes were made of two thousand small pieces of jade tied together with gold wire.

We have now good summaries of the present state of Chinese archaeology among which we mention T. K. Cheng's *Archaeological Studies in Szechwan* (Cambridge, 1957), *Prehistoric China* (Cambridge, 1959), and *New Light on Prehistoric China* (Cambridge, 1966); W. Watson's *China* (London, 1961), *Ancient Chinese Bronzes* (London, 1962), and *Cultural Frontiers in Ancient East Asia* (Edinburgh, 1971); K. C. Chang's *Archaeology of Ancient China* (New Haven, revised edition, 1968); and Judith M. Treistman's *The Prehistory of China: an Archaeological Exploration* (New York, 1972). What is exciting in all these books is not the narrative of finds but the presentation of an entirely new interpretation of Chinese prehistory. Gone is the view of Neolithic and Bronze Age China as remote eastern outposts of the Near East: it is now impossible to deny the independent development of agriculture and bronze-working in China. The new Chinese archaeology, like the development of American archaeology in the last quarter century has made quite out of date the evolutionary unilinear construct which dominated so much of archaeological thought in the second quarter of the twentieth century. Writing of the agricultural innovation in China, Professor Treistman says "Without a doubt the 'invention' took place many times in many places" (*The Prehistory of China*, 41).

2. *Prehistoric Europe*

The progress of archaeology in Europe accelerates every year.

Much the most sensational and publicised event in Palaeolithic European archaeology was the debunking of Piltdown Man. *Eoanthropus dawsonii* is no more: the exposure of this remarkable fraud is well set out by Professor J. S. Weiner in *The Piltdown Forgery* (Oxford, 1955). The Piltdown Man, Smith Woodward's "first Englishman" that never was, was disposed of from 1953 onwards by the brilliant co-operative work of Oakley, Weiner, and Le Gros Clark. The final coup-de-grace was when the bones were conclusively shown by C14 dating to be modern.

Meanwhile some new and genuine finds of early man were being made. Swanscombe man had been found in 1935–36, and another parietal bone was found by Wymer in 1956. In 1947 Mademoiselle G. Henri-Martin found remains of *Homo sapiens* at Fontéchevade in south-west France. Mention has already been made of the discovery at Vértesszöllös in Hungary of *Homo sapiens* with a pebble tool industry—perhaps the oldest European.

The excavations of Mademoiselle S. de Saint-Mathurin and the late Professor Dorothy Garrod (d. 1969) at Angles-sur l'Anglin, in western France, produced, among other things, one of the oldest human portraits in the world—the life-size head and shoulders of a Magdalenian man of about 14,000 years ago—painted in red and black with dark, untidy hair, short beard and tip-tilted nose. During the period covered by this chapter Palaeolithic studies certainly came of age. The centenary of Neantherthal man was celebrated in 1960: the centenary of Les Eyzies, self-styled "capital de la préhistoire" in 1967–68. New discoveries of Upper Palaeolithic art were made since 1940: in Italy, Sicily, and at Ribadasella in northern Spain. Many would claim that Rouffignac in the Dordogne was a sensational new discovery but others have reservations about the authenticity of some or all of the paintings and engravings there (see L-R. Nougier and R. Robert, *The Cave of Rouffignac*, London, 1958, an English translation of the same authors' French book *Rouffignac, ou La Guerre des Mammouths*, Paris, 1957; D. A. E. Garrod, *Antiquity*, 1969; Daniel, *The Hungry Archaeologist in France*, London, 1963, chapter 6). The comparative study of Upper Palaeolithic art has advanced enormously, as can be seen from the following books: Breuil, *Four Hundred Centuries of Cave Art* (1952); Graziosi, *L'Arte dell'Antica Eta della Pietra* (Florence, 1956); A. Leroi-Gourhan, *Préhistoire de l'Art Occidental* (Paris, 1965); J. Maringer and H. G. Bandi, *Art in the Ice Age* (London, 1968); P. J. Ucko and A. Rosenfeld, *Palaeolithic Cave Art* (London, 1967).

Two European Mesolithic excavations deserve special mention. First the excavations between 1949 and 1951 at Star Carr, near Scarborough directed by Professor Grahame Clark with a team of botanists, zoologists and geologists. This was a Maglemosian site of 7538±350 b.c.: it was a seasonally used settlement of three or four families who lived by hunting red deer, aurochs, elk and roe deer. The full publication of this important site, Clark *et al.*, *Excavations at Star Carr* (Cambridge, 1954) has been re-issued (Cambridge, 1971) with a preface bringing the significance of this important site up to date. In 1965 Trifunović and Srejović began work at the site of Lepinski Vir on the southern shores of the Danube in eastern Yugoslavia. It had been discovered by a special reconnaissance carried out on riparian sites before the raising of the level of the Danube by a dam at the Iron Gates. A very remarkable settlement of hunter-fishers was discovered, pre-Starcevo in style, with trapezoidal houses and curious stone sculptures of a style hitherto unknown. For a good account see D. Srejović, *Europe's First Monumental Sculpture: New Discoveries at Lepinski Vir* (London, 1972).

In the last thirty years our knowledge of the Neolithic settlement of Europe, the *landnam* phase of European prehistory, has advanced enormously by excavations such as those at the Greek sites of Nea Nikomedia, Saliagos and Sitagroi, Karanovo in Eastern Bulgaria, Bylany in Czechoslovakia, Barkaer in Denmark, and the work of Bernabò Brea in Arene Candide in Liguria, the Liparis and Sicily.

The spread of farming into Europe—diagnostic of the Neolithic *landnam*—has in the last two decades been accurately dated by C14: these dates were set out graphically by Grahame Clark in *Antiquity*, 1965, 47, and in *Proc. Preh. Soc.*, 1965, 58; a revised map appears in his *World Prehistory: a New Outline* (1969, 121). Sites like Karanovo, Sidari, Neo Nikomedia, Sesklo and Argissa in the Balkans date from before 5200 B.C., Danubian sites from Central Europe to the Low Countries from 5000 to 4000 b.c. while the early Neolithic sites in France, the British Isles and Scandinavia are between 2800 and 4000 B.C. This is a remarkable change from pre-C14 days when Childe in his *Dawn of European Civilisation* and Piggott in his *Neolithic Cultures of the British Isles*

(1954, second edition 1970) dated the beginning of the British Neolithic at about 2000 B.C.

A great deal of work has been done on the Neolithic and later settlements in Italy, Iberia and the west Mediterranean islands and this work can be read in summary form in Bernabò Brea's *Sicily before the Greeks* (1957); J. D. Evans, *Malta* (1959); M. Guido, *Sardinia* (1963); H. N. Savory, *Spain and Portugal* (1968); A. Arribas, *The Iberians* (1963); D. Trump, *Central and Southern Italy* (1966); L. H. Barfield, *Northern Italy* (1966), and L. Pericot y Garcia, *The Balearic Islands* (1972). For a general summary see J. D. Evans and G. E. Daniel, *The Western Mediterranean* (Cambridge, 1967). Grosjean's finds of statue-menhirs and *torri* in Corsica are among the most important in this field, as also the establishment of a clear stratigraphy in the Acropolis site of Lipari by Bernabò Brea and the painstaking work of Evans and Trump in Malta: we now have a clear sequence of monuments and cultures. The Maltese sequence is summarised in detail in Evans, *The Prehistoric Archaeology of Malta* (London, 1971).

The last twenty years has seen a great revival of interest in the Etruscans beginning with the fine exhibition of Etruscan art in 1955 and the reconstruction of the Museum in Rome. The painted tombs of Tarquinia were first discovered in 1892. Recently the study of air photographs and the electrical resistivity survey and periscope photography of the Lerici Foundation has revealed very many more. The British School at Rome has been making a very special study of Etruscan settlement patterns and its Director, J. Ward-Perkins, suggests how the process of synoecization took place in Italy, that a loosely knit group of Villanovan villages became the Etruscan form of Veii.

Mention must be made here of two of the very remarkable archaeological discoveries made in Italy in recent years: Piazza Armerina in Sicily of the later 3rd/early 4th century; and in 1956 the layout of the ancient port of Spina on the Adriatic to the south of Venice was located and photographed from the air. Excavation in the town and some of its cemeteries date the life of the settlement to between 530 and 300 B.C.

The first modern major syntheses of European prehistory were V. G. Childe's *The Dawn of European Civilisation* (first published 1925, sixth edition 1957) and C. F. C. Hawkes's *The Prehistoric Foundations of Europe* (1940). Both Childe and Hawkes in these books take the story down to Mycenaean times but in his Oslo lectures, subsequently published as *Prehistoric Migrations in Europe* (1950), Childe went forward to the Roman Conquest, as did Stuart Piggott in his *Ancient Europe from the Beginning of Agriculture to Classical Antiquity: a Survey*, published in 1965 and now the major work of synthesis available to us. Childe had published posthumously as a paperback *The Prehistory of European Society* (1958). Childe's *Dawn*, as also *The Danube in Prehistory* (1929) were perhaps the most formative influences on thinking about European archaeology in the period 1925–40.

How have the views set out there, on which most European archaeologists of the present generation were brought up, stood up to the last three decades of discovery and change and to the re-dating of the past by C14? In his interpretation of the past Childe had first flirted with the Elliot-Smith/Perry school of Egyptocentric hyper-diffusionism but soon moved to a modified diffusionist position. Avoiding the determinist extravagances of the Elliot-Smith/Perry school and of Lord Raglan he yet believed that most that changed man from a hunting-fishing savage to an agricultural barbarian and from that state of primitive village economy to the civilisation of literate urban cities had occurred in the Most Ancient Near East and that whatever happened in Europe (and for that matter in India or China) was a pale reflection of the Near East. The job of the archaeologist was to discover what in prehistory came from where and to date these cultural borrowings or the arrivals of new people. In Childe's view, and that of his conscious and unconscious disciples, European prehistory was a matter of invasion and diffusion. And yet in his last publication, *The Dawn of European Society* (1958), he was forced to think in terms of possible independent origins.

Since then prehistorians have thought more and more in terms of local development and, while not denying the primacy of South West Asia in many things, are more inclined to view any case of diffusion as something to be proved not assumed, and to envisage the possibilities of independent invention. In his "The Invasion Hypothesis in British History", Grahame Clark challenged the accepted view (*Antiquity*, 1966, 172–89). Radiocarbon dates, and especially when calibrated, have emphasised the antiquity of many European Neolithic and Chalcolithic societies including the builders of megaliths. In a series of publications A. C. Renfrew has argued that copper-working in Eastern Europe and south-eastern Spain may well be earlier than metallurgy in the Near East, that Stonehenge is before Mycenae, and that the earliest megalithic monuments in Malta, Iberia, and Brittany are earlier than the Pyramids of Egypt and the ziggurats of Mesopotamia: that they are, in fact, the oldest architectural monuments in the world.

Two particularly interesting discoveries are to be recorded from the Balkans. In 1949, men digging for clay for a brickworks at Panagurichte, 25 miles from the Sofia-Plovdiv road, found a magnificent treasure of eight vases and a wonderfully carved cup. The treasure belonged to a Thracian king living at the end of the fourth century or the beginning of the third century B.C. It is typical Graeco-Persian art and is thought to come from the coast of Asia Minor. In 1963 N. Vlassa reported (*Dacia*, VII, 1963, 485–94) the discovery of three clay tablets of Protoliterate Mesopotamian type in an "Early Bronze Age" level in the mound of Tartaria in Transylvanian Romania and the nature, interpretation and significance of these tablets has led to much controversy.

From eastern Europe to the west: in 1958 the Tir-au-Pigeon Club of Seville decided to extend their premises on the El Carambolo hill outside the city. Workmen found a remarkable hoard of gold bracelets, plaques, pectorals and a necklace typical of work in Cyprus in the 7th/6th century B.C. This rich find renewed intelligent interpretation of Tartessos: it has even been suggested that the treasure perhaps belonged to Arganthonios who reigned for 80 years and died at the age of 120 in 550 B.C.

A few references to outstanding discoveries and advances in Greek archaeology. In 1953 Michael Ventris announced the decipherment of Linear B. Here was a story as exciting and romantic as any of the nineteenth-century tales of decipherment and it has been well told by John Chadwick, close collaborator of Ventris, in his *The Decipherment of Linear B* (Cambridge, 1959). Ventris (1922–1956), when a schoolboy at Stowe, attended a Christmas lecture in London by Sir Arthur Evans on Minoan archaeology and decided he would try to decipher Linear B. This he did in conjunction with other scholars like John Chadwick. He was himself not a practising classical scholar but an architect and was killed in a car accident at the early age of 34—a sad loss to scholarship.

In the same year as Ventris announced his decipherment of Linear B, Papadimitriou discovered the second circle of royal tombs (Circle B) at Mycenae. British work at Mycenae continued, first under A. J. Wace and later by Lord William Taylour. Blegen published his excavations at Troy and excavated the Palace of Nestor at Pylos. In 1964 N. Platon discovered at Kato Zakro, on the eastern coast of Crete, a new Minoan palace which had been ruined *c.* 1500 B.C.

We can mention only a few discoveries of the European Iron Age. First in Germany the great Hallstatt hillfort of the Heuneberg overlooking the Danube near Sigmaringen in Würtemberg. Five main building phases were distinguished here but at the beginning of Phase II in the sixth century B.C. part of the rampart was reconstructed in the Greek manner with bastions of mud-brick on a stone foundation. Found there were nine amphorae, and Attic Black Figure pottery probably imported from the Greek city of Massalia. Secondly, the remarkable find at Reinheim in the Saar made by Dr Josef Keller in 1954; a Celtic grave of a princess of *c.* 400 B.C. with superb treasures including a gilt-bronze drinking vessel. Thirdly, the discovery in 1963 by Dr Harting Zurn, director of archaeology for Würtemberg of a remarkable stone statue of a Hallstatt warrior at Hirschlanden near Stuttgart. In France the discovery which overshadows all others is that made in 1953 at Vix in Burgundy by René Joffroy, then a Professor in the Lycée at Châtillon-sur-Seine and now Conservateur-en-Chef of the Musée des Antiquités Nationales at St-Germain-en-Laye. Here was a wooden mortuary chamber under a ploughed-out tumulus: it contained a dismantled four-wheeled waggon and was the grave of a young woman, perhaps a local Celtic princess, a gold diadem on her head. Buried with her were many imported objects including an Attic Black Figure Cup of *c.* 525 B.C. and an immense bronze *krater*, 5 feet high; it weighed 200 kg. with a capacity of 1,250 litres and was made in a Corinthian workshop of about 575 B.C.

A notable contribution to the understanding of the Early Iron Age in northern France was R. E. M. Wheeler and K. Richardson, *The Hill Forts of Northern France* (London, 1959). Among excavations of hillforts in Britain that have thrown much light on this period were those of Wheeler at Stanwick in Yorkshire, Richmond and Brailsford at Hod Hill, Dorset, and Savory at

Dinorben. The Dinorben excavations showed that hillforts had been constructed in Britain from the Late Bronze Age.

3. *America*

During the period under review in this chapter American archaeology has most certainly come into its own. Any general books on archaeology written immediately before or during the 1939–45 war paid short shrift to American archaeology. O. G. S. Crawford, who had founded *Antiquity* in 1927 and edited it until his death thirty years later, had no interest whatsoever in pre-Columbian archaeology. Gordon Childe regarded American archaeology as something bizarre, unpalatable and irrelevant, and in *What Happened in History*, which he wrote during the war, he says that he pays little attention to American archaeology because it is "outside that main stream of history". To him, and to many of his generation, the main stream of history was very little different from the four-Empire doctrine of the German historians of the nineteenth century. It was the stream that came from Greece and Rome, and, behind those classical lands, from Palestine, Babylonia and Egypt. The origins of civilisation, and therefore history, was to Childe something that occurred in what he called the Most Ancient East, and Breasted before him had called the Fertile Crescent.

The scientific, systematic and rigorous development of American archaeology has now built up a second stream of history. American archaeology has not merely accumulated new facts; they are facts like those produced by the extension of prehistory to China and Japan which challenge the basic ideas of culture change in the prehistoric and protohistoric past. By today we see very clearly that by the stream of history we mean the progress from savagery through barbarism to civilisation in man's past; there were several parallel streams of history.

Pre-Columbian America received scant treatment in the first edition of this book. Stephens, Catherwood, Charnay and Maudslay were mentioned and there was talk of the finds of projectile points at Folsom. We must make some attempt at redressing the balance now. The history of American archaeology has been well-described by Gordon Willey in his chapter "One Hundred Years of American Archaeology" in (ed.) J. O. Brew,

One Hundred Years of Anthropology (Harvard, 1968), and in his book written with Jerry Sabloff, *The History of American Archaeology* (London and New York, 1973).

Willey has devised for the development of American archaeology an historical scheme of four periods. The earliest was the pioneer or preparatory era, which he calls the Speculative Period, which went from the European discovery of the New World until the middle of the nineteenth century. The second period he calls the Descriptive Period, which runs from the beginning of systematic and descriptive archaeology in the mid-nineteenth century to the early twentieth century. Willey's third period, his "Descriptive-Historic" followed from the second decade of the present century and lasted until 1950. It was the time of what he describes as "the stratigraphic revolution" in American archaeology, and the concerted attack on the problems of chronology.

In this Descriptive-Historic period the most important discovery was that in 1927 of projectile points in association with Pleistocene fauna at Folsom in New Mexico (see p. 275 above). In 1938 the association of man and extinct fauna was reported from the lowest layer of a large stratigraphical sequence in the Straits of Magellan. Kroeber, in the second (1948) edition of his *Anthropology*, says that the earliest man in America might have dated anywhere from 8000 B.C. to 25,000 B.C.

Willey's fourth phase of American archaeology falls entirely within the compass of this chapter: it is since 1950 and this period, from that moment to the present day, he calls the Comparative-Historic. Since 1950, and, to put no finer point on it, since the second edition of Kroeber's *Anthropology*, there are good dates of Clovis hunters between 10000 and 9000 B.C. "The weight of evidence," says Willey, "favours a spread of human cultures and a bifacial flaked blade technology from north-east Asia to America somewhere between 15,000 and 20,000 years ago. . . . There are also some New World finds . . . which have been interpreted as evidence for still earlier peoples. . . . As of 1966, pre-Clovis man in the Americas is a possibility, not a demonstrated fact." Others have not felt prepared to go so far as Willey. Thus Bushnell in *The First Americans* (London, 1968) says: "The earliest dated signs of man in America are at about 9500 B.C." Yet Laguna man in California has been dated well before this.

As early as 1917, H. J. Spinden, in his paper, "The Origin and

Distribution of Agriculture in America" (*Proceedings, Nineteenth International Congress of Americanists*, Washington, D.C., 1917, 269) and again in his *Ancient Civilisations of Mexico and Central America* (New York, 1928), has stated clearly that the ancient civilisations of Peru and Mexico, as well as the cultures peripheral to those areas, were independently developed in America from earlier village farming communities: he alleged that there must have been an American "Neolithic", which, he thought, had its origins in the valley of Mexico. This so-called Archaic hypothesis of Spinden has been shown to be fundamentally right, though the story was not as simple as he supposed. It now seems that no one area was the single source of all New World farming and settled life: there were, in fact, many sources. R. S. MacNeish's excavations in the valley of Tehuacan, a dry valley in southern Mexico, have shown that maize was first cultivated in the highlands of southern Mexico as far back as the fifth millennium B.C., and that maize as a cultigen may well have originated there.

But, at the same time, other food plants were being cultivated in Peru (where maize did not appear until between 1400 and 1200 B.C.), and also in the South American highlands—gourds, lima beans, and subsequently cotton, chili, and two kinds of squash. In southern Tamaulipas, near the Gulf coast in North East Mexico, gourds, pumpkins, runner-beans, chili were being cultivated, and later corn. And in New Mexico, in the southwest of the U.S.A., in the lower levels of the Bat Cave, dated to between 3600 and 2000 B.C., there were primitive corncobs, rinds of gourds, pumpkin seeds and rinds and particles of sunflowers.

MacNeish's Reports of the Tehuacan Archaeological-Botanical Project were published by the Peabody Foundation of Andover in 1961 and 1962. Reference should also be made to D. S. Byers, *The Prehistory of the Tehuacan Valley: I. Environment and Subsistence* (Andover, 1967). For good general accounts of this work see *Science*, 1964, 531 and *Antiquity*, 1965, 87: in these articles MacNeish suggests that there were not only the four independent areas of agricultural origins in America which have already been mentioned, and are set out on the map, but the possibility of a fifth, namely the South American tropical forest, where such crops as bitter and sweet manioc and the yam were experimented with, and domesticated, perhaps even before 1000 B.C., and possibly in lowland Venezuela as early as 2000 B.C.

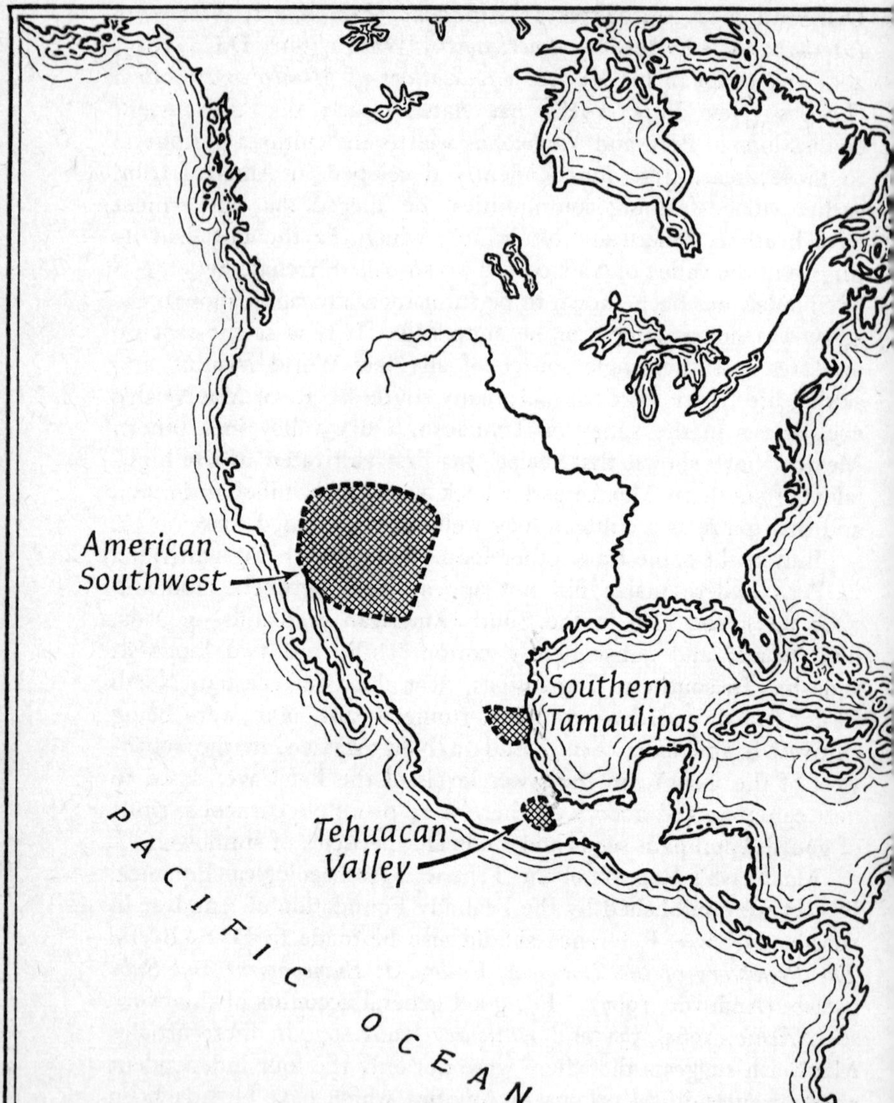

FIG. 7. Areas of independent agricultural invention in America

These early agricultural communities developed into settled villages growing in size and complexity: such a one was Chavín de Huantar in Peru. By about the eighth century B.C. the villages of Chavín type had developed into what is described as the ancient Peruvian civilisation, characterised by massive flat-topped adobe pyramids and palace complexes, modelled art such as the Mohica and Nazca pottery, and metal working in copper, bronze and gold, textile working of great skill and beauty, and a fine stone architecture such as the great monolithic gateway and stairway at Tiahuanaco. For a good account of these prehistoric developments in Peru, reference should be made to G. H. S. Bushnell's *Peru* (2nd edition, London, 1963).

The first civilisation of Mesoamerica, which antedated the Peruvian civilisation, was that of the Olmecs, who flourished on the Gulf coast plain of Mexico in the region of southern Vera Cruz and neighbouring Tabasco. The Olmec civilisation had been known for some time because of its remarkable jade objects and sculptures, many emphasising human infants with snarling, jaguar-like features. The finds of Matthew Stirling at La Venta, a small island, entirely surrounded by swamps, in Tabasco, were followed by further excavations at this and other sites. A complex of three ceremonial centres at San Lorenzo, Tenochtitlan, in southern Veracruz, was excavated between 1966 and 1968, and revealed a long sequence of cultural development going back to *c.* 1500 B.C. Carbon–14 dates from La Venta show that the Olmec civilisation's main period was from 800 to 400 B.C. The most remarkable features of Olmec culture are the colossal basalt heads about 8 feet high; one of the most famous ones from La Venta (where four were found) is now in the Olmec Park at Villahermosa. For an account of the Olmecs see Michael D. Coe *America's First Civilisation: Discovering the Olmec* (Eau Claire, Wisconsin, 1968) and his *Mexico* (London, 1962). Miguel Covarrubias said that the Olmec culture was the foundation on which was built the later Mexican and Mayan civilisations, and Coe writes: "There is now not the slightest doubt that all later civilisations in Mesoamerica, whether Mexican or Mayan, ultimately rest on an Olmec base." Drucker, Heizer and Aquier, however, in their "Excavations at La Venta, Tabasco" (*Bulletin of American Ethnology*, 1959, 170) while emphasising the importance of the Olmec, do not endorse the views of Covarrubias and Coe.

The other civilisations of Mesoamerica revealed by archaeology have been those of Central Oaxaca and the Valley of Mexico. In Oaxaca the main metropolitan site was Monte Alban, dated from between 800 and 300 B.C. This was the country of the Zapotecs, and Monte Alban was their sacred hill town: from this site came stone-reliefs of a remarkable kind called Los Danzantes, and one of these may have a hieroglyph for the name of a person. Certainly the Zapotecs of Ooxaca have produced the oldest glyphs in America: and although these have not been properly deciphered, it is thought they may denote names and dates.

In the valley of Mexico the large cemetery of Tlatilco dates from *c.* 1000 to 500 B.C. As the first millennium came to an end there stood in the valley the great site of Teotihuacan: it covered more than three square miles with a population that grew from 10,000 to 120,000. It began about 100 B.C.; but the main building period was A.D. 150 to 300. A fully urban community, it had a gridded layout of streets, with palaces, temples and pyramids—the Pyramid of the Sun is 700 feet long by 200 feet high and is one of the largest pre-Spanish structures in Mesoamerica.

It is now known that the civilisation of the Maya developed earlier than was previously thought. Tikal was inhabited by 600 B.C. and the earliest temples at Uaxactun date from this time. It still remains curious that the Maya, with their remarkable knowledge of mathematics and astronomy, and their complex calendar, did not have what could properly be called cities: their great centres were, to use Bushnell's phrase, "more akin to cathedral closes". One of their greatest religious centres was Copan: the last hieroglyphic inscription was carved there in A.D. 800.

The Museu d'Anthropologica Nacional in Mexico City was opened in 1960. It is by very general consent one of the two or three finest archaeological museums in the world—brilliant in conception and brilliant in execution. It records not only the past of Mexico on the ground floor but the culture of the present-day peasant communities on the floor above, and one can move easily from the Maya civilisation of the past to the Maya of the present.

For a brief while American archaeology used the divisions of the Thomsen three-age system and Lubbock's neo-Grecist labels in its description of pre-Columbian material, but it became increasingly clear that this system was impractical and nearly meaningless for America, which had no iron age before the Spanish conquest, and no remains from an Old Stone Age comparable with the Palaeolithic of the classic areas of south-west France and northern Spain: and indeed the term "Bronze Age" could only be used in America with uncertainty and was irrelevant to the European Bronze Age. True bronze was used in northern Argentine before A.D. 1000 and the knowledge of bronze-working spread to Peru shortly afterwards. The Aztecs occasionally alloyed copper with tin but bronze was never as important in America as it was in the Old World, and it is therefore quite impossible to use the term Bronze Age in America in any general meaningful sense.

An entirely new system of cultural nomenclature was devised by Willey and Phillips and set out in their *Method and Theory in American Archaeology* (Chicago, 1958). Here they adumbrate five stages which they call Lithic, Archaic, Formative, Classic and post-Classic, and here they are consciously doing for American archaeology what Lubbock did for European Archaeology about a hundred years before. The Lithic and Archaic stages of Willey and Phillips correspond in a very general way to the Upper Palaeolithic and Mesolithic of Europe and the Near East. The Formative Period saw the origins of agriculture and the beginnings of settled village communities. The Classic comprises the ancient civilisations of Peru and Mexico: the post-Classic the Incas. This is a very useful terminology, and one that could perhaps be used in areas outside America except that we could not apply the term "Classic" to the urban bronze-using cultures of Egypt, Mesopotamia and the Indus Valley, without considerable disturbance to those brought up in the extension of the German four-Empire tradition to regard the Classic to be the classical civilisations of Greece and Rome. But such a disturbance might not be unhealthy. Perhaps Egypt, Sumer, Harappa and Shang China might conveniently be called the pre-Classic Civilisations? We are always at a loss to describe in a general way the first peasant village communities of the Near East and Europe, and we labour our material and ourselves with terms such as pre-pottery Neolithic, Chalcolithic, Eneolithic, and the like. These cultures are those which give rise to the ancient civilisations of the most ancient Near East, and which, in Europe, give rise to the near-civilisations of the Celts, Ligurians, Etruscans and Iberians. The

Willey/Phillips word "formative" might be a good way of describing the societies of barbarian Europe between 6000 and 1000 B.C.

If we appear here to digress it is only an example of the inspiration which modern American archaeology in its Comparative-Historic phase has provided to archaeologists in the rest of the world. Jacquetta Hawkes, commenting on the development of American archaeology by Americans, once said: "They were too busy creating their own civilisation to look for older ones"; and this was very true. But once they started, the results produced to date are quite prodigious and not only tell us the story of man in early America, which is in itself a great achievement, but by this work have revolutionised our knowledge and thinking about the development of man in the Old World. Here, without any doubt, there was in the New World a parallel and independent cultural evolution to be set against and beside the developments so far charted in the most ancient Near East.

By saying, deliberately, "parallel and independent", we do not deny the possibility of contacts across the Pacific and the Atlantic in pre-Columbian times. Meggers and others have argued for the presence of Jōmon pottery from Japan in Ecuador, and the voyages of Heyerdahl have demonstrated the possibility of these contacts. But the few proven cultural contacts, and the accepted possibilities of more, do not alter the fact that the existing archaeological evidence shows an independent evolution in America from Lithic/Mesolithic societies to civilisation. This is one of the major achievements of archaeology in the last thirty years. For a detailed study the reader is recommended the following books: G. R. Willey, *An Introduction to American Archaeology: I. North and Middle America* (New Jersey, 1966); *II. South America* (New Jersey, 1972); G. H. S. Bushnell, *The First Americans: the Pre-Columbian Civilisations* (London, 1968), as well as his *Peru* already mentioned; M. D. Coe's *Mexico* (London, 1962) and *The Maya* (London, 1966); B. J. Meggers, *Ecuador* (London, 1900); G. Reichel-Dolmatoff, *Columbia*, (London, 1965); Donald W. Lathrap's *The Upper Amazon* (London, 1970); Irving Rouse and J. M. Cruxent, *Venezuelan Archaeology* (Yale, 1963), and J. E. S. Thompson's, *The Rise and Fall of Maya Civilisation* (2nd ed. Norman, Oklahoma, 1966).

Of course there remain those who, through ignorance or prejudice, reject the archaeological evidence for the independent development of culture in America and turn back to simplistic theories involving the colonisation of the New World by Egyptians, the lost tribes of Israel, the Phoenicians, Greeks, Irish, Welsh, not to mention non-existent Atlanteans and the inhabitants of the mythical continent of Mu, and others who were supposed to have come from extra-terrestial civilisations in flying saucers. All these follies have been beautifully dealt with in Wauchope's *Lost Tribes and Sunken Continents* (Chicago, 1962), a brilliant example of the best in archaeological *haute vulgarisation*. But the simplistic nonsense pours out from the presses: C. M. Boland's *They All Discovered America*, first published in 1961, is now a paperback to be found in bookstalls the length and breadth of America, and two recent examples of these extravagancies are Betty Bugbee Cusack's *Collectors' Luck: Giant Steps into Prehistory* (Stonehaven, Mass, 1968), and Cyrus H. Gordon's *Before Columbus* (New York, 1971). For a discussion of these see *Antiquity*, 1972, 2–5.

We do not deny that there were people who travelled across the Atlantic to North America in pre-Columbian times—not the Irish of St Brendan nor the Welsh under Madoc, but the Vikings. The sagas made this clear and the journey by Leif Eriksson from Helluland (Greenland) to Vinland (somewhere in North America) happened in the tenth century A.D., though it is clear from the sagas that there was never any long occupation of America. It might have been thought unlikely that we should ever find any archaeological evidence of what must have been a very short and very small occupation of some part of eastern America by the Vikings. Certainly the alleged evidence cited by many, such as the Newport Tower, the Minnesota Stone, and other faked runic inscriptions in America, are no help to us. So much nonsense and misrepresentation has surrounded the archaeological attestation of the Vikings in North America that most scholars viewed with caution and disquiet the claim that at L'Anse aux Meadows, on the northern tip of Newfoundland, there had been found a Viking settlement. But years of excavation there have revealed traces of turf-walled houses similar to those from Viking sites in Iceland and Greenland: they yielded a spindle-whorl, iron nails, a smithy with pieces of bog-iron and several pounds of slag.

The radiocarbon dates range from a.d. 700 to a.d. 1080 with a concentration in the late tenth century. We seem at last to have established archaeologically one group of pre-Columbian settlers of America from Europe. The discovery of this Newfoundland site was made by Helge Ingstad and his wife Anne Stine. Mrs Ingstad's preliminary report of the excavations is in *Acta Archaeologica*, XVI, 1970, and for a general account see Helge Ingstad's *Land under the Polar Star* (London, 1966).

For good, scholarly and moderate treatment of pre-Columbian trans-Atlantic crossings, and indeed the whole problem of contacts with the Old and New Worlds in early days, reference should be made to (ed.) Geoffrey Ashe, *The Quest for America* (London and New York, 1971); (eds.), C. J. Riley, C. Kelley, C. W. Pennington and R. L. Rands, *Man Across the Sea: Problems of Pre-Columbian Contacts* (Austin and London, 1971), and S. E. Morison, *The European Discovery of America: I: The Northern Voyages A.D. 500 to 1600* (London, 1971). The publication by the Yale University Press in 1965 of their Vinland map has given rise to much discussion and controversy. The authors of this publication, R. A. Skelton, T. E. Marston and G. D. Painter, *The Vinland Map and the Tartar Relation* (New Haven and London, 1965), came to the conclusion that the map could probably be dated to *c.* A.D. 1440. Most writers are very cautious in their acceptance of the map as genuine: Morison does not accept it. For a full account of modern views about the map see Helen Wallis *et al*, "The Strange Case of the Vinland Map", *Geographical Journal*, 1974, 183–214.

4. *Science and Archaeology*

The thirty years from 1940 to 1970 have certainly seen developments and discoveries in archaeology as far-reaching as those of any period of thirty years described in previous chapters: but the contributions made to archaeology by the natural sciences during this period have made it one of the most memorable and exciting in the history of the subject. There had of course been, long before 1940, known and proved applications of science to archaeology. Baron de Geer had demonstrated geochronology through the counting of clay varves, A. E. Douglass had pioneered dendrochronology, Lennart von Post had demonstrated pollen analysis, and H. H. Thomas was able to show, petrologically, that the "foreign" stones at Stonehenge came from Pembrokeshire.

All this was the beginning of science in archaeology. 1940–70 saw enormous advances. In the second (1969) edition of their admirable *An Introduction to Prehistoric Archaeology* (first published in 1950), Frank Hole and Robert F. Heizer say: "The two decades since 1950 will certainly become known historically as the age of technological innovation in archaeology."

The scientific aids to archaeology now lie in the discovery and survey of archaeological sites, the study of the provenance of artifacts, the conservation and protection of specimens, but most of all in dating. Nothing perhaps has been so important in the last three decades of archaeology as the discovery of C14 dating, announced by Libby in 1949: it is no exaggeration to say that, while the antiquarian and geological revolutions of the early nineteenth century brought modern archaeology into existence, the radio-carbon dating revolution brought archaeological chronology out of uncertainty and guesswork and has provided a firm basis for the new prehistory of the present.

Good summaries of the way in which science is now assisting archaeology are provided by (ed.) E. Pyddoke, *The Scientist and Archaeology* (London, 1963) and (eds.) D. R. Brothwell and E. S. Higgs, *Science in Archaeology* (first published, London, 1963; second edition, 1969). In the preface to the latter book Brothwell and Higgs write: "It will be many years before the impact of scientific applications in archaeology are fully appreciated in all parts of this multifarious discipline. Within the past three or four decades, very great changes have taken place, and the re-orientation towards a more scientific attitude in archaeological research continues at a surprising pace." There now exist at least two institutions in Europe entirely devoted to science and archaeology: one is the Oxford Research Laboratory for Archaeology and the History of Art, brain-child of Lord Cherwell and Professor C. F. C. Hawkes, and directed by E. J. Hall and M. J. Aitken; the second is the Lerici foundation in Milan and Rome. Both these foundations now issue their own journals: *Archaeometry* began in 1958 as the house magazine of the Oxford laboratory and is now a general journal with world-wide circulation: the Lerici Foundation produces *Prospezioni Archeologiche.* A third journal, *Science and Archaeology*, was started in England in March, 1970, and is now edited by F. S. C. Celoria and J. D. Wilcock. A fourth journal was started in March of 1974: it is called *The*

Journal of Archaeological Science and is edited by Professor G. W. Dimbleby, Dr D. R. Brothwell and Dr H. Barker.

In 1947 the Council for British Archaeology issued its *Notes for the Guidance of Archaeologists in Regard to Expert Evidence*, and in 1970 produced an entirely new and revised edition entitled *Handbook of Scientific Aids and Evidence for Archaeologists*, which is a clear and most useful summary. In December, 1970, a joint symposium of the Royal Society and the British Academy was held in London on the relations between the natural sciences and archaeology and the papers at this symposium (which, incidentally, was marking the coming of age of C14 dating) have been published as a book, (ed.) F. R. Hodson, *The Place of Astronomy in the Ancient World* (London, 1974).

The role of science in the discovery of sites and their details has been developed by geophysical methods of prospection, and these are many. Electrical resistivity measurements have been used for the last half century by civil engineers, geologists and geomorphologists. A particular technique of electrical prospecting was developed in large-scale oil-prospection, and this technique, the measurement of the degree of electrical conductivity present in the soil, was first used for the detection of buried archaeological structures by R. J. C. Atkinson at Dorchester in 1946. He showed how a survey could be made, with resistivity meters, of structures, pits and ditches even though they were completely invisible from the surface of the ground. For an account of this pioneer technique see R. J. C. Atkinson's article "Resistivity Surveying and Archaeology", in (ed.) E. Pyddoke, *The Scientist and Archaeology* (London, 1963, 1–30). Magnetic methods were introduced in 1957–58, the magnetometer recording remanent magnetism was invented in England in 1958. The Hald-American mission discovered the site of Sybaris using this technique. Electromagnetic methods were developed from 1962 onwards.

In 1955 Carlo Lerici founded the Institut Polytechnique at Milan, and developed there the technique of inserting into an unexcavated burial chamber a periscope with a camera which took photographs through 360 degrees. In 1956 he began using this method in the Etruscan necropolises of Cerveteri and Tarquinia and the work in the next few years there, and at Vulci, exceeded all expectations.

The geological identification of rocks, begun by H. H. Thomas under the inspiration of O. T. Jones, has been developed in Britain since 1936 with the foundation of the sub-committee of the south-western Group of Museums and Art Galleries, under the chairmanship and inspiration of Alexander Keiller. This Committee classified the materials used in making stone axes and has been able to locate factories from which the rough-outs of axes came; similar work is now being done in France. We should also note here F. R. Matson's microscopic analysis and objective description of the clays from which pottery was made, and the work of Sangmeister, Otto and others on the analysis of metal in the Bronze Age (an analysis which has, admittedly, been received critically in some quarters). Renfrew, Cann and others have developed techniques of analysing obsidian and so finding from what areas it was traded: it has been possible, for example, to show that the obsidian used at Deh Luran came from sources in eastern Anatolia, 900 km to the N.W. A special technique used at Deh Luran was the systematic use of flotation for the recovery of carbonised plant material. The flotation of material from all excavated levels is gradually becoming routine practice. On this technique see Williams, *Antiquity*, 1973, 288–92, and Jarman, Legge and Charles in (ed.) Higgs, *Problems in economic prehistory* (Cambridge, 1972), 39–48.

Many other analytical techniques have been developed such as beta-ray back scattering, electron micro-probing, neutron activation analysis, optical omission spectrometry, X-ray diffraction, X-ray fluorescence spectrometry and many another. Even the list is defeating to archaeologists untrained in the natural sciences: for details of these the reader must turn to the detailed manuals already mentioned.

The scientific techniques of dating the past fall into two groups: those that produce relative dates and those that produce absolute dates. Palynological dating, that is to say dating by pollen analysis, was, as we have said, well known before 1940. Other methods of relative dating have been developed since then, such as nitrogen analysis, fluorine analysis, and uranium analysis. In 1884 an English chemist called James Middleton put forward the idea that fossils contained quantities of fluoride in proportion to their age. At the end of the century the Frenchman Adolphe Carnot took up the idea, but it was not until 1948 that the method was used with great success by Kenneth Oakley in England.

The scientific techniques of absolute dating are Potassium-Argon dating, Dendrochronology, C14 dating, Archaeomagnetism and Thermoluminescence. The technique of potassium-argon dating was developed by Dr J. F. Evernden and Dr G. H. Curtis of Berkeley and was designed to ascertain the age of volcanic materials and other igneous rocks, and of tektites, and hence, by association, the age of deposits in which they occur freshly formed. It is based on the fact that potassium (K40) decays to argon (Ar 10) at a constant rate.

The technique of C14 dating was discovered by Willard F. Libby when Professor of Physics in the University of Chicago: he is now Professor of Chemistry in UCLA and was made a Nobel Prizeman in 1960—as Colin Renfrew has amusingly said, "the first archaeological Nobel Prizeman". The new technique is based on the fact that all living matter contains minute traces of C14, a radioactive isotope of carbon. It is formed at high altitudes by the action of neutrons in atmospheric nitrogen, quickly becomes oxidised to carbondioxide, and intimately mixed with the non-radioactive carbondioxide of the atmosphere. It is thus incorporated in the carbon exchange reservoir and consequently taken up by all living matter in a fixed proportion to that of ordinary carbon (one atom of carbon-14 for every million million atoms of the non-radioactive carbon-12). When an organism dies, this proportion is no longer maintained: the radioactive C14 diminishes at a known rate: the Libby value for the half-life was 5570 ± 30 years (but a new and more accurate value now appears to be 5730 ± 40 years); and while our present instructions are to use the original Libby half-life, dates so constructed may be converted to the basis of the new half-life by multiplying by 1.03.

Many laboratories have been established all over the world to make radiocarbon determinations. There are by now well over 70 laboratories and between 35,000 and 40,000 dates have been determined. The way in which these dates become available to scholars is a very special problem, and for years in the fifties and sixties, archaeologists used to meet each other, rather like the proverbial Stock Exchange operator with the latest dirty joke, and say, "Have you heard this one?", as he produced some startling early C14 date. At first it was proposed to send out punched cards for every date determined and this was being done from Andover, Massachussetts, but this system broke down. The

American Journal of Science for a while printed new dates in a supplement, and this has now become an independent journal called *Radiocarbon*, edited by Irving Rouse. This journal is now an indispensable requisite of every professional archaeologist and archaeological organisation. The radiocarbon laboratories report their dates in years bp (before the present), and the year 1950 has been arbitrally adopted to mean the present, and should be deducted from all bp dates to give ad/bc dates.

The practical limits of C14 dating seem to be reached at between 40,000 and 50,000 years ago. From the moment of the announcement of this technique it was important to realise its limitations. For example, the C14 date of a sample is the date of the removal by death or otherwise of the sample: a piece of timber may have been used for a particular purpose long after the tree was felled, and, of course, wood from near the bark will be younger than that from the centre of the tree.

The C14 dates that were determined in the fifties and early sixties caused considerable confusion among archaeologists. They proposed a much earlier chronology for barbarian Europe than had been traditionally supposed, and canvassed in the writings of Montelius, Sophus Muller, and Childe. Milojčić rejected them *in toto*, and he and many other central and east European prehistorians still persist in the old and shorter chronology based on cross-dating with Egypt and Mesopotamia. In 1952 excavations on a settlement site adjacent to the south bank of the Durrington Walls Henge Monument produced a well-preserved mass of wood charcoal on the land surface beneath the chalk rubble mound of the Henge. Two radiocarbon tests on samples from this charcoal gave a date of *c.* 2620 to 2630 b.c. for the charcoal, and so for the construction of the Henge of Durrington Walls. Professor Stuart Piggott, who published these dates in due course wrote: "This date is archaeologically inacceptable for the following reasons" (*Antiquity*, 1959, 289), and he gave what seemed to all of us, at that time, very good reasons. But now, only just more than a decade after those sensible words were written, most of us are happy to realise that this date is very archaeologically acceptable and that the henge monuments of the British Isles date from the third millennium B.C. Such is the change that has happened in the thinking of archaeologists in the last fifteen years.

The second reason why archaeologists and ancient historians were at first reluctant to accept that revolution in chronology proposed by the acceptance of the C14 dates was that the radiocarbon dates for early protohistoric Egypt did not agree with the dates produced by the accepted Egyptian chronology based on written records. As the Egyptian written records seemed impeccable, was it not therefore right to suppose that something was wrong with C14 dating? Curiously enough, dendrochronology, which no one had much bothered about in the second quarter of the twentieth century, came to the rescue of C14 dating in a dramatic and unexpected way. The technique of tree-ring dating developed in America where the giant sequoias went back 3,000 years. It was the problem of using dendrochronology for the purposes of cross-dating that seemed insoluble. Could tree-ring graphs worked out in America be of any use in the Old World? The applicability of the technique directly used in Europe was, however, splendidly demonstrated for medieval and post-medieval times at Novgorod in Russia, where from the tenth century A.D. onwards the streets were paved with wood, especially pine. (For an account of this see M. W. Thompson, *Novgorod the Great*, London, 1967.)

But it was the tree-ring chronology provided by *Pinus aristata*, the bristle-cone pine growing in eastern California, that established a dendrochronology going back to seven thousand years ago, and showed that the years produced by C14 determination were not, as had been supposed, calendar years. H. E. Suess and M. Stuiver, checking on the chronology of the bristle-cone pines, suggest that the C14 in the earth's atmosphere was not constant, and V. Bucha suggests that this was due to, or that at least one of the reasons for this was, changes in the earth's magnetic field (*Science*, 157, 726). The variation between calendar years and C14 years has been worked out in Philadelphia by Ralph, in Tucson by C. W. Fergusson and by Suess in San Diego. No agreed curve has yet been published but the one reproduced here gives a general picture of the problem. It shows that from 3000 to 4000 B.C. the C14 dates are more recent than they should be, and it resolves the apparent discrepancy between the calendar dates and the C14 dates for early dynastic Egypt. The calibration of C14 dates has produced a new revolution in prehistory, or rather has dramatically emphasised the revolution implicit in the

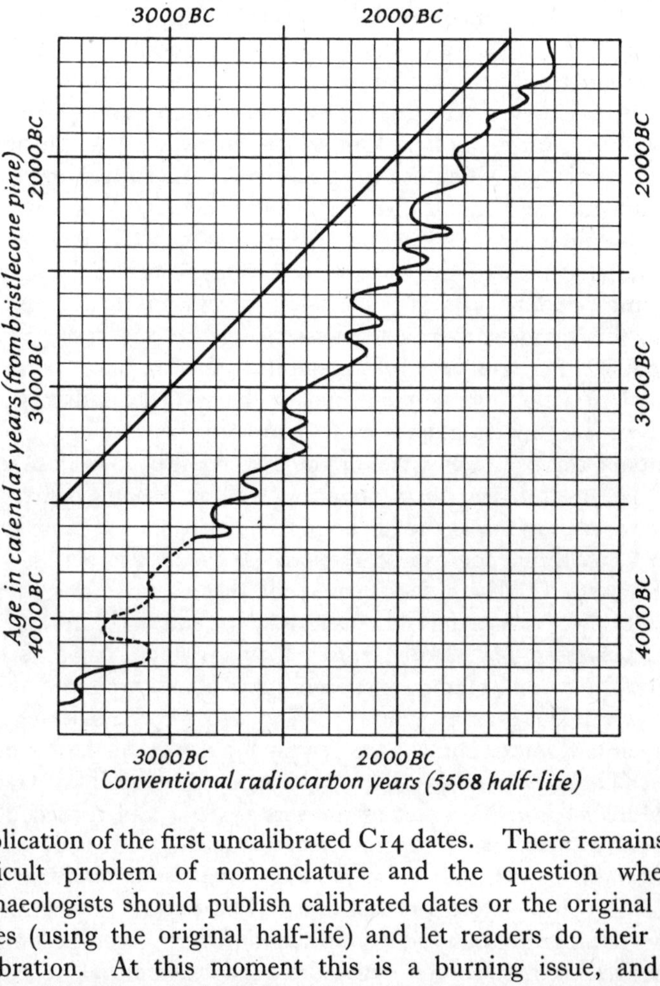

publication of the first uncalibrated C14 dates. There remains the difficult problem of nomenclature and the question whether archaeologists should publish calibrated dates or the original C14 dates (using the original half-life) and let readers do their own calibration. At this moment this is a burning issue, and the archaeological world is divided into three camps, those who will not bother with C14 dates at all, those who accept C14 dates but will not bother with calibration, and those who calibrate away merrily. This is a tiresome state of affairs and must be satisfactorily resolved soon.

The technique of dating by thermoluminescence is, in its way, as novel and startling as C14 and potassium-argon dating. This is based on the emission of light, over and above ordinary red-hot glow, when a substance is heated, and this light represents the release of energy which has been stored as trapped electrons in the crystal lattice of the minerals. The stored energy is acquired by absorption from any nuclear radiation to which the mineral may have been exposed: the amount of thermoluminescence observed (measured with a photomultiplier) is proportional to the overall dose of radiation which has been received. In most pottery there are mineral constituents that have this property of accumulating thermoluminescence. Heating to above 500°C removes the accumulated thermoluminescence and, consequently, the firing of clay into pottery sets the "thermoluminescent clock" at zero. From this moment thermoluminescence grows with time, and by measuring the amounts of uranium, thorium and potassium present in a pottery fragment and in the soil, the radiation dose received by the fragment each year can be calculated. The results of the use of this technique have confirmed the calibrated C14 dating of *Linearbandkeramik*, as well as, among many other things revealing that some of the pots recently sold to museums as from Chalcolithic contexts in Haçilar, are modern forgeries.

Kenneth Oakley has discussed all these, and many another technique of science for providing relative and absolute dates, in his *Framework for Dating Fossil Man* (London, 1960; second edition 1970; one of the most important books produced in this field in the last quarter century. The history of archaeology has been, among other things, the search for a way of dating man's past. The Thomsen-Lubbock system, as developed by Gabriel de Mortillet into the chest of drawers system, and turned into a form of historical dating by the cross-dating techniques developed by Montelius and Childe, seemed to have dated man's past as best one could before the last war. The natural sciences have shown us since the war that we can abandon these earlier techniques and start from absolute dates provided by natural scientists. We are now living in this new archaeology, and exploring and describing a properly dated past.

While the scientific aids to archaeology, and particularly dating the past, increased in such a dramatic way in the years since the Second World War, so did the techniques of reconnaissance and excavation. Just as it was the 1914–18 war that really brought about the origins of archaeological air photography because it involved men like Crawford, Hamshaw Thomas and others in air observation and photography, so it was the 1939–45 war that developed air photography in a wide variety of ways—by the technical development of new and improved cameras, by wide cover of the world hitherto unphotographed and by the training and involvement in military intelligence, and especially military photo-intelligence, of great numbers of archaeologists. There was hardly a photographic intelligence unit anywhere in the world in the last few years of the last war that did not have on its staff, and to its great benefit, several archaeologists. Just as Crawford translated his military experience into civil archaeology in the early twenties, so some of the veterans of the Second World War used their military experience and translated it into the civil archaeology of post-war years.

Such a one was John Bradford, to whom we have already referred. He worked as an air photographic interpreter in the army, mainly in the Central Mediterranean. A series of articles about the way air photography had produced new evidence about the first farmers in southern Italy, on the Etruscans, and on the study of Roman centuriation, culminated in a book, both general and detailed, called *Ancient Landscapes: Studies in Field Archaeology* (London, 1960). Dr J. K. St Joseph who served in the Royal Air Force during the 1939–45 war, was able, after that war, to have special facilities for archaeological air photography. He was created Curator of Aerial Photography in the University of Cambridge, and, slowly, a University department came into being with its own aircraft, pilot and servicing facilities. This Cambridge department, surely the only air photographic department in any University in the world not concerned with exact survey, has worked, not only in Great Britain, Northern Ireland and the republic of Ireland, but also in northern France, Holland, and Denmark with beneficial results to all concerned. The air photographic archive of the Cambridge Committee is now very considerable and is growing in size and value with every season. Some of the members of the Cambridge Committee for Aerial Photography wrote a general book, edited by St Joseph, *The Use of Air Photography: Nature and Man in a New Perspective* (London, 1966), explaining what they were at, and several detailed books have been published by the Cambridge department, namely, M. D. Knowles and J. K. St Joseph, *Monastic Sites from the Air* (Cambridge, 1952); J. K. St Joseph, *Medieval England: an Aerial Survey* (Cambridge, 1958), and E. R Norman and J. K. St Joseph,

The Early Development of Irish Society: the Evidence of Aerial Photography (Cambridge, 1969). These three books are the first in the new series of Cambridge Air Surveys.

It would be an error to suppose that Britain, which, more than any other country, pioneered archaeological air photography in the twenties and thirties, was alone in redeveloping it in the years since 1945. Colonel Barradez traced the north African Roman *limes* by using existing plans and air photographs, and published in 1949 his important monograph entitled *Fossatum Africae: Investigations on the Organisation of the Borders of the Sahara in the Roman Period.* And to select one other area, let us note the outstanding work of Roger Agache in the north of France. Agache is Regional Director of Prehistoric Antiquities for the North of France and Picardy, with his headquarters in Abbeville. The excellence and importance of his work may be seen by consulting some of his articles (e.g. *Antiquity*, 1964, 113–19; and 1972, 117–23) and his *Détection aérienne de vestiges protohistoriques Gallo-Romains et Médiévaux* (Amiens, 1970). Agache has persuaded schoolmasters and the general public of the importance of air photography in seeing and understanding our ancient cultural landscape and, with his co-operation and advice, the Centre Regional de Documentation Pedagogique of the Academie d'Amiens produced in 1971 a publication entitled *Notre Picardie: Archéologie Aérienne de la Picardie* consisting of twenty-four 35-mm lantern slides and a text with illustrated written commentary and plans. This is a model of its kind and all regions should follow suit so that our schools everywhere in the world can show to their pupils the air view of their prehistory and history.

A history of aerial archaeology has long been wanted, and the section in the first edition of this book (pp. 294ff.) was only a short essay towards such a history. Now Leo Duel, who has already put us all in his debt with two books, *The Treasure of Time* and *Conquistadores Without Swords*, has written *Flights into Yesterday: the Story of Aerial Archaeology* (New York and London, 1969), and no one interested in the historical development of archaeology can afford not to read this book. I personally found it of absorbing interest, and while I knew the truth of what he was writing about men like Crawford, Allen, Bradford, St Joseph, Agache, Chombart de Lauwe, Baradez, Chevallier and Adamesteanu, I was not sufficiently aware of the history of American air photography from the pioneer flights of Lindbergh onwards, which Duel tells so well.

In 1925, Salomon Reinach wrote: "The richest museum of the ancient world lies at the bottom of the Mediterranean . . . This museum is, however, still inaccessible." That statement, even then, was not quite true: many treasures had already been recovered from beneath the sea and could be seen, for example, in the National Museum at Athens, and the first organised exploration of a wreck had already taken place off the Tunisian coast at Mahdia between Sfax and Sousse. This was the wreck of a Greek ship found by skin divers forty metres down and explored with the help of the French Navy: the material can be seen in the Bardo Museum at Tunis.

But, by now, that museum to which Reinach referred and many more at the bottom of other seas, lakes and wells, are accessible. The development of techniques of exploration, survey, and excavation beneath the sea, has been one of the most interesting features of archaeology in the last thirty years. Professor George Bass of the University Museum, Philadelphia, whose book, *Archaeology Under Water* (London, 1966), provides an excellent introduction to the subject, deliberately called his book by that title, and does not like the phrase "underwater archaeology". "Archaeology under water, of course," he writes, "should be called simply *archaeology*. We do not speak of those working on the top of Nimrud Dagh in Turkey as mountain archaeologists, nor those at Tikal in Guatemala as jungle archaeologists", and quotes with approval the dictum of Dr Stephen de Borhegyi: "The problems presented by underwater archaeology should be considered only as an extension of those already met and solved for dry-land archaeology."

It is an extension which to most dry-land archaeologists presents many new problems. Helmeted sponge divers have discovered most of the underwater archaeological sites in the Mediterranean. Better equipment for the archaeologist is the self-contained breathing apparatus known as *scuba* of which the most commonly used is the aqualung, developed in 1942 by Emile Gagnan and Jacques-Yves Cousteau. A compromise between standard diving equipment and scuba is the hookah or nargile, named after the Turkish water pipe.

Among the most notable archaeological digs under the

Mediterranean are the work of Cousteau at the Grand Congloué near Marseilles, and Peter Throckmorton and George Bass near Bodrum (the ancient Halicarnassos), which now has a new Museum for underwater archaeology. In the spring of 1958 Throckmorton found a graveyard of ships off the little island of Yassi Ada, and then discovered at Cape Gelidonya the oldest shipwreck ever recorded. Throckmorton, Dumas, Bass and Joan du Plat Taylor worked together on the Cape Gelidonya wreck and established that it was a Bronze Age shipwreck of *c.* 1200 B.C. Throckmorton gives an account of these discoveries in his *The Lost Ships* (London, 1965), and, in the preface to his *Shipwrecks and Archaeology: the Unharvested Sea* (London, 1970) he wrote:

> The Cape Gelidonya excavation was the beginning, you might say, of my professional career as a marine archaeologist, and the end of my career in Turkey. It was there that I made the mistake of firing a Turk whose uncle later became a high Government official. I was "tried" *in absentia* by a secret committee of inquiry, who found me to have been an antiquities smuggler all along. No formal accusations were ever made; press releases were more than enough. Like James Mellaart, the young British archaeologist recently in trouble over the same sort of charges, I struggled along for a couple of years, trying to clear myself. But I never managed to do so and slowly gave up hope of working again in Turkey.

Professor George Bass was more fortunate. The University of Pennsylvania underwater team, led by him, worked at the Byzantine wreck at Yassi Ada from 1961 onwards, developing the mapping of wrecks photogrammetrically with stereo-photographs, and using a two-man submarine, the *Asherah*, launched in 1964 by the Electric Boat Division of General Dynamics in Groton, Connecticut. The *Asherah*, as Bass says, "was not only the first submarine ever built for archaeology, but the first non-military submarine ever sold by the Electric Boat company in its sixty-year history". The work of this and many other expeditions in various parts of the world is summarised in the books already mentioned by Throckmorton and Bass and in (ed.) Joan Du Plat Taylor *Marine Archaeology, Development during*

Sixty Years in the Mediterranean (London, 1965); Mendel Peterson's *History Under the Sea: a Handbook for Underwater Exploration* (Washington D.C., 1965); Philippe Diolé, *4000 Years Under the Sea: Excursions in Undersea Archaeology* (London, 1954); Honor Frost, *Under the Mediterranean* (London, 1963); Dumas Frederic Dumas, *Deep-Water Archaeology* (1962), and (ed.) G. Bass, *A History of Seafaring* (London, 1972). Recently two new journals of marine archaeology have appeared: *The International Journal of Nautical Archaeology and Underwater Exploration*, intended for archaeologists, divers interested in the past and for everybody attracted by the underwater world, produced in London, and the *Cahiers d'Archéologie Subaquatique*, a French journal confined strictly to underwater archaeology.

The excavation of the Gokstad and Oseberg ships has stimulated the interest of Scandinavian archaeologists in wrecked survivals of ancient ships. King Gustav Adolphus II ordered the *Vasa* to be constructed in 1625: she sank in Stockholm Harbour after achieving only a few hundred yards of her maiden voyage. In 1956 Anders Franzen, a petroleum engineer working for the Swedish Admiralty, located the *Vasa* which has since been raised to the surface and is in its own museum in Stockholm. Anders Franzen has written an account of all this in his *The Warship Vasa* (Stockholm, 1966); see also Begt Ohrelius *Vasa: the King's Ship* (London, 1962). At Skuldelev, north of Roskilde, there were discovered in the late sixties, five wrecked Viking ships: a coffer dam was built around them while they were being excavated by Olav Olsen and Crumlin Petersen of the Danish National Museum: a special and very remarkable museum has been built to house the reconstructed ships at Roskilde on the edge of the fjord. Already Wreck I has been completely restored: it is a broad solid vessel with high sides, so far the only example yet found of the type known as *knarr*, a seagoing cargo ship that was sailed across the North Sea to England and across the North Atlantic to Iceland and Greenland. The existence of wrecks of this kind present an entirely new series of problems to archaeologists and to the state, and few countries have been so far-seeing in developing this aspect of marine archaeology as Sweden, Norway and Denmark. The problems of wreck-recovery, conservation and ownership in Great Britain have been well set out by Peter Marsden in his article, "Archaeology at Sea" (*Antiquity*, 1972, 198).

The Oseberg and Gokstad ships stand proudly in the fine ship museum at Bygdoy across the fjord from Oslo. Nearby is Amundsen's *Fran* and Thor Heyerdahl's *Kon-Tiki*. The *Kon-Tiki* expedition captured the imagination of the world when in 1960 Heyerdahl and five companions sailed across the Pacific from Peru in a balsa raft. In 1970 Heyerdahl succeeded in sailing across the Atlantic in a reed boat, the *Ra*. These brave adventures demonstrated that it was possible for Egyptians to sail the Atlantic in a reed boat, and possible for South American Indians to get to Easter Island and South-East Asia in a balsa raft. Of course many people have assumed that the present-day proof of possibility is a demonstration of achievement in prehistoric times, but Heyerdahl's exploits have not proved that Egyptians actually got to America, or that South Americans actually got to South-East Asia in prehistoric times.

5. *Historic Archaeology*

A humanising influence on the discipline of archaeology in the last thirty years has been the gradual realisation that it is not synonymous with prehistory, that it is not concerned only with savage and barbarian Europe and the early civilisations of the ancient near East and of Greece and Rome. A heavy orientation of archaeology to prehistory still exists in some places: David Clarke was able to call his book *Analytical Archaeology* when it was concerned entirely with prehistory. In America such a clear division is made between the study of the material remains of the ancient civilisations, and that of pre-Columbian Indians that an orthographic distinction persists, the former being called archaeology, and the latter archeology (see Richard Watson, *Antiquity*, 1972, 210), and a distinction is made in University teaching: the archaeology of the early civilisations being thought of as humanistic and taught in Departments of Classics and History and Oriental Studies, the archeology of the uncivilised past of men being thought of as "scientific" and taught in Departments of Anthropology.

To some extent this unhappy dichotomy is due to a feeling that archaeology is not the same when it is dealing with literate societies as when it is dealing with the prehistoric past, and this is to an extent true. But the past of man is one and the archaeologist studies all his artifacts. There remains a deep-seated feeling among many that the artifacts of yesteryear are not archaeology, that one's grandmother's goffering iron or an early eighteenth-century port bottle are different in kind and relevance, as well as in form, from a megalithic tomb or an Acheulian handaxe. This attitude may be hardened by museums who classify artifacts of the last two or three centuries as bygones, and perpetuate a distinction between archaeology and folk culture.

One of the most encouraging developments in western European archaeology in the past few decades has been the development of historical archaeology, helped as it has been by the development of "folk" museums in places like Sweden, Norway, Denmark and Wales. In Britain the *Journal of Roman Studies* has been in existence for many years, and now a new journal, *Britannia*, has been started to deal exclusively with Roman Britain. The journal *Medieval Archaeology* was founded in 1957, *Industrial Archaeology* in 1966, and *Post-Medieval Archaeology* in 1967. There is as yet no agreed definition of industrial archaeology; R. A. Buchanan, in a survey of the origins and development of industrial archaeology (*Antiquity*, 1970, 281), gives his own preference for the definition that "it is a field of study concerned with investigating, surveying, recording, and in some cases, with preserving industrial monuments" and these he defines as relics "of an obsolete phase of an industry or transport system". The term was first used in 1963 when there appeared E. R. R. Green's *The Industrial Archaeology of County Down*, a regional survey, and Kenneth Hudson's *Industrial Archaeology*, a general introductory handbook. In the last ten years there has been a spate of general and regional books on industrial archaeology as well as specialist studies. Guides to this literature are Michael Rix, *Industrial Archaeology* (1967); (ed.) K. Hudson, *The Industrial Past and the Industrial Present* (Bath, 1967); (ed.) R. A. Buchanan, *The Theory and Practice of Industrial Archaeology* (Bath, 1968), and Buchanan's article "Industrial Archaeology: Retrospect and Prospect" (*Antiquity*, 1970, 281). It has been said that Industrial archaeology is of course only one aspect of the archaeology of the last two hundred years. This is so, but at least it is one step towards the proper development of the archaeology of recent times.

In America a Society for Historical Archaeology was founded in 1967 and now publishes the *Journal of Historical Archaeology*, and this phrase is now used widely in America to include what was formerly described as "colonial archaeology" and "historic sites archaeology". For a very good account of the aims and methods of this organisation in America, and of the whole problem in general, the reader is recommended to read Ivor Noël Hume's *Historical Archaeology* (New York, 1969), and his subsequent book on *The Historical Artifacts of America* (New York, 1971). Noël Hume himself, who is archaeologist to Colonial Williamsburg, has done a remarkable piece of work at this remarkable site—a classic example of the best in historical archaeology. Colonial Williamsburg is a private enterprise, but close to it are Jamestown and Yorktown, also excellent examples of preservation in historical archaeology which are of outstanding importance.

In the same way as all through this chapter, we can do no more here than mention a few achievements in historical archaeology which are of outstanding importance.

In London, near the Guildhall, excavation took place in 1947 in the large devastated area west of St Paul's Cathedral, under the direction of Professor W. F. Grimes. Near Walbrook, in 1954, Grimes found a Mithraic temple of the second century A.D. This discovery, in some mysterious and fascinating way, electrified the British public, who queued in their thousands to see the remains of this temple, now preserved for posterity on a neighbouring site. The continuing replanning and reconstruction of London after the war has given great opportunities for recovering its past. For surveys made in the sixties see W. F. Grimes, *The Excavation of Roman and Mediaeval London* (1968); R. F. Merrifield, *The Roman City of London* (1965) and *Roman London* (1969), and for a statement of the present position, Martin Biddle and Daphne Hudson, *The Future of London's Past* (1973). A special unit has been set up under Brian Hobley, as Chief Urban Archaeologist, to deal with the archaeological problems of the new development of London. This unit is at the moment part of the Guildhall Museum: shortly the Guildhall Museum and the London Museum will coalesce to form the new Museum of London being built at the moment in the Barbican area.

London may provide a successor to the classic example of urban archaeology in Britain, namely Winchester. Here for many years under the direction of Martin Biddle, the Winchester Research Unit of the Winchester Excavations Committee has been recovering with painstaking care and accuracy the past of this city, and the first volume of a large series of books dealing with this research will shortly be published. In 1963 no less than 190 free-standing oak figurines and ex-voto plaques carved in low relief were found near the Gallo-Roman sanctuary of Sequana at the source of the Seine in north Burgundy. Buried on one occasion towards the middle of the first century A.D., the figures are up to 1.25 metres in height and represent human beings parts of human beings, and animals. All show the great skill of the Gallo-Roman artists in carving wood in the round. An even more dramatic demonstration of Gallo-Roman artistic skill and religious beliefs was provided by the excavations at Chamalières (a suburb of Clermont Ferrand), where, between 1968 and 1971, Professor Claude Vatin found more than five thousand wooden ex-votos. These finds have given us an entirely new view of the art of Celtic and Roman Gaul (*Antiquity*, 1972, 39–42).

In 1959 Michel Fleury, working in the crypt of the Abbey Church of Saint-Denis, found the sarcophagus of a sixth-century Queen, with her name, Arnegunde, on her ring. She was the wife of Clothaire I, who succeeded Clovis in 558 and ruled to 561. She is buried with magnificent clothes and jewels. About the same time Otto Doppelfeld, digging behind the Choir of Cologne cathedral, found the tomb of a Frankish woman and a six-year old boy.

Among the most startling early finds of historical archaeology in Britain were the discovery, by Brian Hope-Taylor, of an Anglo-Saxon Hall (perhaps the one used by Edgar and described by Bede) at Yeavering in Northumberland; the site of the Royal Palace of the Kings of Wessex at Cheddar in 1960–62 by Philip Rahtz, and the excavations by Leslie Alcock, at South Cadbury in Somerset, which reveal an iron age hillfort continuing in occupation into post-Roman times: it might possibly be the Camelot of Arthur.

Great Moravia was the first political organisation of the Slavs, beginning in 822 and lasting for 76 years. Ratislav was one of the first places visited by the mission of St Cyril and St Methodius, which was responsible for the Slavonic Church and the beginnings of the Cyrillic alphabet. In 1948 a small church of this period was found at Stare Mesto, and in the next fifteen years there were found in the Morava valley the remains of seventeen more churches as well as thousands of graves. In 1963 the Czechs celebrated the

1100th anniversary of St Cyril and St Methodius with a splendid exhibition of the arts and artifacts of Great Moravia.

In Denmark Viking camps at Trelleborg and Fyrkat have been excavated and studied with care. In England a special study has been made of deserted villages and of the archaeology of our towns, a study begun by the necessity of reconstruction after bomb damage in the last war, and continued by the necessity of examining what is being revealed by deep excavations of new buildings. A model of such town research has been provided by Martin Biddle's many-season work at Winchester. Those especially interested in these problems and the urgency of their study should read *The Erosion of History* (London, 1972), a remarkably interesting and forceful pamphlet produced by the Council for British Archaeology.

6. *Archaeology, New and False*

When, twenty-one years ago, I wrote the last words of what is now Chapter 10 in this book, I said that "without a sense of history, and of historical problem, archaeology can revert to mere collection" and warned that there was always "the danger of a new antiquarianism". This real danger could have happened: at a time when there seemed no certainty of any absolute chronology in the really distant past, and there were no proven ways of turning the study of artifacts into history, there was necessarily in the forties and fifties despair about whether prehistoric archaeology could ever become history. There was speculation that it would remain an unimportant discipline practised by people who dug for its own sake (some, alas, who never shared their results with the world by publishing them), or who enjoyed the material in itself, wallowing in taxonomies and typologies.

Carbon–14 dating, the extension of prehistory to the world as a whole, and particularly the development of American archaeology, and the realisation that the old models that dominated archaeological thinking for so long were outmoded, have given the subject a new life and a new purpose and firmly established it as what it is, namely, one of the auxiliaries of the human science of history. There has been endless discussion about where archaeology fits in the scheme of knowledge: for a good discussion of this see Bruce Trigger's *Beyond History: the Methods of Prehistory* (New

York, 1968) and his article in "Aims in Prehistoric Archaeology" (*Antiquity*, 1970, 26–37). "Is archaeology science or history?" is the impatiently asked question, and the unfortunate designation by Lord Snow of the "two cultures" has further bedevilled this issue.

In the attractively produced *Larousse L'Archéologie: découverte des civilisations disparues* (Paris, 1969), G. Charles-Picard asks the question "Qu'est-ce que l'Archéologie?" and answers that it is "une science auxiliare de l'histoire". This is a reasonable and workable definition. Edward Bacon, in his *Archaeology: Discoveries in the 1960s* (London 1971), refers to archaeology, in a quick throw-away phrase, as "this curious art-cum-craft-cum science", and this is what it is, except that this tripartite activity is not curious. Archaeology is, first, a craft, and those practitioners who prospect, excavate, conserve and preserve, are skilled craftsmen. It is, secondly, a scientific pursuit in that it uses all manner of scientific disciplines. But the craftsmanship and the scientific techniques fall short of the fulfilment of archaeology unless transmuted by the art of historical interpretation and writing. The thirty years under review in this chapter have shown how archaeology, instead of remaining a rather strange mystique of prehistoric artifacts, has become a main contributor to the writing of history, and more especially the ancient history of man.

But the danger of the new antiquarianism still remains, and Jacquetta Hawkes speaks of this danger in her provocative article "The Proper Study of Mankind" (*Antiquity*, 1968, 255–62). It is really the awareness of this danger that brought into being in America what is now generally referred to as "the new archaeology of the 1960s". For an account of the "new archaeology" the reader is referred to Richard Watson, "The new archaeology of the 60s" (*Antiquity*, 1972, 210–15); (eds.) S. R. and L. R. Binford, *New Perspectives in Archaeology* (Chicago, 1968), and particularly the last chapter of Willey and Sabloff, *History of American Archaeology* (London and New York, 1973). In Europe the nearest approximation to the new American archaeology is provided by David Clarke's *Analytical Archaeology*. This new movement in America stems, of course, from the bareness of the pre-Columbian record of archaeology: for centuries nothing happened of general interest to the student of world history—no Stonehenge, no Maltese temples. American archaeologists, dismayed by their archaeological record, have sought refuge in theory and methodology and spend their time talking about "the elucidation of cultural process" and the production of "laws of cultural dynamics". There is much to praise in this 1960 American movement which stems back to Taylor's *A Study of Archaeology*, a book that was, in the previous chapter, recognised as of such importance: the application of statistics, environmental archaeology, geographical patterns. This new movement of the 1960s needs to be absorbed into standard thought and work: at the present moment it is, especially for non-American workers, bedevilled by jargon and by people who, apparently unable to speak and write in clear English, use such phrases as "the logico-deductive-evolutionary systems paradigm".

We must never forget that these "new" American methods and concepts are developed in the study of the most unrewarding material: no steps were taken to the establishment of a higher culture or civilisation in North America and there were no incentives to persuade students of North American archaeology that they were dealing with events in the main stream of history. In the Old World this was very different. In the last thirty years many things have humanised and made universal the appeal of archaeology. I wrote in 1950: "There are two obvious problems which beset the archaeologist who is trying to reconstruct the early history of culture. The first is the development of economy, and the second is the development of art." I then referred to the work of Renard, Heyman and Bandi and especially to the work of J. G. D. Clark. At that time Clark's work was in the form of papers and articles: since then he has expanded and summarised these, and published them in developed form in his *Prehistoric Europe: the Economic Basis:* he has also set out his general ideas in his British Academy Lecture, *Archaeology and Economy* (London, 1960).

The study of man's economy was the first humanising influence in archaeology: the second was the development of the study of art. A great deal of nonsense has been spoken and written about art and archaeology, and sometimes it has been argued that archaeologists should have nothing to do with art—which is one of the greatest nonsenses of all time. What is called art is the achievement of the past which the present finds agreeable and emotionally exciting and stimulating, or, on the other hand, ugly and horrid. But, either way, it sees it as the surviving product of early societies, as well as a prime document providing information about all sorts of aspects of vanished societies.

Siegfried De Laet, Professor of Archaeology in the University of Ghent, expressed an anti-art point of view in his book *Archaeology and its Problems* (London, 1957). "Works of art," he wrote, "are not, of course, excluded from the province of archaeology, if they can clarify in any way the history of former civilisations. They remain, however, for archaeology, purely historical documents, and archaeology should refrain, *as should the archaeologist*, from formulating a subjective judgment on their aesthetic value. The distance which separates archaeology from art-history, moreover, increases every day." With this viewpoint we cannot agree, and the measure of our difference has been set out in my *Archaeology and the History of Art* (Hull, 1970). I then used De Laet's words as one of three texts for what was an inaugural lecture. The second text was from Seton Lloyd's *The Ancient Art of the Near East:* "In a world of equivocal values, art is an acceptable reality and its contemplation one of the greater privileges of our heredity." The third was the words of George Macaulay Trevelyan: "Even if cause and effect (in human history) could be discovered with accuracy, they still would not be the most interesting part of human affairs. It is not man's evolution, but his attainment, that is the great lesson of the past and the highest theme of history."

At the end of that inaugural lecture I said: "The gap between the dirt archaeologist and the art historian is not widening every day, and it should be narrowed until it does not exist . . . The attainments of man in prehistory, as in history, are the highest themes and the study of artistic achievement one of the highest of those themes, and its study one of our greatest privileges. Socrates said that art was the key to the soul of man. If we keep the study and appreciation of art as a main element in prehistory and protohistory, archaeology will not become a soul-less discipline and we will defeat the fears of a new antiquarianism."

I am delighted that in the last few years there has been a steady flow of books depicting and describing the art of those areas of human history which are normally those of the archaeologist. The first in this new genre were French: Lantier and Hubert's *Les Origines de l'Art Français* (Paris, 1947) and V. Gilardoni's *Naissance de l'Art* (Paris, 1954). Palaeolithic art has been especially well treated: F. Windels published his *Lascaux: 'Chapelle Sixtine' de la Préhistoire* in 1948, and A. Laming and M. Roussel their *La Grotte de Lascaux* in 1950. In the next twenty years there were published G. Bataille's *Prehistoric Painting; Lascaux and the Birth of Art*; Andre Leroi-Gourhan's *The Art of Prehistoric Man in Western Europe* (1968); J. Maringer and H. G. Bandi's *Art in the Ice Age* (London; 1953); Henri Breuil's *Four Hundred Centuries of Cave Art* (Montignac, 1952); C. Zervos's *L'Art de L'Europe du Renne* (Paris, 1959), and Paolo Graziosi's *L'Arte dell'Antica eta della Pietra* (Florence, 1957).

For later periods in France there was A. Varagnac and R. Lantier, *L'Art Gaulois* (Paris, 1950), and the book by M. Pobé and Jean Roubier, translated into English as *The Art of Roman Gaul: a Thousand Years of Celtic Art and Culture* (London, 1960). In Germany, W. Kimmig and H. Hell, *Vorzeit am Rhein und Donau*, included some exceptionally good photographs. In Britain, S. Piggott and the present writer published *A Picture Book of Ancient British Art* in 1950, and Stanley Thomas his *Prehistoric Britain* in 1960. In the last fifteen years some remarkable general surveys of prehistoric art in Europe have been published: the first was W. B. Forman and J. Poulik, *Prehistoric Art* (London, undated, somewhere in the late fifties), followed by T. G. E. Powell *Prehistoric Art* (London, 1966); N. K. Sandars *Prehistoric Art in Europe* (Harmondsworth, 1968), and Torbrugge's *Prehistoric European Art* (London, 1970). Powell's book was in the Thames and Hudson series *The World of Art*, which also contained Seton Lloyd, *The Art of the Ancient Near East* (London, 1961) G. H. S. Bushnell, *Ancient Art of the Americas* (London, 1965); Tamara Talbot Rice, *Ancient Arts of Central Asia* (London, 1960); John Boardman, *Greek Art* (London, 1964), and Sir Mortimer Wheeler, *Roman Art and Architecture* (London, 1964).

The study of the history of archaeology has also been an important humanising element in the development of the subject, but it has taken a long time to persuade some archaeologists that what is preached and practised at the present is not necessarily the truth, but one of many ways of looking at the past. The brash idea that what is said today is the final truth breaks down as one studies the development of ideas, the accumulation of facts, and the promotion of varying models over the last hundred and fifty years. A. Michaelis's *A Century of Archaeological Discoveries* was published in 1908, and the first edition of this present book under the title of *A Hundred Years of Archaeology* in 1950. In the years in between one remembers Casson's *The Discovery of Man* (1939), Joan Evans, *Time and Chance* (1943), H. J. E. Peake, *The Study of Prehistoric Times* (London, 1940), and Sir John Myres, *The Cretan Labyrinth: a Retrospect of Aegean Research* (London, 1933).

This study of the historical development of archaeology has revealed not only the way in which the past was discovered and by whom, but the way in which the discovered past was interpreted. The models of the past are as interesting to the archaeologists as is the present state of thought. It is not difficult to list the models that have been used: first the mythological model which brought Brutus to Britain, then the theological model which sought for answers to the past in the Bible, then the historical model which, rejecting the Bible as a reliable source, hoped for answers in classical writers—here the Ancient Britons and the Druids came into their own, as argued for by Aubrey and Stukeley. The break with the historical model came when Thomsen ordered his museum in Copenhagen according to the three ages of Stone, Bronze and Iron—the technological model of man's remote past, which, in varying forms, still exists and is still useful. Nilsson, Thomsen's Swedish contemporary at Lund, had proposed an economic model.

The nineteenth century was mainly dominated by the technological three-age model; but other models were put forward such as the diffusionist model which was taken to hyperdiffusionist extremes by the Rivers-Elliot Smith-Perry school in the twentieth century. Lewis Morgan produced a development of Nilsson's economic model and this was further developed and canonized by Engels and Marx. The Engels-Marx model has become the official view of prehistory in Russia and many communist countries: it bears no more relation to the truth than any other model. Gordon Childe, as a piece of anti-establishment whimsey, tried out a Marxian model in his *Scotland Before the Scots* (London, 1946). Childe himself was perhaps the person mainly responsible for the model of the past which was made so popular during the period 1925 to 1960. This was the model I have referred to as the modified diffusionist model: its main theme was that most advances in culture had come from the most ancient Near East, where Childe's Neolithic and Urban revolutions had taken place. It was argued that all the main changes in culture in the whole of the Old World had emanated from the nuclear heartland of the most Ancient East. Childe could make out a very good case for Europe, but his case for India and China was very weak and no case really existed at all for America.

Childe had begun writing at a time when the prehistory of pre-Columbian America was still little known. Nowadays it is clear that agriculture and city life developed in America independently of the ancient Near East and China.

The period under review in this chapter saw an enormous increase in the popularity of archaeology, and for this, broadcasting deserves the main credit. A straightforward archaeological quiz entitled *What in the World?* created in Philadelphia by Fro Rainey, was copied all over the world and eagerly watched by hundreds of thousands. In Britain, under the title *Animal, Vegetable, Mineral?*, it ran for six years under the chairmanship of the present writer and with panelists such as Sir Mortimer Wheeler, Sean O Ríordaín, Geoffrey Bushnell, Hugh Shortt, Thomas Bodkin and Stuart Piggott. These men became household names in the fifties, and with them into the house came archaeology as an interesting, amusing and valuable study. Gone, in a year of television, was the idea of archaeologists being white-bearded crackpots looking for treasure.

The BBC itself has played a very important role in the modern popularising of archaeology. Paul Johnstone, who started *Animal, Vegetable, Mineral?* went on to produce an archaeological series *Buried Treasure*, and now a monthly series, called *Chronicle*, run by a permanent archaeological and historical unit. One of the British independent television companies, Anglia, has taken up an interest in archaeology and history and produced series such as *Once a Kingdom*, *Who were the British?* and *The Lost Centuries*. In America, the CBS Network did a programme on Stonehenge which astonished the whole nation with the wide interest it created.

The printed word soon reflected the interest aroused by broadcasting. Books of *haute-vulgarisation* pour from the presses: to mention a few, the books of Henri-Paul Eydoux in France, Robert Silverberg in America, and the works of C. W. Ceram

(Kurt Marek) such as *Gods, Graves, and Scholars* and *The First American* and Geoffrey Bibby's *The Testimony of the Spade.* New journals of interest to the non-professional general reader have sprung up like *The Archaeological News-Letter* and *Current Archaeology* in England, *Archéologia* in France and *Archaeology* in America. The popularisation of archaeology is not a one-way traffic: it is only an informed public that can acquaint the professionals of new discoveries and co-operate in the preservation of ancient monuments threatened with destruction, and we rely on the public when we are faced with problems of public deception and forgery in archaeology.

These problems are ones which constantly beset and worry collectors and curators. A good account of the problems of fakes and forgeries as they appeared seventy years ago was given by Robert Munro in his *Archaeology and False Antiquities* (London, 1905); for more recent treatment see Vayson de Pradenne, *Les Fraudes en Archéologie* (Paris, 1932); Sonia Cole, *Counterfeit* (London, 1955), and Adolf Rieth's *Vorzeit Gefälscht* (Tubingen, 1967: English translation *Archaeological Fakes*, London, 1970).

Calvin Tomkins in his *Merchants and Masterpieces: the story of the Metropolitan Museum of Art* (New York, 1970) is very good in dealing with the problems of that great museum in relation to its disputed works and forgeries. The Met narrowly escaped buying any of Alceo Dossena's work as genuine antiquities but was not so fortunate with its purchases of the three huge terracotta sculptures identified at the time as Etruscan works of art of the sixth century B.C.; but actually made by Riccardo Riccardi and his *mezzo-matto* cousins near Orvieto in the twentieth century A.D. The Met bought in 1923 a Greek Bronze Horse which was accepted by virtually every classical scholar as one of the finest Greek bronzes in existence. Gisela Richter called it "without doubt, artistically the most important single object in our classical collection" and suggested that it was made by Kalamis. The horse appeared in practically every book on Greek art published after 1923, and thousands of plaster replicas were sold in the Museum's sale desk and by Brentanos. It was, in the end, not a curator of Greek art who exposed the horse as a forgery but Joseph V. Noble, the Met's operating administrator. He had come to The Met in 1956 and had walked past the horse to his office many thousands of times. Yet it was not until one morning in 1961 that he noticed, for the first time, a thin line running from the top of the horse's mane down to the tip of the nose, and also down the spine, over the rump and under the stomach. It suddenly occurred to Noble that this mould mark was such as is left when a sculpture is made by sand-casting—a process invented in the fourteenth century A.D. Suspicion grew and the horse was removed from public exhibition; the incontrovertible proof came in 1967 when a gamma-ray shadowgraph showed the inside of the horse with its sand core, and the iron wire used as its framework. Noble gave a public lecture on this sad discovery in which he said of this horse, "It's famous, but it's a fraud." But now we ask, is this proof incontrovertible? At the end of 1972 *The New York Times* revealed that scientific tests have shown that Noble was wrong and that the horse is a genuine antiquity (See *Antiquity*, 1974, 4–5). And, as we correct the proofs of this chapter we learn that many objects from Glozel, long regarded as forgeries of the 1920s, have been dated by thermoluminescence to the last few centuries B.C. (See *Antiquity*, 1974, 265 and 272).

We have already referred to the exposure of Piltdown Man as a forgery and the doubts which many still have about the alleged Upper Palaeolithic paintings from Rouffignac. In 1971 and 1972 the Research Laboratory for Archaeology and the History of Art in the University of Oxford published, in their journal *Archaeometry* the results of their thermoluminescence tests into alleged fakes: these showed that many allegedly genuine finds from Haçilar and many allegedly genuine early Chinese pots now in the main museums of the world, are fakes. The illicit trade in forged antiquities is alarming and so is the illicit trade in genuine objects.

In 1960 the University Museum of Philadelphia put on display a treasure of material comparable with that found by Schliemann at Troy, but unprovenanced. In 1970, as part of its centennial exhibition, the Boston Museum put on show another unprovenanced find of similar treasure from the Aegean Bronze Age. How and whence are these unprovenanced treasures available to the American market? In an astonishing despatch from Nicosia published in *The Times* for 17 August 1971, Peter Hopkirk revealed the extent to which Mycenaean treasures are being plundered from tombs in Cyprus. He wrote: "In a frenzy of tomb robbing, an entire city in Cyprus has been destroyed and thousands of tombs all over the island stripped of their treasures . . . From these tombs a steady stream of treasures is finding its way by secret routes to Europe and America . . . One comparatively small-time "exporter" boasted to me that he made thousands of pounds annually selling antiquities to foreign clients. He showed me a large suitcase that was being sent to Switzerland that afternoon into which he was packing Bronze Age pottery . . . The very best pieces are disposed of privately and often go directly into museum basements in America for a decent interval before being put on exhibition." And for an account of the theft of Maya antiquities see *Antiquity*, 1972, 91–3. We are clearly back to the tomb-robbing days of Belzoni and Rassam. What can be done? In Paris, in November 1970, UNESCO approved a draft convention on the plundering of archaeological sites and the illegal export of antiquities. A year later only one of the sixty-six members of UNESCO, namely Ecuador, had ratified the convention. It must be ratified and implemented as soon as possible by all countries, and certainly by England, the United States of America and Switzerland. The Universities of Pennsylvania and Harvard have already made public declarations of their intentions not to purchase unprovenanced finds in future, and this is a beginning towards a new ethic in archaeology.

It would be thought odd by readers of this book in years to come if they do not find any mention of the Dorak Treasure among our account of the notable moments of archaeology between 1940 and 1970. For a full statement of this *cause célèbre et fantastique* they should read Pearson and Connor, *The Dorak Treasure* (London, 1960). There they will learn that in 1960 James Mellaart, then assistant director of the British School of Archaeology in Turkey, was shown, or believes he was shown, a most remarkable treasure. Dorak is in western Turkey south of the sea of Marmora, and here, according to Mellaart, was found a series of royal tombs of the Copper Age, comparable to, but far richer than, those of Alaça Hüyük. Mellaart's account of what happened would be thought surprising to the point of incredibility in a third-rate detective story. Since he drew these remarkable finds they have never been seen by anyone; indeed we have no evidence that they have ever been seen by anyone, at any time, except Mellaart himself.

Where is the Dorak treasure, if it ever existed? It may be in the safes of a dealer in Zurich awaiting a suitable sale. It may already be in the private collection of an American millionaire. It may be in the basement of an American museum awaiting the right moment to surface. It may be a figment of Mellaart's imagination. These are questions which the next fifty years of archaeology may resolve: it took forty years for the doubts about Piltdown man to be resolved. We must be fair: the Dorak treasure may surface somewhere some day. We end this discussion with the comments of Bray and Trump in their *Dictionary of Archaeology* s.v. Dorak: "This very important material has since vanished in a manner more appropriate to a crime thriller than to archaeological research, and little can be made of it unless it reappears."

Let us not end this chapter, and this book, on a note concerned with fakes, frauds and foregeries and with our concern about the current outbreak of destroying antiquities and looting archaeological sites. These are some of the dangerous and difficult aspects of archaeology and we may take satisfaction in the fact that the world is now well aware of the falsification of antiquities and the illicit trade in genuine antiquities. It is also, now more than ever, well aware of the nature and importance of archaeology. Fifty treasures from the tomb of Tutankhamun were generously lent by the Egyptian Government to Britain for an Exhibition to mark the fiftieth anniversary of the discovery of the tomb by Caernarvon and Howard Carter in 1922. This exhibition was mounted in the British Museum from March to December 1972 and during those nine months 16,000,000 people visited it: the exhibition raised £600,000 for the fund to rescue the temples of Philae from the Nile. 400,000 copies of the catalogue were sold, and at 75p each, raised, as a correspondent pointed out in *The Times* "more than the total gate money for the five Australian Test matches" in 1972.

The following year there was mounted in the rooms of the Royal Academy in Burlington House an exhibition of archaeological finds made in China in the last twenty years. It was not only a remarkable revelation in itself, but attracted even more people than the Tutankhamun exhibition. There is now no question that archaeology occupies, at long last, a proper position in the minds and thinking of many people, and this is important, not only for the pleasure and historical perspective it gives, but because we are now at a time when co-operation of everyone is needed to record our disappearing heritage and preserve what is best in our patrimony. A recent report of the Ancient Monuments Board of the Department of the Environment referred to the year 1972 as one which "witnessed an unprecedented demand for excavation of threatened archaeological sites throughout the country. This stemmed largely from the expanding programme of motorway construction and from the extensive redevelopment schemes affecting major and minor towns whose centres overlie their mediaeval and sometimes Roman counterparts." *Rescue: a Trust for British Archaeology* was brought into existence in 1971 by a group of vigorous and far-thinking young archaeologists, and its first meeting in London of that year was attended by over 700 people—perhaps the largest archaeological meeting that has ever happened.

Now the Department of the Environment is planning and carrying out an extensive rescue organisation, and more money is being devoted to archaeological fieldwork than ever before. There are still those, and there will always be such, who think that "the backward looking curiosity" is of no value to us today; that we should look forward to the future. To them we answer in the words of J. J. S. Worsaae, the first professional archaeologist: "It is inconceivable that a nation which cares about itself and its independence could rest content without reflecting on the past."

GLOSSARY

Artifact. An object made or fashioned by man; an "extra-corporeal limb" (*Crawford*).

Association. Things are said to be in association when they are found in circumstances which suggest that they were deposited together simultaneously.

Barrow. A mound of earth or stones covering one or more burials.

Chronology, absolute. A temporal sequence expressed in exact years.

Chronology, relative. A temporal sequence based on the relationship of artifacts and cultures to each other or to natural events.

Cromlech. A folk-word in Wales for any megalithic monument and in Brittany for a stone circle; generally used in the nineteenth century for any megaliths.

Cross-dating. The dating of artifacts or cultures by their association with artifacts or cultures already dated in other contexts.

Culture. In anthropology this word is used for the sum-total of man's material, moral, mental and spiritual inheritance, or for a particular pattern of inheritance; in archaeology the word is used for an assemblage of artifacts assumed to be the material manifestation of a particular pattern of cultural inheritance.

Dolmen. A folk-word in Brittany and France generally for any megalithic tomb; a word widely used to mean any megalithic tomb, but also, unfortunately, given the specific meaning of certain kinds of megalithic tombs by some writers.

Eolith. A "dawnstone"; a word applied to those rudely chipped stone tools which lie between man's use of stone and his fashioning of stone, many of which, of course, cannot be proved to be man-made.

Ethnography. The descriptive study of the existing pre-literate societies.

Geochronology. The method of obtaining exact dates by means of non-calendric methods, such as clay-varves, etc.

Homotaxy. A word first introduced by T. H. Huxley to indicate the "relative synchronism" of events occupying the same positions in two sequences, but which have different absolute dates. Thus the English Revolution of Stuart times and the French Revolution might be said to be homotaxial.

Industry. A persistent association of artifacts representing the material culture of one group of people.

Megalithic monument. Any structure built of large undressed, or roughly dressed, stones constructed of orthostats (uprights) and capstones.

Menhir. A single standing stone.

Protohistory. The period of human history between prehistory, when no written sources existed, and history *sensu stricto*, when written sources are a main source; the time when history can be written only from an appraisal of many sources—archaeological, literary, linguistic and oral.

Sequence-dating. The labelling of stages in a typological sequence with numbers, giving an independent scheme of reference, though not an absolute chronology.

Sondage. A method of cutting right through a tell to obtain a cross-section of its history.

Stratigraphy. The arrangement of natural or man-made deposits over a long period of time in superimposed strata or layers.

Taxonomy. Classification; the arrangement of artifacts into significant groups on grounds of morphology, and their labelling.

Tell. A mound caused by the accumulation in one spot of several occupation layers by man; other common names in the Near East for these man-made occupation mounds are tepe, huyuk, etc.

Typology. The arrangement of artifacts into sequences showing morphological development.

CHRONOLOGICAL TABLE OF MAIN EVENTS IN THE HISTORY OF ARCHAEOLOGY 1820–1970

NOTE.—Some non-archaeological events of a literary and general interest have been included.

[1819. Danish National Museum opened to the public organised by C. J. Thomsen on the three-age system of Stone, Bronze and Iron.]

1820. Belzoni organises exhibitions in London and Paris and publishes his *Narrative of the Operations and Recent Discoveries within the Pyramids, Temples, Tombs and Excavations in Egypt and Nubia*; Discovery of the Venus de Milo on Melos.

1821. Venus de Milo acquired by France; Rich begins exploring Babylon.

1822. Discovery of Philae obelisk; Champollion announces decipherment of hieroglyphic writing; Daguerre and Bouton invent diorama; Fosbrooke, *Encyclopedia of Antiquities and Elements of Archaeology*.

1823. Buckland excavates the Red Lady of Paviland and publishes *Reliquiae Diluvianae*; present British Museum building, designed by Smirke, begun; Mechanics Institutes founded in Glasgow and London.

1824. Northmore and Trevelyan begin excavating at Kent's Cavern; Champollion, *Précis du système hiéroglyphique des anciens Egyptiens, figuratif, idéographique et alphabetique.*

1825. Foundation of the Royal Society of Northern Antiquaries in Copenhagen; Father MacEnery begins work at Kent's Cavern (which continued until his death in 1841).

1826. Fiedler publishes Cycladic graves with copper tools and marble statuettes; Champollion appointed Keeper of the Egyptian collection in the Louvre.

1828. Italian expedition to Egypt under the direction of Rosellini and Champollion; Tournal publishes his finds from the Grotte de Bize in *Annales des Sciences naturelles.*

1829. French excavations at Olympia under Abel Blouet.

1830. Charles Lyell, *Principles of Geology* (1830–3); Léon de Laborde, *Voyage de l'Arabie Petrée*; Dulrux excavates Kul Oba near Kertsh in the Crimea; opening of Museum in Berlin and the Glyptothek in Munich.

1831. Champollion elected to the first European Chair of Egyptology in the Collège de France; Charles Darwin sets out for his five-year voyage on the *Beagle*; Kingsborough's *Antiquities of Mexico*; foundation of the British Association for the Advancement of Science.

1832. Deaths of Cuvier and Champollion; foundation of *Chambers's Edinburgh Journal*, later *Chambers's Journal*.

1833. Tournal uses *préhistoire* in a paper in the *Annales de chimie et de physique*; the *Bridgewater Treatises*; Schmerling, *Recherches sur les Ossements Fossiles découverts dans les Cavernes de la Province de Liège*.

1834. Nilsson's essay, *Udkast til Jagtens og Fiskeriets Historie i Scandinavien*.

1835. *Monuments d'Egypte et de la Nubie* (–1845).

1836. Publication of the *Ledetraad til Nordisk Oldkyndighed*, the guide to the Danish National Museum, translated into English in 1849 as *A Guide to Northern Antiquities*; discovery of the Regulini-Galassi tomb at Cerveteri; Buckland, *Geology and Mineralogy considered in relation to Natural Theology*; Rich, *Narrative of a Residence in Koordistan and on the site of Ancient Nineveh*; Lartet discovers Pliopithecus at Sansan.

1837. Boucher de Perthes begins collecting flint implements in the Somme gravels; Rawlinson deciphers the Behistun inscription; Vyse and Perring begin work at the Great Pyramid; Alexander Cunningham digs at Sarnath; Lisch advocates the three-age system in his *Frederico-Francisceum*.

1838. Nilson, *Skandinaviska Nordens Urinvånare* (–43); Boucher de Perthes, *De la Création: essai sur l'origine et la progression des êtres* (–41); Edward Robinson begins his travels in Palestine.

1839. Stephens and Catherwood pay their first visit to Central America; Layard first visits Mesopotamia; Wilde and Petrie dig the Lagore crannog near Dunshaughlin, Co. Meath.

1840. Germans begin work at Delphi; Stephens's expedition to Yucatan and Central America; Agassiz's *Études sur les Glaciers*; Lepsius's survey of Nubian antiquities.

1841. J. L. Stephens, *Incidents of Travel in Central America, Chiapas and Yucatan*; *Punch* started; Tract XC.

1842. Worsaae, *Danmarks Oltid*; Botta at Nineveh; American Ethnological Society founded in New York.

1843. Botta at Khorsabad (1843–46); Lepsius's Mission (1843–45); Prichard, *The Natural History of Man*; foundation of Ethnological Society of London and the British Archaeological Association; Macaulay's *Essays*.

1844. Retzius, *On the Form of the Head in Different Peoples*; *Vestiges of the Natural History of Creation*.

1845. Layard at Nimrud (1845–47); Squier and Davis investigate the mound builders; *Mrs Caudle's Curtain Lectures*.

1846. Boucher de Perthes, *De L'Industrie primitive*; Rawlinson, *Behistun Inscription*; Ramsauer begins excavation of Hallstatt; Committee of Torquay Natural History Society formed to explore Kent's Cavern; Worsaae lectures to the Royal Irish Academy.

1847. de Perthes, *Antiquités Celtiques et Antédiluviennes*; *Comic History of England.*

1848. Squier and Davis, *Ancient Monuments of the Mississippi Valley;* Bateman, *Vestiges of the Antiquities of Derbyshire*; Akerman, *Archaeological Index*; Dennis, *Cities and Cemeteries of Etruria*; Layard, *Nineveh and its Remains*; Wakeman, *Archaeologia Hibernia*; Gibraltar skull found; Macaulay's *History* (1848–61).

1849. Lord Ellesmere's translation of *A Guide to Northern Antiquities*; Thom's translation of *The Primeval Antiquities of Denmark*; Botta and Flandin, *Monuments de Ninive* (1849–50); Layard, *The Monuments of Nineveh*; La Tène finds at Tiefenau, Berne.

1850. Mariette sent to Egypt by the Louvre to search for Coptic manuscripts—discovers the Serapeum; Loftus at Warka; Kendrick, *Ancient Egypt under the Pharaohs*; Latham, *The Natural History of the Varieties of Man.*

1851. Layard, *A Popular Account of Discoveries at Nineveh*; Vaux, *Handbook to the Antiquities in the British Museum*; Daniel Wilson, *The Archaeology and Prehistoric Annals of Scotland*; Colonel Lane Fox founds his museum at Bethnal Green; the Great Exhibition.

1852. Excavations in Scythian graves in South Russia; Wright, *The Celt, the Roman and the Saxon.*

1853. Discovery of cemetery at Villanova near Bologna; Rassam finds palace of Assur-bani-pal; Beddoe, *Scottish Ethnology.*

1854. Rigollot, *Mémoires sur les Instruments en Silex trouvés à Saint-Acheul*; discovery of lakeside pile dwellings in Switzerland; Taylor digs at Tell Mukayyar and Abu Shahrein; Worsaae, *Afbildninger fra det Kongelige Museum.*

1855. The Kurnah disaster; Crimean War puts an end to Mesopotamian excavation; Battersea shield found; Spencer, *Principles of Psychology*; Le Play, *Les Ouvriers Européens.*

1856. Bryan Fausset, *Inventorum Sepulchrale*; Norris completes transcription and translation of entire Behistun inscription; discovery of Neanderthal skull.

1857. Oppert, Hincks, Fox Talbot and Rawlinson separately translate cylinder of Tiglath Pileser I; Thurnam, *Crania Britannica*; Wilde's *Catalogue*; Buckle, *History of Civilisation* (1857–61).

1858. Pengelly begins excavating at Brixham; La Tène excavations by Schwab; Falconer visits Boucher de Perthes on the Somme; Wallace and Darwin's papers on Natural Selection to the Linnaean Society; Boutell's *Manual of British Archaeology.*

1859. Darwin, *Origin of Species*; Prestwich's paper, *On the Occurrence of Flint Implements associated with the Remains of Animals of Extinct Species*, to the Royal Society on May 26; MacEnery's *Cavern Researches*; excavations at Brixham completed; Waitz, *Anthropologie der Naturvolker*; Société d'Anthropologie de Paris founded; *Essays and Reviews*.

1860. Lartet digs Massat and finds engravings; Fiorelli directs excavations at Pompeii (1860–75); Renan begins excavating in Phoenicia; Morlot, *Études Géologico-archéologiques en Danemark et en Suisse*; Huxley and Wilberforce at the Oxford meeting of the British Association; first meeting of the Congrès International d'Anthropologie et d'Archéologie Préhistoriques.

1861. Lartet's paper in *Annales des Sciences naturelles* publishing Chaffaud and Massat; Maine, *Ancient Law*; Tylor, *Anahuac*; Müller, *Lectures on the Science of Language*; Bateman, *Ten Years' Diggings*; Perrot begins travels in Galatia and Bithynia and finds Boghaz Keui; excavations at Alesia; Quatrefages, *L'Espèce Humaine*; Bachofen, *Das Mutterrecht*; Herbert Spencer, *First Principles*.

1862. A. H. Rhind, *Thebes*; Bishop Colenso on *The Pentateuch* (1862–79).

1863. Lyell, *The Geological Evidences of the Antiquity of Man*; Kemble, *Horae Ferales*; Huxley, *Man's Place in Nature*; Lartet and Christy begin excavations in the caves of the Vézère; Napoleon III creates the Saint-Germain Museum; Wilson, *Prehistoric Man*; the affair of the Moulin Quignon jaw.

1864. Lartet and Christy, *Les Cavernes du Périgord*; Brouillet and Meillet, *Époques Antédiluviennes et Celtiques du Poitou*; Renan, *Mission en Phénicie*; de Mortillet founds *Matériaux*; Evans, *The Coins of the Ancient Britons*.

1865. Bonstetten, *Essai sur les Dolmens*; Lysons, *Our British Ancestors*; Lubbock, *Prehistoric Times* (in which the words Palaeolithic and Neolithic are coined); Tylor, *Researches into the Early History of Mankind*; Pengelly begins work at Kent's Cavern (1865–83); Congrès International d'Anthropologie et d'Archéologie Préhistoriques founded at Spezzia; *Reliquiae Aquitanicae* (1865–75).

1866. Establishment of Palestine Exploration Fund; Lubbock translates *The Primitive Inhabitants of Scandinavia*; first meeting of Congrès International d'Anthropologie et d'Archéologie Préhistoriques at Neuchâtel; Salzmann and Biliotti in Rhodes; *Antiquités de la Scythie d'Hérodote* (1866–73).

1867. Exposition in Paris; de Mortillet, *Promenades Préhistoriques à l'Exposition Universelle*; Cesnola in Cyprus (1867–76); Abbé Bourgeois's discoveries from St-Prest and Thenay; de Mortillet, *L'Origine de la Navigation et de la Pêche*.

1868. Louis Lartet discovers first cave burial at Cro-Magnon;

Schliemann visits Homeric sites; Nilsson's *Primitive Inhabitants of Scandinavia* translated by Lubbock; von Sacken, *Das Grabfeld von Hallstatt.*

1869. Worsaae acclaims authenticity of Chaffaud at Copenhagen conference; Thurnam, *Ancient British Barrows*; de Mortillet, *Essai de Classification des Cavernes et des Stations sous Abri*; Finlay, *Observations on Prehistoric Archaeology in Switzerland and Greece*; Schliemann digs in Ithaka and publishes *Ithaka, the Peloponnese and Troy.*

1870. Lubbock, *The Origins of Civilisation*; Rivière begins studying the Grimaldi caves at Mentone; Stevens, *Flint Chips*; Hamy, *Précis de Paléontologie humaine.*

1871. Darwin, *Descent of Man*; Tylor, *Primitive Culture*; Dupont, *L'Homme pendant les Ages de la Pierre*; Schliemann begins work at Troy; George Smith, *History of Ashur-bani-pal*; British Museum, *Guide to the Exhibition Rooms of the Departments of Natural History and Antiquities.*

1872. Evans, *Ancient Stone Implements*; Fergusson, *Rude Stone Monuments*; Borlase, *Naenia Cornubiae*; de Mortillet expounds his scheme of classification to the Brussels conference; Darwin, *Expression of the Emotions*; Fustel de Coulanges, *La Cité antique.*

1873. Smith's *The Chaldean Account of the Deluge* and his expedition to Kuyunjik; Conze at Samothrace; Cunningham at Harappa.

1874. Boyd Dawkins, *Cave Hunting*; Schliemann's *Troy*, and he begins digging at Mycenae (1874–76); discoveries of first paintings at Altamira; Geikie, *The Great Ice Age*; Hildebrandt, *Sur la Commencement de l'Age du Fer en Europe*; Pitt-Rivers's lectures on *The Principles of Classification* and *Early Modes of Navigation.*

1875. German excavations at Olympus (1875–81); Sautuola begins digging at Altamira; Von Pulszky proposes a Copper Age; Lukis, *Guide to the Morbihan Monuments*; Pitt-Rivers on *The Evolution of Culture.*

1876. Pengelly, *Kent's Cavern*; Schliemann, *Mycenae*; McLennan, *Studies in Ancient History*; Haeckel, *History of Creation.*

1877. Greenwell and Rolleston, *British Barrows*; French excavations at Delos and at Telloh; Morgan, *Ancient Society*; de Mortillet declares: "C'est l'enfance de l'art, ce n'est pas l'art de l'enfant"; Miocene flints from Puy Corny claimed.

1878. Chiron finds drawings on walls of Chabot (Ardèche); Gardner Wilkinson, *Manners and Customs of the Ancient Egyptians*; Montelius, *Civilisation of Sweden in Heathen Times.*

1879. Discovery of polychrome paintings at Altamira; Vielle excavates at Fère-en-Tardenois; Schliemann's second season at Troy;

Fouqué, *Santorin et ses Eruptions*; Fürtwangler and Loeschcke, *Mykenische Thongefässe.*

1880. Boyd Dawkins, *Early Man in Britain*; Mitchell, *The Past in the Present*; Newton, *Essays in Art and Archaeology*; Schliemann at Orchomenos; Pitt-Rivers begins excavating in Cranborne Chase; Petrie begins work in Egypt; Baye, *L'Archéologie préhistorique.*

1881. Evans, *Ancient Bronze Implements*; Tylor, *Anthropology*; Geikie, *Prehistoric Europe*; Maspero begins work in Egypt; Maudslay's first expedition to Central America; A. and G. de Mortillet, *Le Musée préhistorique.*

1882. Perrot and Chipiez, *Histoire de l'Art antique* (1882–1914); Schliemann's third season at Troy begins; Rhŷs, *Celtic Britain*; Elton, *Origins of English History*; Ratzel, *Anthropo-géographie* (1882–91).

1883. G. de Mortillet, *Le Préhistorique*; Gross, *Les Protohelvètes*; Daleau begins excavating at Pair-non-Pair; Egypt Exploration Fund started; Seebohm, *The English Village Community*; Milchhöfer, *Die Anfänge der Kunst in Griechenland*; Anderson, *Scotland in Pagan Times.*

1884. Dieulafoy at Susa; Schliemann at Tiryns (1884–85); von Pulszky, *Die Kupferzeit in Ungarn*; Pitt-Rivers Museum moved to Oxford; Wright, *The Empire of the Hittites*; Engels, *Origins of the Family.*

1885. Ratzel, *Völkerkunde* (1885–88); Tischler on La Tène; Montelius, *Sur la Chronologie de l'Age du Bronze*; Chantre, *Recherches . . . dans le Caucase.*

1886. Cartailhac, *Les Ages préhistoriques de l'Espagne et du Portugal*; Much, *Die Kupferzeit in Europa*; Gross, *La Tène.*

1887. Pitt-Rivers, *Excavations in Cranborne Chase* (1887–98); Siret, *Les premiers Ages du Métal dans le sudest de l'Espagne*; Americans under Peters and Hilprecht begin work at Nippur; discovery of the Tell el-Amarna tablets; Piette begins excavating at Mas d'Azil.

1888. Sayce, *The Hittites; the Story of a Forgotten Empire*; Vaphio gold cups found; Boule, *Essai de Paléontologie Stratigraphie de l'Homme*; Sophus Müller, *Ordning of Danemarks oldager* (1888–95).

1889. Reinach, *Époque des Alluvions et des Cavernes*; Cartailhac, *La France préhistorique*; Congress of Archaeological Societies holds first meeting; Schliemann's fourth season at Troy begins; Petrie at Gurob; Harrison claims Kentish eoliths; d'Arbois de Jubainvine, *Les Premiers Habitants de l'Europe*; *Biologia Centrali-Americana* (1899–1902).

1890. Petrie at Tell el-Hesi; death of Schliemann; Schuchhardt's *Schliemann's Ausgrabungen*; Schrader and Jevons, *Prehistoric Antiquities of the Aryan Peoples*; *L'Anthropologie* founded;

Munro, *The Lake Dwellings of Europe*; Taylor, *The Origin of the Aryans*; Frazer, *Golden Bough*.

1891. Petrie at Mycenae; Salmon, *Age de la Pierre*; Peabody Expedition to Honduras; *Pithecanthropus erectus* found in Java; Marshall, *Principles of Economics*.

1892. Petrie, *Ten Years' Diggings*; Allen Brown suggests the name Mesolithic; Cartailhac, *Monuments primitifs des Îles Baléares*; Stubel and Uhle, *Die Ruinenstatte von Tiahuanaco*.

1893. Reinach, *Le Mirage Oriental*; Balfour, *Evolution of Decorative Art*; J. W. Gregory recognises Palaeolithic tools in East Africa; Huxley, *Evolution and Ethics*.

1894. Evans, *Cretan Pictographs*; Cyrus Thomas, *Report on Mound Explorations*; de Morgan at Dahshur (1894–95).

1895. Piette, *Hiatus et Lacune*; Rivière discovers engravings at La Mouthe; Montelius, *La Civilisation primitive en Italie*; Reinach, *Les Déesses nues*; British excavations at Tell el-Amarna and Phylakopi; Sergi, *La Stirpe Mediterranea*; Evans, *Eastern Question in Anthropology*; Haddon, *Evolution in Art*; Durkheim founds *L'Année Sociologique*.

1896. Smith, *Historical Geography of the Holy Land*; Blinkenberg, *Antiquités pre-Mycéniennes*; Madsen, *Gravhøje og gravfund fra stenalderen i Danmark*.

1897. Borlase, *Dolmens of Ireland*; du Chatellier, *La Poterie aux Époques préhistoriques . . . Armorique*; Tsountas and Manatt, *The Mycenaean Age*; Hoernes, *Urgeschichte der Menschzeit*.

1898. Montelius, *Die Chronologie der ältesten Bronzezeit*; Petrie, *Diospolis Parva (Hu)*; Chantre, *Mission en Cappadoce*; Gradman, *Das Pflanzenleben der Schwäbischen Alb*; Cambridge expedition to Torres Straits and New Guinea; Hoernes, *Urgeschichte der bildenden Kunst in Europa*.

1899. Deutsche Orient Gesellschaft at Babylon (1899–1914); Myres and Ohnefalsch-Richter, *Cyprus Museum Catalogue*; Montelius, *Der Orient und Europa*; Keane, *Man, Past and Present*; Hogarth, *Authority and Archaeology*.

1900. Evans begins work at Knossos; Sarauw at Mullerup; Ripley, *Races of Europe*; Deniker, *Races of Man*; Rhŷs and Brynmor Jones, *The Welsh People*; Zumoffen, *La Phénicie avant les Phéniciens*; Ingram takes over editorship of *Illustrated London News*.

1901. Mortimer, *Forty Years' Researches*; Heierli, *Urgeschichte der Schweiz*; Breuil, Capitan and Peyrony discover Combarelles and Font-de-Gaume; Dörpfeld *et al.*, *Troja und Ilion*; Penck and Bruckner, *Die Alpen im Eiszeitalter* (1901–9); Douglas begins his dendrochronological researches; Tsountas excavates Sesklo; Schliz, *Das steinzeitliche Dorf Grossgartach*; Viollier, *Les Fibules de l'Age du Fer*.

1902. Cartailhac, *Mea culpa d'un Sceptique*; Schmidt, *Schliemann's*

Sammlung Trojanischer Altertümer; Macalister at Tell Jezer (1902–8); Wood Martin, *Traces of the Elder Faiths.*

1903. Deutsche Orient Gesellschaft at Assur; Montelius, *Die Älteren Kulturperioden im Orient und in Europa*; Myres, *The Early Pot Fabrics of Asia Minor*; Cabre recognises East Spanish Art; Hoernes, *Der diluviale Mensch in Europa.*

1904. Petrie, *Methods and Aims in Archaeology*; Pumpelly and Schmidt at Anau; Abercromby's distribution map of Beakers in Britain; Meyer, *Aegyptische Chronologie*; Windle, *Remains of the Prehistoric Age in England*; Anderson's articles in *Chambers's Encyclopaedia.*

1905. Müller, *Urgeschichte Europas*; de Geer begins his geochronological field work; MacCurdy, *The Eolithic Problem*; Munro, *Archaeology and False Antiquities.*

1906 *Manuel des Recherches préhistoriques*; Niaux discovered; Winckler begins work at Boghazkeui; Evans, *Essai de Classification des Époques de la Civilisation Minoenne*; first archaeological air photographs of Stonehenge; Cartailhac and Breuil, *La Caverne d'Altamira.*

1907. Piette, *L'Art pendant l'Age du Renne*; Rice Holmes, *Ancient Britain and the Invasions of Julius Caesar*; Burrows, *The Discoveries in Crete.*

1908. Michaelis, *A Century of Archaeological Discoveries*; de Mortillet, *Classification Paléthnologique*; volume one of Déchelette's *Manuel d'Archéologie* appears; Pumpelly, Schmidt *et al.*, *Explorations in Turkestan*; Montelius, *Chronology of the British Bronze Age*; Tsountas, *Prehistoric Acropolis of Dimini and Sesklo*; Garstang at Sakje-Geuzu; Hadrian Allcroft, *Earthwork of England.*

1909. Greenwell and Brewis, *The Bronze Spearhead*; Evans, *Scripta Minoa*, vol. i; de Morgan, *Les Premières Civilisations*; Peet, *The Stone and Bronze Ages in Italy and Sicily*; discovery of apparent contemporaneity of Azilian and Tardenoisian at Grotte de Valle near Santander; Breuil, *L'Aurignacien présolutréen.*

1910. Breuil, Capitan and Peyrony, *La Caverne de Font de Gaume*; Prince of Monaco establishes the Institut de Paléontologie Humaine; de Geer, *Geochronology of the Last 12,000 Years*; Mosso, *Dawn of Mediterranean Civilisation*; Brunhes, *La Géographie Humaine*; King, *History of Sumer and Akkad.*

1911. Sollas, *Ancient Hunters*; Piltdown skull found; Bulleid and Gray, *The Glastonbury Lake Village* (1911–12); Belz, *Die La Tène Fibeln*; von Oppenheim begins work at Tell Halaf; Semple, *Influences of Geographic Environment*; Elliot Smith, *The Ancient Egyptians.*

1912. Abercromby, *Bronze Age Pottery of Great Britain and Ireland*; Crawford, *Distribution of Early Bronze Age Settlements*;

Breuil, *Les Subdivisions du Paléolithique Supérieur*; Ray Lankester champions rostrocarinates at Royal Society; Coffey, *New Grange*; Wace and Thompson, *Prehistoric Thessaly*; Petrie, *Revolutions of Civilisation.*

1913. Reinach, *Répertoire de l'Art Quaternaire*; Coffey, *Bronze Age in Ireland*; Schuchhardt, *Westeuropa als alter Kulturkreis.*

1914. Begouen discovers Trois Frères paintings; Geikie, *Antiquity of Man in Europe*; Wright, *Quaternary Ice Age*; Koldewey, *Excavations at Babylon*; Laszlö, *Erösd*; Lankester, *Description of the Test Specimen of the Rostrocarinate Industry.*

1915. Droop, *Archaeological Excavation*; Osborn, *Men of the Old Stone Age*; Parkyn, *Prehistoric Art*; Williams Freeman, *Field Archaeology as illustrated by Hampshire*; Keith, *Antiquity of Man*; Huntingdon, *Civilisation and Climate*; Elliot Smith, *Migrations of Early Culture.*

1916. Obermaier, *El Hombre Fossil*: Fleure and Whitehouse, *Early Valleyward Movement of Population*; Breasted, *Ancient Times*; Dottin, *Les Anciens Peuples de l'Europe*; Wace and Blegen classify pre-Mycenaean pottery into Early, Middle and Late Helladic.

1917. Hrozny, *Die Spreche der Hethiter*; Goury, *L'Origine et Évolution de l'Homme.*

1918. Campbell Thompson and Hall at Ur and Eridu; Perry, *The Megalithic Culture of Indonesia.*

1919. Reid Moir, *Pre-Palaeolithic Man.*

1920. Vouga, *Essai de Classification du Néolithique Lacustre*; Petrie, *Prehistoric Egypt*; H. G. Wells, *Outline of History.*

1921. Evans, *Palace of Minos* (1921–35); Crawford, *Man and his Past*; Breuil accepts Reid Moir's pre-Crag finds at the Liége Conference; Macalister, *Textbook of European Archaeology*; Schuchhardt, *Alteuropa*; Sahni begins work at Harappa; Banerji begins work at Mohenjodaro; Andersson discovers Yang Shao Tsun; Burkitt, *Prehistory.*

1922. Peake, *Bronze Age and Celtic World*; Brunton at Badari (1922–25); Crawford, *Long Barrows of the Cotswolds*; Reinerth, *Pfahlbauten am Bodensee.*

1923. Carter and Carnarvon excavate tomb of Tutankhamen; the *Observer* publishes air photographs of the Stonehenge Avenue and the Celtic fields; Vouga, *La Tène*; Fox, *Archaeology of Cambridge Region*; Childe, *Schipenitz*; Crawford, *Air Survey and Archaeology*; Elliot Smith, *The Ancient Egyptians and the Origin of Civilisation.*

1924. Kidder, *Study of South-western Archaeology*; Caton-Thompson and Gardner in the Fayum (1924–28); MacCurdy, *Human Origins*; Randall McIver, *Villanovans and Early Etruscans*; Ebert, *Reallexikon der Vorgeschichte* (1924–32); Perry, *Growth of Civilisation*; Frankfort, *Studies in Early Pottery of the Near East*; Xanthoudides and Droop, *Vaulted Tombs of the Mesara*; Elliot Smith, *Elephants and Ethnologists.*

1925. Childe, *Dawn of European Civilisation*; Kendrick, *The Axe Age*; Menghin's edition of Hoernes's *Urgeschichte der bildenden Kunst*; Van Giffen, *De Hunnebedden in den Nederlanden* (1925–28); Wheeler, *Prehistoric and Roman Wales*; Hargreaves, *Excavations in Baluchistan*; finds of painted pottery from China described by Andersson and Arne; finds of flint points from Folsom, New Mexico.

1926. Discovery of Royal Tombs at Ur by Woolley; Oriental Institute begins exploration in Central Anatolia; Garrod, *Upper Palaeolithic Age in Britain*; Gjerstad, *Studies in Prehistoric Cyprus*; Jones, *Stone Age in Rhodesia*; Childe, *Aryans*; Tallgren, *La Pontide préscythique*; excavations at Anyang.

1927. Kendrick, *Druids*; Von der Osten and Schmidt at Alishar Hüyük (1927–32); Reid Moir, *Antiquity of Man in East Anglia*; Peake and Fleure begin publishing *The Corridors of Time*; Swedish Cyprus Expedition (1927–31); *Antiquity* founded.

1928. Crawford and Keiller, *Wessex from the Air*; Skara Brae excavated by Childe; Brunton and Caton-Thompson, *Badarian Civilisation*; Brunton excavates at Deir Tasa; Germans at Warka (1928–39); Macalister, *Archaeology of Ireland*; Boule, Breuil, Licent and de Chardin, *Le Paléolithique de la Chine.*

1929. Oriental Institute begins work in Iraq; Schaeffer at Ras Shamra (1929–39); Childe, *Danube in Prehistory*; Mrs Cunnington, *Woodhenge*; Stein, *Archaeological Tour in Waziristan and Northern Baluchistan*; Pericot's excavations at Parpallo (1929–31).

1930. Speiser excavates at Tepe Gawra and Tell Billa; Garstang at Jericho (1930–36); Neuville at El Khiam; Elliot Smith, *Human History*; Myres, *Who were the Greeks?* Peake, *The Flood*: Åberg, *Bronzezeitliche und Früheisenzeitliche Chronologie* (1930–35); Fleure and Peake, *Megaliths and Beakers*; Forde, *Early Cultures of Atlantic Europe*; excavations at Ch'eng Tzu Yai, Lungshan.

1931. Menghin, *Weltgeschichte der Steinzeit*; Eighteenth International Conference of Orientalists at Leiden; Contenau and Ghirshman at Tepe Giyan (1931–32); Schmidt at Tepe Hissar; Marshall *et al.*, *Mohenjodaro and the Indus Civilisation*; Leakey, *Stone Age Cultures of Kenya Colony*; von Oppenheim, *Tell Halaf*; Hawkes, *Hill Forts.*

1932. Fox, *Personality of Britain*; Frankfort, *Archaeology and the Sumerian Problem*; Schmidt, *Cucuteni*; Vassi, *Vinča*; Hubert, *Les Celtes*; Kendrick and Hawkes, *Archaeology in England and Wales, 1914–31*; Clark, *Mesolithic Age in Britain*; Garrod, *Natufian*; Piggott, *Neolithic Pottery of the British Isles*; Bosch Gimpera, *Etnologia de la Peninsula Iberica.*

1933. Mallowan at Arpachiyah; new Iraq antiquities law; Ghirshman at Sialk; Dikaios excavates Erimi; Leeds, *Celtic Ornament*; Dawson, *Age of the Gods*; Toynbee, *Study of History*.

1934. Caton-Thompson and Gardner, *Desert Fayum*; Parrot at Mari; Mallowan at Tell Chagar Bazar and Tell Brak; Poidebard, *La Trace de Rome*; Majumdar, *Explorations in Sind*; Wayland, *Rifts, Rivers, Rains and Early Man in Uganda*.

1935. Contenau and Ghirshman, *Fouilles de Tepé Giyan*; Childe, *Prehistory of Scotland*; Nordman, *Megalithic Culture of Northern Europe*; Mackay digs at Chanhudaro (1935–36); Yale-Cambridge North Indian Expedition.

1936. Clark, *Mesolithic Settlement of Northern Europe*; Childe, *Man Makes Himself*; Lamb, *Excavations at Thermi in Lesbos*.

1937. Garstang excavates at Mersin (1937–40); Garrod and Bate, *Stone Age of Mount Carmel*; MacCurdy (Ed.), *Early Man*; Brunton, *Mostagedda and the Tasian Culture*; de Terra and Movius in Burma; Mahr, *New Aspects and Problems of Irish Prehistory*.

1938. Garrod, *Upper Palaeolithic in Light of Recent Discovery*; Ghirshman, *Fouilles de Sialk* (1938–41); Brønsted, *Danmarks Oldtid* (1938–40); Childe, *The Orient and Europe*; Piggott, *Early Bronze Age in Wessex*; Wu, *Prehistoric Pottery in China*; Mackay, *Further Excavations at Mohenjodaro*.

1939. Pendlebury, *Archaeology of Crete*; de Terra and Paterson, *Studies in the Ice Age in India and Associated Human Cultures*; Poidebard, *Tyr*; O'Brien, *Prehistory of Uganda Protectorate*; Coon, *Races of Europe*; Menghin, *Die ältere Steinzeit*.

1940. Iraq Government excavations at Tell Uquair; Schmidt, *Flights over Ancient Cities in Persia*; Sidney Smith, *Alalakh and Chronology*; Vats, *Excavations at Harappa*; Childe, *Prehistoric Communities of the British Isles*; Hawkes, *Prehistoric Foundations of Europe*; Peake, *The Study of Prehistoric Times*; discovery of cave paintings at Lascaux.

1941. Death of Major George Allen: "an irreparable loss to British archaeology" (O. G. S. Crawford, *Antiquity*, 1941, 89).

1942. V. G. Childe, *What happened in History*; development of aqualung by Emile Gagnan and Jacques-Yves Cousteau; Death of Sir Flinders Petrie at the age of 90.

1943. Seton Lloyd and Sayyid Fuad Safur begin digging at Tell Hassunah; R. E. M. Wheeler, *Maiden Castle*; Joan Evans, *Time and Chance*; discovery of Llyn Cerrig Bach hoard near Holyhead, Anglesey.

1944. Jacobstahl, *Early Celtic Art*; Zeuner, *Dating the Past*; Jessen and Helbaek, *Cereals and Grains in Britain and Ireland in Prehistoric and Early Historic Times*; Childe gives the Rhind

Lectures, subsequently published in 1946 as *Scotland before the Scots.*

1945. Colonel Barradez discovers the "fossatum Africae" raised by Rome on the Saharan borders of Algeria and Tunisia in a study of air photographs.

1946. First use of electrical prospecting for archaeological purposes by R. J. C. Atkinson at Dorchester-on-Thames; excavation of Celto-Ligurian oppidum of Entremont and discovery of sculptures; R. J. C. Atkinson, *Field Archaeology*; Leroi-Gourhan starts work at Arcy-sur-Cure; Willard F. Libby discovers Carbon-14 dating; first issue of *Ancient India.*

1947. Discovery of the first of the Dead Sea scrolls at Qumran; Mademoiselle G. Henri-Martin finds remains of *Homo sapiens* at Fontéchevade; Childe gives his Josiah Mason lectures in Birmingham, later published as *Social Evolution* (1951); excavation of the Pazyryk tombs in the Altai; Kon-Tiki expedition led by Heyerdahl; Braidwood begins work at Jarmo; Seton Lloyd, *Foundations in the Dust.*

1948. Discovery of Slavonic Church at Stare Mesto; K. Oakley applies fluoride test to fossil bones; Schaeffer, *Stratigraphie Comparée et Chronologie de L'Asie Occidentale*; P. Nørlund, *Trelleborg*; W. W. Taylor, *A Study of Archaeology*, A. J. Wace, *Mycenae*; C. F. C. Hawkes, *Britons, Romans and Saxons round Salisbury and in Cranborne Chase*; D. Diringer, *The Alphabet.*

1949. J. G. D. Clark begins excavations at Star Carr, Yorkshire; Discovery of Panagurichte treasure in Bulgaria; Mallowan begins digging at Nimrud; D. A. E. Garrod and S. de Saint-Mathurin start excavating at Angles-sur-L'Anglin.

1950. S. Piggott, *Prehistoric India*; V. G. Childe, *Prehistoric Migrations in Europe*; discovery of Tollund Man in Denmark; Blegen, Boulter, Caskey, Rawson and Sperling, *Troy: Excavations Conducted by the University of Cincinnati, 1932*–8 (4 vols 1950–8); Hope-Taylor's excavations at Yeavering; Third International Congress of Prehistoric and Protohistoric Sciences, Zurich.

1951. L. S. B. Leakey, *Olduvai Gorge*; J. M. Casal starts work at Mundigak; first radiocarbon dates published by Libby and Arnold in *Science*; excavations at Hatra; Henri Frankfort, *The Birth of Civilisation in the Near East.*

1952. Kathleen Kenyon begins work at Jericho; Cousteau explores the wreck at Le Grand Congloué at Marseilles; Arambourg discovers two jawbones of *Atlanthropus* at Terfinine in Algeria; J. G. D. Clark, *Prehistoric Europe: the Economic Basis*; H. Breuil, *Quatre cents siècles d'art parietal*; revolution in Egypt, closing of foreign archaeological schools, expulsion of Drioton.

1953. Ship burial found near Great Pyramid of Cheops; Danish archaeological expedition begins work at Bahrain; debunking of Piltdown Man; O. G. S. Crawford, *Archaeology in the Field*; Michael Ventris (1922–1956) published the decipherment of Linear B, announced the previous year; Papadimitriou discovers the second circle of royal tombs at Mycenae; René Joffroy discovers the Vix burial, near Châtillon-sur-Seine; first fascicule of *Inventaria Archeologia*; Schlumberger begins work at Surkh-Kotal; P. Dikaios, *Khirokitia: Final Report on the Excavations of 1936–46*; Blegen excavates Palace of Nestor at Pylos; Atkinson discovers that some of the stones at Stonehenge were decorated.

1954. Temple of Mithras in the City of London excavated by W. F. Grimes; Piggott, *The Neolithic Cultures of the British Isles*; Wheeler, *Archaeology from the Earth*; Gonheim's excavation of the IIIrd dynasty step pyramid at Saqqara; accidental discovery of chambered tombs at Barnenez in Finistère; Singer, Holmyard and Hall, *History of Technology*, Vol. 1; Clark *et al*; *Excavations at Star Carr;* Fourth International Congress of Prehistoric and Protohistoric Sciences, Madrid.

1955. Cyril Fox, *Offa's Dyke*; J. S. Weiner, *The Piltdown Forgery*; Carlo Lerici founds Institut Polytechnique at Milan; Documentation and Study Centre for the History of the Art and Civilisation of Ancient Egypt set up in Cairo; G. Bailloud and Mieg de Boofzheim, *Les Civilisations néolithiques de la France*; Teilhard de Chardin dies in New York; publication of *Le Phénomène Humain.*

1956. Announcement by Nougier of the discovery of Rouffignac; Lerici begins periscope prospecting of Etruscan tombs; *Vasa* located by Anders Franzen (brought to the surface in 1960); R. J. C. Atkinson, *Stonehenge*; Joan Evans, *A History of the Society of Antiquaries of London*; Emery begins work at Buhen; Spina discovered; Graziosi, *L'Arte dell'Antica eta della Pietra*; M. Ventris and J. Chadwick, *Documents in Mycenaean Greek.*

1957. John Bradford, *Ancient Landscapes*; Mellaart begins work at Haçilar; G. E. Mylonas, *Ancient Mycenae*; first issue of *Medieval Archaeology*; Deaths of O. G. S. Crawford, S. P. Ó Ríordain, J. F. S. Stone, Paul Jacobstahl, Georg Leisner, A. J. Wace, and V. G. Childe.

1958. Discovery of hoard of Tartessian jewllery at El Carambolo near Seville; Willey and Phillips, *Method and Theory in American Archaeology*; magnetometer recording remanent magnetism invented in England; V. G. Childe's posthumous *The Prehistory of European Society*; Erik Wahlgren, *The Kensington Stone, a Mystery Solved*; discovery of St. Ninian's Isle hoard in the Shetlands; J. Mellaart visits Izmir and is shown the Dorak Treasure: John Chadwick, *The Decipherment of Linear B*; Fifth International Congress of Prehistoric and Protohistoric Sciences, Hamburg.

1959. Beginning of UNESCO campaign to salvage Nubia; Michel Fleury discovers tomb of Queen Arnegunde at St. Denis; Doppelfeld's excavations in Cologne Cathedral; Mary Leakey finds a human skull (given name of *Zinjanthropus boisei*) in Bed I at Olduvai dated to a million and three quarters years old; Giot publishes dates of Breton megaliths earlier than 3000 B.C.; Piggott says of the Durrington Walls C14 date "This date is archaeologically inacceptable" (*Antiquity*, 1959, 289).

1960. Royal Commission on Historical Monuments (England), *A Matter of Time*; R. J. Braidwood and B. Howe, *Prehistoric Investigations in Iraqi Kurdistan*; D. Trump digs at Skorba; J. G. D. Clark re-excavates Peacocks Farm, Shippea Hill, Cambridgeshire; discovery of Viking boats at Skuldelev, near Roskilde; G. Bass studies cargo from Late Bronze Age ship at Cape Gelidonya, Turkey; L. H. Palmer throws doubts on the work of Sir Arthur Evans at Knossos (see his *Myceneans and Minoans*, 1961); death of Sir Leonard Woolley.

1961. Juvenile mandible found at Olduvai Gorge close to Bed 1, later labelled *Homo habilis*; J. F. Evernden and G. H. Curtis, discoverers of the Potassium Argon dating method, estimate date at 1.7 million years; Mellaart begins digging at Çatal Hüyük; Ingstadt begins digging at L'Anse aux Meadows, a Viking settlement on Newfoundland; in the Russian mathematical congress at Leningrad it was announced that the Maya hieroglyphs had been deciphered by an electronic computer; death of L'Abbé Breuil.

1962. Re-excavation of Wayland's Smithy, Berkshire, by Atkinson and Piggott; Sixth International Congress of Prehistoric and Protohistoric Sciences in Rome.

1963. Hole and Flannery begin work at Tepe Ali Kosh and Yadin at Masada; Vlassa reports discovery of the Tartaria tablets; Zurn discovers statue of Hallstatt warrior at Hirschlanden near Stuttgart; discovery of oak figurines and plaques in a sanctuary at the source of the Seine in north Burgundy; M. Murray's *My First Hundred Years*; first use of term "industrial archaeology"; the paintings at Lascaux fading and being covered by a green growth.

1964. Platon discovers Minoan palace at Kato Zakro; discovery at Santa Severa of gold tablets with Etruscan inscriptions; excavations by E. Higgs of Palaeolithic material at Asprochaliko and Kastritsa; Cornell University expedition uncovers the supposed tomb of King Gyges at Sardis in ancient Lydia; first issue of *Journal of Industrial Archaeology*; launching of the non-military submarine, the *Asherah*; first publication of

Archaeology in Pakistan; Marshack suggests existence of lunar calendrical notation in Upper Palaeolithic times.

1965. Trifunović and Srejović begin work at Lepinski Vir in Yugoslavia; publication of the Vinland map; Lascaux closed to the public; S. Piggott, *Ancient Europe*; Gerald S. Hawkins, *Stonehenge Decoded*; R. McC. Adams, *Land Beyond Baghdad*; death of G. Bersu.

1966. Excavation of ceremonial centres at San Lorenzo in Southern Veracruz by M. Coe; G. R. Willey, *An Introduction to American Archaeology* (vol. 1: *North and Middle America*; vol. 2, *South America*, 1972); first volume of new Olduvai Gorge series; H. de Lumley begins work at Nice; Seventh International Congress of Prehistoric and Protohistoric Sciences, Prague.

1967. *Current Archaeology* founded; creation of Society for Post-Mediaeval Archaeology; exhibition of Russian archaeology and art in the Hague, Rome and Essen; death of Sir Cyril Fox; first issue of *Origini*, a new publication of the Institute of Palaeoethnology of Rome University; James Mellaart, *Çatal Hüyük: A Neolithic Town in Anatolia*; Hudson, *Handbook for Industrial Archaeologists*; Alcock begins excavating at Cadbury Hill and Wainwright at Durrington Walls; discovery of Lepenski Vir settlement; Atkinson begins BBC-sponsored excavation of Silbury Hill; Renfrew, "Colonialism and Megalithismus", (*Antiquity*, 1967, 276–88); Sheppard Frere, *Britannia* (first volume in new series dealing with the history of the Roman provinces).

1968. *World Archaeology* founded; J. Coles and E. Higgs, *Early Man*; launching of the French archaeological ship, *Archéonaute*; (ed.) J. O. Brew, *One Hundred Years of Anthropology*—five lectures given at the centenary of the Peabody Museum at Harvard; N. K. Sandars, *Prehistoric Art in Europe*; S. Piggott, *The Druids*; death of Dorothy Garrod.

1969. J. G. D. Clark, *World Prehistory, a new Outline*; Hole, Flannery and Neely, *Prehistory and Human Ecology of the Deh Luran Plain*; G. Bibby, *Looking for Dilmun*; Noël Hume, *Historical Archaeology*; W. F. Grimes, *The Excavation of Roman and Mediaeval London*; D. J. Mulvaney, *The Prehistory of Australia.*

1970. Sir Max Mallowan, *Nimrud and its Remains*; Rudenko's *Frozen Tombs of Siberia: the Pazyryk Burials of Iron Age horsemen* (revision of Russian account first published in 1953); Heyerdahl crosses the Atlantic in a reed boat, the *Ra*; UNESCO draft convention on the plundering of archaeological sites and the illegal export of antiquities; centennial exhibition at the Metropolitan Museum, New York and the Boston Museum of Fine Arts: display of unprovenanced Schliemann-type hoard at Boston; Emery discovers the Serapaeum at Saqqara.

A few dates after 1970

1971. A special fund-raising organisation called *Rescue* started at a meeting in London attended by 700; M. D. Leakey, *Olduvai Gorge 3; excavation of Beds I and II*; J. D. Evans, *The Prehistoric Antiquities of the Maltese Islands; a Survey*; Wainwright and Longworth, *Durrington Walls, Excavations 1966–68;* death of W. B. Emery; first issue of *Britannia*, journal of Romano-British and kindred studies; first issue of the *West African Journal of Archaeology*; C. C. Lamberg-Karlovsky, *Excavations at Tepe Yahya, Iran: 1967–69* L. Deuel, *Flights into yesterday;* A. Thom, *Megalithic lunar observatories.* Eighth International Congress of Prehistoric and Protohistoric Sciences, Belgrade.

1972. Srejović: *Europe's first monumental sculpture: new discoveries at Lepenski Vir*; C. Renfrew, *The Emergence of Civilisation: the Cyclades and the Aegean in the Third Millennium B.C.*; first issues of *The International Journal of Nautical Archaeology and Underwater Exploration* and the *Cahiers d'Archéologie Subaquatique*; death of Louis Leakey; (ed.) E. Higgs, *Papers in Economic Prehistory*; J. M. de Navarro: *The Finds from the site of La Tène: I: Scabbards and the Swords found in them*; Richard Leakey announces finding of skull of genus *Homo*, earlier than 2.6 million years ago, in East Rudolf; 1.6 million people visit the exhibition of the Tutankhamen treasure in the British Museum between March and December.

1973. Protection of Wrecks Act; suggested that Charles Dawson forged brick-stamps from Pevensey (Peacock, *Antiquity*, 1973, 138–40); death of van Giffen;

BIBLIOGRAPHY

I give here a long and fairly comprehensive list of books. I have marked with an asterisk a limited number of books and articles to serve as a nucleus for further reading.

No authoritative and definitive history of archaeology has, as yet, been published. A Michaelis, *A Century of Archaeological Discoveries* (1908), was the first attempt at a history: it is mainly concerned with classical archaeology and takes the story up to the end of the nineteenth century. This book was a translation of his *Die archäologischen Entdeckungen des neunzehnten Jahrhunderts* published in Leipzig in 1906. Friedrich von Oppeln-Bronikowski's *Die archäologischen Entdeckungen im 20 Jahrhundert* (Berlin, 1931), takes the story on another thirty years.

An admirable short survey of the development of prehistoric archaeology is provided by H. J. E. Peake, *The Study of Prehistoric Times* (Huxley Memorial Lecture for 1940, Royal Anthropological Institute). My own *The Three Ages* was published in 1943, the first edition of this book as *A Hundred years of Archaeology* in 1950 (reprinted 1952): see also my *The Idea of Prehistory* (1962) and *The Origins and Growth of Archaeology* (1967). Certain aspects and periods of the subject are dealt with by C. W. Ceram (the pseudonym of the late Kurt Marek) in his *Gods, Graves and Scholars* (1952) and his *A Picture History of Archaeology* (1958), and by Geoffrey Bibby in *The Testimony of the Spade* (1957). The long introductory essay to Jacquetta Hawkes's *The World of the Past* (1963) is a very good summary of the history of archaeology. So is George Daux's *Les Etapes de l'Archéologie* (1942) in the *Que-sais-je?* series.

More popular accounts are W. H. Boulton, *The Romance of Archaeology* (London, n.d.); J. Baikie, *The Glamour of Near East Excavation* (1927); R. V. D. Magoffin, *Magic Spades* (1929); R. V. D. Magoffin and E. C. Davis, *The Romance of Archaeology* (1923); D. Masters, *The Romance of Excavation* (1923); A. T. White, *Lost Worlds: Adventures in Archaeology* (1947); G. E. Daniel, *Man Discovers his Past* (1966); C. W. Ceram, *Archaeology* (a small, little known, but excellent book in the Odyssey Library, New York, 1964, London, 1965); H.-P. Eydoux, *History of Archaeological Discoveries* (1966); K. B. Shippen, *Men of Archaeology* (1963), and Henry Garnett, *Treasures of Yesterday* (1964). The general story of archaeology through the discovery of lost cities can be read in Marcel Brion's *La Résurrection des Villes Mortes* (1948) and, more popularly, in Herman and Georg Schrieber, *Vanished Cities* (1958) and Leonard Cottrell's *Lost Cities* (1957).

One of the most fascinating and valuable historical surveys is

Stanley Casson, *The Discovery of Man* (1939), a classic of its kind, which has long been out of print and should be reprinted. It is a general survey of the development of archaeology and anthropology and gives a balanced and inspired picture of the progress of both subjects. A specialist, but most useful account of the development of archaeology and anthropology is provided in (ed.) J. O. Brew, *One Hundred Years of Anthropology* (1968), a volume to celebrate the centenary of the Peabody Museum with essays by G. R. Willey, G. E. Daniel, S. L. Washburn, Fred Eggan and F. G. Lounsbury—all with extensive and detailed bibliographies.

The history of anthropology is of course very closely linked with that of archaeology and there are many books and articles to be recommended on this subject. First, A. C. Haddon, *History of Anthropology* (1910), and its revised edition, A. C. Haddon and A. H. Quiggin, *History of Anthropology* (1934). Secondly R. H. Lowie, *History of Ethnological Theory* (1937). Then T. K. Penniman, *A Hundred Years of Anthropology*, first published in the Duckworth Hundred Years series in 1935, and re-issued in a revised form in 1952 with contributions by Beatrice Blackwood and J. S. Weiner. See also T. Bendyshe, "The History of Anthropology", in *Memoirs of the Anthropological Society of London* for 1865; J. Dieserud, *The Scope and Content of the Science of Anthropology* (1908); P. Mitra, *A History of American Anthropology* (1933); F. Boas, "A History of Anthropology" (*Science*, XX, 1904, 513); J. S. Slotkin, *Readings in Early Anthropology* (1965); M. T. Hodgen, *Early Anthropology in the Sixteenth and Seventeenth Centuries* (1964), and Marvin Harris, *The Rise of Anthropological Theory: a History of Theories of Culture* (1968). For a more popular account see H. R. Hayes, *From Ape to Angel* (1959).

The history of geology is also closely linked with the development of archaeology in the late eighteenth and early nineteenth centuries. For the history of geology see Sir Archibald Geikie, *The Founders of Geology* (1905, 2nd edition); A. C. Ramsey, *Passages in the History of Geology* (1848); H. B. Woodward, *History of Geology* (n.d.) and *History of the Geological Society of London* (1907); C. J. Schneer, "The Rise of Historical Geology in the Seventeenth Century" (*Isis*, 1954, 266); K. V. Zittel, *History of Geology* (1901); (ed.) Cecil J. Schneer, *Toward a History of Geology* (1969); R. Porter, "The Industrial Revolution and the Rise of the Science of Geology", in (ed.) M. Teich and R. Young, *Changing Perspectives in the History of Science* (1973).

For Darwinism and Evolution see J. W. Judd, *The Coming of Evolution* (1910); J. B. Bury, *Darwin and Modern Science* (1909); E. Clodd, *Pioneers of Evolution from Thales to Huxley* (1897), H. F. Osborn, *From the Greeks to Darwin* (1894); Loren Eiseley, *Darwin's Century* (1959); William Irvine, *Apes, Angels and Victorians* (1955); (ed.) S. A. Barnett, *A Century of Darwin* (1958), and Francis C. Haber, *The Age of the World: Moses to Darwin* (1959).

For the history of ideas, particularly in the nineteenth century, in relation to archaeology, and the impact of scientific discoveries upon accepted beliefs, see A. O. Lovejoy, *The Great Chain of Being* (1952), and some of the essays in (foreword H. Grisewood, no editor), *Ideas and Beliefs of the Victorians* (1949)—the text of a series of BBC talks. Also A. D. White, *A History of the Warfare of Science with Theology in Christendom* (1896); C. C. Gillispie's *Genesis and Geology* (vol. LVIII of the *Harvard Historical Studies*, 1951, reprinted as a Harper Torchbook, 1959) with an excellent bibliography; J. B. Bury, *The Idea of Progress* (1920); H. E. Barnes, *An Introduction to the History of Sociology* (1948); G. P. Gooch, *History and Historians in the Nineteenth Century* (1913); E. A. Kirkpatrick, *The Sciences of Man in the Making* (1932), J. T. Merz, *A History of European Thought in the Nineteenth Century* (1896–1914), and W. F. Ogburn and A. Goldenweiser, *The Social Sciences and their Inter-relations* (1927).

For the history of Egyptian archaeology see J. Baikie, *A Century of Excavation in the Land of the Pharaohs* (1926); S. R. K. Glanville, *The Growth and Nature of Egyptology* (1947); J. D. Wortham, *The Genesis of British Egyptology 1549–1906* (1971); Sir Wallis Budge, *The Rosetta Stone in the British Museum* (1929); L. Cottrell, *The Mountains of Pharaoh* (1956); J. Christopher Herold, *Bonaparte in Egypt* (1962); W. R. Dawson and E. P. Uphill, *Who was Who in Egyptology* (1972), and Barbara Hertz, *Temples, Tombs and Hieroglyphs* (1964). For the development of Mesopotamian archaeology: see Sir E. A. Wallis Budge, *The Rise and Progress of Assyriology* (1925); H. Frankfort, *Archaeology and the Sumerian Problem* (1932); H. W. Hodge, *Survey of Recent Assyriology* (1910); R. Koldewey, *The Excavations at Babylon* (1914); A. Parrot, *Archéologie Mésopotamienne: Les Etapes* (1947); Sir Leonard Woolley, *Ur of the Chaldees; a Record of Seven Years of Excavation* (1935); S. Smith, *The Early History of Assyria to 1000 B.C.* (1928); R. Campbell Thompson and R. W. Hutchinson, *A Century of Excavation at Nineveh* (1929), and C. J. Gadd, *The Stones of Assyria* (1936). Quite the best book on the subject, and excellently written, is Seton Lloyd's *Foundations in the Dust* (1947).

For Palestine see R. A. S. Macalister, *A Century of Excavation in Palestine* (1925); W. E. Albright, *The Archaeology of Palestine and the Bible* (1932); J. Elder, *Archaeology and the Bible* (1960); G. L. Harding, *The Antiquities of Jordan* (1959); P. Ilton, *Digging in the Holy Land* (1959); K. M. Kenyon, *Archaeology in the Holy Land* (1961), R. K. Harrison, *Archaeology of the Old Testament* (1963); S. L. Caiger, *Bible and Spade* (1936); F. J. Bliss, *The Development of Palestine Exploration* (1906); H. V. Hilprecht, *Exploration in Bible Lands during the Nineteenth Century* (1903). For some account of discovery in classical and pre-classical Greece see R. M. Burrows, *The Discoveries in Crete* (1907); M. L. Clarke, *Greek Studies in England 1700–1830* (1945), H. R. Hall; *Aegean Archaeology* (1915); F. H. Marshall, *Discovery in Greek Lands* (1920); Sir J. L. Myres, *Who Were the Greeks?* (1930), and *The Cretan Labyrinth: a Retrospect of Aegean Research* (the Huxley Memorial Lecture for 1933 of the Royal Anthropological Society); J. D. C. Pendlebury, *The Archaeology of Crete* (1939), and E. E. Sykes, *The*

Anthropology of the Greeks (1914); William A. McDonald, *The Discovery of Homeric Greece* (1967), and (ed.) M. Platnauer, *Fifty Years of Classical Scholarship* (1954).

Geoffrey Bibby's *The Testimony of the Spade* has already been mentioned in general terms as a history of archaeology. It deals mainly with the development of European prehistory and is especially good on Scandinavian developments. See also I. Undset, "Le Préhistorique Scandinave: ses Origines et son Développement" (*Revue d'Anthropologie*, 1887, 313), and for a completely new treatment of the whole problem O. Klindt-Jensen, *A History of Scandinavian Archaeology* (1975). Colin Simard's *Découverte Archéologique de la France* (1955) deals mainly with the story of French Palaeolithic discovery, as does the Abbé Breuil's *The Discovery of the Antiquity of Man: Some of the Evidence* (the Huxley Memorial Lecture of the Royal Anthropological Institute for 1941, delivered in 1946). See also Breuil, "Découvertes Paléolithiques en France", *Congrès Archéologique de France* (1934); R. Lantier, "Un Siècle d'Archéologie Protohistorique" in *Congrès Archéologique de France* (1935), and S. Reinach, "Esquisse d'une Histoire de l'Archéologie Gauloise" (*Revue Celtique*, 1898, 101 and 292). The development of German archaeology is well described in J. H. Eggers, *Einführung in die Vorgeschichte* (1959). See also A. Stocky, "La Développement de la Science préhistorique tcheque" (*L'Anthropologie*, 1924, 45), and L. Pigorini, *Matériaux pour l'Histoire de la Paléoethnologie Italienne* (1874).

Much has been written on the history of British archaeology. See first Sir Thomas Kendrick's *The Druids* (1927), *British Antiquity* (1950), and "The British Museum and British Antiquities" (*Antiquity*, 1954, 132); then H. B. Walters, *The English Antiquaries of the 16th, 17th and 18th Centuries* (1934). Stuart Piggott has written much of great importance on British antiquaries: see his *William Stukeley* (1950), "Prehistory and the Romantic Movement" (*Antiquity*, 1937, 31), "Stukeley, Avebury and the Druids" (*Antiquity*, 1935, 22), "The Ancestors of Jonathan Oldbuck" (*Antiquity*, 1955, 150), "William Camden and the *Britannia*" (The Reckitt Archaeological Lecture for 1951 (*Proc. Brit. Acad.*, 1951, 199), "Antiquarian Thought in the Sixteenth and Seventeenth Centuries" in (ed.) Levi Fox, *English Historical Scholarship in the Sixteenth and Seventeenth Centuries* (1956), and *The Druids* (1968). See also "The English Antiquaries" by E. Moir (*History Today*, 1958, 781); Joan Evans, *A History of the Society of Antiquaries of London* (1956), and J. Rodden, *A History of British Archaeology* (1975).

A new and standard work on American archaeology is G. L. Willey and G. Sabloff, *A History of American Archaeology* (1974). A good general popular account is C. W. Ceram, *The First American: a Story of North American Archaeology* (1971). See also Gordon C. Baldwin, *America's Buried Past* (1962); H. C. Shetrone, *The Mound Builders* (1930); Paul S. Martin, George I. Quimby, and Donald Collie, *Indians Before Columbus* (1947); Victor von Hagen, *Search for the Maya:*

the Story of Stephenson and Catherwood (1973), and J. B. Griffin "The Pursuit of Archaeology in the United States" (*American Anthropologist* 1959, 379).

For the development of air photography see O. G. S. Crawford and A. Keiller, *Wessex from the Air* (1928); Chombart de Lauwé, *La découverte du Monde aérienne* (1948); R. Chevallier, *L'avion à la découverte du passé* (1964), and *La Photographie Aérienne* (1971); R. Agache, *Détection Aérienne des Vestiges Archéologiques* (1969), and (ed.) J. K. St Joseph, *The Uses of Air Photography* (1966). Leo Deuel's *Flights into Yesterday* (1969) is a fascinating and well written account of the development of air photography. Constance Babington-Smith's *Evidence in Camera* (1958), while dealing with air photography and military intelligence in the 1939–45 war, is full of interesting sidelights on archaeology and archaeologists. A special issue of *Archéologia* entitled *L'Archéologie Aérienne: Vision Fantastique du Passé* was published in 1973 and contains fifteen articles of varied interest dealing with the development of air photography.

For the study of decipherment read J. Chadwick, *The Decipherment of Linear B* (1958 and 1968: translated into 10 languages); Ernst Doblhofer, *Voices in Stone* (1961), and Cyrus H. Gordon, *Forgotten Scripts: the Story of their Decipherment* (1968).

Biographies and autobiographies of archaeologists, geologists and anthropologists provide a useful, illuminating and often amusing source for the history of archaeology. Among biographies, see T. G. Bonney, *Charles Lyell and Modern Geology* (1895); H. Pengelly, *A Memoir of William Pengelly* (1897) and especially the chapter on the scientific work of William Pengelly (written by T. G. Bonney); C. Breasted, *Pioneer to the Past: the Story of J. H. Breasted, Archaeologist* (1948); (ed.) Mrs A. G. Duff, *The Life and Work of Lord Avebury* (1924); (ed.) Warren R. Dawson, *Sir Grafton Elliot Smith: a Biographical Record by his Colleagues* (1938); Sir E. Harrison, *Harrison of Ightham* (1928); V. W. von Hagen, *Maya Explorer: James Stephens and the Lost Cities of Central America and Yucatan* (1947); C. Schuchardt, *Schliemann's Excavations: an Archaeological and Historical Study* (1891); E. Ludwig, *Schliemann of Troy: the Story of a Goldseeker* (1931)—a biassed portrait of the great man to be rectified by reading L. and G. Poole: *One Passion, Two Loves: the Schliemanns of Troy* (1967), which contains much new material; Mrs J. Prestwich, *Life and Letters of Joseph Prestwich* (1899); G. Rawlinson, *A Memoir of Major-General Sir Henry Creswicke Rawlinson* (1938); Mrs Gordon, *Life of William Buckland* (1894); G. H. O. Burgess, *The Curious World of Frank Buckland* (1967); Katherine M. Lyell, *Life, Letters and Journals of Sir Charles Lyell* (1881); P. Chalmers Mitchell, *Thomas Henry Huxley* (1913); A. Ledieu, *Boucher de Perthes* (Paris, 1885); L. Aufrère, *Essai sur les Premières Découvertes de Boucher de Perthes et les Origines de l'Archéologie Primitive, 1838–1844* (1936), (and in this connection see G. E. Daniel, "The Origins of Boucher de Perthes' Archéogeologie" (*Antiquity*, 1972, 317), and Ronald Clark, *Sir Mortimer Wheeler* (1960).

Dr Joan Evans's *Time and Chance* (1943) is not only a chronicle of the remarkable Evans family that produced three Presidents of the Society of Antiquaries of London (Sir John Evans, Sir Arthur Evans, and Dr Joan Evans herself) but a fascinating series of sidelights on the development of archaeology through the last one hundred and fifty years. See also her "Ninety Years Ago" (*Antiquity*, 1949, 115). Unfortunately no biography has yet been written of that most colourful of nineteenth-century archaeologists, General Pitt Rivers, but there is a good memoir by St George Gray in vol. v of *Excavations in Cranborne Chase* (1905). A biography of Louis Leakey by Sonia Cole is to be published in 1975.

There have not been enough autobiographies of archaeologists, but here is a list of some: Boucher de Perthes, *Sur Dix Rois: Souvenirs de 1796 à 1860* (1863–6); Sir E. A. Wallis Budge, *By Nile and Tigris* (1920;) A. A. B. Edwards, *Pharaohs, Fellahs, and Explorers* (1891); H. J. Falconer, *Palaeontological Memoirs* (1868); A. H. Layard, *Autobiography and Letters* (1903); L. S. B. Leakey, *White African* (1937)—this, the first volume of his autobiography was published when he was thirty; second and posthumous volume expected in 1975; O. G. S. Crawford, *Said and Done* (1955); Sir Leonard Woolley, *Spadework* (1953); Sir Mortimer Wheeler, *Still Digging* (1955); J. Beddoe, *Memories of Eighty Years* (1910), Sir Flinders Petrie, *Seventy Years of Archaeology* (1931); Margaret Murray, *My First Hundred Years* (1963), and J. Eric S. Thompson (*Maya Archaeologist*, 1963).

Readers will want to turn to anthologies of extracts from the writings of archaeologists, and most of these I have listed at the end of my own *The Origins and Growth of Archaeology* (1967), itself such an anthology. Since then Robert Silverberg has edited an anthology called *Great Adventures in Archaeology* (1966). In my view the two best are R. F. Heizer, *Man's Discovery of his Past: Literary Landmarks in Archaeology* (first edition: 1962, second, 1969) and Jacquetta Hawkes, *The World of the Past* (1963).

Dictionaries and Encyclopedias of archaeology usually have biographical entries, and especially to be recommended is the *Enzyklopädisches Handbuch zur Ur- und Frühgeschichte Europas* edited by Jan Filip and published in two volumes (A-K, 1966, L-Z, 1969): it not only has good biographical notes but charming drawings of the main figures in the story of archaeology. The volumes of *Antiquity* from 1927, edited by O. G. S. Crawford, and from his death in 1957 by the author of this book, provide a selective chronicle of discovery and change during the last fifty years, and the editorials a personal comment on those events.

INDEX

INDEX